"*The Polyvagal Theory* is at the leading edge of psychosomatic medicine and body-mind therapies. It is a vital contribution to scientifically-informed clinical practice. Psychologists, analysts, physicians, bodyworkers, and educators are provided with an essential map to help guide them in tracking the psychophysiological states of their clients, discern where they are 'stuck,' and help them to heal and move forward in life. Dr. Porges's great contribution is now compiled in this one astounding comprehensive volume. It is a must-read for clinicians and psychobiological researchers."—Peter A. Levine, PhD, author of *In Unspoken Voice; How the Body Releases Trauma and Restores Goodness* and *Trauma Through a Child's Eyes: Awakening the Ordinary Miracle of Healing.*

"Stephen Porges has developed theories of the autonomic nervous system, based on his sound research over many years, which have profound importance for our understanding of human behavior, whether normal or pathological. Based on evolutionary principles, and firmly embedded in neuroanatomy, his work considerably broadens our understanding of the representation of emotion in the brain, reaching parts that most contemporary texts never touch."—Michael Trimble, MD, author of *The Soul in the Brain: The Cerebral Basis of Language, Art, and Belief.*

The Norton Series on Interpersonal Neurobiology
Allan N. Schore, PhD, Series Editor
Daniel J. Siegel, MD, Founding Editor

The field of mental health is in a tremendously exciting period of growth and conceptual reorganization. Independent findings from a variety of scientific endeavors are converging in an interdisciplinary view of the mind and mental well-being. An interpersonal neurobiology of human development enables us to understand that the structure and function of the mind and brain are shaped by experiences, especially those involving emotional relationships.

The Norton Series on Interpersonal Neurobiology will provide cutting-edge, multidisciplinary views that further our understanding of the complex neurobiology of the human mind. By drawing on a wide range of traditionally independent fields of research—such as neurobiology, genetics, memory, attachment, complex systems, anthropology, and evolutionary psychology—these texts will offer mental health professionals a review and synthesis of scientific findings often inaccessible to clinicians. These books aim to advance our understanding of human experience by finding the unity of knowledge, or consilience, that emerges with the translation of findings from numerous domains of study into a common language and conceptual framework. The series will integrate the best of modern science with the healing art of psychotherapy.

A NORTON PROFESSIONAL BOOK

THE POLYVAGAL THEORY

Neurophysiological Foundations of Emotions, Attachment, Communication, and Self-Regulation

STEPHEN W. PORGES

W. W. Norton & Company
New York • London

Note to Readers: Standards of clinical practice and protocol change over time, and no technique or recommendation is guaranteed to be safe or effective in all circumstances. This volume is intended as a general information resource for professionals practicing in the field of psychotherapy and mental health; it is not a substitute for appropriate training, peer review, and/or clinical supervision. Neither the publisher nor the author(s) can guarantee the complete accuracy, efficacy, or appropriateness of any particular recommendation in every respect.

Foreword reprinted with permission from Bessel van der Kolk.

Printed in the United States of America
First Edition

For information about special discounts for bulk purchases, please contact W. W. Norton Special Sales at specialsales@wwnorton.com or 800-233-4830

Manufacturing by Lake Book Manufacturing, Inc.
Production manager: Leeann Graham

Library of Congress Cataloging-in-Publication Data

Porges, Stephen W.
The polyvagal theory : neurophysiological foundations of emotions, attachment, communication, and self-regulation / Stephen W. Porges. — 1st ed.
p. cm. — (The Norton Series on Interpersonal Neurobiology) (A Norton Professional Book)
Includes bibliographical references and index.
ISBN 978-0-393-70700-7 (hardcover)
1. Affective neuroscience. 2. Emotions—Physiological aspects. 3. Vagus nerve. I. Title.
QP401.P67 2011
612.8—dc22 2010044408

ISBN: 978-0-393-70700-7

W. W. Norton & Company, Inc., 500 Fifth Avenue, New York, N.Y. 10110
www.wwnorton.com
W. W. Norton & Company Ltd., 15 Carlisle Street, London W1D 3BS

14 15 16 17 18 19 20

With love and respect
I dedicate this book to Sue Carter,
my wife and intellectual partner.

Contents

Acknowledgments

The polyvagal theory described in this volume evolved from four decades of research. The chapters provide a glimpse into the broad implications of the theory and how the development and expansion of the theory involved many collaborators. The ideas, conceptualized as the polyvagal theory, did not emerge in an intellectual vacuum but were a product of discussions and debates with colleagues and students. The theory is built on solid research and the extensive body of literature on the neural regulation of the autonomic nervous system. The polyvagal theory is not a doctrine but a work in progress. As we learn more, both from our research program and from our colleagues, the theory is updated and expanded. The chapters in this volume illustrate the changing features of the theory as new knowledge is discovered and relevant clinical problems are used to inform the theory.

During my scientific career, I have had the good fortune to meet and to interact with several individuals who have provided important scientific and intellectual guidance. Through these interactions, I became informed by clinical material and learned comparative neurophysiology, evolutionary biology, and time-series analyses. This exposure to perspectives from disparate areas of science provided a rare opportunity to integrate ideas, facts, and methods that led to the discovery of the bold organizing principles on which the polyvagal theory is based.

Several people played important roles in helping me navigate through this uncharted intellectual arena. Publishing this book provides an opportunity to acknowledge their important contributions. First, I want to acknowledge Sue Carter. For 40 years, Sue, as both my wife and intellectual partner, has supported my intellectual curiosity. She has provided me with the confidence to venture into unexplored scientific territories and to successfully find the voice to articulate my scientific and humanitarian vision, both of which are embedded in the theory.

During this process of discovery, there are specific individuals who have functionally "tilted" my thinking and enabled me to expand my perspectives. As a graduate student, David C. Raskin introduced me to the exciting world of psychophysiology with its potential to understand physiological mediators of behavior. Robert E. Bohrer tutored me in time-series statistics and provided me with the confidence to explore my intuitive mathematics. Bob unselfishly worked with me to translate my conceptualizations of the dynamic neural regulation of the autonomic nervous system into the mathematically robust time-series measures that are still the basic metrics used in my research. Stanley I. Greenspan stimulated my interest in psychiatric disorders and provided me with opportunities to deconstruct clinical features into the neurobiological constructs that I study. Peter A. Levine introduced me to the world of trauma research and somatic therapies. His insights into the somatic manifestations of trauma stimulated my passion to understand the neurobiological mechanisms mediating these debilitating effects. Ajit Maiti mentored me in neurophysiology and neuroanatomy. Ajit provided an intellectual bridge between the ancient wisdom of Eastern philosophy and modern Western science. Neil Schneiderman challenged my conceptualization of autonomic measures as psychophysiological indicators by encouraging me to investigate the neural mechanisms mediating heart rate. Hiram E. Fitzgerald shifted my career trajectory toward developmental questions and stimulated my intellectual curiosity to study the autonomic nervous system in young infants. David Crews encouraged me to seek an understanding of the adaptive function of physiological responses from a phylogenetic perspective. Evgeny Sokolov provided a model as a mentor and stimulated me to generate an integrative theory. These insightful and dedicated scientists and clinicians have all been instrumental in framing the intellectual strategies that I used to conceptualize the polyvagal theory. Understanding their contributions unlocks the mystery of the breadth of the theory, which encompasses methodology, mathematics, neuroscience, development, evolution, psychology, and clinical disease. In addition, I want to thank Theo Kierdorf, who encouraged me to integrate several of my papers into a volume on the polyvagal theory. Theo translated and edited several of my papers to create a "polyvagal reader," which was published in German by Junfermann and served as the core of the current volume. I also want to thank Allan Schore, who as editor welcomed this volume into the Norton series on interpersonal neurobiology.

Foreword

Bessel A. van der Kolk

It is an extraordinary experience to hear a new piece of music or a novel scientific idea that makes you sit up in wonder and turns on a bank of lights in your mind that permanently transforms how you understand what life is all about. Seeing Peter Sellers's production of the *Marriage of Figaro,* listening to Elisabeth Kübler-Ross lecture on schizophrenia when I was a medical student, and hearing Steve Maier talk about the neurobiology of inescapable shock at the American College of Neuropsychopharmacology in 1984 were three such unforgettable events for me.

On the morning of May 21, 1999, we had the most memorable series of lectures of the 22 years that I have run the annual Boston trauma conference. The day opened with Bruce McEwen talking about stress and the hippocampus. He introduced the notion of neuroplasticity and showed that Ramon-y-Cahal's dire dictum that anatomy is destiny—that the neuronal connections in the brain are immutably fixed—was incorrect. Jaak Panksepp, whose work has delineated the brain circuits that underlie nurturance, fear, rage, and rough and tumble play, was next. The final speaker that morning was Stephen Porges, who talked about the polyvagal theory of emotions. That lecture caused a fundamental shift in how I and many of my colleagues understand the work we do.

Clinicians and researchers who deal with people with histories of chronic trauma are routinely confronted with fight, flight, or freeze reactions. Our patients (and occasionally colleagues) easily take offense, and they often disorganize their (and our) lives by becoming too angry, too ashamed, and too frozen. Minor irritations easily turn into catastrophes; small failures of communication are difficult to gloss over and easily turn into dramatic interpersonal conflicts. The milk of human kindness, such an essential nutrient in making life bearable, all too often fails to have a significant impact on the despair, rage, and terror of people with histories of trauma and abandonment.

When post-traumatic stress disorder (PTSD) first made it into the diagnostic manuals, we only focused on dramatic incidents like rapes, assaults, or accidents to explain the origins of the emotional breakdowns in our patients. Gradually, we came to understand that the most severe dysregulation occurred in people who, as children, lacked a consistent caregiver. Emotional abuse, loss of caregivers, inconsistency, and chronic misattunement showed up as the principal contributors to a large variety of psychiatric problems (Dozier, Stovall, & Albus, 1999; Pianta, Egeland, & Adam, 1996). One of the most important discoveries in psychology, neuroscience, and psychiatry has been that failure in establishing secure early attachment bonds leads to a diminished capacity to regulate negative emotions. Harlow and his students were the first to show the devastating effects of abandonment and loss on affect regulation in nonhuman primates. Half a century of attachment research has shown that people learn to regulate their emotional arousal largely as a function of the capacity to establish physical and rhythmical attunement with important figures in their early caretaking environment (Trevarthen, 1999). Attachment researchers, starting with John Bowlby, have long shown that the internal regulatory processes of an individual reflect to a large degree the attunement with external sources of regulation early in life (Bowlby, 1973, 1982; Cloitre, Stovall-McClough, Zorbas, & Charuvastra, 2008; Hofer, 2006).

Having a history of chronic misattunement with one's caregivers predisposes people to have difficulties managing negative emotions later in life (Dozier et al., 1999). Sadly, deficient affect regulation caused by early adverse experiences is compounded by the resulting off-putting behaviors in the face of stress, such as temper tantrums and emotional withdrawal (Shaver & Mikulincer, 2002). Dysregulated behavior alienates potential friends and partners and interferes with being able to garner support and accumulate restorative experiences. Lack of affect regulation thus runs the danger of becoming a vicious circle, where deficient self-control leads to abandonment, which in turn makes it even more difficult to regulate negative mood states.

The problem does not end there, since routine psychiatric interventions are quite ineffective in helping people manage their emotions (Cloitre, Stovall-McClough, Miranda, & Chemtob, 2004), and the best that medications generally can do is to dull emotional arousal of any kind, thereby robbing people of pleasure and of pain simultaneously. Traditional psychotherapies also do not offer much immediate relief, since being unable to manage emotional arousal interferes with being able to benefit from treatments such as cognitive behavioral therapy (Jaycox, Foa, & Morral, 1998).

Problems with affect regulation have pervasive effects on the development of mind and brain and lead to significant increases in the utilization of medical, correctional, social, and mental health services (Drossman et al., 1990; Teplin, Abram, McClelland, Dulcan, & Mericle, 2002; Widom & Maxfield, 1996). Many problems of children and adults with histories of chronic trauma and neglect can be understood as efforts to minimize objective threat and to regulate their emotional distress (Pynoos et al., 1987), and hence they are liable to be labeled as "oppositional," "rebellious," "unmotivated," and "antisocial" (Cicchetti

& White, 1990; Widom & Maxfield, 1996; Streeck-Fischer & van der Kolk, 2000).

Our study of patients with abuse and neglect histories was helped enormously by the developments in affective neuroscience, which clarified the underlying neurobiology of many problems seen in these patients. Particularly helpful was Panksepp's (1998) work that elucidated the brain structures and neural circuits involved in the basic emotional systems: seeking, rage, fear, lust, care, panic, and play. But understanding the limbic circuits of emotions still did not account for the precipitous shifts we see in our patients and their lack of responsiveness to the voices and faces of people who care for them, input that helps most people calm down and regain mastery over their senses. The question remained: what causes the emotional systems of some people to be hijacked so easily by slight changes in visual, auditory, kinesthetic, or olfactory input?

More than a decade ago, we became interested in a possible role of heart rate variability (HRV) in the maintenance of these emotional roller coasters. This gave us our first exposure to Porges's polyvagal theory. When we started to measure HRV, we observed that people who maintained relatively stable HRV while remembering horrendous personal events did not seem to suffer from PTSD, whereas people with PTSD generally had poor HRV. Porges's polyvagal theory provided us with an organizing principle for that observation, built on the work of prior scientists such as Charles Darwin and William James, which explained the central role of human interactions and body sensations in our emotional lives.

Up to the time that we learned about the polyvagal theory we had been taught that the autonomic nervous system is organized by the paired antagonism between the sympathetic and the parasympathetic nervous systems, which functionally compete by either increasing or decreasing activity of specific target organs. The introduction of the polyvagal theory vastly expanded this model with an emphasis on the social, myelinated vagus as the fine-tuning regulatory system that opens up a role for the environment to foster or ameliorate stress-related physiological states. Porges proposes that

> phylogenetically, a hierarchical regulatory stress-response system emerged in mammals that not only relies on the well-known sympathetic-adrenal activating system and the parasympathetic inhibitory vagal system, but that these systems are modified by myelinated vagus and the cranial nerves that regulate facial expression which constitute the social engagement system. Thus, phylogenetically, self-regulatory development starts with a primitive behavioral inhibition system, progresses by the evolution of a fight-flight system, and, in humans (and other primates), culminates in a complex social engagement system mediated by facial gestures and vocalizations.

Thus, the mammalian myelinated vagus functions as "an active vagal brake that supports rapid behavioral mobilization, as well as the capacity to physiologically stabilize an individual by means of interoceptive visceral awareness, as well as social interaction." According to Porges, this evolutionary development allows social interactions to stabilize physiological arousal by means of facial expressions, speech, and prosody. When the environment is appraised as being safe, the defensive limbic structures are inhibited. This makes it possible to be socially engaged with calm visceral states.

BREAKDOWN OF AFFECT REGULATION

When that system breaks down, as we witness particularly under conditions of extreme stress, the social vagus no longer can stabilize the organism. The physiological cohesion that forms the basis of the interpersonal neurobiological communication between different organisms breaks down, and the phylogenetically "older" systems will be recruited to regulate metabolic output to deal with environmental challenges. As long as people (and animals) feel threatened, they cannot meaningfully engage with members of their tribe and will resort to more primitive and solipsistic fight-or-flight behaviors (mobilization mediated by the sympathetic nervous system) to ensure survival. Under conditions of inescapable danger even fight or flight breaks down, which leads to immobilization, with a resulting behavioral shutdown, and syncope (via the unmyelinated vagus).

This theory made perfect sense and tied together numerous observations from attachment research, animal ecology, anthropology, and trauma research. To survive and thrive, mammals must be able to distinguish friend from foe, know when a situation is safe or dangerous, and adjust their behavior to the demands of the social group. Porges's observations clarified the mechanisms that allow humans and animals to be physically approached, what ties members of the group together, and how the cohesion of the social group is a central element in managing life's stresses. The polyvagal theory also helps us understand the capacity of the tone of voice and rhythms of speech, as well as faces of our loved ones, to restore our physiological equilibrium.

VISCERAL EXPERIENCES

Another important contribution of the polyvagal theory is a clarification of the relation between visceral state and emotional expression. Trauma researchers understood early on that "the body keeps the score" (van der Kolk, 1994)—that the memory of trauma is encoded in visceral experiences such as heartbreaking and gut-wrenching emotions, in autoimmune disorders, and in skeletal-muscular problems. Porges proposed that afferent feedback from the viscera contributes in a major way to the accessibility of prosocial circuits associated with social engagement. For example, mobilization changes our ability to detect positive social cues, and immobilization may make a person impervious to positive input. Visceral states color our perception of ourselves and our surroundings. The physiological state the person is in precipitates very different outcomes in response to the presentation of the same stimuli.

Internal bodily states are represented in the insula and contribute to subjective feeling states. The insula (which is frequently found to be abnormally activated in neuroimaging studies of traumatized individuals) is involved in the perception of danger and mediates the feedback from the viscera into cognitive awareness. Darwin and James both proposed that visceral experience is a critical element in the experience of emotions and central to their understanding of happiness, fear, anger, disgust, and sadness. Most people are able to gauge danger and love by means of their "gut feelings," which generally accurately detect relative the danger or safety of their situation. People with impaired social engagement systems are prone to misinterpret safety as a threat and objective danger as safety. Their visceral feedback system fails to protect them, or prevents them from engaging in the fullness of what life has to offer.

People who are chronically traumatized have a tendency to become overwhelmed and triggered by their seemingly unmanageable visceral feedback systems that cannot be modified by a functional social engagement system. Consequently they try to inhibit sensory feedback from their bodies and experience the feedback from both their bodies and the world around them as bland and meaningless. Our observation that traumatized individuals habitually engage in body-based defensive maneuvers led us to incorporate the work of such body-based therapists as Peter Levine and Pat Ogden into our treatment armamentarium. In fact, Peter Levine introduced me to Stephen Porges.

IMPLICATIONS FOR TREATMENT

The polyvagal theory of emotions has had a profound effect on helping us organize the treatment of abused children and traumatized adults. True, we might have developed a yoga program for chronically traumatized women anyway, because they so obviously benefit from learning to calm themselves down by learning to manage their breathing and engaging in challenging physical poses that put them in touch with their dissociated bodies. We also probably would have had a theater program in the Boston inner-city schools where traumatized kids learn to play by engaging in rhythmical movements and attuned collaborative exercises. And my friend Tina Packer would have taught Shakespeare to juvenile delinquents anyway, because her profound knowledge of the effects of hexameters and embodying the physical roles of Julius Caesar, Romeo and Juliet, and Richard III compelled her to teach these dysregulated adolescents to engage in and move between deep and varied physiological (and hence mental) states by linking the expressive features of emotion with their visceral responses. My colleagues Robert Macy and Steve Gross would have developed their play techniques and chi qong–based therapies that they apply in inner-city schools and to survivors of tsunamis, earthquakes, and political violence around the world, even if they would never have learned the polyvagal theory.

But the polyvagal theory ties all these disparate unconventional techniques together, in that they all activate situations that in the past have precipitated the participants into uncontrollable flight-or-fight and freeze modes, which, with these various techniques that rely on interpersonal rhythms, visceral awareness and the primary use of vocal and facial communication, attempt to reorganize the perception of danger and capacity to manage emotional engagement.

It is difficult to trace all the sources of one's inspiration, but Porges's polyvagal theory gave us a powerful means of understanding how both bodily states and mental constructs dynamically interact with environmental triggers to precipitate maladaptive behaviors. Porges helped us understand how dynamic our biological systems are and gave us an explanation why a kind face and a soothing tone of voice can dramatically alter the entire organization of the human organism—that is, how being seen and understood can help shift people out of disorganized and fearful states. We had long realized that psychopathological states rarely are static and tend to fluctuate greatly depending on the safety of the environment and the physiological state in which people find themselves. The proposal that our physiological states are flexible, and depend on both our relationship to our visceral experiences and the state of our relationsips promises to decrease our dependence on drug treatment alone to shift people into a different psychological organization. Recognizing the critical role of visceral afferent feedback on the global functioning of the brain inevitably leads to curiosity about the nonpharmacological treatments that have so long been practiced outside of Western medical approaches: age-old traditions of changing mental states with specific breath exercises, body movements (chi qong, tai chi, tae kwon do, and yoga) and rhythmical activities (such as kendo drumming and davening).

Several psychiatric disorders are characterized by difficulties in establishing and maintaining relationships, including difficulty both in expressing social behavior and in reading social cues (i.e., social awareness). Several psychiatric diagnoses are associated with specific deficits in both the behavioral (e.g., poor gaze, low facial affect, lack of prosody) and visceral (difficulties in autonomic regulation resulting in cardiopulmonary and digestive problems) components of the social engagement system.

If physiological mind–brain–viscera communication is the royal road to affect regulation, this invites a radical shift in our therapeutic approaches to a number of psychopathological states, such as anxiety, attention deficit/hyperactivity disorder, autism, and trauma-related psychopathology. Such a shift (for which there appears to be increasing support with increased funding by both the Department of Defense and the National Institutes of Health of such approaches as yoga, martial arts, and acupuncture studies) would ask us to cultivate interpersonal rhythms, nurture the capacity for people to use their voices and faces to regulate emotional states, and explore various body–mind techniques that integrate visceral and emotional experiences. The polyvagal theory legitimates the study of age-old collective and religious practices such as communal chanting, various breathing techniques, and other methods that cause shifts in autonomic state. The polyvagal theory implies that more attention needs to be paid to the development of interventions that either promote activation of the social vagus or dampen sympathetic tone. One major implication is the need to pay closer attention to the therapeutic use of play, rough and tumble behaviors that serve as preliminary exercises to develop adaptive defensive and aggressive behaviors, as a means of shifting people out of fight-or-flight reactions into loving and mutually engaged mobilization.

The Polyvagal Theory

Introduction: Why Is There a Polyvagal Theory?

The polyvagal theory emerged from a dialectic between my curiosity in biobehavioral systems and my dissatisfaction with the prevalent models that integrated physiological state with behavior. When I started my scientific career, I was intrigued with the possibility of using physiological measures to understand the psychological states of others. In the late 1960s, when I was in graduate school, I had the vision that monitoring physiological state would be a helpful guide to the therapist during the clinical interaction. This vision is still part of my research agenda. I am still working on developing a polyvagal monitor, which will provide feedback in real time to clinicians of the dynamic interplay between the three neural circuits described in the polyvagal theory.

In the 1960s, the constructs and models relating physiology to behavior were limited. Dominant in the human and psychophysiological literature was a construct of arousal. The defining features of arousal were vague. However, psychophysiologists assumed that arousal was mediated by the sympathetic nervous system. Early psychophysiologists, such as Chester Darrow, proposed continuity between cortical activation measured through electroencephalography (EEG) and sympathetic arousal measured by the galvanic skin resistance response on the hands. This view of a peripheral indicator of brain processes was consistent with Pavlov's use of autonomic measures in his classical conditioning experiments. For Pavlov, the "classically" conditioned autonomic responses were indices of changes in brain circuits. Arousal is still used in sleep research to describe cortical activation and in research on deception in which traditional polygraphs are used.

The specific physiological and neurophysiological mechanisms underlying arousal are often associated with the sympathetic nervous system and the hypothalamic-pituitary-adrenal (HPA) axis. An inferred connection between the sympathetic nervous system and the HPA axis has resulted in similar research methods being used to study both arousal and stress. This sympathetic-centric view has been translated into the popular press and public consciousness as a cliché that a limited amount of stress is "good" and too much stress is "bad." But what were the thresholds of stress necessary for health or illness? In addition, consistent with this sympathetic-centric view, we all were taught that the stress-related sympathetic excitation had evolutionary origins in mammalian fight-or-flight behaviors. Thus, we were taught that the increased sympathetic tone to novelty and danger was a reflection of our evolutionary history.

At the time of my introduction to psychophysiology, physiological measures were proposed as a portal into psychological processes without requiring conscious awareness or verbal responses. This exciting discipline, however, was constrained by a limited understanding of the neural mechanisms regulating the physiological measures being monitored and an adequate understanding of the mediating neural mechanisms linking peripheral autonomic responses to the psychological processes of interest to the psychophysiologist.

Psychophysiology was established in the early 1960s as a discipline merging features of psychology, medicine, physiology, and engineering. The Society for Psychophysiological Research was formed in 1960 and the first issue of society's journal, *Psychophysiology*, was published in 1964. During its early years, psychophysiology distinguished itself from physiological psychology by focusing on physiology as a dependent variable and psychological factors (e.g., threat, novelty) and processes (e.g., attention, mental effort, emotion) as independent variables. In contrast, physiological psychology manipulated physiology (independent variable) and monitored changes in behavior and psychological processes (i.e., dependent variable). In general, psychophysiologists studied human subjects in their research paradigms, whereas physiological psychologists studied animals. I joined the Society for Psychophysiological Research in 1968 and attended my first meeting in 1969. The early meetings were exciting, and many of the initial pioneers in the society had been successful scientists in other domains. During my more than 40 years of membership, I was involved in the society as a member of the board, secretary-treasurer, and president. During this period, research interests and methods shifted from peripheral measures of the autonomic nervous system to measures of brain function employing EEG, event-related potentials, and functional magnetic resonance imaging methods. Current issues of *Psychophysiology* reflect this trend and focus on measures of brain function during cognitive and affective challenges.

As an important consequence of this history, physiological variables were seen as correlates of psychological processes. This view allowed researchers to study parallels between physiology and behavior without understanding the underlying relationship between these domains. Basically, there are two global domains in the biobehavioral sciences: (1) behavior (observable) and psychological (subjective) and (2) physiological (peripheral autonomic) and neural (brain). Paradigms that correlate physiology and behavior or use physiological variables as a biomarker of a clinical disorder are the consequence of a modern Western scientific solution to the historical remnant of the mind–body problem. The current scientific solutions of dualism are not solutions, but merely objective descriptions of parallel functions with exquisite technologies. Many scientists and disciplines are stuck in the dualism trap. New disciplines have emerged such as cognitive neuroscience, affective neuroscience, social neuroscience, health psychology, and several subdisciplines within public health that use the methods that were developed in psychophysiological research to provide biomarkers of illness. Currently, measures of heart rate variability and neuroendocrine activity (e.g., cortisol, oxytocin, vasopressin) are frequently described as potential biomarkers of clinical health and risk. The polyvagal theory challenges this implicit dualism by providing a bidirectional brain–body model that interprets the brain regulation of peripheral physiology (e.g., neural regulation of both cardiovascular and endocrine function) as providing a neural platform for emergent adaptive social and defensive behaviors (see chapter 8).

The academic arena of the late 1960s had a limited conceptualization of the brain's role in regulating peripheral physiology. Because the details of potential mechanisms mediating the link between psychological processes and physiology were unknown, scientists were comfortable with investigations applying physiological measures as correlates of psychological processes and potential biomarkers of mental and physical health. In 1970, I matriculated into this academic arena with my doctorate and started conducting independent research as an assistant professor

The roots of the polyvagal theory emerged while conducting research on heart rate correlates of attention for my master's thesis (Porges & Raskin, 1969). In this study, I noted that when subjects focused their attention on the task demands, the beat-to-beat heart rate pattern stabilized. The publication of the master's thesis became the first quantitative description of heart rate variability as a response variable sensitive to psychological manipulations. My dissertation followed this theme by testing the relation between heart rate variability and reaction time performance. The dissertation confirmed that greater reductions in heart rate variability were associated with faster reaction times. Moreover, the study identified that individual differences in heart rate variability predicted reaction time performance and the degree to which heart rate variability was suppressed while attending (Porges, 1972). Throughout the following 40 years, although methodologies and research questions have changed, my laboratory research has continued to conduct studies monitoring heart rate and quantifying heart rate variability.

How did an observation that heart rate stabilized during attention lead to the polyvagal theory? There were a few intervening conceptualizations. First, I had to link the changes in heart rate variability to vagal mechanisms. This was accomplished through two stages: first, the development of quantification techniques to characterize the rhythms in the beat-to-beat heart rate pattern, and second, conducting validation studies to demonstrate that the amplitude of the respiratory rhythm in heart rate (i.e., respiratory sinus arrhythmia) was a valid indicator of vagal influences to the heart. By the early 1980s, this was in place. The ideas coalesced and the concept of vagal tone was concretized in a vagal tone monitor and software to enable other laboratories to use this sensitive index.

Although developed 30 years ago, the method I created for quantifying heart rate variability is still being used in more than 100 laboratories worldwide. The method has survived because it has five advantages over the scores of methods that have been proposed during the intervening decades to quantify heart rate variability: (1) the method enables dynamic monitoring of the shifts in vagal control of heart over short periods of time, (2) it conforms to the statistical assumptions necessary for parametric statistics, (3) it enables reliable estimates even when the baseline of heart rate drifts and violates the assumption of stationarity, (4) it is not moderated by respiration rate, and (5) the metric reflects the same changes in vagal function across time and laboratories.

Once the quantification procedures were developed, validated, and packaged in software and hardware, I thought the research world of autonomic psychophysiology would expand. I believed that the sensitive quantification methods would enable scores of scientists to investigate and study the critical role that cardiac vagal tone played in physical and mental health and in moderating social, affective, and cognitive behaviors and motor activity. With these tools dozens of studies were conducted in laboratories around the world with a common metric, and vagal tone became a familiar measure in psychological and psychophysiological research.

Everything seemed relatively simple. Once there was a good measure of parasympathetic activity (i.e., vagal tone), the sympathetic-centric worldview would be challenged and constructs such as autonomic balance, arousal, and stress, introduced decades before, could be studied within a more complete physiological model that included dynamic measures of vagal tone. Interest in vagal tone and heart rate variability grew, and several other metrics of vagal tone derived from heart rate variability developed by other scientists also became available to researchers. The movement from sympathetic-centric to dual sympathetic-parasympathetic measures provided a comfortable haven for researchers who had learned autonomic neurophysiology from a paired-antagonism perspective (i.e., the balance between sympathetic and parasympathetic influences). Thus, my research provided a critical measurement tool that would enable researchers to study the dynamically changing interplay between the sympathetic and the parasympathetic components of the autonomic nervous system. This conceptualization of cardiac vagal tone did not challenge the existing dogma presented in textbooks of the autonomic nervous system as a paired-antagonistic system.

VAGAL PARADOX

Although I had vested interests in vagal regulation, I was not uncomfortable with the paired-antagonism model of the autonomic nervous system. By 1990, I saw my contribution to psychophysiology and psychobiology as presenting the other side of autonomic function to a sympathetic-centric research world. I saw the importance of tonic levels of vagal activity as an index of general neural health and as a protective feature. In my writings I started to discuss the autonomic nervous system as a bidirectional system that involved potent visceral feedback (see chapter 5) and central structures in the regulation of physiological and emotional state (see chapter 9).

In the early 1990s I had not incorporated into my research perspective the three important points that led to the conceptualization of the polyvagal theory. First, although I wrote about the importance of having high vagal tone as a positive health index, I did not conceptualize autonomic reactions as being hierarchical. For example, I did not conceptualize the vagus as being inhibitory of the sympathetic regulation of the heart. Second, I had no understanding of how the neural regulation of the autonomic nervous system changed during evolution and how these changes would be related to adaptive physiological and behavioral functions in mammals. Third, although I knew that vagal pathways originated from two brainstem nuclei (dorsal motor nucleus of the vagus and the nucleus ambiguus), I did not think too much about their relative functions.

By 1992, I was confident that my research was on the right track and looked forward to expanding my projects and collaborations with the technologies I had developed. I thought the hard work was done and looked forward to new discoveries applying these technologies to clinical populations. I had no intention of developing a theory that would require a deep understanding of evolution and the adaptive behavioral functions that covaried with the phylogenetic changes in neural regulation of the autonomic nervous system. I had no intention to challenge either the prevalent theoretical models of the autonomic nervous system (i.e., paired antagonism) or the application of physiological monitoring as correlates of psychological processes and as potential "biomarkers" for health and disease.

My intellectual complacency did not last. The jolt came in the form a complimentary letter from a neonatologist that I received shortly after I published an article in September 1992 (see chapter 4). The neonatologist wrote that although he liked my article, it was not consistent with what he learned in medical school. The paper described evidence that measuring cardiac vagal tone (i.e., respiratory sinus arrhythmia) derived from the beat-to-beat heart rate in newborn infants provided a sensitive index of clinical status. The study reported consistently higher cardiac vagal tone in healthy full-term newborns, while lower cardiac vagal tone at about the time of discharge for premature infants. In his letter he stated that he had learned that high vagal tone was bad for newborns and could kill them, and he ended by stating that perhaps too much of a good thing is bad. Something was not right with this conclusion. Having conducted research in newborn nurseries since 1970, I tried to understand his statements from his training and observations. When I took his perspective, I immediately realized that risk to the newborn was associated with vagal-mediated bradycardia. Bradycardia is a massive slowing of heart rate that if prolonged, may result in depriving the brain of needed oxygen. In contrast, I was looking at a protective feature of the vagus, the beat-to-beat variability that had a respiratory rhythm. By the time I published this paper, we had collected sufficient data from both human newborns and fetuses to realize that bradycardia occurred only when the tonic pattern of beat-to-beat heart rate was relatively flat (i.e., no or very low-amplitude respiratory sinus arrhythmia). I had interpreted this pattern as a lack of vagal influence to the heart. Now I understood why obstetricians and neonatologists, who used beat-to-beat heart rate variability as a biomarker of clinical status, made no inference regarding mechanism.

I was in an intellectual quandary. I had been arguing that cardiac vagal tone was a positive clinical index that could be measured by respiratory sinus arrhythmia. Now there was the possibility that there were two heart rate measures with vagal origins, one protective and the other potentially lethal. Among neonatologists and obstetricians there was an acceptance that beat-to-beat heart rate variability had clinical significance, although the neural mechanisms mediating this clinically relevant biomarker were not known and there appeared to be no motivation to identify the mechanisms. In contrast, rapid massive bradycardias were clearly mediated by transitory vagal surges.

How could the vagal regulation of the heart be an index of resilience and health when it was represented in high-amplitude respiratory sinus arrhythmia and an index of risk when it was represented in bradycardia? This question challenged my understanding of the autonomic nervous system. I placed the letter from the neonatologist in my briefcase, where it remained for about 2 years as I formulated the basis for the polyvagal theory. I labeled this contradiction in our understanding of the vagus the vagal paradox. My motivation to solve the vagal paradox led to new conceptualizations of the autonomic nervous system and the formulation of the polyvagal theory. Only with the new understandings gained from the polyvagal theory would the vagal paradox be deciphered and the hierarchical nature of the neural regulation and the adaptive functions of in the autonomic nervous system understood.

From fall 1992 through fall 1994, I worked on integrating the literature on the autonomic nervous system and extracting a series of organizing principles that became the core of the theory. During this period, in addition to my professorship at the University of Maryland, I was a visiting scientist at the National Institutes of Health (NIH). As such, I had access to the excellent NIH library and the National Library of Medicine. With these resources, I immersed myself in the literature and read hundreds of articles and numerous books on the neural regulation of the autonomic nervous system in vertebrates. The polyvagal theory was the product of this work and was presented on October 8, 1994, in my presidential address to the Society for Psychophysiological Research (see chapter 2).

Since the initial presentation, the theory has been refined and expanded (see Porges, 2001a, 2007a). By selecting and editing previously published papers, the chapters in this book provide an opportunity to share the discoveries of the theory. The chapters include the presentation of the initial theory (see chapter 2) and the expansion and elaboration of ideas dependent on the theory, including vagal brake (see chapter 7), self-regulation (see chapter 6), development (see chapter 8), emotion (see chapters 9 and 10), evolution and dissolution (see chapter 10), immobilization without fear (see chapter 11), the social engagement system (see chapters 11, 12, and 13), attachment (see chapter 12), love and monogamy (see chapter 11), neuroception (see chapters 1 and 12), prosody and vocal communication (see chapter 13), clinical applications (see chapters 14, 15, 16, and 17), and our current work redefining social neuroscience (see chapters 18 and 19). Chapter 3 has been included as a succinct summary of the major points of the theory (e.g., vagal paradox, dissolution, social engagement system, neuroception) and may be helpful in clarifying chapters in which the presentation of the theory has been abridged.

PART I

THEORETICAL PRINCIPLES

CHAPTER 1

Neuroception: A Subconscious System for Detecting Threat and Safety

What determines how two human beings will act toward each other when they meet? Is this initial response a product of learning from culture, family experiences, and other socialization processes? Or is the response the expression of a neurobiological process that is programmed into the very DNA of our species? If the response has a neurobiological basis, are there specific features of the other person's behavior that trigger either feelings of safety, love, and comfort or feelings of danger? Why do some children cuddle and warmly conform to embraces, yet others stiffen and pull back from the same overture? Why do some children smile and actively engage a new person, while others avert their gaze and withdraw?

Does knowledge of human biology help us understand the triggers and mechanisms of these behaviors during normal development? If we learn how behavioral features trigger neural circuits that facilitate social behavior, will we be better able to help children with severe developmental disabilities, such as autism, improve their social behavior?

By processing information from the environment through the senses, the nervous system continually evaluates risk. I have coined the term *neuroception* to describe how neural circuits distinguish whether situations or people are safe, dangerous, or life-threatening. Because of our heritage as a species, neuroception takes place in primitive parts of the brain, without our conscious awareness. The detection of a person as safe or dangerous triggers neurobiologically determined prosocial or defensive behaviors. Even though we may not be aware of danger on a cognitive level, on a neurophysiological level, our body has already started a sequence of neural processes that would facilitate adaptive defense behaviors such as fight, flight, or freeze.

A child's (or an adult's) nervous system may detect danger or a threat to life when the child enters a new environment or meets a strange person. Cognitively, there is no reason for them to be frightened. But often, even if they understand this, their bodies betray them. Sometimes this betrayal is private; only they are aware that their hearts are beating fast and contracting with such force that they start to sway. For others, the responses are more overt. They may tremble. Their faces may flush, or perspiration may pour from their hands and forehead. Still others may become pale and dizzy and feel precipitously faint.

This process of neuroception would explain why a baby coos at a familiar caregiver but cries at the approach of a stranger, or why a toddler enjoys a parent's gentle embrace but interprets the same gesture from a stranger as an assault. We can see the process at work when two toddlers encounter each other in a playground sandbox. They may decide that the situation and each other are safe if the sandbox is familiar territory, if their pails and shovels have roughly similar appeal, and if they (the toddlers) are about the same size. The toddlers may then express positive social engagement behaviors—in other words, they may start to play.

"Playing nice" comes naturally when our neuroception detects safety and promotes physiological states that support social behavior. However, prosocial behavior will not occur when our neuroception misreads the environmental cues and triggers physiological states that support defensive strategies. After all, "playing nice" is not appropriate or adaptive behavior in dangerous or life-threatening situations. In these situations, humans—like other mammals—react with more primitive neurobiological defense systems. To create relationships, humans must subdue these defensive reactions to engage, attach, and form lasting social bonds. Humans have adaptive neurobehavioral systems for both prosocial and defensive behaviors.

What allows engagement behaviors to occur, while disabling the mechanisms of defense? To switch effectively from defensive to social engagement strategies, the nervous system must do two things: (1) assess risk, and (2) if the environment looks safe, inhibit the primitive defensive reactions to fight, flee, or freeze.

By processing information from the environment through the senses, the nervous system continually evaluates risk. As evolution has proceeded, new neural systems have developed. These systems use some of the same brain structures that are involved in defense functions to support forms of social engagement. Neuroception now may encourage the development of social bonds and provide the opportunity for reproduction.

SOCIAL ENGAGEMENT AND DEFENSIVE BEHAVIOR: ADAPTIVE OR MALADAPTIVE STRATEGIES?

Social engagement and defense behaviors may be adaptive or maladaptive, depending on the level of risk that is present in the environment. From a clinical perspective, the defining features of psychopathology may include either a person's inability to *inhibit* defense systems in a safe environment or the inability to *activate* defense systems in a risky environment—or both. Only in a safe environment is it adaptive and appropriate to simultaneously inhibit defense systems and exhibit positive social engagement behavior. Faulty neuroception—that is, an inaccurate assessment of the safety or danger of a situation—might contribute to the maladaptive physiological reactivity and the expression of defensive behaviors associated with specific psychiatric disorders. In typically developing children, however, neuroception detects risk accurately. Children's cognitive awareness of risk matches their "gut response" to danger.

When our nervous system detects safety, our metabolic demands adjust. Stress responses that are associated with fight and flight—such as increases in heart rate and cortisol mediated by the sympathetic nervous system and hypothalamic-pituitary-adrenal axis—are dampened. Similarly, a neuroception of safety keeps us from entering physiological states that are characterized by massive drops in blood pressure and heart rate, fainting, and apnea—states that would support "freezing" and "shutdown" behaviors.

How does the nervous system know when the environment is safe, dangerous, or life-threatening? What neural mechanisms evaluate risk in the environment? New technologies, such as functional magnetic resonance imaging, have identified specific neural structures that are involved in detecting risk. Specific areas of the brain detect and evaluate features, such as body and face movements and vocalizations that contribute to an impression of safety or trustworthiness. Researchers have identified an area in the cortex that becomes activated when we see familiar faces and hear familiar voices. This process of identifying familiar and trustworthy people and evaluating the intentions of others based on "biological movements" of face and limbs seems to be located in the temporal lobe of the cortex. If neuroception identifies a person as safe, then a neural circuit actively inhibits areas of the brain that organize the defensive strategies of fight, flight, and freeze. Slight changes in the biological movements that we see can shift a neuroception from "safe" to "dangerous." When this shift occurs, the neural systems associated with prosocial behavior are disrupted, and the neural systems associated with defensive strategies are triggered.

In the presence of a safe person, then, the active inhibition of the brain areas that control defense strategies provides an opportunity for social behavior to occur spontaneously. Thus, the appearance of a friend or caregiver would subdue the neural circuits in the brain that regulate defensive strategies. As a consequence, closeness, physical contact, and other social engagement behaviors become possible. In contrast, when situations appear risky, the brain circuits that regulate defense strategies are activated. Social approaches are met with aggressive behavior or withdrawal.

IMMOBILIZATION WITHOUT FEAR

As we have seen, humans have three principal defense strategies—fight, flight, and freeze. We are familiar with fight and flight behaviors, but know less about the defense strategy of immobilization, or freezing. This strategy, shared with early vertebrates, is often expressed in mammals as "death feigning." In humans, we observe a behavioral shutdown, frequently accompanied by very weak muscle tone. We also observe physiological changes: heart rate and breathing slow, and blood pressure drops.

Immobilization, or freezing, is one of our species's most ancient mechanisms of defense. Inhibiting movement slows our metabolism (reducing our need for food) and raises our pain threshold. But in addition to freezing defensively, mammals immobilize themselves for essential prosocial activities, including conception, childbirth, nursing, and the establishment of social bonds. For example, when an infant nurses, the mother has to restrain her movements. When a child is embraced, the child is functionally immobilized. Reproductive behaviors also involve a degree of immobilization. However, immobilization with fear elicits profound, potentially lethal, physiological changes (i.e., dramatic slowing of heart rate, cessation of breathing, and dropping of blood pressure). Through the process of evolution, neural circuits in the brain that were originally involved in freezing behaviors were modified to serve intimate social needs. Over time, these brain structures grew receptors for a neuropeptide known as oxytocin. Oxytocin is released during the birth process and nursing. It is also released in the brain during activities that help establish social bonds. Thus, when we sense that our environment is safe, the release of oxytocin allows us to enjoy the comfort of an embrace without fear. But if our nervous system identifies someone as dangerous, although oxytocin may be released, we struggle against the attempted embrace.

SOCIAL ENGAGEMENT: THE PREAMBLE TO A SOCIAL BOND

To develop a social bond, it it not enough to inhibit defense systems. People must also be physically close to each other. This is true whether they are a mother and baby forming an attachment relationship or two adults forming a social bond. There are, of course, major differences between the contexts in which mother–infant attachment and the social bonds of reproductive partners are established. Consider mobility, for example. Due to immature neural development, the baby has limited ability to move either toward or away from the mother. In contrast, two adults who may become reproductive partners are likely to have similar behavioral repertoires.

If the creation of social bonds depended on voluntary motor behaviors, then the human newborn would be greatly disadvantaged: The neural regulation of the spinal motor pathways is immature at the time of birth and takes several years to develop fully. Fortunately, social engagement does *not* depend on how well we can regulate our limbs and move our bodies. Voluntary limb and trunk movement require neural pathways linking the cortex to spinal nerves (i.e., corticospinal pathways). Social engagement depends, rather, on how well we can regulate the muscles of our faces and heads via pathways linking the cortex with the brainstem (i.e., corticobulbar pathways). These are the muscles that give expression to our faces, allow us to gesture with our heads, put intonation into our voices, direct our gaze, and permit us to distinguish human voices from background sounds. Corticospinal pathways to spinal nerves regulate the muscles that control the trunk and limbs; corticobulbar pathways to cranial nerves regulate the muscles of the face and head. The neural pathways from the cortex to these nerves (i.e., corticobulbar) are myelinated sufficiently at birth to allow the infant to signal a caregiver by vocalizing or grimacing and to engage the social and nutrient aspects of the world by gazing, smiling, and sucking.

The neural regulation of the muscles of the face and head influences how someone perceives the engagement behaviors of others. More specifically, this neural regulation can reduce social distance by allowing humans (including infants) to:

- make eye contact;
- vocalize with an appealing inflection and rhythm;
- display contingent facial expressions; and
- modulate the middle-ear muscles to distinguish the human voice from background sounds more efficiently.

Alternatively, when the tone of these muscles is reduced, which occurs spontaneously in response to a neuroception of danger or a life threat in the external environment (e.g., a dangerous person or situation) or the internal environment (e.g., fever, pain, or physical illness) environment:

- the eyelids droop;
- the voice loses inflection;
- positive facial expressions dwindle;
- awareness of the sound of the human voice becomes less acute; and
- sensitivity to others' social engagement behaviors decreases.

It is important to remember that neuroception of danger or a threat to life can occur with respect to the external environment (e.g., a dangerous person or situation) or the internal environment (e.g., fever, pain, or physical illness). Even flat (rather than angry) facial affect might prompt a neuroception of danger or fear and disrupt the development of normal spontaneous interactive and reciprocal social engagements. For example, the flat affect of a depressed parent or the flat affect of an ill child might trigger a transactional spiral that results in compromised emotional regulation and limited spontaneous social engagement.

POLYVAGAL THEORY: THREE NEURAL CIRCUITS THAT REGULATE REACTIVITY

Where do humans' intricate neurobehavioral systems for prosocial and defensive behaviors come from? As we have suggested earlier, mammals—including humans—must distinguish friend from foe, evaluate the safety of the environment, and communicate with their social unit. According to the polyvagal theory (see chapters 2, 5, 10, and 11; Porges, 2001a), mammals—especially primates—have evolved brain structures that regulate both social and defensive behaviors. In other words, evolutionary forces have molded both human physiology and human behavior. As the vertebrate nervous system became more complex during the course of evolution, its affective and behavioral repertoire expanded. A product of this phylogenetic process is a nervous system that provides humans with the ability to express emotions, communicate, and regulate bodily and behavioral states.

The polyvagal theory links the evolution of the neural regulation of the heart to affective experience, emotional expression, facial gestures, vocal communication, and social behavior that is responsive to the behavior of others. The theory points out that the neural control of the heart is neuroanatomically linked to the neural control the muscles of the face and head.

The polyvagal theory describes three stages in the development of a mammal's autonomic nervous system. Each of the three major adaptive behavioral strategies is supported by a distinct neural circuit involving the autonomic nervous system.

1. Immobilization
   - Feigning death, behavioral shutdown.
   - The most primitive component, shared with most vertebrates.
   - Dependent on the oldest branch of the vagus nerve (an unmyelinated portion originating in an area of the brainstem known as the dorsal motor nucleus of the vagus).
2. Mobilization
   - Fight-or-flight behaviors.
   - Dependent on the functioning of the sympathetic nervous system, a system associated with increasing metabolic activity and increasing cardiac output (e.g., faster heart rate, greater ability of the heart to contract).
3. Social communication or social engagement
   - Facial expression, vocalization, listening.
   - Dependent on the myelinated vagus, which originates in an area of the brainstem known as the nucleus ambiguus. The myelinated vagus fosters calm behavioral states by inhibiting the influence of the sympathetic nervous system on the heart.

Infants, young children, and adults need appropriate social engagement strategies in order to form positive attachments and social bonds. At the University of Illinois at Chicago, we have been developing a model that links social engagement to attachment and the formation of social bonds through the following steps.

1. Three well-defined neural circuits support social engagement behaviors, mobilization, and immobilization.

2. Independent of conscious awareness, the nervous system evaluates risk in the environment and regulates the expression of adaptive behavior to match the neuroception of an environment that is safe, dangerous, or life-threatening.
3. A neuroception of safety is necessary before social engagement behaviors can occur. These behaviors are accompanied by the benefits of the physiological states, associated with social support.
4. Social behaviors associated with nursing, reproduction, and the formation of strong pair bonds requires immobilization without fear.
5. Oxytocin, a neuropeptide involved in the formation of social bonds, makes immobilization without fear possible by blocking defensive freezing behaviors.

NEUROCEPTION AND MENTAL HEALTH DISORDERS

So far, we have been discussing neuroception that works. Ideally, a baby's neuroception of her environment shows her a safe place to explore. But even if her neuroception warns her—accurately—of danger from a "frightened or frightening" caregiver, the baby can take some defensive measures, even though they are likely to be ineffective and are almost certain to be psychologically costly. What happens when neuroception itself is impaired? From a theoretical perspective, faulty neuroception—that is, an inability to detect accurately whether the environment is safe or another person is trustworthy—might lie at the root of several psychiatric disorders.

- Areas in the temporal cortex that are assumed to inhibit fight, flight, or freeze reactions are not activated in people with autism or schizophrenia, who have difficulty with social engagement.
- Individuals with anxiety disorders and depression have compromised social behavior; difficulties in regulating heart rate, as reflected in measures of vagal control of the heart and reduced facial expressiveness.
- Maltreated and institutionalized children with reactive attachment disorder tend to be either inhibited (emotionally withdrawn and unresponsive) or uninhibited (indiscriminate in their attachment behavior; Zeanah, 2000). Both types of behavior suggest faulty neuroception of the risk in the environment.

Recent research on children raised in Romanian orphanages has stimulated interest in reactive attachment disorders and in finding ways to remediate the devastating disturbances in their social development. If the behavior of these children suggests faulty neuroception of risk in the environment, are there features in the environment that might help the children feel safer and then begin to move toward more normal social behavior?

A study of Romanian toddlers being raised in an orphanage (Smyke, Dumitrescu, & Zeanah, 2002) illustrates the usefulness of the construct of neuroception in understanding the development of normal and atypical attachment behaviors. Researchers evaluated two groups of institutionalized children and compared them to children who had never been institutionalized. One group of institutionalized children (the standard unit) was cared for according to prevailing standards: 20 different caregivers worked rotating shifts, with approximately 3 caregivers for 30 children on each shift. A second group of children, the pilot unit, consisted of 10 children with 4 caregivers. If we apply our concept of neuroception to this study, we would hypothesize that familiar caregivers would be essential to children's neuroception of safety—which, in turn, would be essential for the promotion of appropriate social behavior. Specifically, a child's ability to recognize a caregiver's face, voice, and movements (the features that define a safe and trustworthy person) should set in motion the process of subduing the limbic system and allowing the social engagement system to function.

The data from the Smyke et al. (2002) study supports our hypothesis. The higher the number of caregivers children had contact with, the higher the incidence of reactive attachment disorder among these children. The standard-unit children were more likely than the other two groups to have reactive attachment disorder. On some indices of reactive attachment disorder, the pilot-group children did not differ from the children who had never been institutionalized. These findings suggest that once we understand the contextual and social features that inhibit the neural circuits which mediate defensive behavioral strategies, we can "optimize" the development of prosocial behavior.

At the University of Illinois at Chicago, we are using a newly developed biologically based behavioral intervention based on principles derived from the polyvagal theory. We are testing this approach with children with autism and individuals with language and social communication problems. Our model assumes that for many children with social communication deficits, including those diagnosed with autism, the social engagement system is neuroanatomically and neurophysiologically intact. Yet these children do not engage in voluntary prosocial behaviors. To improve spontaneous social behavior, we have reasoned, an intervention must stimulate the neural circuits that regulate the muscles of the face and head. The polyvagal theory predicts that once the cortical regulation of the brainstem structures involved in the social engagement are activated, social behavior and communication will spontaneously occur as the natural emergent properties of this biological system. The intervention "stimulates" and "exercises" the neural pathways involved in listening and simultaneously stimulates the function of other aspects of the social engagement system. The intervention provides acoustic stimulation that has been computer altered to systematically modulate the neural regulation of the middle-ear muscles. Theoretically, the middle-ear muscles need to be regulated during listening, and the nerves that regulate these muscles are linked to the nerves that regulate the other muscles of the face and head involved in social engagement. Preliminary results are promising. They suggest that interventions designed to improve spontaneous social behavior should: (1) ensure that the context elicits in participants a neuroception of safety that will allow the social engagement system to function; and (2) exercise the neural regulation of the social engagement system.

CONCLUSIONS

According to the polyvagal theory (including the concept of neuroception), our range of social behavior is limited by our human physiology, which has evolved from that of more primitive vertebrates. When we are frightened, we are dependent on the neural circuits that evolved to provide adaptive defensive behaviors for more primitive vertebrates. These neural circuits provide physiological mechanisms that reflexively organize mobilization or immobilization behaviors before we are consciously aware of what is happening. When, on the other hand, neuroception tells us that an environment is safe and that the people in this environment are trustworthy, our mechanisms of defense are disabled. We can then behave in ways that encourage social engagement and positive attachment.

Focusing on biologically based behaviors common to all humans allows practitioners to imagine new intervention paradigms to help children whose social behavior and attachment are compromised. We can alter the caregiving environment so that it will appear—and be—safer for children and less likely to evoke mobilization or immobilization responses. We can also intervene directly with children, exercising the neural regulation of brainstem structures, stimulating the neural regulation of the social engagement system, and encouraging positive social behavior.

CHAPTER 2

Orienting in a Defensive World: Mammalian Modifications of Our Evolutionary Heritage

A Polyvagal Theory

The systematic investigation of mind–body relations forms the scientific basis for the science of psychophysiology. Unlike the correlative view of mind–body evaluations that dominates psychology and psychiatry, psychophysiology emphasizes a continuity between neurophysiological and psychological processing. Psychophysiologists assume that the nervous system provides the functional units for the bidirectional transduction of psychological and physiological processes. Thus, from a psychophysiological perspective, it is possible to link psychological processes with neurophysiological processes and brain structures by measurement and not just theory.

This chapter will focus on neural regulation of the heart by the vagus and how this regulation evolved to facilitate specific psychological processes. The polyvagal theory, as described in this chapter, provides an explanation of how the vagal pathways regulate heart rate in response to novelty and to a variety of stressors. The theory proposes that through evolution mammals developed two vagal systems: a phylogenetic relic of amphibians and reptiles and an evolutionary modification unique to mammals. According to the polyvagal theory, the two vagal systems are programmed with different response strategies and may respond in a contradictory manner. Explanations for several psychophysiological phenomena and psychosomatic disturbances will be proposed. The theory is based on an established literature in neurophysiology, neuroanatomy, and psychophysiology.

AROUSAL THEORY: HISTORICAL LEGACY

Early psychophysiological research assumed that peripheral autonomic measures provided sensitive indicators of arousal or activation (Darrow, Jost, Solomon, & Mergener, 1942; Duffy, 1957; Lindsley, 1951; Malmo, 1959). This view was based on a rudimentary understanding of the autonomic nervous system in which changes in electrodermal activity and heart rate were assumed to be accurate indicators of sympathetic activity. As the activation-arousal theory developed, a continuity between peripheral autonomic responses and central mechanisms was assumed. According to this assumption, any organ influenced by sympathetic efferent fibers, such as the sudomotor, vascular, or cardiac systems, was a potential indicator of limbic or cortical activity.

Although the specific pathways relating these various levels were never outlined and are still sketchy, electrodermal and heart rate measures became the primary focus of research during the early history of the Society for Psychophysiological Research. This was due to their presumed sympathetic innervation and, in part, to their measurement availability. By default, this emphasis created a research environment that neglected several important factors: (a) parasympathetic influences, (b) interactions between sympathetic and parasympathetic processes, (c) peripheral autonomic afferents, (d) central regulatory structures, (e) the adaptive and dynamic nature of the autonomic nervous system, and (f) phylogenetic and ontogenetic differences in structural organization and function.

The neglect of these concepts and an emphasis on a global construct of *arousal* still abide within various subdisciplines of psychology, psychiatry, and physiology. This outdated view of arousal may restrict an understanding of how the autonomic nervous system interfaces with the environment and the contribution of the autonomic nervous system to psychological and behavioral processes. In contrast, more recent neurophysiological data promote a more integrative view of the autonomic nervous system.

BRAIN-HEART COMMUNICATION: HISTORICAL PERSPECTIVE

When we view living organisms as a collection of dynamic, adaptive, interactive, and interdependent physiological systems, it is no longer appropriate to treat the autonomic nervous system as functionally distinct from the central nervous system. We start to recognize that peripheral organs do not "float in a visceral sea." Rather, they are anchored to central structures by means of efferent pathways and are continuously signaling central regulatory structures along their abundant afferent pathways. Thus, the bidirectional connections between autonomic and central brain structures are becoming apparent. Accordingly, new theories and research strategies must incorporate the dynamic and interactive constructs that link central structures with peripheral organs.

Darwin (1872) provided historical insight into the potential importance of the vagus in bidirectional communication between the brain and the heart. Although Darwin focused on facial expressions in defining emotions, he acknowledged the dynamic relationship between the vagus and the central nervous system activity that accompanied the spontaneous expression of emotions. He speculated that there were identifiable neural pathways that provided the necessary communication between specific brain structures and peripheral organs to promote the unique pattern of autonomic activity associated with emotions. For example:

> when the mind is strongly excited, we might expect that it would instantly affect in a direct manner the heart; and this is universally acknowledged . . . when the heart is affected it reacts on the brain; and the state of the brain again reacts through the pneuma-gastric [vagus] nerve on the heart; so that under any excitement there will be much mutual action and reaction between these, the two most important organs of the body. (p. 69)

For Darwin, when an emotional state occurred, the beating of the heart changed instantly, the change in cardiac activity influenced brain activity, and the brainstem structures through the cranial nerves (i.e., vagus) stimulated the heart. He did not elucidate the neurophysiological mechanisms that translate the initial emotional expression to the heart. Our current knowledge of the origin of the brainstem and the neurophysiological function of the various branches of the vagus was not available to Darwin. At that time, it was not known that vagal fibers originate in several medullary nuclei and that the branches of the vagus exert control over the periphery through different feedback systems. However, Darwin's statement is important, because it emphasizes the afferent feedback from the heart to the brain, independent of the spinal cord and the sympathetic nervous system, and the regulatory role of the pneumogastric nerve (renamed the vagus at the end of the 19th century) in the expression of emotions.

Darwin attributed these ideas to Claude Bernard as an example of nervous system regulation of *le milieu interieur*. Consistent with more contemporary psychophysiology, Claude Bernard viewed the heart as a primary response system capable of responding to all forms of sensory stimulation. He explicitly emphasized the potency of central nervous system pathways to the heart (Cournand, 1979). These ideas are expressed in the following quotation (Claude Bernard [1865] quoted in Cournand, 1979):

> In man the heart is not only the central organ of circulation of blood, it is a center influenced by all sensory influences. They may be transmitted from the periphery through the spinal cord, from the organs through the sympathetic nervous system, or from the central nervous system itself. In fact the sensory stimuli coming from the brain exhibit their strongest effects on the heart. (p. 118)

Although seldom acknowledged as founders of modern psychophysiology, Bernard and Darwin have contributed to the theoretical basis for a neuropsychophysiology of the autonomic nervous system. The quotations document their view that the heart provided not only an output system from the brain, capable of indexing sensory processing, but also that the heart was a source of afferent stimulation to the brain, able to change or contribute to psychological state. Consistent with this theoretical bias, psychophysiologists during the past century have investigated the functional sensitivity of heart rate measures to sensory and affective stimuli (e.g., Darrow, 1929; Graham & Clifton, 1966; Lacey, 1967) and the dynamic feedback between the brain and the heart in regulating both psychological state and the threshold for sensory stimuli (e.g., Lacey & Lacey, 1978).

Contemporary psychophysiology gained much of its current theoretical perspective from intriguing ideas about the interaction between autonomic and sensory processes introduced by Sokolov (1963). The Sokolov model contained all the requisite components of an integrative theory relating autonomic function to psychological state. The model included (a) an acknowledgment of both afferents and efferents in both autonomic and somatic systems, (b) an autonomic feedback loop (i.e., autonomic tuning) to regulate sensory thresholds, (c) an interface between autonomic processes and psychological phenomena (i.e., orienting and defensive reflexes), and (d) brain regulation of autonomic reactivity by habituation.

The Sokolov model included bidirectional communication between brain and periphery. In the Sokolov model, autonomic processes contributed to the tuning of receptor systems to engage or disengage with the external environment. Consistent with the Sokolov view, the Laceys (e.g., Lacey, 1967; Lacey & Lacey, 1978) emphasized the bidirectional communication between the cardiovascular system and brain in the regulation of cardiac function and sensory threshold. In contrast to this emphasis on bidirectional communication, Obrist (1976) focused on the general concordance between metabolic demands and heart rate. Both arguments have merit. For example, afferent stimulation of the baroreceptors has immediate effects on both peripheral cardiovascular function and central arousal state (Gellhorn, 1964), and the metabolic demands associated with exercise have deterministic influences, through vagal withdrawal, on heart rate (Obrist, 1981; Rowell, 1993).

HEART RATE RESPONSES: A NEUROGENIC EMPHASIS

Throughout the history of the Society for Psychophysiological Research, psychophysiologists have been studying robust phenomena such as the autonomic components of the orienting reflex, often without explanatory neurophysiological models. This chapter is in response to this need in providing a theoretical model based on the evolution of neural structures and the neural regulation of autonomic processes to explain several psychophysiological phenomena, including orientation, attention, and emotion.

The orienting reflex provides an excellent point of embarkation. Based on the convergent theoretical approaches of Sokolov (1963), Lacey (1967), and Graham and Clifton (1966), the orienting reflex is assumed to have a cardiac component. This component is characterized by a heart rate deceleration that functionally influences perceptual thresholds in facilitating the processing of information about the external environment. However, what are the neural mechanisms mediating the cardiac orienting response? Or, as Obrist (1976) argued, is heart rate deceleration merely an epiphenomenon associated with decreased metabolic demands accompanying the reduced motor activity that defines orienting and attending behaviors? The time course of the response, the effects of neural blockades, and studies with clinical populations support the contention that the cardiac orienting response is neurogenic. First, heart rate deceleration associated with the cardiac orienting response is rapid, occurring within a few seconds, and usually returns rapidly to baseline. Second, the latency characteristics of the cardiac orienting response are similar to other neurogenic bradycardic reflexes such as optovagal, vasovagal, baroreceptor-vagal, and chemoreceptor-vagal.

Blockade studies with atropine demonstrate that short latency bradycardia associated with both orienting reflexes and classical conditioning are mediated by cholinergic pathways along the vagus (e.g., Berntson, Cacioppo, & Quigley, 1994; Obrist, 1981; Schneiderman, 1974). Studies with the aged and other clinical populations with peripheral neuropathies or autonomic regulatory problems (e.g., diabetes) document deficits in vagal function (De Meersman, 1993; Gribben, Pickering, Sleight, & Peto, 1971; Weiling, van Brederode, de Rijk, Borst, & Dunning, 1982; Weise & Heydenreich, 1991). In addition, studies of individuals with unilateral brain damage demonstrate that heart rate responses are diminished more in individuals with right-side damage (Yokoyama, Jennings, Ackles, Hood, & Boller, 1987). This latter finding is consistent with evidence that neurophysiological regulation of heart rate is primarily along the right vagus to the sinoatrial node and that heart rate is under the control of higher ipsilateral structures in the brain (Warwick & Williams, 1975). Although vagal influences producing heart rate deceleration may interact synergistically with sympathetic withdrawal, short latency decelerations are determined primarily by the vagus. Thus, it may be argued that, because short latency heart rate reactivity is mediated by the vagus, the magnitude of the cardiac orienting response is an index of vagal regulation.

THE VAGAL PARADOX

In attempting to structure a neurogenic model of vagal regulation to explain psychophysiological phenomena, there is an obvious inconsistency between data and theory. Physiological theory attributes the chronotropic control of the heart (i.e., heart rate) and the amplitude of respiratory sinus arrhythmia (RSA) to direct vagal mechanisms (e.g., Jordan, Khalid, Schneiderman, & Spyer, 1982; Katona & Jih, 1975). However, although there are situations in which both measures covary (e.g., during exercise and cholinergic blockade), there are other situations in which the measures appear to reflect independent sources of neural control.

Several arguments have been made to explain this discrepancy. First, it has been argued that RSA and average heart rate (during sympathetic blockade) reflect different dimensions of vagal activity. For example, average heart rate might be viewed as reflecting tonic vagal influences and RSA as reflecting phasic vagal influences (e.g., Berntson, Cacioppo, & Quigley, 1993b; Jennings & McKnight,

1994; Malik & Camm, 1993). Second, it has been argued that the discrepancy is caused by variations in respiratory parameters (Grossman, Karemaker, & Wieling, 1991), with RSA being confounded by respiratory frequency and tidal volume. Third, it has been argued that variation in quantification methods may contribute to the divergence between RSA and heart rate (Byrne & Porges, 1993; Porges & Bohrer, 1990). Fourth, it has been argued that RSA does not reliably measure parasympathetic tone because it decreases with baroreflex stimulation (Goldberger, Ahmed, Parker, & Kadish, 1994). And fifth, it has been argued that average heart rate is influenced by a complex and dynamic interaction between sympathetic and vagal systems, making it difficult to extract a vagal tone dimension (Berntson, Cacioppo, & Quigley, 1991, 1993a).

The arguments often have been linked to a definition of vagal tone as being determined by neural blockade. The functional effect of the neural blockade on heart rate has been used as the criterion measure of vagal tone or parasympathetic control (e.g., Katona & Jih, 1975). Researchers have argued that RSA is not an accurate index of vagal tone, because individual preblockade levels of RSA do not accurately map into pre/post-change in heart rate (Grossman & Kollai, 1993). Contrary to this argument, Porges (1986) argued that the discrepancy was in part based on the criterion measure selected. He demonstrated that RSA exhibited a more sensitive dose-dependent response curve to vagal blockade with atropine than to heart rate. This suggests the possibility that RSA, monitored during periods of spontaneous breathing, may provide a better criterion variable than heart rate. Neurophysiological support may be offered for this proposal. RSA is a vagal phenomenon in contrast to heart rate, which is determined by several sources, including vagal, sympathetic, and mechanical factors. Thus, the efficacy of change in heart rate following cholinergic blockade as an index of vagal tone may be challenged.

These arguments have created a volatile environment for debating the neurophysiological interpretation of RSA and the efficacy of specific methods to quantify RSA. Common to these arguments is the assumption that there is one central source of cardiac vagal tone. The arguments attribute differences, not to central mechanisms, but to the response characteristics of heart rate and RSA. Thus, divergence has been attributed to either the transfer function of the sinoatrial node that would attenuate high-frequency oscillations (Saul, Berger, Chen, & Cohen, 1989) or the statistical transfer function of the method of quantifying RSA (Byrne & Porges, 1993) and not as a function of differential neural output.

However, independent of the quantification methodology and during periods of stable respiratory parameters, data have accumulated that demonstrate that RSA and heart rate (independent of sympathetic influences) often respond differently. Although both the neurogenic bradycardia and the suppression of RSA or heart rate variability observed during attention are assumed to be vagal in origin, they often appear independent of each other or in an apparent physiological contradiction (Porges, 1972; Porges & Raskin, 1969; Richards & Casey, 1991). Similar disparities between levels of heart rate and RSA have been observed during inhalant anesthesia when RSA exhibits a massive depression, whereas heart rate is not altered (Donchin, Feld, & Porges, 1985). Additional examples of convergence and divergence between RSA and heart rate can be observed in both within- and between-subjects designs. For example, individual differences in heart rate and RSA monitored during resting conditions provide independent contributions to measures of cardiac vagal tone derived from vagal blockade (e.g., Grossman & Kollai, 1993). However, convergence may be observed within an individual during exercise when monotonic increases in metabolic load are reflected in both faster heart rate and lower RSA (Billman & DuJardin, 1990) or during neural blockade with atropine when both cardiac indices diminish in a dose-response manner (Cacioppo et al., 1994; Dellinger, Taylor, & Porges, 1987; Porges, 1986).

The relationship between RSA and heart rate may change within and between individuals. In our laboratory, we have observed that the relationship between RSA and heart rate varies with behavioral state (Riniolo, Doussard-Roosevelt, & Porges, 1994). Twenty-four-hour ambulatory monitoring of adults indicates that during states of drowsiness and sleep the correlation between RSA and heart rate is significantly lower than during alert states. Thus, at times RSA and heart rate appear to reflect the same physiological processes, whereas at other times they appear to reflect independent processes.

In contrast to the observable data, neurophysiological research argues for a covariation between these two parameters, because vagal cardioinhibitory fibers to the heart have consistent functional properties characterized by bradycardia to neural stimulation and a respiratory rhythm (e.g., Jordan et al., 1982). This inconsistency, based on an assumption of a single central vagal source, is labeled the *vagal paradox* and is outlined in Table 2.1.

The vagal paradox is critical to the interpretation of several psychophysiological and clinical conditions. For example, if the bradycardia occurring during orienting reflexes is vagal, then why is bradycardia often observed during periods of reduced RSA, also an index of both attention and vagal control of the heart? If vagal tone is a positive indicator of health of a fetus or neonate when monitored with RSA, then why is vagal tone a negative indicator of health when it is manifested as bradycardia? If bradycardia and RSA can both be removed by severing the vagus or by pharmacological blockade, then are they both manifestations of vagal tone? If bradycardia and RSA are both indices of vagal tone, then why do they respond differently? This apparent paradox provides the stimulus for the following inquiry and the development of the proposed polyvagal theory that speculates that, in mammals, there are two anatomically based vagal response systems.

TABLE 2.1. The Vagal Paradox: A Common Central Source?

1. Increased vagal tone produces neurogenic bradycardia.
2. Decreased vagal tone produces suppression of RSA.
3. Bradycardia occur during periods of suppressed RSA.

MAMMALIAN POLYVAGAL SYSTEM

To understand the proposed polyvagal theory, it is necessary to provide additional information regarding the neuroanatomy and neurophysiology of the vagus in mammals. First, the vagus is not one nerve but a family of neural pathways originating in several areas of the brainstem. Second, there are several branches of the vagus. Third, the vagus is not solely an efferent or motor pathway; rather, approximately 80% of the vagal fibers are afferent (Agostoni, Chinnock, DeBurgh Daly, & Murray, 1957). Fourth, the vagus is lateralized with nerve trunks originating in the left and right sides of the brainstem. Fifth, the vagus is asymmetrical, with the left and right sides performing different tasks, with the right vagus most potent in the chronotropic regulation of the heart. These points are summarized in Table 2.2.

Mammals are polyvagal. The different vagi have different roles in the regulation of visceral function and originate in different brainstem nuclei with their respective viscerotropic organization. The different vagi may have oppositional outputs to the same target organ. For example, it is possible that during orienting there is an increase in vagal outflow from one branch to produce bradycardia and a withdrawal of vagal outflow from another branch to produce a suppression of RSA (e.g., Richards & Casey, 1991). Thus, the concept of vagal tone may not be generalized to all vagal efferent pathways or even to the same target organ (e.g., heart), as has been assumed (e.g., Grossman & Kollai, 1993), but may need to be limited to a specific branch or subsystem of the vagus being evaluated. And the intriguing concept of autonomic space proposed by Berntson et al. (1991, 1993a) to deal with dynamic sympathetic-parasympathetic interactions may require an additional dimension to deal with potential vagovagal interactions.

The polyvagal theory proposes that neurogenic bradycardia and RSA are mediated by separate branches of the vagus. Thus, the two commonly used, but not interchangeable, measures of cardiac vagal tone may represent different dimensions of vagal tone.

In mammals, the primary motor fibers of the vagus originate from two separate and definable nuclei in the medulla: the dorsal motor nucleus of the vagus (DMNX) and the nucleus ambiguus (NA). The DMNX is in the dorsomedial medulla. The NA is ventral to the DMNX in the ventrolateral reticular formation (Warwick & Williams, 1975). The name *ambiguus* emphasizes the initial difficulties associated with determining its borders and connections within the

TABLE 2.2. Mammalian Polyvagal System

1. Efferent fibers originate primarily in two medullary nuclei (NA, DMNX).
2. Vagal efferent fibers are clustered into several branches.
3. Approximately 80% of vagal fibers are afferent.
4. The vagus is lateralized.
5. The vagus is asymmetrical with a right bias.

reticular formation (Mitchell & Warwick, 1955). A third medullary nucleus, located near the DMNX, the nucleus tractus solitarius (NTS), is the terminus of many of the afferent pathways traveling through the vagus from peripheral organs. This trinity of neural structures in the medulla forms the primary central regulatory component of the vagal system. The relative locations of these medullary nuclei are illustrated in Figure 2.1.

Most cells originating in the DMNX project to subdiaphragmatic structures (e.g., stomach, intestines, etc.). In contrast, only the rostral portion of the NA provides vagal innervation of subdiaphragmatic structures (Kalia & Masulam, 1980), whereas most cells in NA project to supradiaphragmatic structures (larynx, pharynx, soft palate, esophagus, bronchi, and heart).

Neurotracing and electrophysiological techniques with mammals provide additional evidence that the two vagal nuclei may function independently and have different central connections. These studies have demonstrated that there are no apparent connections between the two nuclei, although both nuclei have input from the NTS, central nucleus of the amygdala, and hypothalamus (Hopkins, 1987; Leslie, Reynolds, & Lawes, 1992). It is well accepted that in mammals the primary cardioinhibitory motoneurons are located in the NA. However, motor fibers from the DMNX join the cardiac vagus (Bennett, Ford, Kidd, & McWilliam, 1984).

Cardioinhibitory and bronchoconstrictor neurons located in the NA have myelinated vagal axons that conduct in the fast B fiber range (McAllen & Spyer,

FIGURE 2.1. Primary brainstem nuclei of the vagus. Nuclei are bilateral, and only one of each bilateral pair is illustrated.

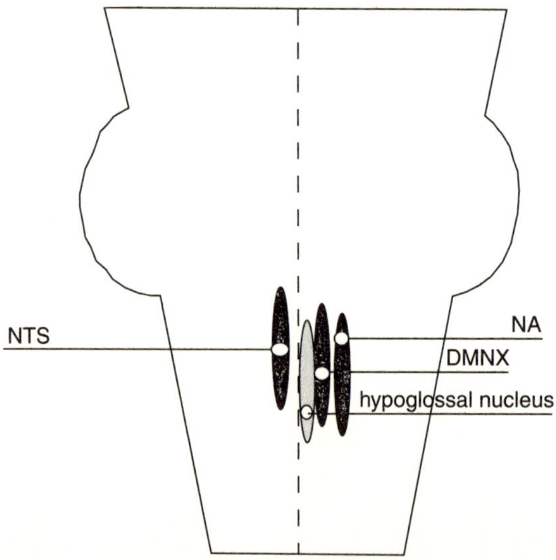

1976, 1978). In contrast, neurons located in the DMNX have axons projecting to the cardiac vagal branches that are nonmyelinated and conduct in the slower C fiber range. Although there are reports of cardioinhibitory vagal neurons with efferent axons conducting in the B fiber range being located in both the DMNX and the NA, neurons with axons conducting in the C fiber range are restricted to the DMNX (Jordan et al., 1982). The role of these nonmyelinated vagal fibers on the heart is not well understood. In research with cats (Ford, Bennett, Kidd, & McWilliam, 1990) and dogs (Donald, Samueloff, & Ferguson, 1967), stimulation of these fibers did not affect heart rate. However, although unsubstantiated at this time, the function of these fibers may be dependent on the outflow of the myelinated NA fibers and may change during conditions such as hypoxia. For example, the influence of the unmyelinated fibers on the heart may be potentiated when the outflow from the myelinated NA fibers is blocked. In contrast, in the rabbit, stimulation of the nonmyelinated vagal fibers results in heart rate slowing (Woolley, McWilliam, Ford, & Clarke, 1987).

The cytoarchitecture of the NA illustrates that the dorsal portion contains source nuclei for special visceral efferents (i.e., voluntary motor fibers) and that the ventral portion contains source nuclei for general visceral efferents (i.e., involuntary motor fibers). Motor projections from the dorsal portion go to target organs including the larynx, pharynx, soft palate, and esophagus. Motor projections from the ventral portion go to several target organs, including the heart and the bronchi. In fact, these projections account for the primary cardiac and bronchomotor pathways and far outnumber the pathways originating in the DMNX.

There is an obvious distinction between the viscerotropic organization of the two vagal nuclei. The DMNX provides the primary vagal efferents to subdiaphragmatic organs that regulate digestive and alimentary processes. In contrast, the NA provides the primary vagal efferents to the supradiaphragmatic target organs, including the soft palate, pharynx, larynx, esophagus, bronchi, and heart.

THE POLYVAGAL THEORY

The polyvagal theory is based on several premises. Some are firmly grounded in neurophysiological and neuroanatomical data and others are more speculative. The first premise articulates the neural regulation of bradycardia and RSA. Based on the initial premise, it is hypothesized that the neurogenic bradycardia associated with the orienting reflex are mediated by the DMNX and that the suppression of heart rate variability (i.e., reduced amplitude of RSA) is mediated by the NA.

Premise 1: Neurogenic bradycardia and RSA are mediated by different branches of the vagus and need not respond in concert.

Physiological support for the hypothesis that the DMNX can contribute to neurogenic bradycardia, independent of the NA, is provided by lesion studies. Machado and Brody (1988) reported that chronic bilateral lesions of the NA reduced but did not totally block baroreceptor reflex-mediated bradycardia in conscious rats. Thus, the DMNX contains vagal neurons capable of producing bradycardia with a response latency associated with the baroreceptor reflex. This is supported by Jerrell, Gentile, McCabe, and Schneiderman (1986), who argued that differential Pavlovian conditioning of bradycardia in rabbits following sinoaortic denervation was mediated along DMNX pathways. The results pose the possibility that vagal pathways, originating in both the DMNX and the NA, have the potential to influence heart rate.

Phylogenetic Development of the Polyvagal System

Investigations of the phylogenetic development of the vagus provide support for the first premise. Because our interests are in mammals, specifically humans, this chapter will focus on the evolution of vagal regulation of cardiac function from reptiles to mammals. There are two questions: Do reptiles produce heart rate patterns during orienting that are similar to the neurogenic bradycardia observed in mammals? Do reptiles produce a phenomenon similar to RSA?

The phylogeny of the vagus illustrates two phenomena: one neuroanatomical and the other physiological. On a neuroanatomical level, differentiation of the visceral efferent column of the vagus into dorsal motor nucleus (i.e., the DMNX) and a ventrolateral motor nucleus (i.e., the NA) is first seen in reptiles. In turtles (e.g., *Chelone mydas* and *Domonia subtrijuga*), there is still a connection between the two nuclei, but in lizards (e.g., *Varanus salvator*) and crocodiles (e.g., *Caiman crocodilus*), the separation between the DMNX and the NA is as complete as it is in mammals (see Barbas-Henry & Lohman, 1984).

Behavioral orienting in reptiles is characterized by a focusing of exteroceptors and a freezing of gross motor activity. Paralleling these behaviors, neurogenic bradycardia has been observed. Belkin (see Regal, 1978) reported that bradycardia is part of a fear response in iguanas. In addition, McDonald (1974) reported bradycardia in the hog-nosed snake during death-feigning. Most researchers found these data incompatible with the prevalent emphasis on arousal and the use of heart rate as an indicator of arousal. How could bradycardia reflect increased arousal within the context of a sympathetic nervous system–oriented arousal theory? In contrast, RSA has not been observed in reptiles. Research investigating the spectral components of reptilian heart rate has failed to identify heart rate oscillations associated with ventilation (Gonzalez Gonzalez & de Vera Porcell, 1988).

Phylogenetic development not only illustrates changes in the neuroanatomy of the vagus but also parallels changes in behavior. One of these behavioral shifts is the addition of active or voluntary attention and complex emotions. In confronting the defensive world, mammals, like reptiles, have an initial reflexive response to novelty, the orienting reflex. However, mammals have additional behaviors in their repertoire. Following or independent of reflexive orienting, mammals may voluntarily respond with sustained attention to foster detailed information processing or with facial expressions and vocalizations to foster communication. Thus, reptiles orient; mammals may first orient and then elect to attend or communicate.

The differences between the reptilian and mammalian cardiac systems provide insight into the phylogenetic origin of behaviors such as reptilian orienting and mammalian attention and emotion. The cardiac output and thus energy production of mammals far exceeds that of reptiles. Mammals have metabolic demands four to five times that of reptiles. The metaphor of a machine or vehicle has been proposed by Else and Hulbert (1981) to compare the efficiency and function of the mammalian and reptilian metabolic systems. According to Else and Hulbert (1981), when idling, the average mammal requires four to five times more fuel than the average idling reptile, even when body weight and ambient temperature are controlled. Elaborating on this metaphor, reptiles represent vehicles with 1-L engines and mammals represent vehicles with 4- or 5-L engines. Thus, as in the story about the race between the tortoise and the hare, reptiles locomote with a reliable but underpowered engine and mammals locomote with a supercharged engine that can function for only short periods without refueling.

The energy production capacities of reptiles and mammals contribute to their respective ways of life. There is a bias among reptiles toward passive feeding strategies. Reptiles tend to be sit-and-wait feeders, slow cruisers, and sluggish browsers. In contrast, mammals with four-chambered hearts can actively hunt and graze and adapt to changing environments (Regal, 1978). To support their behavioral niche and to ensure their adaptive success, reptiles and mammals use different vagal strategies to promote their survival. Being underpowered, reptiles do not maintain a vagal brake on the heart, which would further reduce energy production during unchallenged situations. For reptiles, during periods of either quiescence or apnea, usually associated with behavioral freezing or diving, vagal influences via the DMNX are profound and heart rate is even slower. In contrast, vagal control of the heart is virtually removed during periods of breathing and other motor activities (Jacob & McDonald, 1976).

The underpowered reptiles use vagal efferents from the DMNX to the heart to deal with specific challenges: to orient and freeze in response to predator or prey and to conserve oxygen while submerged for lengthy periods. In contrast to underpowered reptiles, supercharged mammals use vagal efferents from the NA as a persistent brake to inhibit the metabolic potential of this high-powered system. The high NA vagal tone keeps mammals from, literally, bouncing off the walls. Thus, in contrast to that observed in reptiles, in mammals vagal tone is highest during unchallenged situations such as sleep, and vagal tone is actively withdrawn in response to external demands, including metabolically demanding states such as exercise, stress, attention, and information processing. For example, in humans, psychological states perceived as life threatening, such as panic and rage, are characterized by virtually no NA vagal tone when indexed with the amplitude of RSA (George et al., 1989). Metaphorically, and consistent with the model, antisocial and pathological behavioral patterns associated with rage and hyperreactivity without conscious self-regulation have been labeled "reptilian."

If terrestrial mammals adopted the reptilian strategy of reflexive increases in vagal activity to produce massive neurogenic bradycardia, the result would be catastrophic to the oxygen-hungry mammalian cortex and myocardium. This strategy would rapidly produce cardiac ischemia and cortical anoxia. The result of this sequence would be death. Although still dependent on oxygen, aquatic mammals use a diving reflex characterized by a regulated neurogenic bradycardia to reduce metabolic demands. To survive, aquatic mammals have complex mechanisms, not available to terrestrial mammals, to manage oxygen resources and shift priorities for oxygen while submerged for long periods.

It is possible that for mammals during states of stress, when metabolic demands are great and vagal tone from the NA is removed, that the cardiac pacemakers (SA and AV) may be prone to neurogenic bradycardia mediated by the DMNX. The neurogenic bradycardia may be massive and lethal. This may be the case in fetal distress, when bradycardia is observed during hypoxic episodes or as a factor in either sudden infant death syndrome or sudden death in adults. Consistent with this model, it has been demonstrated in the dog that progressive asphyxic hypoxia not only elicits increased cardiac vagal activity but also the sensitivity of the sinoatrial node to vagal efferent influences is potentiated (Potter & McCloskey, 1986). Thus, during hypoxia, large bradycardia may be maintained with limited or reduced vagal efferent activity.

The polyvagal theory provides a potential explanation for the massive neurogenic bradycardia observed during fetal distress and in high-risk neonates who have virtually no observable RSA. For example, as illustrated in Figure 2.2, when massive bradycardia is observed during fetal distress (Figure 2.2a), there is a background of low beat-to-beat variability (Figure 2.2b). Similarly, neonates with the lowest amplitude RSA are at greatest risk for apnea and bradycardia (Sostek, Glass, Molina, & Porges, 1984). Thus, the diminished vagal influences from the NA, responsible for depressed RSA amplitude, seem to be associated with a vulnerability to large neurogenic bradycardia. Potter and McCloskey (1986) provided an explanation of how depressed central nervous system function associated with hypoxia might result in massive neurogenic bradycardia. They reported a complex feedback system between duration of hypoxia, vagal efferent discharge, and potentiation of the vagal output on the heart. This system is able to maintain bradycardia, despite the massive decline in the vagal firing associated with hypoxia, by potentiating the influence of the vagal firing on the SA node. Under these conditions, although the bradycardia is mediated through a branch of the vagus, the magnitude of the bradycardia is determined by a peripheral mechanism and no longer reflects a centrally mediated vagal tone. Although Potter and McCloskey (1986) did not monitor RSA, we must assume that RSA is low in their preparation because the animals were anesthetized prior to the surgical, electrical, and hypoxic manipulations and because both hypoxia and anesthesia are associated with depressed beat-to-beat heart rate variability, including RSA (e.g., Donchin et al., 1985; Nelson, 1976).

Additional support for this bifurcation of vagal influences is demonstrated by

FIGURE 2.2 (a) Bradycardia during fetal distress. (b) Background heart period variability at time of bradycardia.

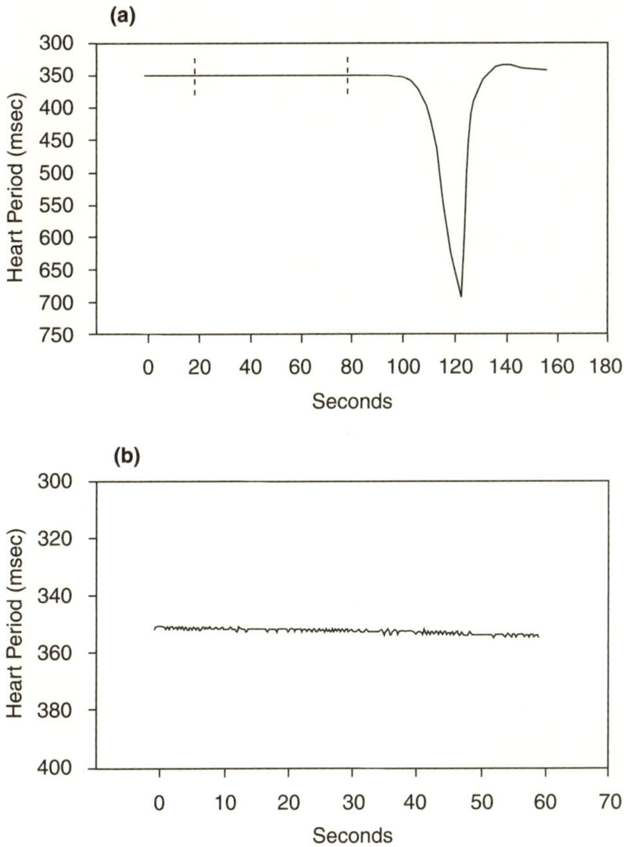

electrical stimulation of the dorsal motor nucleus in the rabbit. As illustrated in Figure 2.3, electrical stimulation of the DMNX results in bradycardia without an increase in RSA. This is in contrast to the effect of stimulation of the aortic depressor nerve, which communicates with both the NA and the DMNX. Figure 2.4 shows that, in a similarly anesthetized rabbit, stimulation of the aortic depressor nerve results in an increase in RSA and a massive bradycardia (e.g., McCabe, Yongue, Porges, & Ackles, 1984).

The polyvagal theory argues that the vagal fibers from the DMNX and NA are distinguishable in structure and function. Specifically, it has been argued that the vagal efferent fibers from the NA are myelinated and contain a respiratory rhythm, and the vagal efferent fibers from the DMNX are unmyelinated and do not express a respiratory rhythm. However, there are some inconsistencies in the proposed distinction. For example, Jordan et al. (1982) reported that there are

FIGURE 2.3. Bradycardia elicited by electrical stimulation of the DMNX in an anesthetized rabbit.

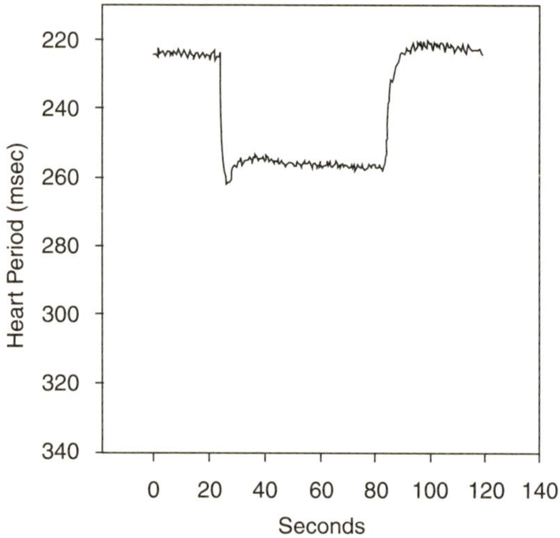

cardioinhibitory vagal neurons originating in the DMNX, with efferent axons conducting in the B fiber range, and are, therefore, myelinated. Moreover, Jordan et al. reported that these had a respiratory rhythm. Although the Jordan et al. findings support the proposed dual source of vagal efferents, their findings confound the proposed functional distinction.

FIGURE 2.4. Bradycardia elicited by aortic depressor nerve stimulation in an anesthetized rabbit.

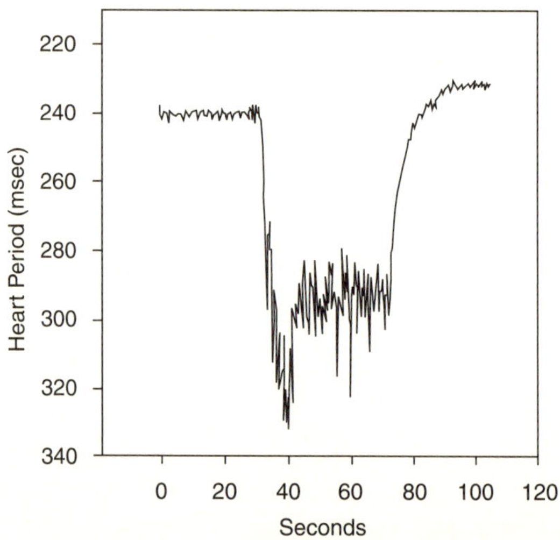

There are several potential explanations for the inconsistency identified by Jordan et al. (1982). The first may be method. The Jordan et al. study used standard neurophysiological stimulation and recording techniques to identify cell bodies. According to Schwaber (1986), many vagal fibers previously assumed to originate in the DMNX have been identified with newer methods, such as retrogradely labeled horseradish peroxidase, as being located in the NA. Schwaber (1986) also stated that, because axons from the NA pass very near the border of the DMNX, it is difficult to stimulate or lesion the DMNX without NA involvement confounding electrical stimulation studies. Thus, additional research with more accurate labeling techniques may demonstrate that all neurons in the B fiber range originate in the NA. Our rabbit data reported in Figures 2.3 and 2.4 provide additional support for the possibility of mislabeling. According to Jordan et al. (1982), all neurons excited by aortic depressor nerve stimulation produced a respiratory rhythm in their ongoing discharge. Similarly, as illustrated in Figure 2.4, stimulation of the aortic depressor nerve resulted in both bradycardia and increased RSA. However, stimulation of the DMNX produced only an attenuated bradycardia. These findings suggest that vagal fibers discharging following stimulation of the DMNX did not have a respiratory rhythm. Moreover, the bradycardia was immediate and similar in latency to that observed following aortic depressor nerve stimulation. The magnitude of bradycardia was about 50% of the magnitude elicited by aortic nerve stimulation, a technique assumed to recruit vagal fibers from both the NA and the DMNX. The attribution of 50% of the magnitude of the heart rate component of the baroreceptor reflex to each vagal system is consistent with Machado and Brody (1988). A second possibility is that there are species differences in the organization and function of the DMNX. For example, to facilitate freezing behavior, the rabbit may have evolved unique myelinated vagal pathways from the DMNX that were independent of respiratory function. According to this explanation, the DMNX would have B fibers, but they would not express a respiratory rhythm. Alternatively, some mammalian species may have neurons in or near the DMNX that are part of a common cardiopulmonary oscillator (Richter & Spyer, 1990).

Future research will determine whether or not the proposed functional and structural distinctions between DMNX and NA efferents as articulated in the polyvagal theory are accurate. An additional concern relates to generalizing across mammalian species. Most of the neurophysiological and neuroanatomical research on the mammalian vagus has been conducted with rat, rabbit, cat, and dog. Studies investigating vagal regulation with humans have been limited to pharmacological blockade studies with measures of peripheral physiology. The few neuroanatomical studies of human brainstem, however, are often conducted on patients who have died of disease or trauma. Thus, one may question the generalizability of a polyvagal model developed from investigations of rodent brainstem to the human. However, existing data illustrate phenomena such as clinical bradycardia in the absence of RSA in the human fetus (see Figure 2.2), shifts in RSA independent of heart rate change during inhalant anesthesia (e.g.,

Donchin et al., 1985), and short latency responses from both systems (see Figures 2.3 and 2.4) that argue for a polyvagal model.

Vagal Strategies in Mammals and Reptiles

Reptilian and mammalian vagal systems have contradictory strategies. Reptiles are characterized by low ambient vagal tone and transient increases in vagal tone in response to environmental challenges. In contrast, mammals are characterized by high ambient vagal tone and transient decreases in vagal tone in response to environmental challenges (Table 2.3).

To adapt to the hostile world, the reptiles' behavioral repertoire is driven by survival. Most behaviors are associated with foraging, stalking, and feeding. Only limited time and energy are dedicated to social interactions such as parenting and reproduction. In the reptiles' defensive world, neurogenic bradycardia is adaptive and does not compromise physiological status. Reptiles have smaller metabolically active body organs, have different metabolic mechanisms, are less oxygen-dependent than mammals, and can go for long periods without oxygen. In contrast, the adaptive strategy of reptiles is lethal for mammals. In the defensive world of mammals, it is necessary to increase metabolic output to foster fight-or-flight behaviors. Therefore, reflexive neurogenic bradycardia to novelty for a prolonged period would reduce oxygen resources and metabolic output and compromise the fight-or-flight potential of mammals. The consequences of reduced oxygen resources also would depress central nervous system function, reduce behavioral complexity and competent execution of complex behaviors, induce unconsciousness, damage vital organs, and finally, if persistent, result in death. Thus, the cardiac component of the orienting reflex must be of short duration and be replaced by a physiological response that does not compromise the oxygen-needy nervous system of mammals. The withdrawal of vagal tone originating in the NA serves this purpose.

Phylogenetic Origins of Vagal Response Patterns

The neurogenic bradycardia controlled by the DMNX and observed in reptiles and mammals during orienting may have evolved from the gustatory response system of primitive vertebrates. Gustation is the primary method for identifying prey (including other appropriate food sources) and predators in aquatic environments. For example, in fish, an undifferentiated vagal lobe controls gustatory,

TABLE 2.3. Vagal Strategies

	Reptile	Mammal
Ambient state	low DMNX	high NA/low DMNX
Response to novelty	increase DMNX	decrease NA/increase DMNX

digestive, and alimentary processes (Finger & Dunwiddie, 1992). A reflexive increase in vagal tone would affect several organs: the heart, where it would reduce metabolism and enable the animal to freeze momentarily; the organs containing gustatory receptors, where it would orient toward the source of stimulation and regulate threshold to detect novelty; and the digestive and alimentary systems, where it would stimulate gastric secretion and motility.

With phylogenetic development, the viscerotropic organization of the vagal system has become more complex by incorporating pathways from other cranial nerves, including trigeminal, facial, accessory, and glossopharyngeal. Thus, more specialized functions, such as head rotation to orient sensory receptors toward the source of stimulation, mastication to ingest food, and salivation to initiate gustatory and digestive processes, are integrated into the vagal system.

The motor component of the vagus shares evolutionary origins with four cranial nerves (trigeminal, facial, accessory, and glossopharyngeal). The vagus not only innervates smooth and cardiac muscle, but, similar to the other four cranial nerves, it contains motor pathways that innervate somatic muscles. Vagal pathways that innervate somatic muscle often are not included in the neurophysiology of the autonomic nervous system. These fibers are called *special visceral efferents* to distinguish them from *general visceral efferents*, the motor pathways innervating smooth and cardiac muscle. The critical difference between the two types of motor pathways is that somatic muscle regulation may be conscious and voluntary, whereas smooth muscle regulation is reflexive and unconscious. Because the special visceral efferents innervate voluntary muscles, they are usually excluded from the autonomic nervous system. Traditionally, only the general visceral efferents from both sympathetic and parasympathetic branches are used to define the autonomic nervous system.

The somatic muscles innervated by the five cranial nerves arise from the branchial arches, embryologically known as the primitive gill arches (Warwick & Williams, 1975). These muscles are critical to several mammalian behaviors. For example, the somatic muscles innervated by the trigeminal, arising from the first branchial arch, are involved in mastication, retraction of the lower jaw, and closing the mouth. The special visceral efferents from the facial nerve, arising from the second branchial arch, innervate the muscles of the face, scalp, and neck to enable facial expressions. The facial nerve also innervates muscles in the floor of the mouth.

Although the trigeminal and facial nerves originate from branchial arches and have communications with the other three cranial nerves originating from the branchial arches, the source nuclei of the special visceral efferents for the glossopharyngeal, vagus, and accessory nerve originate in the same medullary nucleus, the NA. Thus, the efferent fibers travel through three different cranial nerves, but they originate in the same source nucleus.

As a function of phylogenetic development, the source nuclei for the special visceral efferent pathways in the glossopharyngeal, vagus, and accessory nerves migrate to form the NA. In mammals, the NA controls the complex coordination of pharynx, soft palate, larynx, and esophagus. Of special note to psychophysiological processes is that the third gill arch also gives rise to the carotid body, containing peripheral chemosensitive receptors sensitive to oxygen and carbon dioxide levels (Warwick & Williams, 1975). In addition, the accessory nerve contains fibers originating in the cervical spinal cord that innervate the positioning of the neck. The critical carotid arteries, internal jugular veins, and vagus nerves run deep in these muscles (Warwick & Williams, 1975). Thus, this complex also has the ability to orient visceral receptors through somatic muscles, to coordinate structures related to ingestion and expulsion, and to regulate facial expression and emotion. These motor nuclei receive input from cortex to coordinate complex behaviors with cardiopulmonary function. Thus, phylogenetically, even when the gill arches evolve into the branchiomeric muscles common to all mammals, oxygenation of blood through a coordination of breathing and heart rate during interactions with the environment remains a primary functional objective.

The processes associated with NA control of supradiaphragmatic organs appear to be uniquely mammalian. For example, this subsystem of the vagus coordinates the complex sequence of sucking, swallowing, and breathing that allows mammals to feed and breathe actively and voluntarily. Moreover, the NA provides the primary chronotropic control of the heart and controls the intonation of vocalizations. Thus, NA efferent projections are involved with processes associated not only with feeding and breathing but also with movement, emotion, and communication. These behaviors contribute to the unique social and survival behaviors observed in mammals. The NA vagus provides the vagal brake that mammals remove instantaneously to increase metabolic output to foster fight-or-flight behaviors. The NA vagus provides the motor pathways to shift the intonation of vocalizations (e.g., cry patterns) to express emotion and to communicate internal states in a social context.

The behavioral derivatives of the two branches of the vagus suggest a typology in which one branch of the vagus deals with unconscious reflexive vegetative functions and the other is involved in more conscious, voluntary, flexible, and often social activities. There is neuroanatomical support for this typology. The DMNX contains only general visceral efferents that innervate smooth and cardiac muscle fibers and regulate glandular secretion. In contrast, the NA contains special visceral efferents that innervate the somatic musculature of the soft palate, larynx, pharynx, and esophagus.

Somatomotor and Visceromotor: Coupled Systems

In mammals, we observe two evolutionary strategies that link autonomic function with somatic muscle activity. First, there is an anatomical linkage between the segmentation of the spinal nerves and the sympathetic chain. This linkage is reflected in the motor-related increases in sympathetic tone that have dogged psychophysiologists by confounding motor and autonomic responses. The evolution of the segmented sympathetic nervous system parallels the evolution of voluntary motor activities. The sympathetic nervous system regulates vasomotor tone to direct blood flow and, thus, oxygen to the specific muscles being challenged. In addition, there are sudomotor links to hydrate and protect the skin from tearing. This coupling between sympathetic activity and movement has been the cornerstone of arousal theory and hypotheses associating autonomic function with temperament and psychopathologies. It was not many years ago that Obrist (1976) challenged Lacey's (1967) notion that autonomic state was independent of motor activity (i.e., metabolic demands). There is no doubt that the effects of motor activity are profound on the autonomic nervous system, yet this profound effect does not mitigate the importance of other relationships that may be sensitive to specific psychological processes, independent of movement.

Second, there is an anatomical linkage between the somatic muscles that arise from the cranial nuclei and parasympathetic function. We can observe this clearly in the viscerotropic organization of the NA. The NA provides the source nuclei for somatic muscle fibers that innervate larynx, pharynx, trachea, and esophagus. Moreover, ventral to these source nuclei, in an area of the NA known as NA_{EX}, are general visceral efferents that control the resistance of the bronchi (Haselton, Solomon, Motekaitis, & Kaufman, 1992) and heart rate (Bieger & Hopkins, 1987). The ventral portion also projects to other visceral organs (e.g., Brown, 1990).

Based on neuroanatomical studies, it has been demonstrated that visceromotor functions regulated by the ventral part of NA provide the parasympathetic support for the somatomotor projections from NA and trigeminal and facial nerves. Neuroanatomical studies suggest that, unlike the DMNX, which receives primary sensory input through the NTS, the NA has the trigeminal nerve as an important source of sensory input. Moreover, the rostral region of the NA communicates with the facial nucleus. This coupling of the NA with facial and trigeminal nuclei provides additional evidence of the coordination of the visceromotor regulation through the NA with somatomotor functions such as swallowing (Brown, 1974), sucking (Humphrey, 1970), and, perhaps, facial expressions. Thus, the organization of the mammalian brainstem has evolved to have a ventral vagal complex, consisting of NA and the nuclei of the trigeminal and facial nerves, that coexists with the dorsal vagal complex, consisting of the DMNX and NTS, that regulates vegetative processes and is observed in reptiles.

To foster motor movement, visceromotor (i.e., autonomic) processes are associated with somatomotor activities. In the periphery, this is done primarily by the sympathetic chain; in special cases, such as those related to reproduction and elimination, the sacral branch of the parasympathetic nervous system contributes. However, in the rostral part of mammalian anatomy (i.e., the head), the somatic muscles that regulate facial expression, mastication, vocalization, swallowing, and sucking are matched with general visceral efferents, projecting from the ventral portion of NA, that exert potent influences on the heart and the bronchi. These motor fibers effectively slow heart rate and increase respiratory resistance to conserve oxygen exchange. Neuroanatomical studies performed on human embryos and fetuses suggest that these visceromotor neurons may have migrated from the DMNX (Brown, 1990).

As observed through both embryological research and phylogenetic comparisons, in mammals the primitive gill arches evolve into muscles and nerves controlling the face, bones of the mouth, jaw, pharynx, larynx, soft palate, esophagus, and trachea. The nerves innervating these muscles uniquely arise not from the anterior horns of the spinal cord but from the source nuclei of five cranial nerves (trigeminal, facial, glossopharyngeal, vagus, and accessory). Because of their uniqueness, these motor systems are known as special visceral efferents. And, because of their voluntary aspects, these pathways have been excluded from traditional concepts of the autonomic nervous system. Facial expressions characteristic of mammals, such as sucking, swallowing, and vocalizations, reflect the unique mammalian adaptation of special visceral efferent control of the visceral muscles evolving from the branchial arches.

However, similar to the synergistic relationship between the sympathetic nervous system and skeletal muscles of the extremities, there is a synergistic relationship between the traditional general visceral efferents of the vagus and the somatic muscles controlled by these cranial nerves. Thus, increased outflow of these somatic muscles produce specific visceral shifts. For example, chewing will produce salivation in the absence of food, and head rotation, by means of accessory special visceral efferents, will impact on cardiovascular action along the vagus.

Phylogenetic development of the central nervous system has progressed in mammals to produce a brain with a large neocortex (e.g., MacLean, 1990). The neocortex is very vulnerable to shifts in oxygen. Evolutionary pressures have resulted in autonomic strategies that optimize the availability of oxygen to the cortex. However, these uniquely mammalian strategies coexist with the ancestral reptilian strategies. Thus, premise 2 is consistent with MacLean's view that the advanced mammalian brain contains its phylogenetic heritage.

Premise 2: Neurogenic bradycardia associated with orienting is a phylogenetic vestigial relic of the reptilian brain and is mediated by the DMNX.

Although phylogenetic development has modified several brain structures, the evolved brain of advanced mammals maintains several structures and systems that are virtually identical to those observed in primitive reptiles. These primitive structures have extensive interconnections and functional dependencies, although each is capable of specific independent functions. Thus, in mammals, the DMNX still maintains its reptilian functions of facilitating digestion and slowing heart rate. Mammals utilize an additional brainstem structure, the NA, to supply general visceral vagal efferents that provide the prominent control of the heart and the bronchi. The cells of origin of these fibers efficiently communicate with limbic and other higher centers and allow for the conscious and voluntary selection of novelty. In contrast, the DMNX is more directly regulated by hypothalamic communication, often triggered by survival-oriented stimuli

(Hopkins, 1987; Leslie et al., 1992). Thus, as stated in premise 3, the regulation of vagal efferents by NA mechanisms contributes to the mammalian ability to detect novelty, actively engage with the environment, and socially communicate.

Premise 3: Withdrawal of cardiac vagal tone through NA mechanisms is a mammalian adaptation to select novelty in the environment while coping with the need to maintain metabolic output and continuous social communication.

To summarize the reptilian-mammalian evolutionary evidence, phylogenetic development of the neural regulation of the heart provides insights into an apparent contradiction or paradox in vagal control of the heart. In most reptiles, the neuroanatomy demonstrates (a) a lack of anatomically distinguishable boundaries between the DMNX and NA, and (b) cardiac vagal efferent pathways originating only in the DMNX. In mammals, the neuroanatomy demonstrates (a) a distinct separation of the DMNX and NA; (b) cardiac vagal efferent pathways originating primarily, but not exclusively, in the NA; (c) direct neural connections between the central nucleus of the amygdala and NA; and (d) a clustering of medullary neurons in the NA capable of regulating the somatic muscles related to vocalizations, facial expression, and coordinating breathing with sucking and swallowing.

Smart and Vegetative Vagi

The polyvagal theory proposes that the evolutionary shift resulting in both an NA that is distinct from the DMNX and the evolutionary development of special visceral efferents changed the role of the vagus. The general visceral efferent pathways from the DMNX vagus are part of a passive reflexive motor system associated with vegetative function and, thus, a vegetative vagus. The special visceral efferent pathways from NA create an active voluntary motor system associated with the conscious functions of attention, motion, emotion, and communication, and, thus, a smart vagus.

The polyvagal theory requires a reconceptualization of the vagal system and the construct of vagal tone. The theory focuses on the cytoarchitecture of the medullary source nuclei of the cranial nerves. The theory takes an evolutionary approach and investigates, through embryology and phylogenetic comparisons, the common origins of the special visceral efferents and focuses on the shared medullary structures for the cell bodies of these fibers. The theory acknowledges that the vagal system is complex and should be organized not in terms of bundles of fibers leaving the medulla but rather in terms of the common source nuclei of several of these pathways. Functionally, the common source nuclei provide a center to coordinate and regulate the complex interactions among various end organs and are related to optimizing cardiopulmonary function.

Mammals, with their oxygen-hungry metabolic systems, require a special medullary center to coordinate cardiopulmonary functions with behaviors of ingestion (e.g., mastication, salivation, sucking, and swallowing), oral or esophageal expulsion (vomiting), vocalizations (e.g., cries and speech), emotions (e.g., facial expressions), and attention (e.g., rotation of the head). The NA plays this role and serves as the cells of origin of the smart vagus. The potent link between the NA and cardiopulmonary function observed in mammals is not observed in reptiles. In reptiles, which do not have nerves to regulate facial expression, the NA does not play a major role in visceromotor regulation.

Medullary Contributions to a Common Cardiopulmonary Oscillator

The NA is a continuum of interconnected subdivisions, beginning rostrally at the level of the facial nucleus and extending caudally to the spinal medullary junction. As illustrated in Figure 2.5, the rat NA has several subdivisions. The subdivisions are the compact (NA_C), semicompact (NA_{SC}), loose (NA_I), and external (NA_{EX}) formations (Bieger & Hopkins, 1987). The dorsal division consists of the NA_C, NA_{SC}, and NA_I. The dorsal division is the source of special visceral efferents innervating the soft palate, pharynx, larynx, and esophagus. The ventral division consists of the NA_{EX} and is the source of general visceral efferents innervating the thoracic viscera, primarily the bronchi and the sinoatrial node. Vagal fibers originating in the NA_{EX} and terminating in both the bronchi (Haselton et al., 1992) and the sinoatrial node (Spyer & Jordan, 1987) have a respiratory rhythm, thus suggesting that RSA may reflect a common respiratory rhythm originating in or at least incorporating the NA.

After investigating the neuroanatomical centers associated with laryngeal, pulmonary, and cardiac function, Richter and Spyer (1990) arrived at a convergent conclusion that NA was a contributor to a common respiratory rhythm. They also speculated that mammals, with their great need for oxygen, have a medullary center to regulate cardiopulmonary processes. They proposed that a common cardiorespiratory oscillator evolved to foster coordination between cardiac and respiratory processes. In their model, the respiratory rhythm is dependent on the interaction between two groups of neurons, one in the NTS and the other in the NA. Accordingly, the "common" oscillator producing respiratory frequencies is a manifestation of a neural network comprised of interneu-

FIGURE 2.5. Topographic organization of the nucleus ambiguus (NA) in the rat (Bieger & Hopkins, 1987).

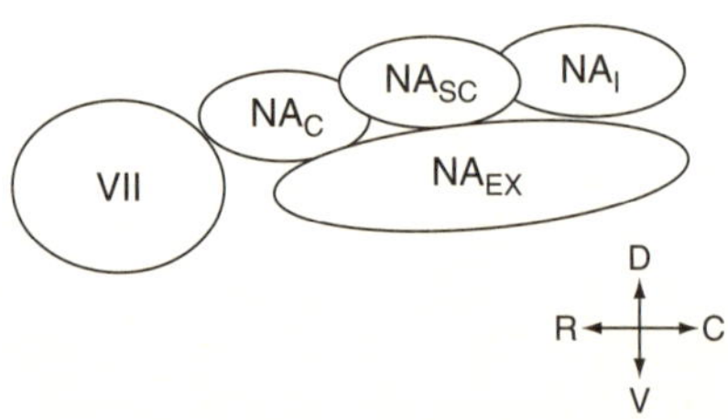

rons between areas containing the motoneurons regulating respiratory, laryngeal, and cardiac functions. The cardiorespiratory oscillator does not involve the DMNX. To support their hypotheses, Richter and Spyer (1990) reported cross-correlational studies of single units. Thus, the NA is part of the cardiorespiratory oscillator network, and the period of the oscillations in heart rate (the period of RSA) provides a valid index of the output frequency of the cardiopulmonary oscillator.

Other researchers have emphasized the importance of additional brain structures as contributors to the regulation, if not the generation, of a cardiopulmonary rhythm. For example, Harper and associates demonstrated that "respiratory rhythms" can be observed in several nuclei in the brainstem, midbrain, and forebrain. Harper's group, by employing cross-correlation techniques, reported units firing on a breath-by-breath basis in periaqueductal gray (Ni, Zhang, & Harper, 1990), central nucleus of the amygdala (Frysinger, Zhang, & Harper, 1988), hippocampus (Frysinger & Harper, 1989), and the anterior cingulate (Frysinger & Harper, 1986). In addition, they reported that stimulation of the amygdala can influence the respiratory cycle (Harper, Frysinger, Trelease, & Marks, 1984).

The covariation of the bronchi with heart rate oscillations (e.g., RSA), mediated by the NA, may have a functional influence on the oxygenation of blood. As stated earlier, the primary objective of the phylogenetic derivatives of the primitive gill arches is to maintain oxygenation. Thus, one might speculate that oscillations in vagal tone to the bronchi and the heart might influence oxygenation. Perhaps coherent rhythmic shifts between bronchial tone and heart rate, with a fixed-phase lag, maximize oxygen diffusion. To answer this question, research would need to confirm a relationship between oxygen saturation and RSA, independent of the average heart rate and respiration rate. Currently, only anecdotal data exist that demonstrate that clinical conditions in which oxygen saturation is low tend to be conditions in which RSA also is depressed. Support for this hypothesis is obtained from research demonstrating that vagotomy disrupts the oxygen consumption-oxygen delivery relationship (Scherlel, Brourman, Kling, Schmall, Tobias, & Myerowitz, 1994).

Measurement of NA Status: Quantification of RSA

For psychophysiologists, interest is primarily in the behaviors and psychological processes associated with special visceral efferents. Most research has been directed toward processes that require the ability to monitor and mediate complex behaviors, such as attention, motion, emotion, and communication; these processes are neurophysiologically dependent on the special visceral efferents of the NA and facial and trigeminal nerves. Yet many of us measure only general visceral efferents from both the parasympathetic and sympathetic branches, although we are interested in the special visceral efferents that regulate vocalizations and facial expression. We are not at a total loss, because there is interneuronal communication between the dorsal and ventral segments of the NA. Thus, by the nature of the NA having general visceral efferents that regulate heart and bronchi, it is possible to monitor continuously the vagal output or tonus of the smart vagus. This leads to the fourth premise of the polyvagal theory.

Premise 4: The ability of NA to regulate special and general visceral efferents may be monitored by the amplitude of RSA.

The vagal fibers originating in the NA_{ex} have a characteristic respiratory frequency that reflects a waxing and waning of influence. For example, the vagal fibers from the NA that have an inhibitory action on the sinoatrial node also wax and wane in inhibitory influence at the respiratory rhythm and produce RSA. Thus, it is possible to monitor continuously the general status of the NA by evaluating RSA. Similarly, NA fibers to the bronchi that elevate lung resistance also wax and wane in their inhibitory influence (Haselton et al., 1992).

RSA is a measure of the general visceral efferents of the NA and thus is an index of the smart vagus. RSA is not a global measure of vagal tone or even a measure of "total" vagal control of the heart as previously proposed (Fouad, Tarazi, Ferrario, Fighaly, & Alicandro, 1984; Katona & Jih, 1975; Porges, 1992). There are other vagal and nonvagal influences on the heart that contribute to both heart rate level and rhythm. For example, there are DMNX projections and monosynaptic cholinergic pathways within the heart, sympathetic pathways, and intrinsic factors. However, the primary, if not sole, source of respiratory rhythms on the sinoatrial node is due to projections from the NA.

To evaluate NA regulation of the sinoatrial node, the parameters of RSA must be accurately extracted. We have approached this problem by evaluating the period and amplitude of RSA, independent of slower oscillations and trends, with a moving polynomial approach (Porges & Bohrer, 1990). In our research, we have obtained correlations between respiration rate and period of RSA approaching 1.0. These findings support the notion of a common cardiorespiratory oscillator as described by Richter and Spyer (1990). RSA, with its amplitude representing visceromotor tone and its period representing the common cardiorespiratory drive frequency, is the functional consequence of the output of vagal fibers originating in NA and terminating on the sinoatrial node. Thus, to emphasize the relationship between RSA and the vagal tone from the NA to the heart, a better designation for the vagal tone index (Porges, 1986) would be V_{NA}.

Quantification of RSA requires only an accurate determination of the amplitude and period of these oscillations. Additional experimental constraints to regulate breathing rates might confound the visceral-medullary feedback system, which determines central respiratory rhythms. For example, because paced breathing requires an awareness of breathing parameters, cortical influences on brainstem structures might modulate the gain of the feedback and influence the amplitude of RSA, and paced breathing may shift respiratory parameters, such as rate, amplitude, inspiration-expiration ratio, interbreath pause, and resistance, from brainstem setpoints. Data illustrating that paced breathing may influence RSA (Sargunaraj, Lehrer, Carr, Hochron, & Porges, 1994) have been reported.

Various manipulations or conditions that depress special visceral efferents, such as inhalant anesthesia, have profound influences on RSA (Donchin et al., 1985). Recovery of function of special visceral efferents is paralleled by a recovery of RSA. In neurology, diagnosis is often based on the evaluation of the special visceral efferents. In our research, we noted that RSA amplitude before neurosurgery was an effective diagnostic of neurological recovery following neurosurgery (Donchin, Constantini, Szold, Byrne, & Porges, 1992). Additional neurological data demonstrate consistent depression of RSA in individuals who are diagnosed as brain dead (Mera, Wityk, & Porges, 1995).

High-risk preterm neonates have problems coordinating breathing, sucking, and swallowing (i.e., processes regulated by the NA). These infants have low levels of RSA (Porges, 1992). Many of these infants have severe bradycardia. The bradycardia is often paralleled by apnea, and a drop in available oxygen may be assumed to reflect neurogenic vagal regulation by the DMNX. This response, in dealing with decreased resources, is adaptive for reptiles but potentially lethal for humans. This also is observed during fetal distress, when there is severe hypoxia associated with a loss of RSA and a pronounced neurogenic bradycardia.

Vagal Competition and Autonomic Dysfunction

The concept of competition between sympathetic and parasympathetic inputs is well known. For example, Levy (1984; Vanhoutte & Levy, 1979) has clearly documented the ability of vagal efferents to inhibit sympathetic influences. Similarly, Berntson et al. (1991) modeled the interactions between sympathetic and parasympathetic efferents to the heart. However, there may be a different type of competition in which the two vagal branches are conveying contradictory information to the target organs. As both vagal pathways are capable of regulating heart rate, there may be competition on the sinoatrial node. Due to the rate of acetylcholine degradation on the nodal tissue (Dexter, Levy, & Rudy, 1989), the continuous stimulation of the sinoatrial node by NA pathways may functionally protect the heart from massive neurogenic bradycardia mediated by the DMNX. Thus, the observations of massive pathophysiological bradycardia in hypoxic fetuses and neonates, who have very low amplitude RSA, may reflect the loss of NA protection on the sinoatrial node. Similarly, sudden death following exercise might reflect a similar process associated with the depression of NA input to foster metabolic activity and a surge of DMNX input in response to decreased oxygen resources.

The vagal competition hypothesis may be generalized and tested to explain other autonomic diseases such as asthma. The vagal competition hypothesis proposes that all target organs with smooth and cardiac muscle have dual innervation from both the DMNX and the NA. This has been documented in animal preparations for heart, lungs, esophagus, and abdominal viscera including pancreas, liver, and stomach (Brown, 1990). However, as with the heart, the two vagal inputs may innervate in a contradictory manner. Just as a DMNX surge coupled with low RSA may result in sudden death, bronchial asthma may be produced by a similar mechanism. In the case of asthma, NA efferent control of bronchi results in the bronchi exhibiting a rhythmic waxing and waning with breathing. This continuous stimulation of the bronchi by NA pathways may functionally protect the bronchi from pathophysiological DMNX influences. It is possible that without NA influences, the bronchi become vulnerable to vagal surges from the DMNX. This would be an adaptive response for a primitive brainstem attempting to conserve oxygen but would be lethal for the oxygen-hungry mammal. The asthma attack, similar to lethal neurogenic bradycardia, may be a product of a primitive vagovagal reflex. In this type of reflex, not only do the motor fibers originate, but the afferent fibers terminate, in DMNX. There is an anatomical basis for a monosynaptic vagovagal reflex. There are reports that dendritic processes from DMNX neurons extend into the boundaries of the NTS. Thus, vagal afferent fibers may communicate directly with DMNX neurons (Neuheuber & Sandoz, 1986). Because afferents terminate in DMNX, the name *motor nucleus* is not accurate, and *dorsal nucleus of the vagus nerve* has been suggested instead (Nara, Goto, & Hamano, 1991). In most vagal reflexes involving the bronchi, the afferents terminate in the NTS and influence the NA to provide a fail-safe feedback system.

Based on the polyvagal theory, the assumption of vagal competition promotes the following testable hypotheses.

Nucleus ambiguus (vagal) protection hypothesis. Vagal projections originating in the NA and terminating in visceral organs provide tonic influences that promote health, growth, and restoration.

Nucleus ambiguus (vagal) withdrawal hypothesis. Removal of the NA vagal brake for short periods of time promotes metabolic output to foster locomotion. Removal of these influences for long periods places the organ at risk.

Emotion

The polyvagal theory provides a set of predictions regarding the relation between autonomic responses and emotion. Darwin (1872) carefully described facial expressions as the primary defining characteristics of emotion. The special visceral efferents, associated with the facial nerve, control movements of facial expression. Reptiles cannot modulate facial expression. The facial nerve in mammals not only regulates facial muscles but also interacts with the NA and the vagal system. Thus, it is logical that emotional expression, which requires somatic muscles controlled by special visceral efferents, is coupled to the visceromotor regulation of cardiopulmonary function by NA vagal efferents. In addition, special visceral efferents originating in NA regulate the larynx and control intonation. Thus, the following premise is stated.

Premise 5: Emotion, defined by shifts in the regulation of facial expressions and vocalizations, will produce changes in RSA and bronchomotor tone mediated by the NA.

As a construct, emotion is heterogeneous. Therefore, correlations between specific emotions and physiological states may be a function of the type of emotion. Even Darwin (1872) distinguished between primary or neurally based emotions and social or culturally based emotions. Darwin (1872) suggested that certain emotions have as their substrate an innate neural basis and, because these emotions are neurally based, they are universally expressed and understood across cultures. These primary emotions include anger, fear, panic, sadness, surprise, interest, happiness (ecstasy), and disgust (Ross, Homan, & Buck, 1994). Because the prevalent hypotheses suggest a strong physiological basis for primary emotions, we will focus on relating primary emotions to the polyvagal theory.

There are two important aspects linking the polyvagal theory to the study of emotion: first, there is a parallel between cortical asymmetry and autonomic asymmetry; second, the branchial arches have evolved into the structures that mammals use to express emotion (i.e., facial muscles and larynx).

The literature documents the relationship between right brain function and primary emotions (Heilman, Bowers, & Valenstein, 1985). The medullary source nuclei and efferent pathways of the vagus also are lateralized with a right bias. The right NA by means of the right cardiac vagus provides the primary chronotropic output to the heart. The special visceral efferents, which provide the behaviors that are used to define emotion (facial expression and vocalization) also have a right bias and are linked neuroanatomically to the general visceral efferents, originating in the NA, that regulate the bronchi and heart, organs that are assumed to be sensitive to emotion and stress. It is difficult to predict the influence of this right bias on actual facial expressions. Because the face is controlled by upper motor neurons that are crossed and lower motor neurons that are uncrossed (Rinn, 1984), facial expression may not be systematically lateralized. In fact, research on facial asymmetry and emotion has not been consistent. There have been reports of facial expressions not being lateralized, being lateralized on the left, and being lateralized on the right (e.g., Hager & Ekman, 1985).

The functional dominance of the right side of the brain in regulating autonomic function and emotion may have implications for the specialization of motor and language dominance on the left side of the brain. The right-sided responsibilities of regulating homeostasis and modulating physiological state in response to both internal (i.e., visceral) and external (i.e., environmental) feedback may contribute to the development of motor and language functions on the left side of the brain.

A partitioning of central control of voluntary processes, independent of emotional-homeostatic processes, would enable the individual to express complex voluntary levels of communication and movement, from the left side of the brain, and more intense emotional-homeostatic processes, from the right side of the brain. If these processes are lateralized, they might have a degree of autonomous regulation. This would enable simultaneous activation of global functions associated with emotional-homeostatic processes and language-voluntary movement processes.

Given the strong theoretical relationships between lateralized autonomic and hemispheric function and between the neurons that control RSA and those that control facial expression and vocal intonation (see Figure 2.5), research should be directed at evaluating the relationship between RSA and the primary emotions. Recall that the source nucleus of the facial nerve is the border of the NA and afferents from the trigeminal nerve provide a primary sensory input to the NA. Thus, the ventral vagal complex, consisting of the NA and the nuclei of the trigeminal and facial nerves, is clearly related to the expression and experience of emotion.

Based on the polyvagal theory, one would expect shifts in affective state to parallel RSA. For example, the elicitation of a negative primary emotion would result in a systematic withdrawal of vagal tone along NA to promote fight-or-flight behaviors. In contrast, a shift to a more pleasant affective state would be associated with an increase in RSA. A study by Bazhenova and colleagues (2001), in emphasizing the dynamics of RSA change during shifting affective states, supports this speculation. Manipulation of the affective state resulted in RSA deceases when an infant shifted to a more negative state. Moreover, when the infant shifted to a more positive affective state, RSA increased above the affectively neutral base level.

The polyvagal theory does not neglect the important role of the DMNX in the emotional experience. For example, the DMNX is critical in the regulation of digestive polypeptides and gastric motility (Uvnas-Moberg, 1989), dimensions of physiological activity that parallel emotive experiences and stress. Consistent with the polyvagal theory, which emphasizes the importance of NA and the ventral vagal complex in overt emotional expressiveness and regulation, the theory would acknowledge the importance of less conscious survival-oriented processes that are mediated by the dorsal vagal complex, which consists of the NTS and the DMNX. A complementary theory has been proposed by Uvnas-Moberg (1987, 1994). The Uvnas-Moberg theory emphasizes the role of the DMNX in the regulation of gastrointestinal hormones and during emotional states including stress, hunger, and satiety.

SUMMARY AND CONCLUSION

The following seven points summarize the polyvagal theory.

1. *The vagal system does not represent a unitary dimension.* The vagal system includes general visceral efferent fibers regulating smooth and cardiac muscle and special visceral efferent fibers regulating the somatic muscles of the larynx, pharynx, and esophagus. These somatic muscles control vocalization, sucking, and swallowing and interface these processes with breathing. The vagal system also is linked neuroanatomically to the source nuclei that control facial expression, mastication, and head turning.

2. *There are two vagal motor systems.* One vagal system is the vegetative vagus, which originates in the dorsal motor nucleus and is associated with passive reflexive regulation of visceral functions. The other vagal system is the smart vagus,

which originates in the NA and is associated with the active processes of attention, motion, emotion, and communication. The two systems are neuroanatomically distinct, have different ontogenetic and phylogenetic origins, and employ different adaptive strategies.

3. *In mammals, the concept that vagal tone represents a single or summed system may have limited physiological or heuristic value.* For example, in mammals, high tone from the dorsal motor nucleus vagal system may be lethal, whereas high tone from the NA vagal system may be beneficial. Based on the proposed polyvagal theory, an accurate measure of the NA system is critical to the evaluation of psychophysiological relationships.

4. *The functional output of the NA vagus on the heart may be monitored by RSA.* NA is part of a common neuronal network producing a cardiorespiratory rhythm. Thus, the output from the branch of the vagus originating in NA and terminating on the sinoatrial node of the heart conveys a frequency common to both respiratory and cardiac systems. In contrast, the output from the dorsal motor nucleus does not convey a respiratory rhythm.

5. *The magnitude of neurogenic bradycardia is mediated by the dorsal motor nucleus.* Rapid heart rate changes, such as conditioned anticipatory heart rate deceleration and decelerations associated with orienting, are neurogenic bradycardia. Additional neurogenic bradycardia are reflexes such as optovagal and chemovagal. In the absence of NA influences to the sinoatrial node, local conditions such as hypoxia may greatly potentiate the vagal effect.

6. *There is a common cardiopulmonary oscillator.* The common respiratory rhythm observed in heart rate and breathing is produced by a network of interneurons located in the NTS and NA, which communicate with the motor neurons that control respiratory, laryngeal, and cardiac function.

7. *Primary emotions are related to autonomic function.* Because the primary emotions are often related to survival, they must be integrated into cardiopulmonary regulation. Moreover, primary emotions have a right-hemisphere bias, ipsilateral with the regulatory bias of the medullary structures controlling visceral function.

Based on the polyvagal theory, additional hypotheses may now be tested by evaluating the relationship between RSA (the measure of NA vagal tone, V_{NA}) and processes and states dependent on the coordination of cardiopulmonary processes with the special visceral efferents of the cranial nerves. This, of course, includes all processes associated with vocalizations, feeding, breathing, and facial expression.

In developing the polyvagal theory, the most striking insights came from the phylogenetic approach. Not only does a phylogenetic approach explain the vagal paradox in terms of the medullary source nuclei of the dorsal motor nucleus and NA, but it also highlights the importance of oxygen needs in the evolving nervous system. As the nervous system gets more complex, there are greater demands for oxygen. Oxygen needs may have provided a major environmental pressure leading to the evolution of the adaptive and sophisticated autonomic nervous system found in mammals. Thus, constructs such as orienting, attention, emotion, and stress are by-products of the evolutionary pressure to optimize oxygen resources.

Appendix A: Title of the Chapter

The title was selected to emphasize the concept that evolutionary processes have sculpted the neural regulation of autonomic function. Evolution has provided obvious divergences in behavior and appearance and has had an impact on the autonomic strategies related to the detection of novelty in the environment.

The aim of this chapter was neither a theory of orienting nor an attempt to distinguish between the autonomic components of orienting or defensive reflexes, but rather the neurogenic regulation of cardiac responses by two vagal responses systems. A primitive system inherited from reptiles produced a rapid neurogenic bradycardia that reduced the activity of our cardiopulmonary system to conserve oxygen. This is the strategy of sit-and-wait feeders common in reptiles. In contrast, the evolution of the energy-demanding mammal required two autonomic behavioral shifts: mammals needed to (a) obtain great amounts of food and (b) protect their nervous systems from oxygen loss. These two objectives are linked. In the evolution of mammals, success in obtaining food resources was dependent on the ability to detect threat. Thus, mobilization and attention became two important behavioral dimensions. Unlike reptiles, which orient in response to novelty and attack or return to a quiescent state or lumber off, mammals orient and then attend. Following this phase of attention, a mammal may rapidly depart or approach (attack) within the context of the classic fight-or-flight response. With the increasing complexity of behavior, there is a parallel increase in complexity in the organization and function of the autonomic nervous system.

The title was also intended to emphasize the concept that evolution has placed mammals in a defensive world. The survival systems of reptiles and other nonmammalian vertebrates can be organized into orienting and defensive dimensions. Mammals, to survive in this defensive and reactive world, had to circumvent these potentially lethal reactions of other species. The evolution of the mammalian nervous system enables mammals to escape danger rapidly and to use neural resources for the complex information processes required to detect subtleties in the environment. Moreover, evolution promoted additional motor systems related to communication. Motor systems developed to communicate conditions related to survival with facial expressions and vocalizations associated with primary emotions. The evolutionary modifications had to coexist with the oxygen-hungry metabolic system, and, by increasing the complexity of motor behaviors, there was an additional increase in oxygen needs. Thus, there is a link between the special visceral efferent actions regulating the communicative processes of emotion (and later, language) with the general visceral efferent actions regulating cardiopulmonary function. The ability to detect subtleties in the environment coupled with the ability to communicate threat or comfort through facial expressions and vocalizations contributed to within-species social behavior, parenting, and pair bonding. These complex functions evolved while the demanding oxygen needs of mammals were programmed into the background of nervous system function by the autonomic nervous system.

Appendix B: Personal Retrospective

In discussing any theoretical perspective, it is important to place the ideas and speculations in the context of earlier research conducted by the investigator. My early research focused on the use of heart rate measures as indicators of attention. While conducting research for my master's thesis (Porges & Raskin, 1969), I noted that attention-demanding tasks produced heart rate response patterns with two prominent characteristics. First, heart rate exhibited a rapid transitory directional change in response to task onset and stimulus changes. Second, when subjects became involved in the task and focused their attention on the task demands, heart rate variability was reduced. I was intrigued with these observations and speculated on the possible physiological mechanisms. This evolved into a two-component theory of attention in which the components were labeled *phasic or orienting* and *tonic or attention* responses (Porges, 1972). These findings stimulated me to investigate neural mechanisms of heart rate regulation and to develop the vagal tone index (V) of RSA, which I believed would help provide insight into the mechanisms mediating the more tonic sustained attention response.

The preceding sections of this chapter provide the basis for the polyvagal theory and enable an interpretation of the two heart rate components associated with attention. The first component, associated with orienting and neurogenic bradycardia, is determined reflexively by the vegetative vagus, originating in the dorsal motor nucleus. The second component, associated with voluntary engagement with the environment and depression of RSA, is determined by the smart vagus, originating in the NA. Thus, after years of studying heart rate patterns, a speculative two-component psychophysiological model of attention is evolving into the neuroanatomically and neurophysiologically based polyvagal theory.

CHAPTER 3

The Polyvagal Theory: New Insights Into Adaptive Reactions of the Autonomic Nervous System

HISTORICAL PERSPECTIVES ON THE AUTONOMIC NERVOUS SYSTEM

Central nervous system regulation of visceral organs is the focus of several historic publications that have shaped the texture of physiological inquiry. For example, in 1872 Darwin acknowledged the dynamic neural relationship between the heart and the brain:

> when the heart is affected it reacts on the brain; and the state of the brain again reacts through the pneumo-gastric [vagus] nerve on the heart; so that under any excitement there will be much mutual action and reaction between these, the two most important organs of the body. (p. 69)

Although Darwin acknowledged the bidirectional communication between the viscera and the brain, subsequent formal description of the autonomic nervous system (e.g., Langley, 1921) minimized the importance of central regulatory structures and afferents. Following Langley, medical and physiological research tended to focus on the peripheral motor nerves of the autonomic nervous system, with a conceptual emphasis on the paired antagonism between sympathetic and parasympathetic efferent pathways on the target visceral organs. This focus minimized interest in both afferent pathways and the brainstem areas that regulate specific efferent pathways.

The early conceptualization of the vagus focused on an undifferentiated efferent pathway that was assumed to modulate "tone" concurrently to several target organs. Thus, brainstem areas regulating the supradiaphragmatic (e.g., myelinated vagal pathways originating in the nucleus ambiguus and terminating primarily above the diaphragm) were not functionally distinguished from those regulating the subdiaphragmatic (e.g., unmyelinated vagal pathways originating in the dorsal motor nucleus of the vagus and terminating primarily below the diaphragm). Without this distinction, research and theory focused on the paired antagonism between the parasympathetic and sympathetic innervation to target organs. The consequence of an emphasis on paired antagonism was an acceptance in physiology and medicine of global constructs such as autonomic balance, sympathetic tone, and vagal tone.

More than 50 years ago, Hess (1954) proposed that the autonomic nervous system was not solely vegetative and automatic but was instead an integrated system with both peripheral and central neurons. By emphasizing the central mechanisms that mediate the dynamic regulation of peripheral organs, Hess anticipated the need for technologies to continuously monitor peripheral and central neural circuits involved in the regulation of visceral function.

THE VAGAL PARADOX

In 1992, I proposed that an estimate of vagal tone, derived from measuring respiratory sinus arrhythmia (RSA), could be used in clinical medicine as an index of stress vulnerability (see chapter 4). Rather than using the descriptive measures of heart rate variability (i.e., beat-to-beat variability) frequently used in obstetrics and pediatrics, the article emphasized that RSA has a neural origin and represents the tonic functional outflow from the vagus to the heart (i.e., cardiac vagal tone). Thus, it was proposed that RSA would provide a more sensitive index of health status than a more global measure of beat-to-beat heart rate variability reflecting undetermined neural and non-neural mechanisms. The article presented a quantitative approach that applied time-series analyses to extract the amplitude of RSA as a more accurate index of vagal activity. The article provided data demonstrating that healthy full-term infants had RSA of significantly greater amplitude than did preterm infants. This idea of using heart rate patterns to index vagal activity was not new, having been reported as early as 1910 by Hering. Moreover, contemporary studies have reliably reported that vagal blockade via atropine depresses RSA in mammals (Porges, 1986, 2007a).

In response to this article (Porges, 1992), I received a letter from a neonatologist who wrote that, as a medical student, he learned that vagal tone could be lethal. He argued that perhaps too much of a good thing (i.e., vagal tone) could be bad. He was referring, of course, to the clinical risk of neurogenic bradycardia. Bradycardia, when observed during delivery, may be an indicator of fetal distress. Similarly, bradycardia and apnea are important indicators of risk for the newborn.

My colleagues and I (Reed, Ohel, David, & Porges, 1999) further investigated this perplexing observation by studying the human fetus during delivery. We observed that fetal bradycardia occurred only when RSA was depressed (i.e., a respiratory rhythm in fetal heart rate is observable even in the absence of the large chest wall movements associated with breathing that occur postpartum).

This raised the question of how vagal mechanisms could mediate both RSA and bradycardia, as one is protective and the other is potentially lethal. This inconsistency became the "vagal paradox" and served as the motivation behind the polyvagal theory.

With regard to the mechanisms mediating bradycardia and heart rate variability, there is an obvious inconsistency between data and physiological assumptions. Physiological models assume vagal regulation of both chronotropic control of the heart (i.e., heart rate) and the amplitude of RSA (Jordan, Khalid, Schneiderman, & Spyer, 1982; Katona & Jih, 1975). For example, it has been reliably reported that vagal cardioinhibitory fibers to the heart have consistent functional properties characterized by bradycardia to neural stimulation and a respiratory rhythm (Jordan et al., 1982). However, although there are situations in which both measures covary (e.g., during exercise and cholinergic blockade), there are other situations in which the measures appear to reflect independent sources of neural control (e.g., bradycardic episodes associated with hypoxia, vasovagal syncope, and fetal distress). In contrast to these observable phenomena, researchers continue to argue for a covariation between these two parameters. This inconsistency, based on an assumption of a single central vagal source, is what I have labeled the *vagal paradox*.

THE POLYVAGAL THEORY: THREE PHYLOGENETIC RESPONSE SYSTEMS

Investigation of the phylogeny of the vertebrate autonomic nervous system provides an answer to the vagal paradox. Research in comparative neuroanatomy and neurophysiology has identified two branches of the vagus, with each branch supporting different adaptive functions and behavioral strategies. The vagal output to the heart from one branch is manifested in RSA, and the output from the other branch is manifested in bradycardia and possibly the slower rhythms in heart rate variability. Although the slower rhythms have been assumed to have a sympathetic influence, they are blocked by atropine (Porges, 2007a).

The polyvagal theory (see chapters 2, 10, 11, and 12; Porges, 2001a, 2007a) articulates how each of three phylogenetic stages in the development of the vertebrate autonomic nervous system is associated with a distinct autonomic subsystem that is retained and expressed in mammals. These autonomic subsystems are phylogenetically ordered and behaviorally linked to social communication (e.g., facial expression, vocalization, listening), mobilization (e.g., fight-or-flight behaviors), and immobilization (e.g., feigning death, vasovagal syncope, and behavioral shutdown).

The social communication system (see description below of the social engagement system) involves the myelinated vagus, which serves to foster calm behavioral states by inhibiting sympathetic influences to the heart and dampening the hypothalamic-pituitary-adrenal (HPA) axis (Bueno et al., 1989). The mobilization system is dependent on the functioning of the sympathetic nervous system.

The most phylogenetically primitive component, the immobilization system, is dependent on the unmyelinated vagus, which is shared with most vertebrates. With increased neural complexity resulting from phylogenetic development, the organism's behavioral and affective repertoire is enriched. The three circuits can be conceptualized as dynamic, providing adaptive responses to safe, dangerous, and life-threatening events and contexts.

Only mammals have a myelinated vagus. Unlike the unmyelinated vagus, originating in the dorsal motor nucleus of the vagus with pre- and postganglionic muscarinic receptors, the mammalian myelinated vagus originates in the nucleus ambiguus and has preganglionic nicotinic receptors and postganglionic muscarinic receptors. The unmyelinated vagus is shared with other vertebrates, including reptiles, amphibians, teleosts, and elasmobranchs.

We are investigating the possibility of extracting different features of the heart rate pattern to dynamically monitor the two vagal systems. Preliminary studies in our laboratory support this possibility. In these studies we have blocked the nicotinic preganglionic receptors with hexamethonium and the muscarinic receptors with atropine. The data were collected from the prairie vole (Grippo, Lamb, Carter, & Porges, 2007), which has a very high ambient vagal tone. These preliminary data demonstrated that, in several animals, nicotinic blockade selectively removes RSA without dampening the amplitude of the lower frequencies in heart rate variability. In contrast, blocking the muscarinic receptors with atropine removes both the low and respiratory frequencies.

CONSISTENCY WITH JACKSONIAN DISSOLUTION

The three circuits are organized and respond to challenges in a phylogenetically determined hierarchy consistent with the Jacksonian principle of dissolution. Jackson (1958) proposed that in the brain, higher (i.e., phylogenetically newer) neural circuits inhibit lower (i.e., phylogenetically older) neural circuits and "when the higher are suddenly rendered functionless, the lower rise in activity." Although Jackson proposed dissolution to explain changes in brain function due to damage and illness, the polyvagal theory proposes a similar phylogenetically ordered hierarchical model to describe the sequence of autonomic response strategies to challenges.

Functionally, when the environment is perceived as safe, two important features are expressed. First, bodily state is regulated in an efficient manner to promote growth and restoration (e.g., visceral homeostasis). This is done through an increase in the influence of mammalian myelinated vagal motor pathways on the cardiac pacemaker that slows the heart, inhibits the fight-or-flight mechanisms of the sympathetic nervous system, dampens the stress response system of the HPA axis (e.g., cortisol), and reduces inflammation by modulating immune reactions (e.g., cytokines). Second, through the process of evolution, the brainstem nuclei that regulate the myelinated vagus became integrated with the nuclei that regulate the muscles of the face and head. This link results in the bidirectional coupling between spontaneous social engagement behaviors and bodily states. Specifically, an integrated social engagement system emerged in mammals when the neural regulation of visceral states that promote growth and restoration (via the myelinated vagus) was linked neuroanatomically and neurophysiologically with the neural regulation of the muscles controlling eye gaze, facial expression, listening, and prosody (Figure 3.1; see Porges, 2007a, for review).

The human nervous system, similar to that of other mammals, evolved not solely to survive in safe environments but also to promote survival in dangerous and life-threatening contexts. To accomplish this adaptive flexibility, the human nervous system retained two more primitive neural circuits to regulate defensive strategies (i.e., fight-or-flight and death-feigning behaviors). It is important to note that social behavior, social communication, and visceral homeostasis are

FIGURE 3.1. The social engagement system. Social communication is determined by the cortical regulation of medullary nuclei via corticobulbar pathways. The social engagement system consists of a somatomotor component (special visceral efferent pathways that regulate the muscles of the head and face; solid blocks) and a visceromotor component (the myelinated vagus that regulates the heart and bronchi; dashed blocks). Solid blocks indicate the somatomotor component. Dashed blocks indicate the visceromotor component. Reprinted from Porges (2007a), with permission from Elsevier.

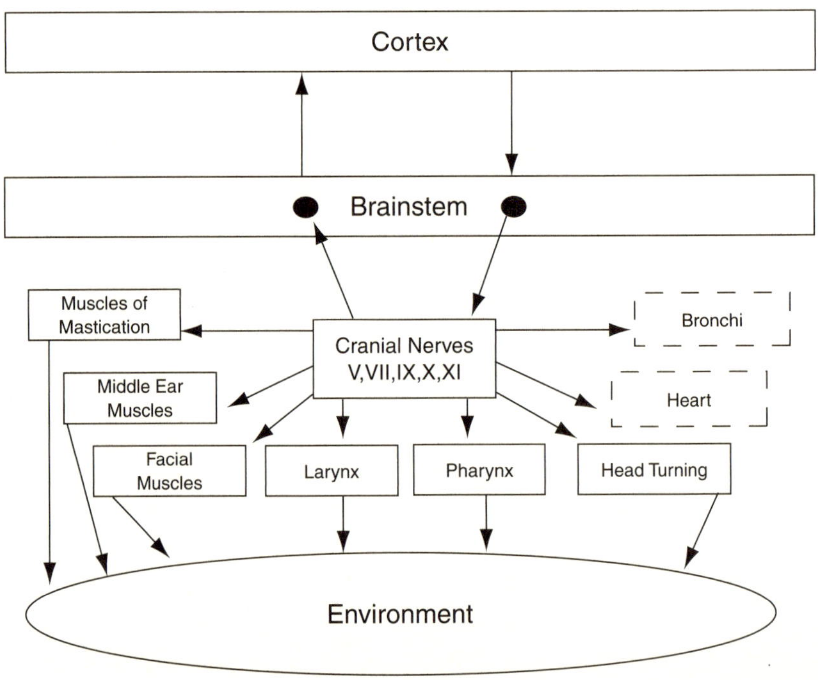

incompatible with the neurophysiological states and behaviors promoted by the two neural circuits that support defense strategies. Thus, via evolution, the human nervous system retains three neural circuits, which are in a phylogenetically organized hierarchy. In this hierarchy of adaptive responses, the newest circuit is used first; if that circuit fails to provide safety, the older circuits are recruited sequentially.

Investigation of the phylogeny of regulation of the vertebrate heart (Morris & Nilsson, 1994; Taylor, Jordan, & Coote, 1999; see also chapters 2 and 10) has led to extraction of four principles that provide a basis for testing of hypotheses relating specific neural mechanisms to social engagement, fight-or-flight, and death-feigning behaviors:

- There is a phylogenetic shift in the regulation of the heart from endocrine communication to unmyelinated nerves and finally to myelinated nerves.
- There is a development of opposing neural mechanisms of excitation and inhibition to provide rapid regulation of graded metabolic output.
- A face–heart connection evolved as source nuclei of vagal pathways shifted ventrally from the older dorsal motor nucleus to the nucleus ambiguus. This resulted in an anatomical and neurophysiological linkage between neural regulation of the heart via the myelinated vagus and the special visceral efferent pathways that regulate the striated muscles of the face and head, forming an integrated social engagement system (Figure 3.1; for more details, see Porges, 2007a, and chapter 12).
- With increased cortical development, the cortex exhibits greater control over the brainstem via direct (e.g., corticobulbar) and indirect (e.g., corticoreticular) neural pathways originating in motor cortex and terminating in the source nuclei of the myelinated motor nerves emerging from the brainstem (e.g., specific neural pathways embedded within cranial nerves V, VII, IX, X, and XI), controlling visceromotor structures (i.e., heart, bronchi) as well as somatomotor structures (muscles of the face and head).

NEUROCEPTION: CONTEXTUAL CUEING OF ADAPTIVE, MALADAPTIVE PHYSIOLOGICAL STATES

To effectively switch from defensive to social engagement strategies, the mammalian nervous system needs to perform two important adaptive tasks: (1) assess risk, and (2) if the environment is perceived as safe, inhibit the more primitive limbic structures that control fight, flight, or freeze behaviors.

Any stimulus that has the potential for increasing an organism's experience of safety has the potential of recruiting the evolutionarily more advanced neural circuits that support the prosocial behaviors of the social engagement system.

The nervous system, through the processing of sensory information from the environment and from the viscera, continuously evaluates risk. Since the neural evaluation of risk does not require conscious awareness and may involve subcortical limbic structures (Morris, Ohman, & Dolan, 1999), the term *neuroception* (see chapter 1) was introduced to emphasize a neural process, distinct from perception, that is capable of distinguishing environmental (and visceral) features that are safe, dangerous, or life-threatening. In safe environments, autonomic state is adaptively regulated to dampen sympathetic activation and to protect the oxygen-dependent central nervous system, especially the cortex, from the metabolically conservative reactions of the dorsal vagal complex. However, how does the nervous system know when the environment is safe, dangerous, or life-threatening, and which neural mechanisms evaluate this risk?

Environmental Components of Neuroception

Neuroception represents a neural process that enables humans and other mammals to engage in social behaviors by distinguishing safe from dangerous contexts. Neuroception is proposed as a plausible mechanism mediating both the expression and the disruption of positive social behavior, emotion regulation, and visceral homeostasis (see chapter 1; Porges, 2007a). Neuroception might be triggered by feature detectors involving areas of temporal cortex that communicate with the central nucleus of the amygdala and the periaqueductal gray, since limbic reactivity is modulated by temporal cortex responses to the intention of voices, faces, and hand movements. Thus, the neuroception of familiar individuals and individuals with appropriately prosodic voices and warm, expressive faces translates into a social interaction promoting a sense of safety.

In most individuals (i.e., those without a psychiatric disorder or neuropathology), the nervous system evaluates risk and matches neurophysiological state with the actual risk of the environment. When the environment is appraised as being safe, the defensive limbic structures are inhibited, enabling social engagement and calm visceral states to emerge. In contrast, some individuals experience a mismatch and the nervous system appraises the environment as being dangerous even when it is safe. This mismatch results in physiological states that support fight, flight, or freeze behaviors, but not social engagement behaviors. According to the theory, social communication can be expressed efficiently through the social engagement system only when these defensive circuits are inhibited.

Other Contributors to Neuroception

The features of risk in the environment do not solely drive neuroception. Afferent feedback from the viscera provides a major mediator of the accessibility of prosocial circuits associated with social engagement behaviors. For example, the polyvagal theory predicts that states of mobilization would compromise our ability to detect positive social cues. Functionally, visceral states color our perception of objects and others. Thus, the same features of one person engaging another may result in a range of outcomes, depending on the physiological state of the target individual. If the person being engaged is in a state in which the social engagement system is easily accessible, the reciprocal prosocial interactions are likely to occur. However, if the individual is in a state of mobilization, the same engaging response might be responded to with the asocial features of withdrawal or aggression. In such a state, it might be very difficult to dampen the mobilization circuit and enable the social engagement system to come back on line.

The insula may be involved in the mediation of neuroception, since it has been proposed as a brain structure involved in conveying the diffuse feedback from the viscera into cognitive awareness. Functional imaging experiments have demonstrated that the insula plays an important role in the experience of pain and the experience of several emotions, including anger, fear, disgust, happiness, and sadness. Critchley (2005) proposes that internal body states are represented in the insula and contribute to states of subjective feeling, and he has demonstrated that activity in the insula correlates with interoceptive accuracy.

SUMMARY

The polyvagal theory proposes that the evolution of the mammalian autonomic nervous system provides the neurophysiological substrates for adaptive behavioral strategies. It further proposes that physiological state limits the range of behavior and psychological experience. The theory links the evolution of the autonomic nervous system to affective experience, emotional expression, facial gestures, vocal communication, and contingent social behavior. In this way, the theory provides a plausible explanation for the reported covariation between atypical autonomic regulation (e.g., reduced vagal and increased sympathetic influences to the heart) and psychiatric and behavioral disorders that involve difficulties in regulating appropriate social, emotional, and communication behaviors.

The polyvagal theory provides several insights into the adaptive nature of physiological state. First, the theory emphasizes that physiological states support different classes of behavior. For example, a physiological state characterized by a vagal withdrawal would support the mobilization behaviors of fight and flight. In contrast, a physiological state characterized by increased vagal influence on the heart (via myelinated vagal pathways originating in the nucleus ambiguus) would support spontaneous social engagement behaviors. Second, the theory emphasizes the formation of an integrated social engagement system through functional and structural links between neural control of the striated muscles of the face and the smooth muscles of the viscera. Third, the polyvagal theory proposes a mechanism—neuroception—to trigger or to inhibit defense strategies.

PART II

BIOBEHAVIORAL REGULATION DURING EARLY DEVELOPMENT

CHAPTER 4

Vagal Tone: A Physiological Marker of Stress Vulnerability

Routine medical procedures are often stressful and produce periods of physiologic and behavioral instability. However, given the same treatment, all children do not respond alike. Some children exhibit prolonged periods of instability, while other children are virtually insensitive to the treatment. Although clinicians are concerned with the potential vulnerability associated with stressful events, a standard approach does not exist to address both the measurement of stress and the indexing of stress vulnerability.

Research on stress has often focused on the description of events that are considered stressful (e.g., life stress scales) and not on the functional impact of these events on physiology. In contrast, in pediatrics, stress is assumed to be a physiologic construct that is observed when behavior becomes disorganized and homeostatic processes are disrupted. In clinical settings this is often labeled physiologic instability.

Although we are aware that there are individual differences in vulnerability to the same medical procedures, current definitions of stress emphasize either the treatment or the response to treatment and not the neurophysiologic status prior to treatment. However, it is this neurophysiologic state that may index the stress vulnerability of the child.

This chapter proposes a method to assess on an individual basis both the stress response and the vulnerability to stress. This method monitors the neural control of the heart via the vagus (i.e., vagal tone) as an index of homeostasis. The method permits the assessment of the effects of disrupting homeostatic processes (i.e., stress) and the vulnerability of homeostasis to disruption by various clinical treatments (i.e., stress vulnerability).

STRESS: A STATE OF AUTONOMIC NERVOUS SYSTEM COMPROMISE

The autonomic nervous system (ANS) regulates homeostatic function. The ANS is composed of two subsystems, the parasympathetic (PNS) and sympathetic nervous systems (SNS). The PNS and SNS represent neural systems that originate in the brainstem and contribute to the regulation of a variety of target organs, including the eyes, lacrimal glands, salivary glands, sweat glands, blood vessels, heart, larynx, trachea, bronchi, lungs, stomach, adrenal, kidney, pancreas, intestine, bladder, and external genitalia. In general, the PNS promotes functions associated with a growth and restorative system. In contrast, the SNS promotes increased metabolic output to deal with challenges from outside the body.

In general, when a visceral organ is innervated by both the SNS and PNS, the effects are antagonistic. For example, SNS neurons dilate the pupil, accelerate the heart, inhibit intestinal movements, and contract the vesical and rectal sphincters. The PNS neurons constrict the pupil, slow the heart, potentiate peristaltic movement, and relax the vesical and rectal sphincters.

The PNS deals primarily with anabolic activities concerned with the restoration and conservation of bodily energy and the resting of vital organs. This view was clearly stated by Cannon (1929a):

> A glance at these various functions of the cranial division reveals at once that they serve for bodily conservation; by narrowing the pupil they shield the retina from excessive light; by slowing the heart rate they give the cardiac muscle longer periods for rest and invigoration; and by providing for the flow of saliva and gastric juice, and by supplying the necessary muscular tone or the contraction of the alimentary canal, they prove fundamentally essential to the processes of proper digestion and absorption by which energy-yielding material is taken into the body and stored. To the cranial division belongs the great service of building up reserves and fortifying the body against time of need and stress. (pp. 31–32)

Stimulation of the SNS prepares the individual for the intense muscular action required to protect and defend in response to external challenges. The SNS quickly mobilizes the existing reserves of the body. The eyes dilate, the rate and force of the heart contractility increase, blood vessels constrict, and blood pressure increases. Blood is drained from the intestinal reservoir to foster availability and transport of oxygenated blood to the skeletal muscles, lungs, heart, and brain. Peristalsis and alimentary secretion are inhibited, and sphincter contractions block urinary and rectal outlets.

The SNS and PNS are reciprocally innervated, and their responses are coordinated to provide the appropriate internal state to meet shifts in both internal and external demands. The PNS is modulated primarily by internal changes in the viscera. The SNS is primarily activated by exteroceptive impulses via somatic afferent fibers in response to changes in the external environment.

The PNS facilitates digestion and conserves energy by slowing heart rate. In the absence of external challenges (e.g., ambient temperature shifts, noise, pain, pyrogenic agents, etc.), the PNS optimizes the function of the internal viscera. In contrast, by increasing metabolic output to deal directly with external challenges, the SNS attempts to optimize the organism's relationship with the environment, Thus, increases or decreases in ambient temperature, noise, pain, and pyrogenic agents will produce attenuated PNS tone and increased SNS activity. Consistent with this functional description of the ANS, Gellhorn (1967) labeled the PNS as a trophotropic system and the SNS as an ergotropic system.

Early investigators defined the ANS as purely visceral motor (Langley, 1921). This limited definition did not acknowledge the contribution of visceral afferents. The afferent fibers accompany most visceral efferent fibers and form the afferent limb for visceral reflexes. The contemporary view of the ANS is that it is a complex system containing both peripheral efferent and afferent fibers as well as central neural structures, Thus, as Hess (1954) stated, the function of the ANS reflects more a visceral nervous system than a vegetative or automatic nervous system. It is because the ANS is an integrated system with both peripheral and central neurons that measurement of peripheral visceral activity provides a window to the brain structures that regulate visceral function and state.

The ANS responds to both internal and external stimuli. Although the ANS is often viewed as a motor system controlling visceral organs, most autonomic neurons are afferent. In the maintenance of bodily functions and in the reaction to stressful situations, ANS afferents are crucial. Afferent feedback from visceral organs often regulates PNS tone and has little impact on SNS tone. For example, distension of the stomach or stimulation of baroreceptors will result in reflexive increases in PNS tone. Afferent feedback from sensory organs produces a different response profile. Autonomic responses to external stimuli, including nociception or attention, produce a decrease in PNS tone. There is a complementary increase in SNS tone only if the stimulus is of high intensity and prolonged duration or is associated with conditions of nociception or intense stimulation. In response to metabolic demands, the two branches of the ANS often function synergistically to maximize cardiovascular output. For example, during exercise, there is a progressive decrease in PNS tone and a parallel increase in SNS tone. There are unique situations in which the autonomic response is characterized by either dual activation or dual inhibition. For example, in human adults, sexual arousal is characterized by a dual excitation.

The ANS is not merely a response system, quiescently awaiting challenges from the external environment. Rather, the ANS is continuously servicing the visceral afferents in an attempt to maintain homeostasis and promote physiologic stability. This regulatory process is primarily mediated by the PNS. Unfortunately, there are disease states that compromise the regulatory function. Some disease states (e.g., hypertension) are characterized by a depression of PNS tone with a compensatory SNS excitation. Other disease states (e.g., diabetes) are characterized by a depression of the PNS tone without eliciting a reciprocal SNS excitation, while other disease states may be characterized by dual inhibition.

The ANS is involved in the physiologic expression of stress. Shifts in ANS activity that disrupt homeostatic processes seem to characterize the common theme associated with physiologically based definitions of stress. More specific investigation of the literature suggests that the PNS, virtually independent of the SNS, regulates homeostatic processes and would thus be most sensitive to stress.

STRESS AND HOMEOSTASIS: NEW DEFINITIONS

There have been many definitions of stress. Because most definitions are structured in terms of the causal influences (i.e., stimulus or context) and not in terms of the variables commonly measured in a clinical setting, the definitions tend to be limited in their use in the medical environment. Often the definitions are circular because stress is defined both in terms of the context (e.g., medical treatment) and the response (e.g., behavioral and physiologic responses). For example, is the medical treatment stressing because it elicits an increase in blood pressure and heart rate? Or do increases in blood pressure and heart rate reflect stress independent of the specific medical treatment? Or do the physiologic responses reflect stress because the clinician assumes that there is stress associated with the medical treatment? The definition is further confounded because we assume that there are individual differences in responsiveness or vulnerability to the stressful event. Thus, the stressful treatment might not elicit a stress response in one patient while a nonstressful treatment might elicit a stress response in another patient.

Current definitions of stress are not very useful in the clinical setting. Even if stress were operationally defined by labeling the stressing stimulus as the stressor and the behavioral and physiologic response to the stressor as *stress*, at least two problems would remain: (1) the definitions of stress and stressor would be circular, and (2) there would be situations in which individual differences and state might mediate the degree of responsivity (i.e., *stress*) of a patient to constant medical treatments (i.e., *stressor*). For example, the same treatment that may physiologically compromise one patient may not produce a discernible behavioral or physiologic response in another patient or even in the same patient a second time. Alternatively, the same treatment that did not produce a response during the first administration may result in a massive physiologic compromise during subsequent administrations. Thus, stress must not be conceptualized simply in terms of the stressor and observed response but also in terms of the physiologic state of vulnerability of the patient at the time of treatment.

New definitions of stress and stress vulnerability can be derived and operationally defined based on the function of the ANS. Physiologically based measures can be objectively assessed within clinical settings with online monitoring of stress and stress vulnerability. In developing this approach, two essential areas must be discussed: (1) the rationale for evaluating specific autonomic variables as indices of stress, and (2) the measurement technology necessary to measure the autonomic indices of stress online in a clinical setting.

AN ANS DEFINITION OF STRESS: A RATIONALE

The ANS deals both with servicing the needs of the internal viscera and with responding to external challenges. The central nervous system mediates the distribution of resources to deal with internal and external demands. Perceptions and assumed threats to survival, independent of the actual physical characteristics of the stimulation, may promote a massive withdrawal of PNS tone and a reciprocal excitation of SNS tone. The trade-off between internal and external needs may be used in developing definitions of stress and homeostasis. Based on this model, stress and homeostasis are interdependent. Homeostasis reflects the regulation of the internal viscera, and stress reflects the subjugation of internal needs in response to external needs. Thus, measurement of PNS tone may provide the indexing variable for defining stress and stress vulnerability.

The concept of homeostasis is not new. Walter Cannon (1929b) coined the term and stated that "the coordinated physiological reactions which maintain most of the steady states in the body are so complex, and so peculiar to the living organism, that it has been suggested that a specific designation for these states be employed—*homeostasis*" (p. 400). Cannon's views are dependent on the earlier work of Claude Bernard. Bernard's construct of "le milieu interieur" included physiologic mechanisms responsible for the maintenance of the constancy of the internal environment. As Bernard's work evolved, he emphasized the dynamic and oscillatory nature of the nervous system in maintaining the "internal milieu" within a limited range (Bernard, 1878–79).

Homeostasis as a construct was never meant to reflect a static state. Rather it defined the dynamic feedback and regulation processes necessary for the living organism to maintain internal states within a functional range. Over time the concept has lost much of its rich meaning and has often been interpreted to represent a static internal level. Clinically, stasis or lack of endogenous variability in neurally mediated peripheral systems, such as gastric motility and heart rate, is a sign of severe physiologic compromise.

In the proposed model, the PNS fosters visceral needs (i.e., homeostasis) and the SNS responds to external challenges. Thus, status of the PNS state parallels homeostasis. Alternatively, withdrawal of PNS tone in response to a challenge may define stress, and PNS tone prior to the challenge may represent physiologic or stress vulnerability. With this physiologic model, SNS state is not the defining characteristic of stress or stress vulnerability; stress responses and stress vulnerability may be indexed in the absence of major shifts in SNS tone. It is important to note that in many situations with healthy children, the transitory withdrawal of PNS tone will be paralleled by an increased expression of SNS tone. In contrast, severely compromised children may not exhibit SNS reactivity and SNS tone might be low. Moreover, these children would have low PNS tone, virtually no PNS reactivity, and would be clinically assessed as being chronically stressed or exhibiting physiologic instability.

This view suggests that homeostasis may be defined as the autonomic state that fosters visceral needs in the absence of external challenge. This state would be defined by a high degree of PNS tone. Stress may be defined as the autonomic state that reflects a disruption of homeostasis. This state would be defined by the withdrawal of PNS tone. Thus, the degree of stress can be quantified on a physiologic level. Moreover, the chronic autonomic state before a clinical event would index the patient's stress vulnerability; individuals exhibiting problems of homeostasis will have the greatest stress vulnerability.

THE ASSESSMENT OF STRESS: VAGAL TONE MONITORING

Given the foregoing justification, it is necessary to identify and quantify an index of PNS activity. The most readily indexed measure of PNS activity is derived from the heart rate pattern. The amplitude of respiratory sinus arrhythmia (RSA) provides a validated and easily obtainable index of PNS tone via the cardiac vagus (Porges, 1986). In the following sections this will be described as an index of cardiac vagal tone. With modern technology it is possible to monitor online the changing influence of the vagus on the heart and to estimate shifts in general vagal tone (Porges, 1985).

Physiologic and behavioral processes are dependent on neural feedback. Information is received at the periphery and transmitted to the central nervous system, and appropriate physiologic reflexes or overt behaviors are emitted. Feedback loops typical of many homeostatic processes produce a rhythmic pattern characterized by phasic increases and decreases in neural efferent output to organs such as the heart. In many physiologic systems, efficient neural control is manifested as rhythmic physiologic variability, and within normal parameters the greater the amplitude of oscillation, the healthier the individual. Thus, the amplitude of rhythmic physiologic processes may index the status of the individual's nervous system and capacity to respond. In other words, the greater the amplitude of *organized* rhythmic physiologic variability, the greater the response potential or possible range of behavior. Individuals with attenuated physiologic variability would then exhibit a lack of physiologic and behavioral flexibility in response to environmental demands. This is observed in very ill infants. Thus, in terms of stress reactions, one would expect these individuals to lack the self-regulatory capacity to adjust rapidly to stressful stimuli.

Research in areas of cardiology, gerontology, physical therapy, and diabetology demonstrate that general PNS deficits are reflected in cardiac vagal tone. Moreover, stimulation of other PNS afferents results in reflexive increases in cardiac vagal tone (Cottingham, Porges, & Lyon, 1988; DiPietro & Porges, 1991). Since cardiac vagal tone reflects the general PNS input to the viscera, it may be used to monitor stress and index individual differences in stress vulnerability.

As a noninvasive measure of cardiac vagal tone, we have standardized a method to quantify the amplitude of RSA (Porges, 1986). RSA indexes the nervous system modulation of heart rate activity via the vagus. RSA reflects rhythmic vagal efferent influences on the cardiac pacemaker modulated by respiratory processes in the medulla. Heart rate patterns, like behavioral processes, are dependent on the status of the nervous system and the quality of neural feedback. Stress results in a disorganization of the rhythmic structure of both behavior and autonomic state. Thus, measures of cardiac vagal tone, such as the amplitude of RSA, provide an important window into the central control of autonomic processes and by inference into the central processes necessary for organized behavior.

Cardiac vagal tone is reflected in the amplitude of a heart rate rhythm associated with frequency of spontaneous breathing. This rhythmic process has been observed and studied for more than 100 years. Speculations regarding the neural mechanisms were reported as early as 1910, when a relation between RSA and vagal tone was proposed by Hering (1910). Hering clearly stated that "it is known with breathing that a demonstrable lowering of heart rate . . . is indicative of the function of the vagi." Derivations of this method with paced breathing techniques are currently used to diagnose peripheral neuropathy in diabetic patients. Contemporary research has provided empirical evidence that the amplitude of RSA accurately maps the efferent influence of the vagus nerve on the heart. Based on electrophysiologic studies of vagal efferents, it has been proposed that central respiratory drive gates the source nuclei of the vagal cardioinhibitory fibers (Jordan, Khalid, Schneiderman, & Spyer, 1982).

If cardiac vagal tone is a sensitive index of the functional status of the nervous system, then we would predict that individuals with greater vagal tone would exhibit a greater range of competent behaviors. We would also expect that conditions that compromise the central nervous system (e.g., medical complications, anesthesia, and illness) would result in an attenuation of vagal tone.

In building a model that relates cardiac vagal tone to stress, we first describe a global metaphor characteristic of homeostatic processes and then more specific pathways related to the vagus. Heart rate in a healthy human is not steady. The pattern of heart rate reflects the continuous feedback between the central nervous system and the peripheral autonomic receptors. The primary source of heart rate variability is mediated by phasic increases and decreases in neural efferent output via the vagus to the heart (Porges, McCabe, & Yongue, 1982). Under most conditions, like other measures of homeostatic control, the greater range of the phasic increases and decreases, the "healthier" the individual. For example, with high-risk neonates, there is an attenuation of the range of homeostatic function. Paralleling this process is a reduction in cardiac vagal tone (Fox & Porges 1985; Porges 1988).

Heart rate variability is a marker of the efficiency of neural feedback mechanisms and may index health status or the individual's capacity to organize physiologic resources to respond appropriately. Thus, the better the "organized" physiologic variability, the greater the range of behavior. Organized variability is due to dynamic feedback and thus is characterized by rhythmic deviations from a constant level. An optimum feedback system allows large deviations from the mean with negative feedback occurring at constant intervals. Neural regulation of the heart in healthy individuals is similar to the optimal feedback system already described. In the neural control of the heart, the vagus serves as the primary negative feedback mechanism. Thus, states of attenuated heart rate variability would have attenuated vagal influences on the heart. Returning to our metaphor, states characterized by attenuated vagal influences should be paralleled by reduced behavioral flexibility in response to environmental demands.

STRESS VULNERABILITY IN THE NEONATE: AN EXAMPLE OF VAGAL TONE MONITORING

Figure 4.1 illustrates 2 minutes of the heart rate pattern and the amplitude of RSA for two sleeping neonates. The top panel illustrates the pattern of a high-risk

FIGURE 4.1. Beat-to-beat heart rate and respiratory sinus arrhythmia (RSA). Top panel illustrates data from a high-risk preterm neonate monitored at approximately term. Bottom panel illustrates data from a healthy normal full-term neonate monitored within 36 hours of delivery. Data were collected during sleep. In both panels, the top line illustrates the beat-to-beat heart rate and the bottom line illustrates RSA calculated for sequential 10-second segments. RSA values are in natural logarithm units per millisecond squared.

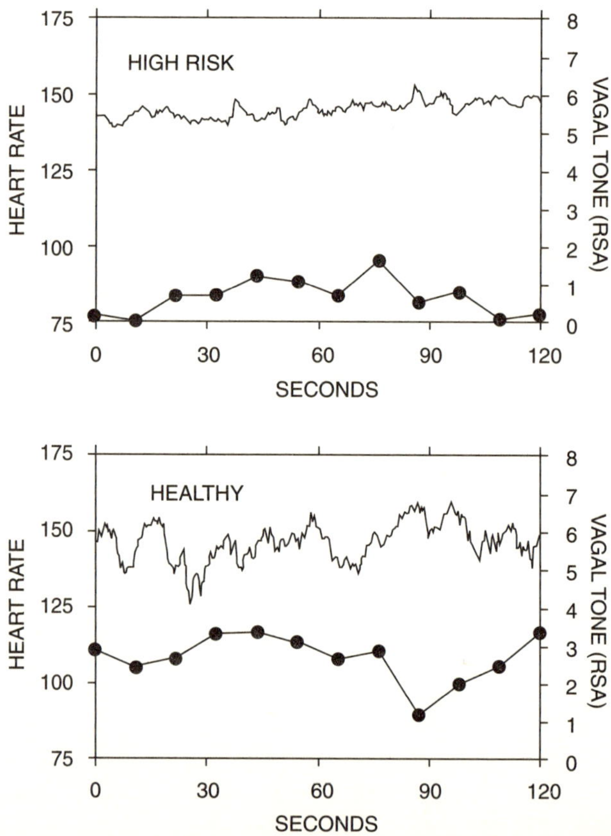

FIGURE 4.2. Distribution of respiratory sinus arrhythmia (RSA) for normal full-term neonates and neonates in the NICU. RSA values are in natural logarithm units per millisecond squared.

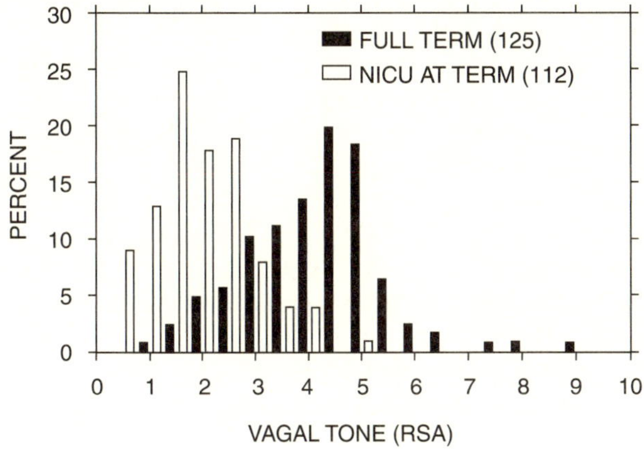

preterm neonate monitored at approximately term. The bottom panel illustrates the pattern of a healthy term neonate monitored within 36 hours of delivery. The top line on each panel illustrates the continuous heart rate over the 2 minutes. The bottom line on each panel represents the amplitude of RSA calculated for each sequential 10 seconds within the 2 minutes. Clarification of the vagal tone concept may be obtained by observing the differences between the top and bottom panel. Notice that even during sleep, heart rate is not constant. Although the heart rate levels are similar for the two neonates, the healthy term neonate has much greater beat-to-beat variability relative to the high-risk preterm. Close inspection of the two beat-to-beat patterns identifies a striking difference in the rapid changes in heart rate that occur every 1 to 3 seconds. These oscillations are associated with respiration and reflect cardiac vagal tone. Cardiac vagal tone is indexed by the amplitude of these rapid oscillations (i.e., RSA) and is reported in natural logarithm units.

Figure 4.2 illustrates the frequency distributions of the amplitude of RSA for both high-risk and normal full-term neonates. The subject samples were 125 full-term neonates and 112 neonatal intensive care unit (NICU) residents. The full-term neonates were all residents of a full-term normal nursery and were tested during the second day following delivery. RSA values for the premature NICU neonates were derived during the first recording made with the neonates not using the ventilator and breathing room air. RSA was assessed during sleep when the NICU neonates were between 35 and 37 weeks corrected gestational age.

From the data in Figure 4.2, it is obvious that high-risk neonates, as a group, have significantly lower vagal tone than do full-term neonates ($F[1, 235] = 226.3$, $p < .0001$). Since respiration frequency might influence the quantification of RSA, respiration was monitored on a subset of 47 full-term and 62 NICU neonates. Respiration was significantly faster for the NICU neonates ($F[1, 107] = 23.5$, $p < .0001$). However, even when this significant influence was removed with analysis of covariance, there was still a highly significant difference between the two groups ($F[1, 107] = 82.2$, $p < .0001$). The group classification (full-term vs. NICU) accounted for 53.1% of the variance in the statistical model. When the influence of respiration was removed, group classification accounted for 43.7%.

Research in our laboratory suggests only subtle maturational increases and great stability of these estimates under standard sampling conditions during residency within the NICU. For example, a sample of 16 preterm neonates was tested during sleep on 5 separate days starting at least 1 day following delivery. Although there was a significant relationship between severity of clinical condition and RSA (i.e., healthier neonates had higher amplitude RSA), the average correlation among the RSA values approached 0.9.

This example illustrates how monitoring of vagal tone in the NICU by quantifying RSA may provide a sensitive index of stress vulnerability. Data from our laboratory and the laboratories of others demonstrate that the more compromised NICU residents have lower cardiac vagal tone. Consistent with the model of stress and stress vulnerability, the NICU neonates have limited PNS tone to regulate their internal state and are simultaneously confronted with demands from the environment, including the necessity to thermoregulate and to deal with sensory stimuli including medical procedures assumed to be painful.

The vagal system is responsive to the changing needs of the organism. Often the vagal system will react by selectively increasing or decreasing its influence on the periphery. This might be observed as a withdrawal of vagal tone to increase heart rate to support metabolic demands or an increase in vagal tone to regulate digestive polypeptides and gastric motility. The adaptive success of the infant is not based merely on the tonic level of the ANS but on the ability of the ANS to respond appropriately to environmental and interval challenges. For example, during painful medical manipulations, such as circumcision, cardiac vagal tone is suppressed (Porter, Porges, & Marshall, 1988). In contrast, during gavage feeding of premature neonates, cardiac vagal tone is increased (DiPietro & Porges, 1991). If infants exhibited a vagal tone increase during gavage feeding and a depression of vagal tone below pregavage levels following feeding, they were discharged approximately 2 weeks earlier than were infants who did not exhibit this response. These effects were independent of birth weight, gestational age at birth, and other clinical factors. Although pregavage vagal tone was not related to the response pattern or discharge, it did predict weight gain trajectories. Thus, vagal reactivity provides another dimension related to clinical risk.

Measures of vagal tone provide an important window to the central modulation of autonomic function. Measures of vagal tone during sleep or nonchallenging conditions provide an index of normal homeostatic feedback, while measures during sensory or cognitive challenges provide an indication of adaptive functioning. Thus, low levels of vagal tone are associated with high-risk populations, while atypical vagal responsivity even in infants with normal basal levels of vagal tone seems to identify a subset of infants who have behavioral and regulatory problems (DeGangi, DiPietro, Greenspan, & Porges, 1991; DiPietro & Porges, 1991).

VAGAL TONE SHIFTS DURING STRESS: THE COST OF DOING BUSINESS

The ANS has many physiologic responsibilities. It must regulate the blood pressure to ensure that enough blood reaches the brain. It also monitors the blood gases. If there are shifts in oxygen and carbon dioxide, changes in cardiopulmonary parameters are immediately implemented by the direct neural modulation of the heart, vasomotor tone, and lungs. While these cardiopulmonary processes are being regulated, the ANS is also controlling digestion and metabolism. The actions of the ANS are related to life support: ergotropic (i.e., work) and trophotropic (i.e., growth) functions (Gellhorn, 1967).

The vagal system is critical to the regulation of both ergotropic and trophotropic process. Increases in vagal tone not only result in increases in metabolic output but modulate the digestive polypeptides and gastric motility (Uvnas-Mober, 1989). The vagus is also critical in the facilitation of trophotropic process. The vagus can have direct inhibitory influences on sympathetic excitation of the myocardium (Levy, 1977). Moreover, the limbic system, assumed by psychophysiologists to modulate autonomic arousal solely through sympathetic excitation, has direct inhibitory influences on the cells of origin of the vagus (Schwaber, Kapp, & Higgins, 1980). The brainstem regions controlling the vagal efferents act to express greater vagal tone, thus maintaining trophotropic states, or to allow withdrawal of vagal tone to facilitate the immediate mobilization of the organism.

Research with other species demonstrates that cardiac vagal tone increases during development (Larson & Porges, 1982). Paralleling this increase in vagal tone are increases in self-regulatory and exploratory behaviors. In research with infants high cardiac vagal tone is associated with better visual recognition memory (Linnemeyer & Porges, 1986; Richards, 1985). An overview chapter summarizes the research on cardiac vagal tone and affect (Porges, 1990).

DiPietro and Porges (1991) also evaluated in preterm neonates the relationship between cardiac vagal tone and behavioral reactivity to gavage feeding. In this study, individual differences in cardiac vagal tone were significantly correlated with behavioral reactivity to the gavage method of feeding, Similarly, Huffman et al. (1998) observed that 3-month-old infants with high cardiac vagal tone habituated more rapidly to novel visual stimuli and exhibited more sustained attention than did infants with low cardiac vagal tone.

Drugs that depress vagal tone also seem to have a degrading effect on sustained attention, For example, in a study evaluating the effects of atropine sulfate on sensorimotor performance, we reported not only dose-dependent depression of vagal tone but also dose-dependent decrements in performance (Dellinger, Taylor, & Porges, 1987). We also have conducted research on the effects of inhalant anesthesia on the parallel between alertness and cardiac vagal tone. Inhalant anesthesia depressed cardiac vagal tone, and as the patients regained consciousness, there was a parallel increase in cardiac vagal tone (Donchin, Feld, & Porges, 1985).

With the ability to monitor cardiac vagal tone by quantifying the amplitude of RSA, we have been able to obtain a more accurate assessment of vagal mechanisms and the relationship between vagal tone and autonomic reactivity. Studies using the vagal tone index support the hypothesis that vagal tone may index stress and stress vulnerability. Porter et al. (1988) demonstrated, in a sample of normal newborns, massive withdrawal of cardiac vagal tone during circumcision. Moreover, individual differences in cardiac vagal tone were correlated with heart rate reactivity to circumcision. Neonates with higher cardiac vagal tone exhibited not only larger heart rate accelerations but also lower fundamental cry frequencies during surgical procedures. Porter and Porges (1988) also demonstrated in premature infants that individual differences in cardiac vagal tone were related to heart rate responses during lumbar puncture procedures.

CONCLUSION

There is a physiologic basis for defining stress and stress vulnerability. The concepts of stress and homeostasis are interdependent and manifested in the activity of the PNS. In contrast to traditional models of stress, the PNS is proposed as the modulator of stress vulnerability and reactivity. The model proposed suggests that accurate monitoring of PNS state will provide a window allowing the assessment of stress.

A physiologic justification is presented for the use of PNS, rather than or in addition to SNS, activity in the description of both stress vulnerability and stress reactivity. The quantification of cardiac vagal tone from spontaneous heart rate oscillations is described as a method for assessing the changing PNS state. The quantification of cardiac vagal tone provides a standard instrument with statistical parameters that are comparable between patients and throughout the life span. The method is not dependent on stages of motor or cognitive development and thus is practical for use even with neonates. This noninvasive method will allow the assessment of the stressful impact of various clinical treatments on the young infant and permit the identification of individuals with vulnerabilities to stress.

In conclusion, the usefulness of contemporary definitions of stress is limited, in part by circularity and in part by a tendency within stress research to focus narrowly on the contribution of the SNS. Cardiac vagal tone, measured by quantifying the amplitude of RSA, is proposed as novel index of stress vulnerability and reactivity with applications in all branches of medicine, and with particular value in pediatrics.

CHAPTER 5

The Infant's Sixth Sense: Awareness and Regulation of Bodily Processes

Life is a sensory experience. During every moment of our lives, we experience the world through our varied sensory systems. Sensory experiences drive our behavior and contribute to the organization of our thoughts and emotions. Immediately after birth, the infant is bombarded with a variety of new sensory stimuli. These provide important information about the characteristics and potential demands of the baby's new environment. The infant must immediately detect, discriminate, and adapt to this information. Successful adaptation to the rapidly changing environment and the ability to cope with changing demands depend on the infant's ability to detect and interpret sensory information. Thus, when we study infant behavioral patterns, vocalizations, and physiological reactivity, we attempt to understand how the young infant uses sensory systems to detect information from the environment and to integrate this information into motor, affective, and cognitive schema to successfully interact and adapt to a changing environment.

We have learned that humans have five primary sense modalities: smell, vision, hearing, taste, and touch. We know that even a newborn can respond to these sensory modalities. These responses are obvious to the parent and clinician (although only a few decades ago, scientists were unaware of the sensory capacities of young infants). However, this traditional method of categorizing sensory information does not account for the vast amount of sensory information being conveyed to the brain from the numerous sensors located inside our body. Even current clinical models of infant regulation (e.g., Ayres, 1972; Greenspan, 1991) that emphasize the importance of sensory processing in the emotional and cognitive development of the infant, and individual differences among infants in the ease with which they detect and interpret sensory information, focus primarily on three sense modalities that describe the external environment—that is, touch, vision, and hearing. These models do not deal with internal sensations that provide information about the physiological regulation.

Although neurophysiologists and neuroanatomists describe sensory systems that regulate our internal organs, this research has had little influence on either our common language or the clinical terminology we use to describe bodily processes. At present, there are only a few easily understood descriptors that characterize internal senses and states—for example, pain, nausea, and arousal. Yet in spite of this linguistic handicap, our experiences provide us with an awareness of bodily sensations and an appreciation of how these sensations can contribute to mood state and psychological feelings.

Missing from our language and our science is the ability to describe internal states. In our day-to-day interactions we choose vague terms, such as "feelings," to describe the psychological consequences of bodily changes. Behavioral scientists often attempt to objectify these terms by operationalizing concepts such as state, mood, and emotion with verbal reports and elaborate coding systems. Clinical practitioners infer these feelings and use terms descriptive of emotional tone. However, whether we are talking about feelings, emotions, states, or moods, we are always attempting to describe the internal states that are continuously being monitored and regulated by the nervous system.

The goal of this chapter is to introduce an additional sense modality that monitors bodily processes. A variety of terms may be used to describe this sensory system. Classic physiology describes this sensory system as interoception. Interoception is a global concept which includes both our conscious feelings of and unconscious monitoring of bodily processes, Interoception, like other sensory systems, has four components:

1. Sensors located in various internal organs to "sense" internal conditions;
2. Sensory pathways that convey information to the brain regarding the internal conditions;
3. Brain structures to interpret sensory information and organize systems to respond to the changing internal conditions; and
4. Motor pathways that communicate from the brain back to the internal organs that contain the sensors to change directly the state of the internal organ. Brain structures evaluate interoceptive information, categorize it, associate it with other sensory information, and store the associations in memory.

INTEROCEPTION IS THE SIXTH PRIMARY SENSE

The five classic senses already described are categorized based on the sensors located on the external surface of the body, or exteroceptors. However, we are aware that the external senses (e.g., vision, audition, sound, touch, smell, and taste) are not the sole source of stimulation directing the infant's behavior, thoughts, and emotions. The ability to sense internal states and bodily processes—through interoceptors located on the heart, stomach, liver, and other organs inside the body cavity—constitutes a sixth sense that is crucial to the infant's survival.

This sixth sense represents a functional awareness, with both conscious and unconscious dimensions, of what is happening inside the body. For example, on a conscious level, digestive processes may provide sensory information that the infant interprets as hunger when the stomach is empty, or as pain when the stomach is severely distended due to gas. The cardiovascular and respiratory systems also provide conscious feedback. Alertness changes as a function of shifts in both blood pressure associated with posture (when, for example, a baby brightens when picked up and held upright against a parent's shoulder) and blood gas concentrations of carbon dioxide and oxygen. On an unconscious level, internal organs have sensors which send continuous information to brain structures. This unconscious awareness fosters stability (i.e., homeostasis) in internal physiology by rapidly adjusting to support specific motor behaviors and psychological processes.

Although bodily sensations are paramount to the infant's successful survival, developmental specialists are currently more concerned with the infant's capacity to sense external stimuli. For example, clinical assessment tools, such as neurological and neuropsychological examinations, focus only on the processing of external stimulation. Similarly, our current childrearing and intervention strategies are not at all geared to helping young children sense their internal physiological states. We do not provide infants and young children with descriptive or symbolic tools to represent internal states, nor are caregivers taught to perceive specific behavioral or physiological indicators of gradations in the infant's bodily sensations. This remains the case even though we know that the status of bodily functions (such as digestion) and infants' reactions to difficulties in these processes (such as colic) are derived via important sensory systems. Moreover, the sensory information from continuously monitoring bodily functions can influence the infant's ability to perform specific behaviors, perceive external stimuli, and organize information into mental representation of cognitions and emotions.

EVALUATING SENSORY PROCESSING

For the five classic sensory modalities, we can evaluate the competence of the child to process sensory information by direct observation of behavior and through verbal reports. We can observe adaptive and dysfunctional strategies. We can identify problems by observing hyporesponsiveness and hyperresponsiveness in response to specific sensory challenges. We can evaluate developmental patterns in the child's ability to integrate sensory information. In addition, we can evaluate intervention procedures delivered by professionals such as speech and hearing specialists, ophthalmologists, nurses, occupational therapists, physical therapists, psychologists, psychiatrists, and pediatricians.

In contrast, interoceptive competence has not been systematized. Other than estimates of pain severity, there are no methods to quantify perception of bodily processes or to test unconscious interoceptive feedback. There are no scales to identify developmental landmarks.

But whether or not we know how to describe or measure them, sensations from inside the body are a strong influence on the infant's behavior in the world. From birth, the infant's need of sleep, food, water, and warmth are monitored via internal sensors. This information drives much of the infant's behavior. The infant's behavior then provides cues to the caregiver. In other words, stimulation of specific sensors inside the body of the young infant results in behavioral responses that prompt the caregiver to interact with the infant, to comfort, and to reduce the cause of these bodily sensations. For example, feeding the infant reduces hunger, burping relieves flatulence after feeding, and sucking may stimulate digestion and reduce constipation.

INTEROCEPTION: THE INFRASTRUCTURE OF HIGHER ORDER BEHAVIOR

Interoception is dependent on a complex feedback system that starts with sensors located in various body organs and ends with the higher order social interaction with the caregiver. Faulty sensors or a dysfunction in any component of the sensory system (i.e., sensor, sensory pathway to the brain, motor pathway from the brain, or areas in the brain that interpret the sensory information and control the motor output to the organ) may not only contribute to physiological problems but also negatively impact on the psychological and interactive experiences of the infant. Thus, the quality of interoceptive processes may contribute to individual differences in information processing (e.g., cognitive processes), emotional expressiveness, and social behavior.

I have conceptualized the dependency of complex behaviors on successful bodily processing in a hierarchical model with four levels (see Porges, 1983). Each level requires successful functioning on the preceding level of organization. Although the model includes complex social behaviors, the substrate of the model depends on the organizational competence of the nervous system.

- Level I is characteristic of homeostatic processes of physiological systems regulating the internal organs. Homeostatic regulation requires the bidirectional interoceptive process of monitoring and regulating the internal organ via sensory and motor pathways between the brain and the internal organ.
- Level II processes require cortical, conscious, and often motivated influences on the brainstem regulation of homeostasis.
- Level III processes are observable behaviors that can be evaluated by the quantity, quality, and appropriateness of motor behavior.
- Level IV reflects the coordination of behavior, emotional tone, and bodily state to successfully negotiate social interactions.

This model assumes that complex behavior, including social interactions, depends on physiology and how appropriately the nervous system regulates bodily processes. In this model, interoception becomes the foundation of physical, psychological, and social development. Interoception serves as the neurophysiological substrate of the higher processes, included in Level III and Level IV, that have been elaborated by many other researchers, practitioners, and theorists of child development.

LEVEL I PROCESSES: PHYSIOLOGICAL HOMEOSTASIS

Underlying the vague concept of "feelings" is a physiological process that depends on interoception. By explaining and measuring the functional regulation of physiological processes dependent on interoceptive mechanisms, we can identify functional vulnerabilities in the infant's ability to regulate on the most basic level. If the infant is insensitive to his or her own bodily calls for care, nurturance, and protection, how will the infant appropriately function and respond to social needs?

Level I processes provide the physiological mechanisms for state regulation, including emotional regulation and expression. They also provide the infrastructure for the child's successful interaction with the challenging social demands of the world.

In the proposed hierarchical model, Level I processes represent the successful regulation of internal bodily process via neural feedback systems. To maintain homeostasis, interoceptors originating in the body cavity (e.g., gastric, hepatic, enteric, cardiac, vascular, and pulmonary systems) transmit information via nerves to brainstem structures. The brainstem structures interpret the sensory information and regulate the internal physiological organs. They do this by stimulating nerves that either directly control internal organs (e.g., increase or decrease heart rate, constrict or dilate blood vessels, inhibit or facilitate peristaltic activity, etc.) or indirectly manipulate the organs by releasing specific hormones or peptides (e.g., adrenalin, insulin, oxytocin, vasopressin, gastrin, somatostatin, etc.).

Level I is associated with the organization and neural feedback mechanisms that characterize the maintenance of homeostasis. These homeostatic processes can shut down when either internal conditions or external challenges require maximum output of energy. For example, fever, severe thermo-stress, extreme emotional distress, and aerobic exercise can reflexively inhibit Level I feedback systems. States associated with severe illness (e.g., physiological compromise and instability) are also characterized by a down-regulation of the neural control of bodily processes. Alternatively, up-regulation may occur when the interoceptors are directly stimulated (e.g., the filling of the stomach with food) or when other sensory modalities reflexively influence bodily processes. For example, the smell of appetizing food initiates signals from the nose to the brainstem structures that in turn stimulate glands in the mouth and stomach to produce digestive secretions even before the food enters the mouth.

LEVEL II PROCESSES: COST OF DOING BUSINESS

The autonomic nervous system is the division of the nervous system that senses the condition of internal organs and regulates their activity. The autonomic nervous system deals with: (1) servicing the needs of the organs inside the body, and (2) responding to external challenges. We can define adaptive behavioral strategies and homeostasis in terms of the child's ability to trade off between internal and external needs. Based on this model, homeostasis and response strategies to environmental demands are interdependent. Homeostasis reflects the regulation of the physiological conditions within the body. Response strategies reflect the stage when internal needs become less important than external needs—when the baby (fed, burped, and changed) is ready and eager to interact with the world of people and things.

The autonomic nervous system has two branches, the sympathetic and the parasympathetic. In general, the parasympathetic branch promotes functions associated with growth and restoration. In contrast, the sympathetic branch promotes increased output of energy to deal with challenges from outside the body. When there are no environmental demands, the autonomic nervous system services the needs of internal organs to enhance growth and restoration. However, in response to environmental demands, homeostatic processes are compromised and the autonomic nervous system supports increased output of energy, by down-regulating parasympathetic function and often stimulating sympathetic function to deal with these external challenges.

The central nervous system mediates the distribution of resources to deal with internal and external demands. Perceptions and assumed threats to survival (independent of the actual physical characteristics of the stimulation) may promote a massive withdrawal of parasympathetic tone and a reciprocal excitation of sympathetic tone. This trade-off between internal and external needs is monitored and regulated by the central nervous system.

Level II represents the integration of interoceptive systems with other sensory modalities and psychological processes. Unlike the reflexive integration described in Level I, Level II involves higher brain processes. Level II processes include voluntary approaches to the source of stimulation or an awareness of the need to problem solve and engage in information processing. To foster the contact with the stimulus or to process information, the internal bodily state is changed. Level II is characterized by the appropriate adjustment (i.e., gradations in inhibition) of homeostatic processes during states of attention, the processing of information, and social behavior.

When other senses—for example, hearing, sight, or touch—are stimulated, the autonomic responses are a secondary process. Under these conditions, after the baby detects sensory information, his or her brain structures regulate autonomic organs to facilitate the processing of the sensory information. These physiological states may support the baby's ability simply to pay attention to the sensory stimulus, or, by increasing metabolic output, the physiological state may support the child's physical movement toward or away from the stimulus.

Sensory information from the external environment triggers changes in internal regulation that are maintained via accurate interoception. Without accurate interoception, the down-regulation of internal physiological processes may compromise survival—for example, by inhibiting digestion or by disturbing electrolyte or blood gas levels. Defects in interoception may also be at the base of regulatory disorders (Greenspan, 1991). Regulatory disorders reflect a broad spectrum of dysfunction in young children and include difficulties in bodily processes such as eating and sleeping, difficulties in processing sensory and affective information, and difficulties in state regulation.

PHYSIOLOGICAL AND BEHAVIORAL HOMEOSTASIS: PARALLEL CONCEPTS

As a construct, physiological homeostasis is consistent with the behavioral homeostasis observed by Greenspan (1991). Greenspan has described a developmental period from birth to 3 months during which the infant masters homeostatic processes. In this model, homeostasis requires the appropriate regulation of sleep and behavioral states as well as the ability to incorporate appropriate visual, auditory, and tactile stimulation. Thus, children defined as having regulatory disorders have difficulties in sleep, feeding, and sensory integration.

Greenspan's model, however, focuses on the external sensory modalities—hearing, sight, and touch. I am suggesting that physiological homeostasis (Level I) and the regulation of physiological homeostasis to support sensory processing of environmental stimuli (Level II) are necessary substrates for the behavioral homeostasis. In other words, the regulatory disorders defined by Greenspan may have a physiological substrate (Porges & Greenspan, 1991). Empirical research provides support for this hypothesis (e.g., DeGangi, DiPietro, Greenspan, & Porges, 1991; Porges, Doussard-Roosevelt, Portales, & Suess, 1994). We are demonstrating that physiological measures of homeostasis are related to behavioral problems in infants. Our findings suggest the possibility that clinicians will be able to use physiological measures that reflect interoceptive competence diagnostically to identify Level I and Level II vulnerabilities in infants and young children.

ASSESSMENT OF LEVEL I AND LEVEL II PROCESSES

In general, homeostatic processes are regulated by the parasympathetic nervous system via the vagus nerve, a large nerve with several branches enabling bidirectional communication between brain structures and internal organs. The vagus, with its sensory and motor pathways, is the primary component of the interoceptive system. The vagus and its branches account for approximately 80% of the parasympathetic nervous system. Approximately 80% of the vagal fibers are sensory and thus directly service interoceptors within the body cavity. Thus, measurement of vagal activity provides information on interoception in maintaining homeostasis (i.e., Level I processes) and the regulation of homeostasis to support environmental challenges (i.e., Level II processes).

It is possible to monitor vagal activity by quantifying specific rhythmic changes in heart rate (see Porges, 1992). Level I processes may be evaluated by measuring vagal control of the heart during rest or sleep; this provides a measure of the infant's interoceptive capacities to maintain homeostatic control. Level II processes may be evaluated by measuring the change in vagal control of the heart during environmental challenges; this provides a measure of the infant's capacity to down-regulate the vagal system to deal with environmental demands.

Our research program provides data supporting the hypothesis that the ability to sense and regulate internal physiological state is at the base of competencies in higher order behavioral, psychological, and social processes. Currently, we are developing laboratory procedures to profile the infant's capacity to regulate internal physiological systems during a variety of sensory processing demands. Our long-term goal is to provide a standardized clinical instrument to evaluate interoception. This instrument would complement neurological, neuropsychological, and other sensory evaluations. The assessment would index interoceptive processes through the measurement of vagal influences on the heart by quantifying rhythmic changes in the beat-to-beat heart rate pattern (i.e., respiratory sinus arrhythmia as a measure of cardiac vagal tone). The instrument will have the capacity to evaluate two dimensions of interoception:

1. The capacity to monitor and maintain homeostasis in the absence of environmental challenges (i.e., Level I processes); and
2. The capacity to alter homeostasis to support behaviors required by environmental challenges (i.e., Level II processes).

The ability to measure interoception, the sixth sense, opens a new window to the infant's sensory experiences. This window allows us to observe and to understand the internal feelings of the infant and how these internal states change during illness, mental processing, and social behavior.

CHAPTER 6

Physiological Regulation in High-Risk Infants: A Model for Assessment and Potential Intervention

Birth is the greatest challenge to human survival. When an infant is born, the supportive environment of the womb is gone. Parturition functionally disrupts the fetus's dependency on maternal physiology and expels the fetus from this secure environment. Thus, birth marks a transition as the management of autonomic regulation shifts from the maternal placental-fetal system to the newborn. In this demanding environment, the newborn must have skills to regulate autonomic processes (e.g., breathe, feed, digest, thermoregulate, etc.) and to communicate autonomic state needs to caregivers (e.g., cry). Within minutes of birth, these skills are challenged. Difficulties in expressing physiological competence are life-threatening. Even with healthy full-term newborns, there is great concern by health care professionals and parents about an infant's physiological regulation competency in negotiating this complex transition. Postpartum adaptation is more difficult for the high-risk infants who experience a variety of risk factors, including prematurity and delivery complications. These high-risk infants, often limited by a less mature or a damaged nervous system, are compromised in performing these self-regulatory tasks.

The study of the high-risk neonate provides a real-life laboratory to evaluate the unique contribution of autonomic regulation to development. Research can evaluate the relation between specific physiological vulnerabilities and subsequent develop mental problems in behavioral organization, social behavior, and cognitive function.

A model of neural regulation of autonomic processes that focuses on the high-risk neonate might address two research questions. First, is it possible to assess the relative risk that an individual newborn faces following the birth process;

and second, how do we help the high-risk newborn negotiate the transition from a physiological dependency on maternal systems to the physiological self-regulation required in the extrauterine world?

Successful adaptation of the newborn to the extrauterine environment requires a dynamic and complex repertoire of responses. These responses occur on several levels. Although self-regulatory physiological strategies require complex neurophysiological systems, involving feedback between the brain and peripheral physiology, several systems may be monitored by careful visual surveillance of the newborn. For example, the Apgar scale (Apgar, 1953) codifies the status of physiological self-regulation via a standard observational scale. Similarly, neurological examinations during the newborn period assess neural function through the systematic elicitation of observable reflexes.

In the day-to-day care of the high-risk infant, clinical management attempts to compensate for the immature or compromised nervous system and its limited abilities to regulate physiological homeostasis. For example, radiant heaters use the neonate's core temperature in a feedback loop to compensate for an inability to thermoregulate; ventilators are used to ensure sufficient oxygen when the respiratory system is either too premature or depressed; orogastric or nasogastric (i.e., tube) feeding is used to compensate for the neonate's inability to actively suck and to coordinate sucking, swallowing, and breathing.

The attentiveness of staff in the neonatal intensive care unit (NICU) emphasizes the importance of observable physiological systems, such as body movements, breathing, thermoregulation, and sucking to detect shifts in clinical status. Thus, although technology has contributed to the evaluation of physiological self-regulation through specialized biomedical monitoring equipment (e.g., computerized oxygen saturation, blood pressure, temperature, and heart rate monitors), the primary clinical indicators of autonomic regulation that promote homeostasis are still obtained through clinical observations.

Before the infant can master complex behavioral interactions with the environment, the infant must competently regulate autonomic processes. A goal of mammalian development is to become independent of the caregiver. There are several constraints on the development of self-regulatory skills, including the status of neurons, neurophysiological systems, motor behavior control, and the availability and contingency of socioenvironmental stimulation. Although assessments of self-regulatory skills usually focus on global levels of motor and social behavior, these abilities are dependent on physiological systems. In turn, physiological systems are dependent on a neuronal substrate, which provides the boundary conditions. If there is damage to neural tissue, the ability to regulate both motor and visceral processes is limited. Neurons can be damaged by hypoxia, fever, trauma, and other insults, such as drugs. Although neurons cannot be measured noninvasively in the infant, the functional output of populations of interconnecting neurons produce physiological responses such as sucking, breathing, and heart rate, which are easily monitored.

SELF-REGULATION AND THE NERVOUS SYSTEM

Implicit in the evaluation of clinical status in the newborn is the assumption that the assessment reflects the quality of nervous system function. Although many assessments do not require detailed physiological monitoring, the systems observed (e.g., regularity of respiration, body movements, sucking responses, coloration of skin, etc.) provide insight into the competence of the nervous system and its ability to orchestrate complex self-regulatory physiological processes. Thus, underlying most assessment strategies is the assumption that the nervous system provides the management skills necessary to regulate internal physiological systems and plays a pivotal role in determining the newborn's success in navigating through the changing environment.

Self-regulation characterizes physiological systems. Weiner (1948) proposed a model of nervous system self-regulation to explain homeostasis. According to Weiner, homeostasis is an emergent property of a system that, via bidirectional communication, monitors and regulates the status of an organ to maintain an output level within a specific functional range. As illustrated in Figure 6.1, the system would include a central regulator that would determine the motor output to an organ after interpreting the information from the sensor (e.g., afferent feedback) that monitors the status of the organ.

To maintain physiological homeostasis, sensory pathways originating in peripheral organs (e.g., chemoreceptors and baroreceptors in the carotid sinus) convey information regarding physiological status, and motor pathways (e.g., vagal and sympathetic pathways to the heart) change the output of peripheral organs. The sensory pathways from visceral organs originate in the periphery and usually terminate in the brainstem; however, many of the motor pathways originate in the brainstem and terminate in the periphery.

Physiological systems could be described as being composed of sensors that input information about the external (outside the body) and internal (within the body) environments, motor systems that control behavioral and visceral activity,

FIGURE 6.1. Schematic representation of bidirectional communication between central regulator and peripheral organ characteristic of physiological homeostasis.

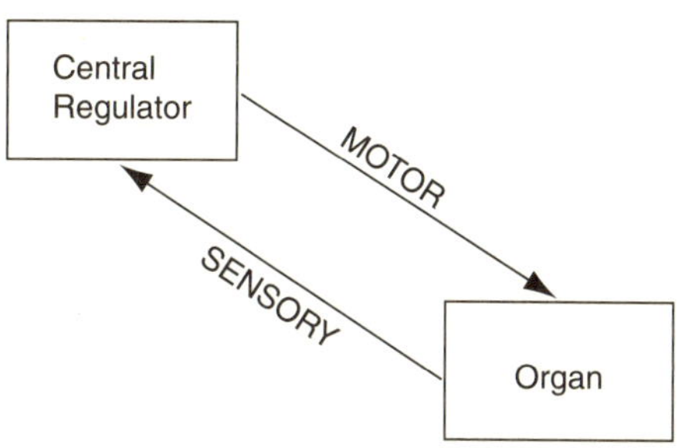

and an integrative mechanism that evaluates the input from the sensors and determines the specifics of the motor output.

The study of normal psychological and behavioral development emphasizes the importance of the external environment. For example, individual differences in development are often associated with socioeconomic status, family function, nutrition, and stress factors. In contrast, partially because psychopathology can be observed in "healthy" environments, the study of psychopathological development emphasizes the importance of the internal environment (e.g., the brain and neural regulation of physiological systems). For example, pathological development is often associated with problems in brain development and dysfunctional physiological systems. This interest in organismic variation promotes research questions evaluating mechanisms through which feedback from visceral organs contributes to the organization and development of emotional, cognitive, and behavioral processes.

Self-Regulation: A Negative Feedback System

Physiological systems regulating visceral state (e.g., heart rate, temperature, blood pressure) are self-regulatory. Self-regulatory systems adjust output to the changing input through a process known as feedback. When the feedback opposes the state of the system, it is known as negative feedback. When the feedback augments the state of the system, it is known as positive feedback. The room thermostat provides a functional metaphor for a negative feedback system. The room thermostat contributes to the temperature regulation by evaluating sensors to determine when the room temperature deviates from a predetermined range (i.e., homeostasis). If the room temperature drifts outside this range, the thermostat will trigger "motor" mechanisms to heat or cool the room to obtain a temperature within the previously defined "homeostatic" range.

The regulation of blood pressure represents a physiological feedback system with an objective to maintain levels within healthy limits. Because brain function requires a continuous supply of oxygenated blood, any drop in blood pressure is critical to survival and requires a rapid and appropriate physiological adjustment. In the healthy individual, drops in blood pressure are instantaneously detected by baroreceptors in the blood vessels. The baroreceptors send information to the brainstem, and the brainstem sends a motor command to the heart to increase heart rate rapidly. As soon as blood pressure returns to normal limits, neural feedback slows heart rate. However, there are individuals who have defective feedback. For example, in the elderly or individuals using specific medications, the blood pressure feedback system may be depressed. For these individuals, when the blood pressure drops because of a posture shift, they may experience severe dizziness or even syncope. This experience is common in the elderly and frequently contributes to falls and severe injuries.

In contrast to the negative feedback systems, which characterize self-regulatory processes, there are also positive feedback systems. A malfunctioning room thermostat providing positive feedback would continue to augment the temperature until the system ceased functioning due to extreme heat or extreme cold. Thus, prolonged positive feedback is destructive to systems. For example, rage, severe anger, or panic might be viewed as a behavioral consequence of physiological positive feedback that promotes increased metabolic output. Consistent with the feedback model, the physiological cost of prolonged periods of positive feedback might compromise the health of the individual.

The characteristics of physiological feedback may change as a function of physiological, emotional, cognitive, or behavioral demands. For example, during periods requiring massive metabolic output, such as exercise, the feedback system must be vigilant and efficient to support the changing oxygen needs of the cardiovascular system. During less motorically demanding conditions, such as periods of drowsiness and sleep, the pattern of neural feedback may change and go through periods of dissociation. Additionally, it is possible that the ability to express emotional sensitivity or behavioral contingency might be related to the "gain" or "amplification" of the feedback from the viscera. Therapeutic drugs, such as clonidine, used for panic disorders, may alter the neural feedback system by dampening the impact of the afferent feedback from visceral organs. Thus, the study of abnormal development and psychopathology may prompt attention to the study of the development of normal feedback systems and the relation between physiological systems and emotional, cognitive, and behavioral development (see Cicchetti, 1993).

Homeostasis: Signs and Signals of Competent Neural Self-Regulation

For the newborn, maintaining physiological homeostasis is crucial for survival. Homeostasis is not a passive process in which physiological systems remain constant. Rather, homeostasis is an active, neurally modulated process in which physiological systems vary within viable ranges.

The quality of homeostasis may be assessed with measures that are related to clinical status. When the output of a system is above the functional level, output is decreased until the level drops into the functional range. The output level progressively decreases through the functional range. When the output drops below the functional level, the output is progressively increased to reach and pass through the functional range. This process of waxing and waning of output reflects the negative feedback property of our nervous system. Thus, healthy physiological systems have a characteristic rhythm that provides an important observable window of the status of the nervous system. For example, respiration, blood pressure, heart rate, and temperature exhibit rhythms that provide important clinical information.

The rhythms provide indicators of the quality of feedback characterizing the system as it attempts to maintain homeostasis. The physiological rhythms produced by central-autonomic feedback loops have two dynamic characteristics:

(a) a period of time of constant reflecting the temporal latency of the system to adjust or respond, and (b) a magnitude dimension reflecting the degree to which the system can deviate from a specific state. Both dimensions are modulated by higher brain structures and limited by neurochemical processes. Thus, by the nature of brain-autonomic regulation, autonomic response systems are time series, characterized by oscillations, with a period determined by the duration of the feedback loop, and an amplitude determined by central regulatory control.

Measures of heart rate oscillations, such as respiratory sinus arrhythmia (RSA), which are often used to assess cardiac vagal tone, dynamically reflect the bidirectional communication between the peripheral cardiovascular system and the brain. Under specific demand situations requiring shifts in metabolic output (e.g., stress- or survival-motivated responses, attention or social engagement, activity, fever, disease) the characteristics of the feedback, magnitude, valence, and period may change. Thus, the interest in monitoring cardiac vagal tone during demand situations, and as a marker of physiological self-regulation, is justified.

There are times when the nervous system is compromised and the neural feedback regulating cardiopulmonary and thermoregulatory processes is deficient. The occurrence of apnea and bradycardia signal dysfunction in the neural regulation of cardiopulmonary function. Similarly, difficulties in maintaining body temperature when ambient temperatures are changing reflect difficulties in thermoregulation.

The care of the high-risk infant often requires interventions to regulate physiological processes that are no longer under appropriate neural control (i.e., efficient negative feedback). Following apnea and bradycardia, interventions such as physical movement of the infant, serve as potent stimuli to reengage neural regulation of cardiopulmonary processes. When an infant has difficulty thermoregulating, rather than relying on neural feedback to vascular and cardiac processes, technology may use feedback from sensors that monitor body temperature to regulate ambient temperature. The common use in the NICU of heating units controlled by the newborn's body temperature is a functional example of a negative feedback system that compensates for defective self-thermoregulation.

The well-managed diabetic provides another example of external manipulation of a deficient internal feedback system. The diabetic has a defective feedback system that does not adequately regulate blood sugar through the endogenous release of insulin. To compensate for this problem, the diabetic must supplement the endogenous feedback system. To provide afferent feedback, blood is sampled and the amount of sugar in the blood is assessed. The individual's brain and associated cognitions interpret the afferent feedback and determine the appropriate amount of insulin required to regulate blood sugar within a functional level. To complete the feedback loop, motor systems are recruited to administer the insulin.

The human nervous system functions as a collection of several interacting self-regulatory negative feedback systems, each with a specific role. Sensors or receptors are located on the surface of the body to assess environmental changes and within the body to assess internal conditions. Motor systems control body movements and visceral organs. The feedback from internal sensors is interpreted by brainstem structures that contribute to the regulation of autonomic state (e.g., nucleus tractus solitarius, dorsal motor nucleus of the vagus, nucleus ambiguus). The nervous system provides the infrastructure for all levels of self-regulation. Self-regulatory processes characterize various domains ranging from the overt behavioral strategies of the infant demanding caregiver attention to subtle physiological shifts related to changes in thermoregulation, digestion, or cardiopulmonary function.

Self-Regulation of Physiological Systems: Primary Survival Agenda

In the proposed model, the effectiveness of an assessment is dependent on its sensitivity to measure the status of the nervous system. The success of an intervention is dependent on the functional enhancement of the nervous system. Although developmental follow-up studies of high-risk infants focus on the complex regulation of motor, social, and cognitive behaviors, survival of the high-risk infant in the NICU is based on successful regulation of the physiological systems that support growth and restorative processes. Initially, this regulation may involve extraneural feedback provided by external monitoring of critical care variables (e.g., temperature, heart rate, respiration, oxygen saturation). Then, based on the monitored condition, clinical interventions (e.g., ventilation, ambient temperature, medication) are administered to aid physiological regulation. If these interventions were successful, the clinical course would reflect a shift from a dependence on extraneural regulation to neural self-regulation. Thus, assessment should be directed at evaluating the nervous system structures and functions that promote physiological states fostering growth and restorative processes. Moreover, when methods are developed to accurately monitor these systems, interventions could be developed that specifically enhance neural feedback and improve the function of these systems.

The Vagal System: An Indicator of Survival-Related Self-Regulation

The proposed model for assessment and intervention focuses on the vagal system, a physiological system uniquely important for the survival of the high-risk infant. The vagal system contributes to the regulation and coordination of survival processes, including breathing, sucking, swallowing, heart rate, and vocalization. Dysfunction in these processes places the infant at survival risk and produces clinical indicators of risk, such as apnea, bradycardia, difficulties in sucking and swallowing, and weak, high-pitched cries.

Although the clinical indicators just listed appear to reflect divergent processes, they share an important neuroanatomical and neurophysiological substrate. The following four points highlight our knowledge and understanding of this substrate and justify why knowledge of this system may contribute to the development of psychophysiological assessment and clinical intervention strategies (a detailed and documented review of the physiological substrate of this system is described in chapter 2).

First, from a neuroanatomical level, sucking, swallowing, vocalizations, heart rate, and bronchial constriction are regulated by a common brainstem area. The regulation of these processes is dependent on motor fibers emerging from a medullary nucleus known as the nucleus ambiguus. These myelinated motor fibers originate in the nucleus ambiguus and travel through the tenth cranial nerve, the vagus.

Second, the vagus contributes sensory and additional motor fibers to the self-regulation of physiological systems. The vagus contains sensory fibers that provide feedback and motor fibers originating in the dorsal motor nucleus of the vagus. Sensory fibers compose approximately 80% of vagal fibers. The vagal sensory fibers originate in several visceral organs (e.g., heart, lungs, stomach, pancreas, liver, intestines) and terminate in a brainstem area known as the nucleus tractus solitarius. The vagal motor fibers originating in the dorsal motor nucleus of the vagus, unlike the myelinated motor fibers originating in the nucleus ambiguus, are unmyelinated and provide the primary motor control of the digestive system. However, the dorsal motor nucleus also projects to the bronchi and heart.

Third, nucleus tractus solitarius integrates sensory information from visceral organs and communicates, via interneurons, with the primary source nuclei of the vagus (i.e., nucleus ambiguus and dorsal motor nucleus). As illustrated in Figure 6.2, this feedback system regulates digestive and cardiopulmonary processes to foster growth and restoration. The afferent and efferent pathways conveying the bidirectional communication between the peripheral organs and the brainstem travel through the vagus. Note that the model describes potential feedback modulation (changing the magnitude or direction of the feedback) by other brain structures.

Fourth, neurophysiological research suggests that respiration rate is determined by a brainstem system that also outputs the respiratory rhythm to the heart and the bronchi. This neurophysiological drive to breathe is, in part, dependent on the emergent properties of interneuronal communication between the nucleus ambiguus and the nucleus tractus solitarius. According to Richter and Spyer (1990), the interneuronal communication between the nucleus ambiguus and the nucleus tractus solitarius is the source of a rhythmic generator producing a cardiopulmonary rhythm that results in oscillations in bronchial constriction and heart rate at a frequency similar to spontaneous breathing. The rhythmic concordance among these processes may functionally enhance diffusion of oxygen, and coordinate breathing and heart rate with other processes dependent on nucleus ambiguus motor fibers, such as sucking, swallowing, and vocalization.

The foregoing overview of the vagal system emphasizes the importance of vagal fibers in self-regulatory processes. The neuroanatomical descriptions and neurophysiological information regarding vagal function have been organized in the polyvagal theory (see chapter 2). The polyvagal theory provides a theoretical

FIGURE 6.2. Feedback model of vagal regulation of autonomic state. Model illustrates the brainstem mechanisms that regulate vagal control of cardiopulmonary and digestive processes.

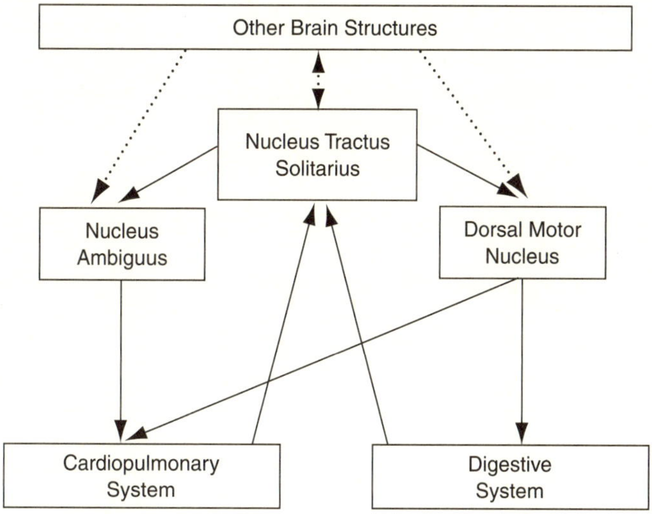

basis for specific clinical assessments and interventions in the NICU. Based on the polyvagal theory, interventions may be developed that will not jeopardize the clinical status of the vulnerable infant. In contrast, the polyvagal theory also explains how stimulation of specific sensory systems may elicit life-threatening vagal reflexes. For example, oral-esophageal stimulation, commonly occurring during suction or during the insertion of the orogastric tube for gavage feeding, may elicit potent bradycardia.

Polyvagal Theory

The polyvagal theory emphasizes the functional difference between vagal fibers originating in two areas of the brainstem: the nucleus ambiguus and the dorsal motor nucleus of the vagus. The two types of pathways have different embryological origins, promote different response strategies, and provide the neurophysiological justification for new definitions and explanations of stress, distress, and distress vulnerability. The polyvagal theory explains the stress and distress experienced by the high-risk infant within the context of the evolution of the mammalian autonomic nervous system. Because of the evolutionary pressures associated with obtaining and maintaining oxygen resources and transporting oxygenated blood to the brain, a neomammalian vagal system developed from fibers originating in or migrating to the nucleus ambiguus. The neomammalian vagal system provides the neural control of the muscles that evolved from the primitive gill arches. The gill arches throughout evolution have been associated with the extraction of oxygen from the environment. Somatomotor pathways from the neomammalian vagal system innervate the larynx, pharynx, and esophagus and coordinate vocalizations, breathing, and sucking. Additionally, visceromotor pathways from this vagal system regulate bronchial constriction and heart rate. Thus, this system is still involved in obtaining oxygen from the environment, diffusing oxygen in the blood, and maintaining cerebral blood flow by regulating blood pressure. The evolutionarily older reptilian vagal system involves fibers originating in the dorsal motor nucleus.

The polyvagal theory emphasizes that the two vagal systems (neomammalian and reptilian) respond differently to a stressor. For healthy mammals, the initial response is mediated by the neomammalian vagus and is characterized by a rapid withdrawal of vagal tone. This functionally removes the potent *vagal brake* from the heart and facilitates an instantaneous increase in metabolic output (i.e., increased heart rate) to mobilize energy resources for the classic flight-or-fight response. Removal of the vagal brake increases strength and speed to deal with stress and to aid in obtaining oxygen resources. However, withdrawal of the vagal brake functionally degrades (i.e., reduces control in) the motor systems involving the nucleus ambiguus. Thus, stress would not only be associated with faster heart rate, but also with higher pitch vocalizations (e.g., cries) and difficulties in coordinating sucking, swallowing, and breathing. This, of course, is commonly observed in physiologically stressed or compromised infants.

The Removal of the Vagal Brake Is the Neomammalian Vagal Response to Stress

According to this model, stress characterized by removal of the vagal brake is not necessarily detrimental to the survival of the individual. Removing the vagal brake occurs often as an adaptive response to increase metabolic output to mobilize and react to survival-related demands. For example, the vagal brake will be removed during exercise, pain, attention, and even during the appetitive phases of eating. Successful postpartum adaptation is related to the infant's skill and neurophysiological capacity to regulate the vagal brake to differentially engage and disengage with the environment. Therefore, the high-risk infant who exhibits a systematic regulation of the vagal brake to environmental demands should have more positive social and cognitive outcomes (e.g., Doussard-Roosevelt, McClenny, & Porges, 2001; Doussard-Roosevelt, Porges, Scanlon, Alemi, & Scanlon, 1997; Hofheimer, Wood, Porges, Pearson, & Lawson, 1995).

Removal of the vagal brake places the mammalian nervous system in a vulnerable state because: (a) it compromises homeostatic functions, including those associated with blood pressure regulation, thermoregulation, food intake, and digestion; and (b) it places the nervous system at risk for reptilian vagal reactions. When the neomammalian vagus is in control, the heart and bronchi are protected from the reptilian vagus, and blood is appropriately oxygenated and transported to the brain. In the healthy infant, transitory behavioral states such as crying are characterized by a disengagement and self-soothing as a reengagement of the vagal brake. Infants with greater neomammalian vagal tone tend to be more reactive to the environment (DeGangi, DiPietro, Greenspan, & Porges, 1991; Porges, Doussard-Roosevelt, Portales, & Suess, 1994; Porter, Porges, & Marshall, 1988; Stifter & Fox, 1990) and more able to self soothe and calm (Fox, 1989; Huffman et al., 1998). Moreover high-risk newborns with greater neomammalian vagal tone have fewer risk factors (see chapter 4; Porges, 1995) and have more optimal cognitive outcomes (Fox & Porges, 1985).

In contrast to the self-regulatory characteristics of the neomammalian vagus and the function of the vagal brake in staging responses as a function of environmental demands, the reptilian vagus responds with massive increases in vagal tone that slow the heart and constrict the bronchi. By reducing metabolic output, the reptilian vagus contributes to the conservation of available oxygen and promotes adaptive responses such as submerging and diving in aquatic environments or behaviorally freezing (i.e., feigning death) in terrestrial environments. Unfortunately, these response strategies, which are adaptive for reptiles, are potentially fatal for mammals. In mammals, this maladaptive strategy is observed in clinical settings as potentially lethal bradycardia and apnea. Based on the polyvagal theory, it has been proposed (see chapter 2) that fetal distress and sudden death, including sudden infant death syndrome, due to their neurogenic origins, are potential examples of the noxious impact of the reptilian vagal surge.

In a clinical setting, it may be possible to evaluate the status of the neomammalian vagus to indicate stress and distress vulnerability. Vagal fibers to the heart from the nucleus ambiguus produce a respiratory rhythm (i.e., RSA). By applying time-series statistics to the beat-to-beat heart rate pattern (Porges, 1985; Porges & Bohrer, 1990), it is possible to extract a measure of RSA that accurately represents vagal influences from the nucleus ambiguus.

In the absence of nucleus ambiguus stimulation to the heart, the heart is vulnerable to surges in vagal tone from the dorsal motor nucleus that produce bradycardia. Data from my laboratory support this conclusion. We have observed that bradycardia in the fetus and newborn occur during periods of depressed RSA, the measure of vagal tone from the nucleus ambiguus (Reed, Ohel, David, & Porges, 1999). Moreover, the observed meconium in the amniotic fluid of fetuses who have suffered from hypoxia (i.e., fetal distress) provides additional support for this model, because vagal stimulation via the dorsal motor nucleus of the vagus to the lower digestive track produces meconium (Behrman & Vaughan, 1987). Thus, during fetal distress, when we know RSA is depressed, the fetus exhibits a dorsal motor nucleus vagal surge as evidenced by the expression of massive bradycardia and meconium.

In support of these conclusions, neuroanatomical research suggests that sudden infant death syndrome may be related to a delayed maturation of the myelinated fibers of the vagus (Becker, Zhang, & Pereyra, 1993). The neomammalian vagal motor fibers are myelinated, as are many of the vagal sensory fibers. Hypoxia or other neurophysiological insults that may impede vagal myelination or contribute to demyelination would result in defects in the negative feedback system regulating the neomammalian vagus. The engagement and disengagement of the vagal brake would be unreliable. Defects in this system are critical to survival, because the nucleus ambiguus is involved in the generation of respiratory rhythms and the coordination of sucking, swallowing, and breathing. Thus, evaluation of nucleus ambiguus function may map into a continuum of deficits in self-regulation processes.

Hierarchical Model of Self-Regulation

Self-regulation processes observed in mammals may be organized into a hierarchical model with four levels (Porges, 1983). The hierarchical model emphasizes the dependence of higher order behavioral systems on more primary physiological systems. The model assumes that behaviors such as the organized motor activity associated with feeding, or the appropriate emotional regulation during social interaction, are dependent on a more primary physiological substrate related to the systematic regulation of autonomic state. The model has four levels and is hierarchical because each level requires successful functioning on the preceding level of organization (see Table 6.1).

Level I is characteristic of homeostatic processes of physiological systems regulating the internal organs. Homeostatic regulation requires bidirectional processes of monitoring and regulating the internal organ via sensory and motor pathways between the brain and the internal organs. Level II processes require cortical, conscious, and often motivated influences on the brainstem regulation of homeostasis. Level III processes are observable behaviors that can be evaluated by the quantity, quality, and appropriateness of motor behavior. Level IV reflects

TABLE 6.1. Hierarchical Model of Self-Regulation

Level I:	Neurophysiological processes characterized by bidirectional communication between the brainstem and peripheral organs to maintain physiological homeostasis.
Level II:	Physiological processes reflecting the input of higher nervous system influences on the brainstem regulation of homeostasis. These processes are associated with modulating metabolic output and energy resources to support adaptive responses to environmental demands.
Level III:	Measurable and often observable motor processes, including body movements and facial expressions. These processes can be evaluated in terms of quantity, quality, and appropriateness.
Level IV:	Processes that reflect the coordination of motor behavior, emotional tone, and bodily state to successfully negotiate social interactions. Unlike those of Level III, these processes are contingent with prioritized cues and feedback from the external environment.

the coordination of behavior, emotional tone, and bodily state to successfully coordinate social interactions.

Unique to this model is the assumption that complex behaviors, including social interactions, depend on physiology and how appropriately the nervous system regulates autonomic state. Thus, the regulation of autonomic state, via bidirectional communication between the brain and visceral organs, becomes the linchpin of physical, psychological, and social development. This chapter elaborates only on Level I and Level II processes, because these processes provide a developmentally antecedent substrate of emotional, cognitive, and behavioral regulation and must be mastered by all infants to ensure survival and successful adaptation in the postpartum environment.

Level I Processes: Physiological Homeostasis

Level I processes represent the successful regulation of internal bodily processes via neural negative feedback systems composed of interoceptors or sensory receptors monitoring internal bodily state and their respective neural pathways. To maintain homeostasis, interoceptors originating in the body cavity (e.g., gastric, hepatic, enteric, cardiac, vascular, and pulmonary systems) transmit information via neural pathways to brainstem structures. The brainstem structures interpret the sensory information and regulate the visceral state by triggering motor pathways that either directly manipulate various organs via neural pathways (e.g., increase or decrease heart rate, constrict or dilate blood vessels, inhibit or facilitate peristaltic activity) or trigger the release of specific hormones or peptides (e.g., adrenalin, insulin, oxytocin, vasopressin, gastrin, somatostatin). Level I is associated with the organization and neural feedback mechanisms that characterize the maintenance of homeostasis.

Level II Processes: Cost of Doing Business

The autonomic nervous system deals both with servicing the needs of the internal viscera and with responding to external challenges. Competence in the ability to trade off between internal and external needs may be used in developing definitions of adaptive behavioral strategies and homeostasis. Based on this model, response strategies to environmental demands and homeostasis are interdependent. When there are no environmental demands, the autonomic nervous system services the needs of the internal viscera (e.g., internal organs such as the heart, lungs, and gut) to enhance growth and restoration. However, in response to environmental demands, homeostatic processes are compromised and the autonomic nervous system supports increased metabolic output by down-regulating "growth and restoration" functions to deal with these external challenges. The central nervous system mediates the distribution of resources to deal with internal and external demands. This trade-off between internal and external needs is monitored and regulated by the central nervous system.

Survival Tasks of the High-Risk Newborn: In the NICU and Post-NICU

Survival in the NICU is dependent on achievement of Level I and Level II self-regulatory processes. Competence in regulating these processes enables the newborn to maintain and regulate homeostatic processes, such as temperature, breathing, feeding, blood pressure, and sleeping. All other systems, including neurophysiological systems associated with cortical function, sensory integration, and motor control of observable behavior are dependent on successful regulation of these more primary homeostatic functions. A similar argument can be made regarding the importance of brainstem control systems (e.g., nucleus ambiguus, nucleus tractus solitarius, dorsal motor nucleus of the vagus) as an infrastructure for emotional regulation, social behavior, and cognitive development. Thus, clinical care of the high-risk newborn should include assessments to evaluate and intervention strategies to foster development of nucleus ambiguus function.

Discharge from the NICU is directly related to competent self-regulation of Level I and Level II processes. In contrast, survival post-NICU is dependent on processes attributed to Level III and Level IV. Successful adaptation post-NICU not only requires competent Level I and Level II processes but is dependent on the Level III and Level IV processes that require the regulation of motor behavior, emotional expression, cognitive processes, and social interactions.

The concept that early difficulties in self-regulation lead to problems in emotional and social development evolves from the clinical and theoretical work of Greenspan (1992). Greenspan has described a sequence of developmental milestones that may be equated with the hierarchical levels presented here. Although his work focuses on Level IV processes, he acknowledges the importance of more primary physiological systems related to sensory feedback and motor control. Greenspan has proposed that difficulties in these primary neurophysiologically dependent systems contribute to problems in impulse control, attention, concentration, creative thinking, affect integration, and social interactions. The current detailed descriptions of Level I and Level II processes and their dependence on the nucleus ambiguus provide a neurophysiological model that complements these clinical observations.

Global Assessment Strategy

With the view that nucleus ambiguus function is critical to the survival risk of the newborn and our knowledge of how to monitor this function via RSA, we have the tools for a global neurophysiological assessment. A noninvasive assessment strategy might use a baseline or sleep measure of RSA to assess a Level I process and a feeding test to challenge the system to evaluate a Level II process. In older children, the autonomic substrate (i.e., Level I and Level II) might be evaluated during baseline and tasks associated with higher order processes. Baseline measures followed by tasks requiring Level III and Level IV processes, such as manipulating motor (e.g., activity level), cognitive (e.g., attentional), or social demands might be used to evaluate the child's autonomic tone (i.e., Level I) and ability to regulate autonomic state (i.e., Level II) to support higher level processes.

Level I Assessments

To assess Level I, we have measured RSA during periods of minimal environmental demand (e.g., sleep or quiet states) in the neonatal nursery. Research with this assessment procedure has reliably distinguished between high-risk and full-term newborns (Porges, 1992) and between risk groups of preterm newborns matched for gestational age (see chapter 4). Consistent with the hierarchical model, research has demonstrated that the RSA measure of vagal function in the NICU is related to cognitive outcome at 3 years of age (Doussard-Roosevelt et al., 1997). Similarly, preterm newborns with greater amplitude RSA exhibited more social behavior and attention in the NICU (Hofheimer et al., 1995).

Level II Assessments

To assess Level II, we have measured changes in RSA during periods of well-defined environmental demands (e.g., feeding) in the neonatal nursery. Three studies have been conducted to evaluate the effect of a feeding challenge on the pattern of RSA. In one study, an apparatus provided water or sucrose in solution when a newborn sucked (Porges & Lipsitt, 1993). In response to increased sweetness, the heart rate increased, the amplitude of RSA decreased (lower nucleus ambiguus vagal tone), and the sucking frequency increased. In a second study, RSA was evaluated during bottle feeding in a sample of NICU newborns (Portales et al., 1997). During the bottle feeding, RSA was depressed and heart rate increased. Following feeding, the levels returned to prefeeding baseline levels. A third study (Suess et al., 2000) illustrated a relationship between RSA recovery following feeding and degree of prematurity. In addition, outcome studies using the feeding challenge with older infants are currently being conducted in my laboratory. These studies will determine if infants who have a history of excessive crying and difficulties in regulating behavioral state also have difficulties in regulating the vagal control of the heart mediated by the nucleus ambiguus. In these studies, the pattern of vagal reactivity, monitored by RSA, to the feeding challenge and recovery following feeding are used as Level II assessment indices. These assessments will be evaluated to determine whether they are related to clinical risk factors and developmental outcome.

General Intervention Strategy

Measurement of RSA provides the capability to assess individual differences in neural regulation of homeostatic function in terms of nucleus ambiguus control. It is now possible to answer two questions: (a) whether individual differences in neural regulation are related to intervention effectiveness, and (b) whether interventions are beneficial or detrimental to survival-related physiological regulation. Thus, our knowledge regarding neurophysiological function may be useful in designing intervention strategies to promote increased nucleus ambiguus function.

Beneficial intervention strategies would stimulate specific visceral sensors to increase the function of the neomammalian vagus. The intervention would stimulate motor outflow and enhance the regulation and coordination of heart rate, respiration, vocalization, sucking, and swallowing. Positive developmental outcomes (e.g., weight gain, improved state regulation, longer periods of alertness, improved neurological development) would be the product of the improved regulation and coordination.

In contrast, detrimental intervention strategies would stimulate sensors that would increase the function of the reptilian vagus. Under conditions during which the dorsal motor nucleus vagus becomes dominant, the intervention might result in bradycardia, apnea, and digestive problems and produce compromised outcomes.

The sensory components of the trigeminal nerve (cranial nerve V) and the facial nerve (cranial nerve VII) provide the primary sensory input to the nucleus ambiguus. Therefore, interventions that provide sucking opportunities, oral stimulation, and facial movement would provide regulation challenges to the nucleus ambiguus vagal system and may be beneficial. In contrast, interventions that may trigger dorsal motor activity may be potentially dangerous. For example, shifting the posture of an infant will elicit baroreceptor responses including a heart rate change mediated via the vagus to regulate blood pressure. In the low-risk infant, this intervention exercises a negative feedback system that maintains cerebral blood pressure and contributes to the regulation of behavioral state. The system includes motor control of the cardiovascular system from the dorsal motor nucleus and the nucleus ambiguus. In the high-risk infant, with depressed nucleus ambiguus function, posture shifts may result in a massive bradycardia and loss of consciousness similar to the vasovagal syncopes observed in older adults with low nucleus ambiguus vagal tone (i.e., low-amplitude RSA).

Similarly, abdominal massage or pelvic manipulations may be detrimental to the high-risk infant. These interventions, similar to the posture shifts, may stimulate sensory pathways that activate both nucleus ambiguus and dorsal motor nucleus. Thus, in the presence of low nucleus ambiguus tone (a characteristic of the high-risk infant), these interventions also might elicit massive bradycardia and loss of consciousness.

Caution: It is extremely important to emphasize that many high-risk infants are in a compromised physiological state, defined by low nucleus ambiguus vagal tone. Interventions applied to these infants such as abdominal pressure during massage, baroreceptor stimulation by posture shifts, or lower esophageal stimulation during either suction or orogastric feeding might trigger massive dorsal motor nucleus reflexes and, in turn, bradycardia, apnea, and even loss of consciousness.

CONCLUSION

Although the methods described have focused on the high-risk infant during the neonatal period, the model may be generalized to study older children and even adults with behavioral and psychological problems. Associated with various psychological and psychiatric disorders are symptoms related to difficulties in state regulation. For example, hyperactivity or forms of attentional problems are associated with an inability to regulate the physiological substrate to support appropriate attentive and social behaviors. Similarly, individuals with inappropriate expressions of panic, terror, or rage, with their defining massive physiological responses, provide examples of an inability to self-regulate physiological state to self-soothe or to be contingent with social gestures being expressed by others to help calm them.

In support of the foregoing generalizations, several studies have monitored RSA and investigated Level I and Level II processes in clinical populations. Level I assessments have been used to determine whether individual differences in tonic state of the vagal system measured via RSA (e.g., assessed during sleep or quiescent periods) are related to clinical risk factors. Level I methodology also has been used in specific experimental manipulations to evaluate potential mechanisms that may mediate psychopathology, such as panic disorders, or to evaluate the autonomic impact of the pharmacological treatments commonly used for psychiatric disorders. Level II assessments, involving the quantification of the pattern of vagal tone regulation in response to a clearly defined challenge, also have been used in clinical research.

Examples of Level I Assessments

In an attempt to understand the mechanisms of how the nervous system regulates autonomic state during panic, George et al. (1989) evaluated RSA during hyperventilation and sodium lactate infusion, manipulations known to elicit panic. They reported that both manipulations produced a massive decrease in RSA. Based on the assessment model, these data reflect a severe deficit in Level I processes. Thus, consistent with the clinical observations of elicited panic and severe anxiety, the assessment would predict that self-regulatory physiological and behavioral functions would be compromised.

Other research has attempted to evaluate how psychotropic medication influences Level I processes. Based on the assessment model, the degree that medication depresses RSA would affect behavioral and psychological outcome. For example, it would be predicted that if medication depressed RSA it would compromise higher level processes, and behavior would not improve. Alternatively, it would be predicted that if medication increased or did not decrease RSA, the psychotropic effect on behavior would be optimized. McLeod, Hoehn-Saric, Porges, and Zimmerli (1992) demonstrated that the effectiveness of imipramine on general anxiety disorders (i.e., measured by the Hamilton scale), was directly related to the influence imipramine had on RSA. If imipramine, due to its known anticholinergic effects, reduced RSA, then imipramine did not have beneficial effects. In contrast, if the patient did not exhibit depressed RSA in response to imipramine, behavioral outcome was optimized. Thus, if medication disrupted Level I processes, the higher level processes also were compromised.

The focus of this chapter has been on clinical applications of the proposed psychophysiological assessment model. There have been several investigations that demonstrate the utility of Level I assessments in clinical settings. As discussed in chapter 4, high-risk neonates have significantly lower amplitude RSA. Moreover, individual differences in RSA from another another high-risk sample have been related to clinical condition and predict cognitive outcome (Doussard-Roosevelt et al., 1997, 2001). Consistent with these findings, Donchin, Constantini, Byrne, and Porges (1992) reported that in adults preneurosurgical levels of RSA predicted clinical course (i.e., neurological and cognitive outcomes).

Examples of Level II Assessments

Level II assessments have been designed to evaluate the individual's ability to regulate the component of the vagal tone system originating in the nucleus ambiguus. Level II assessments assume that the regulation of vagal pathways originating in the nucleus ambiguus is mediated by higher central mechanisms that influence brainstem feedback to promote either immediate mobilization of energy resources or calming. Level II assessments are important in dealing with populations that appear to exhibit normal Level I activity. For example, we have reported that independent of resting levels of RSA, children who do not systematically depress RSA during attention-demanding tasks are more likely to have behavioral regulation problems (DeGangi et al., 1991). In a second sample we observed that this inability to regulate RSA at 9 months of age predicted behavioral problems at 3 years (see chapter 7). Consistent with the hierarchical model, both studies demonstrate that measures of RSA regulation are predictive, when baseline RSA, an indicator of Level I processes, does not predict outcome. Other research has evaluated the acute and tonic influences of alcohol and narcotics on the ability to regulate vagal reflexes. For example, Hickey, Suess, Newlin, Spurgeon, and Porges (1995) demonstrated that children exposed to opiates in utero, characterized by attentional problems, also exhibited difficulties in regulating vagal tone during sustained attention.

Research with Level II processes has been conducted to investigate the parallel between autonomic state regulation and affective regulation in infants. To evaluate individual differences in the dynamic covariation of affect tone and RSA, Bazhenova, Plonskaia, and Porges (2001) challenged Level II processes by eliciting various affective states. The Bazhenova et al. study demonstrated that infants who exhibited a systematic parallel between shifts in affect tone and RSA exhibited more optimum social behavior and state regulation.

Research in my laboratory with newborn infants has focused on evaluating the feeding challenge as a Level II assessment. Preliminary research with feeding challenges demonstrates individual differences in RSA regulation while bottle feeding (Portales et al., 1997), sucking (Porges & Lipsitt, 1993), or during orogastric feeding (DiPietro & Porges, 1991). We have developed a standardized Level II assessment for infants that evaluates nucleus ambiguus vagal tone (i.e., RSA) regulation during feeding. The assessment procedure evaluates Level I processes from a baseline recording of RSA during a calm state and Level II processes from the RSA response to the feeding challenge. We are also testing the generality of the assessment model to evaluate RSA regulation (Level II processes) in older children in a variety of challenges related to sustained attention, emotion regulation, and social interactions.

SUMMARY

The methods for assessment and intervention described in this chapter focus on a specific physiological system originating in the nucleus ambiguus. The nucleus ambiguus is a brainstem nucleus that coordinates sucking, swallowing, vocalizing, and breathing via vagal pathways. Moreover, vagal pathways from nucleus ambiguus provide the primary neural control of heart rate. Thus, nucleus ambiguus regulation of the heart is the neurophysiological substrate for all behaviors requiring a regulation of metabolic output to engage, disengage, and reengage dimensions of the environment. By monitoring a rhythmic heart rate pattern (i.e., RSA) mediated by the nucleus ambiguus, it is possible to assess shifts in the competence of neural regulation in the infant, child, or adult. The methodology for assessing nucleus ambiguus function is available and can be generalized to older children and adults by devising tasks that require the individual to regulate nucleus ambiguus output to mobilize and cope with transitory environmental demands. Therefore, this technology may be used to noninvasively monitor nucleus ambiguus function in high-risk infants or other clinical populations, to assess relative risk, and to evaluate the effectiveness of specific interventions. Although this chapter has emphasized assessment, there is a great need to develop appropriate interventions. Research needs to be directed at designing age-specific interventions that will efficiently enhance the neural feedback critical to the function and regulation of the vagal system.

CHAPTER 7

Infant Regulation of the Vagal "Brake" Predicts Child Behavior Problems: A Psychobiological Model of Social Behavior

Cardiac vagal tone is a construct that describes the functional relationship between the brainstem and the heart. Research in several domains has related cardiac vagal tone to a variety of clinical and behavioral dimensions. For example, cardiac vagal tone is related to clinical risk factors in infants (chapter 4), to outcomes in neurosurgical patients (Donchin, Constantini, Szold, Byrne, & Porges, 1992), to depth of anesthesia (Donchin, Feld, & Porges, 1985) to individual differences in temperament (Porges & Doussard-Roosevelt, 1997; Porges, Doussard-Roosevelt, Portales, & Suess, 1994). Most studies have evaluated cardiac vagal tone during steady-state conditions, while few studies have investigated dynamic changes in cardiac vagal tone and how these changes relate to social behavior and emotional regulation (see chapter 9; DeGangi, DiPietro, Greenspan, & Porges, 1991) in children. This chapter proposes that the development of appropriate social behavior is dependent on the ability to regulate cardiac vagal tone. The model presents two contrasting roles of the vagus. In one role, the vagus supports homeostatic functions, while in the other, the vagus serves as a mediator of motor responses to environmental challenges.

Although cardiac vagal tone is relatively stable under steady-state conditions such as quiet baseline (Fracasso, Porges, Lamb, & Rosenberg, 1994; Izard et al., 1991; Porges et al., 1994), it is sensitive to environmental demands and stimulation (e.g., DiPietro & Porges, 1991; Hofheimer, Wood, Porges, Pearson, & Lawson, 1995; Porges & Lipsitt, 1993; Porter, Porges, & Marshall, 1988). Rapid changes in cardiac vagal tone often parallel shifts in the cardiac output required to match metabolic demands (i.e., withdrawal of vagal tone promotes increased heart rate and cardiac output). For example, the increased sucking rate observed during feeding requires a shift in metabolic resources to support ingestive behavior. This shift is observed as parallel increases in heart rate, decreases in cardiac vagal tone, and increases in sucking rate (Porges & Lipsitt, 1993). Similarly, cardiac vagal tone is withdrawn, increasing cardiac output, to support behavioral mobilization during painful situations such as circumcision (Porter et al., 1988).

FUNCTIONAL ROLES OF VAGAL TONE

Vagal tone has two roles. First, during states of low environmental demand (e.g., sleep or quiet states), vagal tone fosters physiological homeostasis to promote growth and restoration. Second, during states characterized by environmental challenges, the vagus acts as a brake to rapidly regulate cardiac output and thus metabolic output. The "vagal brake" functionally keeps the heart rate slow by increasing vagal output to the heart and actively inhibiting sympathetic influences (Levy, 1984; Vanhoutte & Levy, 1979). Releasing the vagal brake reduces vagal inhibition on the cardiac pacemaker (sinoatrial node), and heart rate increases due to the intrinsic rate of the pacemaker, mechanical reflexes, and sympathetic influences. The vagal brake is not an all-or-none construct. Rather, the vagal brake represents the graded inhibition of the cardiac pacemaker by vagal efferent fibers. Because heart rate is not totally determined by the graded impact of the vagal brake, changes in cardiac vagal tone are not always highly correlated with changes in heart rate. During environmental interactions, metabolic output must be rapidly regulated to foster the behavioral and psychological processes required to engage and disengage with the environment. This chapter focuses on the latter role of vagal tone, mediating behavioral responses to environmental challenges and empirically evaluates the vagal brake hypothesis. The relation between infant regulation of the vagal brake and later social developmental outcomes requiring engagement and disengagement is examined.

THE AUTONOMIC NERVOUS SYSTEM: A VISCERAL FEEDBACK SYSTEM

The mammalian brainstem, via the autonomic nervous system, regulates homeostatic processes to foster growth and restoration. This role has been well documented by the functional neuroanatomy of the autonomic nervous system in which visceromotor neurons communicate between the brainstem and visceral organs. Weiner (1948), in proposing the concept of a feedback system, used the autonomic nervous system as his example. According to Weiner, homeostasis is an emergent property of a system that via bidirectional communication monitors and regulates the status of an organ to maintain an output level within a specific functional range. Consistent with Weiner's model, the autonomic nervous system includes a central regulator (brainstem source nuclei) that determines motor output (parasympathetic or sympathetic nerves) to a visceral organ (heart, lung, stomach) after interpreting the information from the sensor that monitors the status of the organ (afferent feedback). To maintain physiological homeostasis, sensory pathways originating in peripheral organs (chemoreceptors and baroreceptors in the carotid sinus) convey information regarding physiological status, while motor pathways (vagal and sympathetic pathways to the heart) change the output of peripheral organs. The sensory pathways from visceral organs originate in the periphery and usually terminate in the brainstem, whereas many of the motor pathways originate in the brainstem and terminate in the periphery.

The cardiac branch of the vagus, although a component of the autonomic nervous system, may be defined as a feedback system. The cardiac vagal system contains the requisite components of afferent and efferent pathways, brainstem source nuclei, and a visceral target, the heart.

EXTEROCEPTIVE AND INTEROCEPTIVE FEEDBACK: COMPETING DEMANDS ON THE VAGAL SYSTEM

The nervous system receives sensory feedback from receptors that sense conditions within the body (i.e., interoceptors) to support homeostasis and from receptors that sense conditions outside the body (i.e., exteroceptors) to deal with environmental challenges. Cardiac vagal output is related to both. In general, cardiac vagal tone is increased to support homeostatic functions, and cardiac vagal tone is decreased to increase cardiac output to support specific motor behaviors in response to environmental challenge.

The conceptual link between the autonomic nervous system and homeostasis has contributed to a limited definition of the autonomic nervous system as a sluggish "vegetative" system with the primary responsibility of maintaining homeostasis. However, components of the autonomic nervous system, such as the vagal system, play a dynamic role in fostering behavioral and psychological interactions with the environment. The vagal system rapidly regulates metabolic output (Rowell, 1993) to foster motor and psychological processes associated with appropriate engagement and disengagement with the environment. To interact with the environment, the priorities of the visceral feedback system change from optimizing visceral state to foster growth and restoration (i.e., homeostasis) to optimizing metabolic output to support the motor behavior required by external challenges. This shift in priorities, from internal visceral feedback to external environmental feedback, has survival consequences. For example, in dealing with the external environment, the organism may effectively respond to environmental demands related to threat, work, communication, and social behavior. However, in serving these environmentally driven priorities, physiological homeostasis may be compromised. When up-regulating metabolic output to serve environmental needs (e.g., fight-or-flight behaviors) the organism must down-regulate visceral needs, thereby disrupting homeostasis.

The vagal system deals both with servicing the needs of the internal viscera and with responding to external challenges. Competence in the ability to trade off between internal and external needs may be used in developing definitions of adaptive behavioral strategies and homeostasis. Based on this model, response strategies to environmental demands and homeostasis are interdependent. When there are no environmental demands, the vagal system services the needs of the internal viscera (e.g., heart, lungs, stomach, intestines) to enhance growth and restoration. However, in response to environmental demands, homeostatic processes are compromised, and the vagal system supports increased metabolic output by down-regulating growth and restoration functions to deal with these external challenges. The central nervous system mediates the distribution of resources to deal with internal and external demands. The trade-off between internal and external needs is monitored and regulated by the central nervous system and can be monitored via the dynamic regulation of the heart by the vagus. This dynamic regulation provides a graded inhibition of the vagal brake with a resultant shift in cardiac output.

THE POLYVAGAL THEORY

The polyvagal theory (see chapter 2) introduces and provides the theoretical justification for studying the vagal brake. The theory proposes that the successful adaptation of mammals is dependent on systematic and reliable withdrawal and reengagement of the vagal brake as a mechanism to rapidly regulate metabolic output in response to environmental demands. The theory, based on comparative neuroanatomy and embryology, proposes that mammals have two vagal systems, a neomammalian system and a more vegetative "reptilian" system, controlled by different medullary nuclei. The mammalian vagal system is controlled by the nucleus ambiguus, and the more vegetative reptilian system is controlled by the dorsal motor nucleus.

The two systems have different response strategies. The nucleus ambiguus (mammalian) vagal system is myelinated and provides a rapid adjustment of metabolic output by regulating heart rate via the sinoatrial node. Usually this is observed as rapid vagal withdrawal and concomitant heart rate acceleration. In contrast, the dorsal motor nucleus (reptilian) vagal system is unmyelinated and appears to have little impact on cardiac output in most conditions. However, under compromising conditions of low oxygen availability, it is hypothesized that the reptilian system fosters resource conservation by stimulating massive bradycardia and apnea. Thus, several lethal phenomena such as cardiac arrest, massive bradycardia producing sudden death, and exercise-induced syncope appear to be the vestigial remnants of a physiological response with adaptive consequences for reptiles but with lethal consequences for mammals.

Because the nucleus ambiguus is an integral component of the medullary system generating the respiratory rhythm (Richter & Spyer, 1990), the output of the vagal fibers terminating on the heart are characterized by a respiratory rhythm of increasing and decreasing tone (Porges, 1995). The functional consequence of this rhythmic modulation of nucleus ambiguus vagal tone to the sinoatrial node is to produce the respiratory oscillations in the heart rate pattern known as respiratory sinus arrhythmia (RSA). Thus, the quantification of the amplitude of RSA provides an index of the dynamically changing status of the vagal brake.

VAGAL BRAKE AND THE DEVELOPMENT OF SOCIAL BEHAVIOR

The current study focuses on the nucleus ambiguus vagal system and evaluates the hypothesis that appropriate withdrawal of the vagal brake during infancy is a marker variable for developmental outcome. Specifically, it is proposed that appropriate regulation of the vagal brake during infancy reflects an ability to selectively engage and disengage with the environment. The vagal brake provides the mechanism for the infant to contingently interact with objects and people. Thus, the vagal brake provides a neurophysiological mechanism that may promote the development of appropriate social behavior. In the current study, 9-month-old infants were evaluated for cardiac vagal tone regulation during the administration of the Bayley Scales of Mental Development (i.e., whether the vagal brake was withdrawn during the test). Administration of the Bayley Scales places a complex set of demands on the infant. The infant must engage and disengage with each changing stimulus within the context of a social interaction with the experimenter. Social behavior problems were assessed at 3 years of age with the Child Behavior Checklist for Ages 2–3 (Achenbach, 1988).

METHOD

Subjects

Twenty-four (12 male, 12 female) subjects were tested initially during infancy (7–9 months). All subjects were evaluated for behavioral problems at 36 months. Subjects were recruited from the metropolitan Washington, DC, area via advertisements in local doctors' offices and newspapers inviting mothers of 7- to 9-month-olds to participate in the research project. Separate advertisements elicited mothers with difficult infants and mothers with nondifficult infants to ensure a broad range of infant behavior. All infants were born full-term with no major medical complications. Mothers ranged in age from 20 to 39 years (M = 32) and had an average of 16 years of education (range = 10–21 years).

Procedures

At the 9-month assessment, the physiological monitoring and developmental testing procedures were explained and informed consent obtained from the mother. Development was evaluated with the Bayley Scales of Infant Development (Bayley, 1969). Electrocardiogram (ECG) was recorded during a 3-minute baseline in which the infant sat quietly on the mother's lap and during the first 7 minutes of the Bayley administration, during which the infant was presented with a variety of attention-demanding tasks. Mothers completed the Infant Characteristics Questionnaire (Bates, 1984) and the Fussy Baby Questionnaire (Greenspan, Porges, Portales, & Walker, 1987) at the 9-month assessment. The difficultness subscale of the Infant Characteristics Questionnaire was included as a predictive variable in the data analyses. This subscale was chosen based on its stability (Bates, 1980) as well as its theoretical linkage to cardiac vagal tone (DeGangi et al., 1991). In addition, information from the two infant questionnaires as well as the Infant Behavior Record of the Bayley Scales was used to classify infants as Regulatory Disordered or non–Regulatory Disordered according to the diagnostic criteria established by the National Center for Clinical Infant Programs (Zero to Three, 1994).

When the child was 3 years of age, the mother completed the Child Behavior Checklist for Ages 2–3 (CBCL/2–3; Achenbach, 1988). The CBCL/2–3 is a parent rating scale consisting of 99 items describing behavioral/emotional problems.

Quantification of Behavior Problems Data

Scores were derived from the CBCL/2-3 (Achenbach, 1988) for total problems and for the six narrow-band syndrome scales (social withdrawal, depressed, sleep problems, somatic problems, aggressive, and destructive). The narrow-band syndrome scales have been derived via factor analysis and the scale scores standardized to determine cutoffs associated with clinical psychopathology (McConaughy & Achenbach, 1988).

Quantification of Heart Rate Data

The ECG was monitored via three AgCl electrodes placed on the infant's chest. The output of the ECG amplifier was stored on a Vetter C-4 FM tape recorder (A. K. Vetter, Rebersberg, PA). The ECG data were quantified offline by replaying the tapes into a Vagal Tone Monitor (Delta-Biometrics, Bethesda, MD). The Vagal Tone Monitor detected the peak of the R-wave to the nearest millisecond and timed sequential heart periods. The sequential heart periods were stored in a file on a PC. The amplitude of RSA,was calculated offline. The amplitude of RSA provides an accurate description of medullary influences on the heart via the nucleus ambiguus branch of the vagus nerve (see chapter 2; Porges, 1995).

MXedit software (Delta-Biometrics) was used to visually display the heart period data, to edit outliers, and to quantify the heart period and RSA. MXedit incorporates the Porges (1985) method of calculating the amplitude of RSA. This method contains a detrending algorithm to remove from the heart rate pattern the variance associated with the complex changing level and oscillations slower than RSA. The detrending algorithm requires heart period values measured to the nearest millisecond and includes the resampling of the heart period data every 250 ms, a moving polynomial filter (third-order 21-point) and a band-pass filter (0.24–1.04 Hz). The analysis represents the variance of the residual series output from the detrending algorithm and is reported in units of $\ln(\text{ms})^2$. In this study each heart rate parameter (i.e., heart period and RSA) was calculated for sequential 30-sec. epochs within each condition. The mean of the within-condition epochs was used in the data analyses.

Design

To evaluate individual differences in the disengagement of the vagal brake during the Bayley test, RSA and heart period reactivity were assessed by calculating difference scores in which the values derived during the Bayley tests were subtracted from the baseline condition values. Change scores were positive when levels during the Bayley tests were lower than the baseline. More positive difference scores reflected greater decreases in RSA and heart period. To test the hypothesis that the functioning of the vagal brake during infancy is related to behavior problems during childhood, correlational analyses were conducted to assess the relation of the outcome measures from the CBCL/2–3 years of age with the RSA and heart period reactivity scores. It was hypothesized that subjects who exhibited larger decreases in RSA during the Bayley test, relative to the baseline condition, would have fewer behavioral problems at 3 years of age. Negative correlations between the change in RSA and behavioral problems (i.e., fewer problems associated with greater depression of RSA) would support this hypothesis.

RESULTS

Physiological Response Patterns

Gender × condition repeated measures analyses of variance evaluated whether or not gender differences existed in either the baseline levels or the pattern of change in heart period and vagal tone across conditions. Gender was not related to level or pattern of reactivity. There was a significant condition effect for heart period. Mean heart period significantly increased (i.e., heart rate slowed) from baseline (445 ms) to Bayley test (463 ms), $F(1,22) = 10.1, p < .01$. Mean levels in RSA did not differ between the conditions, $F(1,22) = 0.6, p > .1$. Inspection of the individual differences indicated that most subjects increased their heart period ($n = 19$) during the test. However, the RSA response was more heterogeneous with 13 subjects decreasing and 11 subjects increasing levels during the test.

The magnitude and direction of the heart period and RSA responses were related to baseline levels. As illustrated in Figure 7.1, higher amplitude RSA during baseline was associated with larger decreases (i.e., more positive change scores) in RSA and heart period during the Bayley test, $r(22) = .42, p < .05$ and $r(22) = .48, p < .05$, respectively. Similarly, longer baseline heart periods, although not correlated with changes in RSA, were correlated with greater de-

FIGURE 7.1. Scatterplots relating baseline RSA to RSA changes (a) and to heart period changes (b). Change scores represent values during the baseline minus values during the Bayley test. Positive change scores reflect decreases from baseline to Bayley condition.

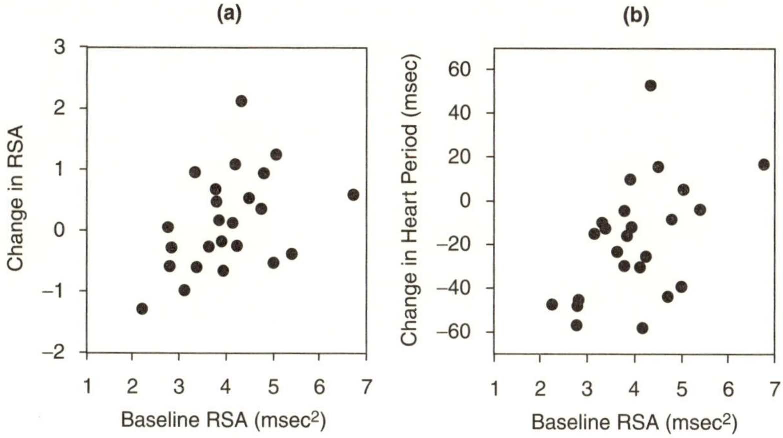

creases in heart period during the Bayley test, $r(22) = .60$, $p < .01$. The magnitude of individual differences in the two change scores was also correlated. Subjects who expressed a greater decrease in RSA also responded with a greater decrease in heart period, $r(22) = .49$, $p < .05$.

THE VAGAL BRAKE AND OUTCOME BEHAVIORS AT 3 YEARS OF AGE

To evaluate the relationship between the vagal brake and outcome behaviors at 3 years of age, correlational analyses were conducted. Analyses examined the relation between 9-month heart period and RSA values (baseline and change scores) and 3-year behavior problems coded on the CBCL/2–3 (total problems and six narrow-band syndrome scores). As listed in Table 7.1, there were consistent relationships between the decrease in RSA during the Bayley test (i.e., magnitude of the change score) and behavior problems at 3 years. Greater decreases in RSA (i.e., the appropriate regulation of the vagal brake during attending demanding tasks) were associated with fewer total behavior problems, $r(22) = -.50$, $p < .05$. Further, greater decreases in RSA were associated with more optimal outcomes on the three narrow-band syndrome scales associated with social behavior (i.e., social withdrawal, depressed, and aggressive behavior). Greater decreases in RSA were correlated with fewer social withdrawal problems, $r(22) = -.42$, $p < .05$, fewer depressed behaviors, $r(22) = -.45$, $p < .05$, and fewer aggressive behaviors, $r(22) = -.53$, $p < .01$. Inspection of the univariate correlations indicates that heart period and changes in heart period were not related to any of

TABLE 7.1. Correlations Between 9-Month Physiological Variables and 3-Year Behavioral Outcome Variables

	Physiological Variables			
Outcome Variables	Baseline Vagal Tone	Change in Vagal Tone	Baseline Heart Period	Change in Heart Period
Total behavior problems	–.37	–.50*	–.15	–.38
Social withdrawal	–.20	–.42*	–.17	–.07
Aggressive	–.31	–.53**	–.09	–.31
Depressive	–.43*	–.45*	–.08	–.20
Destructive	–.39	–.16	–.27	–.27
Somatic problems	–.28	–.11	–.15	–.14
Sleep problems	–.57**	–.28	–.35	–.40

*$p < .05$.
**$p < .01$.

the outcome behaviors. Baseline levels of RSA were related to the depressed, sleep problems, and destructive scales. Infants who had lower amplitude RSA had more problems on the depressed, $r(22) = -.43$, $p < .05$, sleep problems, $r(22) = -.57$, $p < .01$, and destructive, $r(22) = -.39$, $p = .06$, scales. Gender was not related to outcome, nor did gender influence the correlations between the change in RSA and the outcome measures.

For comparison purposes, correlations of the outcome measures with 9-month Bayley Mental Development Index and Infant Characteristics Questionnaire difficultness scores are presented in Table 7.2. The Bayley score was associated with somatic problems, $r(22) = -.44$, $p < .05$, and sleep problems, $r(22) = -.47$, $p < .05$, while the difficultness score was not predictive of later behavior.

TABLE 7.2. Correlations Between 9-Month Behavioral Variables and 3-Year Behavioral Outcome Variables

	Behavioral Variables	
Behavioral Variables	Bayley Mental Development Index	Infant Characteristics Questionnaire Difficultness Score
Total behavior problems	–.30	.19
Social withdrawal	–.28	–.07
Aggressive	–.20	.26
Depressive	–.36	.10
Destructive	–.10	–.09
Somatic problems	–.44*	–.02
Sleep problems	–.47*	.02

*$p < .05$.

MULTIPLE REGRESSION MODELS

Multiple stepwise forward-regression models were tested with the four physiological variables (baseline RSA, RSA change score, baseline heart period, heart period change score) and the two behavioral variables (Bayley Mental Development Index, Infant Characteristics Questionnaire difficultness score) entered into each predictive model. Alpha-to-enter and alpha-to-remove levels were set at .10. For the total behavior problem score, only RSA change scores were a significant predictor of outcome. Once RSA change was entered into the model, no additional variable (i.e., baseline RSA, baseline heart period, change in heart period, Bayley Mental Development Index, difficultness) significantly contributed to the model. This was also true for the social withdrawal, depressed, and aggressive narrow-band syndrome scores.

The models for the other three narrow-band syndrome scales were not consistent. For the destructive syndrome score, there was no significant predictor. The Bayley Mental Development Index score was the only predictor of the somatic syndrome score. And the sleep problems score was best predicted by a model which included baseline RSA and the difficultness score, $F(2,21) = 7.41$, $p < .01$.

DISCUSSION

Infant Vagal Tone and Child Behavior Problems

The best predictor of behavioral problems on CBCL/2–3 at 3 years of age was the infant's ability to decrease cardiac vagal tone during the Bayley test. The infants who expressed the greatest decrease in RSA had the fewest behavioral problems. Thus, the ability to regulate the vagal brake in the hypothesized direction was a significant predictor of positive developmental outcome. Decreases in RSA were associated with the global measure of total behavior problems and also with three of the narrow-band syndrome scales (i.e., social withdrawal, depressed, aggressive). Inspection of the items on these three scales suggests that the scales are uniquely sensitive to social behavior. The social withdrawal scale focuses on difficulties in the initiation and engagement of social interactions. The depressed scale focuses on affect regulation during social interactions. The aggressive scale focuses on aggressive and uncooperative social interactions. The intercorrelations among the narrow-band scales confirm that the three scales are significantly correlated and that aggressive and depressed are the only scales correlated with social withdrawal. In contrast, the three scales that were not related to 9-month regulation of the vagal brake appear to include items more sensitive to visceral regulation, state regulation, and/or awareness of the environment (i.e., sleep problems, somatic problems, destructive behavior). These observations foster the speculation that the vagal brake may be uniquely related to the successful performance of behaviors associated with social interactions, while baseline vagal tone may be more sensitive to endogenous homeostatic function.

The linkage between specific narrow-band syndrome scales and the two measures of vagal tone reflects the two postulated roles of vagal tone described above. The first role is maximized during states characterized by low environmental demand, when vagal tone fosters physiological homeostasis to promote growth and restoration. Thus, higher levels of baseline vagal tone should be, and are in this study, significantly related to fewer sleep problems (i.e., lower scores on the sleep problems scale) and tend to be related to fewer somatic problems (i.e., lower scores on the somatic problems scale) and a greater awareness of and reactivity to the environment (i.e., lower scores on the destructive scale).

Research on clinical populations supports the speculation that low baseline vagal tone is related to illness and health risk (e.g., see chapter 4; Donchin et al., 1992). In addition, research also supports the speculation that subjects who have higher vagal tone are more reactive and aware of the environment (e.g., see chapter 9; Porges, 1991). The second role of vagal tone is maximized during states characterized by environmental challenges, such as social interactions, when the vagus acts as a brake to regulate cardiac output. Thus, greater reductions in vagal tone during tasks that require social interaction and/or focused attention to an external stimulus should be, and are in this study, related to fewer social behavioral problems (i.e., lower scores on the social withdrawal and aggressive scales) and more positive and appropriate affective responsivity to people (i.e., lower scores on depressed scale).

The behavior of the infants at 9 months was not related to the CBCL/2–3 rating at 3 years. Ratings at 9 months on the difficultness scale of the Infant Characteristics Questionnaire were not correlated with the CBCL/2–3 scores. Additionally, based on the Zero to Three diagnostic manual, the 9-month behaviors were coded to determine whether any of the children would be assessed as regulatory disordered. Four infants fit the clinical criteria of severe regulatory disorders. These infants did not exhibit any unique deficits in either measure of vagal tone, nor did they exhibit severe behavioral problems at 3 years of age. In fact, a rank order of the CBCL/2–3 scores indicates one regulatory disordered child in each of the four quartiles. Additionally, none of the four regulatory disordered infants exhibited a CBCL/2–3 score above the clinical cutoff. Thus, the infant measures of behavioral difficulties were not correlated with the vagal tone measures, nor were they predictive of child behavior problems.

VAGAL TONE AND THE REGULATION OF THE VAGAL BRAKE: TWO TIERS OF A MULTILEVEL NEGATIVE-FEEDBACK SYSTEM

The dual functions of vagal tone may be conceptualized within a two-tiered neural feedback system, The first tier coincides with the vagal contribution to visceral homeostasis. Driven by visceral afferents, the first tier represents a basic negative feedback system (see Weiner, 1948). As illustrated in Figure 7.2, the

FIGURE 7.2. Schematic representation of a basic negative feedback model.

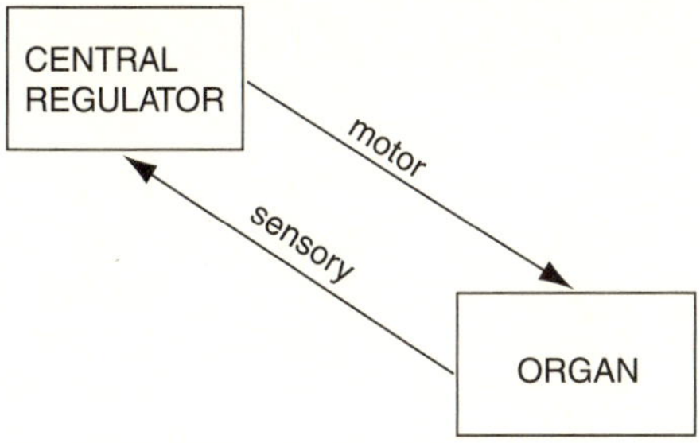

basic negative feedback system includes a central regulator that determines the motor output to an organ after interpreting the information from the sensory input that monitors the status of the organ.

The first tier of the vagal regulation model is a slight modification of the basic negative feedback model. As illustrated in Figure 7.3, the general flow is the same as Figure 7.2, although the specific cranial nerve, brainstem nuclei, and target organ are identified. On the first tier, the central regulator consists of two nuclei in the brainstem, the nucleus ambiguus and the nucleus tractus solitarius, and their interneuronal connections. The vagus nerve contributes both the motor and sensory pathways between the central regulator (brainstem) and the visceral organ (heart). The vagal efferents to the heart originate in the nucleus ambiguus (NA) and the vagal afferents from the heart terminate in the nucleus tractus solitarius (NTS).

As illustrated in Figure 7.3, the vagus provides a bidirectional connection between the brainstem and the heart. The two-way vagal communication between the brainstem and the heart enables the brainstem to monitor and to regulate heart rate and cardiac output. Within this negative feedback model, the efferent vagal pathways contribute to homeostasis by providing negative feedback follow-

FIGURE 7.3. Schematic representation of a negative feedback model for vagal control of the heart.

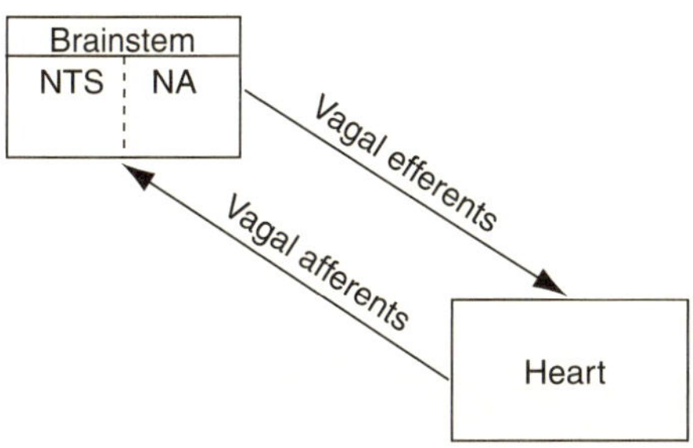

ing the brainstem's interpretation of cardiac state from the afferent vagal pathways. Two-way communication between the brainstem and the heart has long been acknowledged. Darwin (1872) describes the bidirectional communication and attributes this information to Claude Bernard. The interneuronal communication between the brainstem source nuclei of both the efferent and afferent vagal pathways regulating the heart is the topic of current electrophysiological and neuroanatomical research (Richter & Spyer, 1990).

The second tier of the vagal regulation system requires vagal tone changes which modulate cardiac output to match metabolic needs determined by environmental challenges. The second tier is characterized by the cortical inhibition of the brainstem structures controlling vagal output to the heart. The second tier regulates metabolic output by inhibiting vagal tone, which increases heart rate and cardiac output, to foster metabolically demanding motor behaviors. To increase metabolic output, the cortical structures actively inhibit the vagal support of homeostatic functions. To decrease metabolic output, the cortical structures disinhibit the brainstem structures regulating vagal output; vagal output is increased to support homeostatic functions and cardiac output is decreased. Gradations in cortical inhibition of vagal activity enable a fine-tuning of the rapid changes in cardiac output required to foster specific behaviors associated with environmental interactions. This dependency of Tier 2 functions (behavioral interactions with the environment) on Tier 1 functions (homeostasis) requires bidirectional neuronal communication between cortical and brainstem structures. As illustrated in Figure 7.4, this is modeled as a dynamic interaction between cortical and brainstem structures to monitor and regulate visceral tone and metabolic output. The functional interaction between the two tiers provides a neurophysiological mechanism which is capable of either increasing cardiac output to support fight-or-flight behaviors or decreasing cardiac output to calm and self-soothe.

As illustrated in Figure 7.4, the second tier also includes the basic components of a negative feedback system: the monitoring of environmental stimulation via sense receptors (i.e., exteroceptors), the interpretation of the sensory information by brain structures (i.e., cortex), and the selective output of specific observable behaviors. The objective of the second tier is to maximize goal-directed (i.e., motivated) behaviors that, in general, minimize unpleasant or life-threatening experiences and follow the law of effect (Thorndike, 1911). For example, via appropriate negative feedback, positive sensory experiences (e.g., pleasure) will promote engagement with the environment, and negative sensory experiences (e.g., pain) will result in a disengagement with the environment. In understanding or evaluating social behavior, the second tier choreographs the quality and temporal dynamics of approach-withdrawal sequences. The second tier regulates when and with whom or with what an individual behaviorally engages and disengages.

The two-tiered model is hierarchical with priority given to the demands of the

FIGURE 7.4. Schematic representation of a two-tiered negative feedback model. The two-tiered model provides a theoretical framework to explain the operations of the vagal brake in response to environmental challenges (e.g., social interactions). Note the bidirectional communication between cortical and brainstem structures.

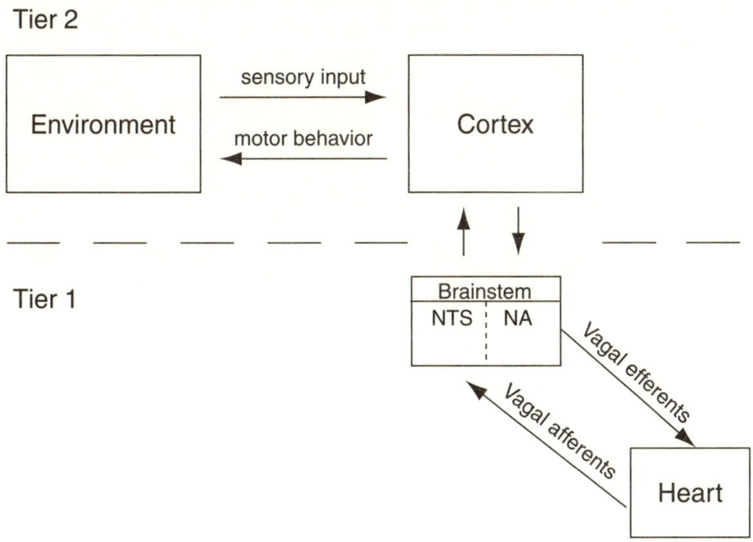

second tier. However, without the first tier functioning adequately and regulating homeostasis to maximize life-support processes such as digestion, oxygenation, thermoregulation, and perfusion, there would be no "energy" resources available for second-tier functions. As a metaphor, the measurement of vagal tone level during a steady state as an index of Tier 1 regulation represents "potential energy." Similarly, the change in vagal tone from a steady-state baseline to a metabolically challenging state as an index of Tier 2 would represent "kinetic energy."

The data illustrated in Figure 7.1 support this metaphor relating baseline vagal tone to vagal reactivity. Infants with greater baseline vagal tone (an index of Tier 1 function) exhibited greater decreases in cardiac vagal tone and heart period during the Bayley test. These findings are consistent with other studies that have reported a relationship between individual differences in baseline cardiac vagal tone and the magnitude of heart period and vagal tone reactivity (DeGangi et al., 1991; Porges & Lipsitt, 1993; Porter & Porges, 1988).

Behavior is metabolically costly. For example, behaviors such as fight-or-flight responses often require massive and instantaneous increases in metabolic output. To successfully accomplish tasks of engagement and disengagement with the environment, the nervous system must divert energy resources from visceral homeostasis (e.g., smooth muscle) to observable behaviors (e.g., striate muscle) that deal directly with the environment. The regulation of the vagal brake provides an index of this shift in resources. By instantaneously releasing the vagal brake, cardiac output increases to support the metabolic demands required by the behavior. Thus, the priority of the two-tiered system subjugates the homeostatic needs in favor of the immediate environmental demands.

CONSTRUCTS OF VAGAL TONE AND THE VAGAL BRAKE

The construct of vagal tone, a Tier 1 process, represents the magnitude of vagal efferent output on the heart. Within Tier 1, optimal homeostatic function, at least in terms of the heart, would be associated with greater vagal tone, reflecting greater negative feedback. There is an abundance of data supporting the notion that greater vagal tone is associated with more optimal physiological state. Low heart rate variability or low cardiac vagal tone has been identified as a risk factor in infants (see chapter 4), in neurosurgery patients (Donchin et al., 1992), and in individuals with cardiovascular risk (Bigger, Fleiss, & Rolnitsky, 1993). The data from this study not only are convergent with these findings, but demonstrate that low levels of cardiac vagal tone during infancy are related to visceral and behavioral state regulation in childhood.

The construct of the vagal brake described within the second tier represents the systematic decrease and increase in vagal efferent output to the heart. In our research, the decrease in cardiac vagal tone reflects a reduction in the vagal inhibitory effect on heart rate. Release of the vagal brake increases heart rate and cardiac output. There have been reliable reports of decreases in indices of cardiac vagal tone (i.e., measures of heart rate variability) in response to environmental demands (e.g., Allen & Crowell, 1989; Mulder & Mulder, 1987; Porges, 1972).

Social behavior requires the second-tier system. Social interactions require a shift in metabolic resources to foster the appropriate behaviors. Thus, the infant's ability to release the vagal brake during a social-attention task might reflect a physiological strategy that would promote social development and fewer subsequent behavioral problems. The data from this study confirm this speculation. Infants who exhibited a greater decrease in cardiac vagal tone (i.e., greater release of the vagal brake) during the social-attention task exhibited fewer social behavior problems in childhood.

SUMMARY

The nucleus ambiguus vagal system deals both with servicing the needs of the internal viscera and with responding to external challenges. Competence in the ability to trade off between homeostatic (internal) and environmental (external) needs is required for successful development. This chapter introduces the vagal brake as a metaphor to describe regulation of visceral tone in response to environmental challenges. Although there is an extensive literature evaluating baseline vagal tone, the relation between dynamically changing vagal tone and behavioral reactivity has been theoretically vague. This chapter, by introducing a two-tiered neural feedback model, provides the first theoretical model to explain the relation between vagal tone during steady states and vagal reactivity (i.e., the vagal brake) in response to environmental challenges.

Co-authors for this chapter were J. A. Doussard-Roosevelt, A. L. Portales, and S. I. Greenspan.

CHAPTER 8

The Early Development of the Autonomic Nervous System Provides a Neural Platform for Social Behavior

During the last trimester and continuing through the first year postpartum, the autonomic nervous system is rapidly changing. These changes ensure that the infant can breathe, obtain food, and maintain body temperature. Coupled with the development of these abilities to obtain basic biological needs is a progressive change in the infant's ability to regulate physiological and behavioral state through interactions with another person (e.g., mother). We propose that the developmental changes in the neural pathways that regulate autonomic state provide a neural platform to support the expanding abilities of the infant to engage objects and people in a dynamically changing environment. Thus, the emerging behavioral repertoire and social-interactive needs of the rapidly developing young infant should be studied within the context of the maturational changes in the autonomic nervous system.

In contrast to the hypothesized dependence of social behavior on the autonomic nervous system, the autonomic nervous system has played a limited role within predominant theories in developmental psychology. Similarly, given the critical role that the autonomic nervous system plays in the infant's survival during the transition from prenatal to postnatal environments, it is surprising that an understanding of the central mechanisms mediating the autonomic nervous system has been tangential to pediatric medicine. In general, measures of autonomic activity have been conceptualized as a correlate of motivated or adaptive behaviors within psychology and as indices of health risk in medicine.

We propose, from a biobehavioral perspective, that the maturational shifts in neural regulation of the autonomic nervous system provide a developing resource, which, in part, mediate much of the dynamic interaction that the infant has with both objects and others. Within this perspective, we identify sequential, developmental, neurophysiological processes, which provide the biological basis to explain how and why individual and developmental differences in vagal control of the heart are related to social behavior and, when relevant, clinical outcome.

DEPENDENCE ON OTHERS: PARALLELS WITH MATURATION OF THE AUTONOMIC NERVOUS SYSTEM

At birth, mammalian infants are incapable of caring for themselves. The newborn is vulnerable and dependent on the mother, or a concerned caregiver, to survive. Support from others is required to obtain basic biological needs, such as food, warmth, and protection. This dependence on other decreases as the infant develops. This decrease in dependence is paralleled by changes in neural regulation of the autonomic nervous system. During development, as higher brain circuits begin to regulate the brainstem nuclei, which control the autonomic nervous system, the infant becomes more independent and is increasingly capable of initiating social interactions with others to regulate physiological state. As these self-regulatory skills develop, the dependence on the caregiver to elicit ingestive-vagal reflexes (i.e., feeding) as a primary strategy of regulation decreases. Behaviorally, the infant appears to be more socially skilled and better able to spend time alone. This is observed as the infant's ability to both rapidly calm after disruptive challenges and to remain calm for longer periods, even in the absence of others.

Developmentally, as skills of state regulation improve, the central nervous system expands to promote enhanced cognition and greater control over peripheral motor systems. These global systems (autonomic, cognitive, and motor) mature in combination and enable the maturing infant to become more independent and explorative in a complex environment.

Similar to most mammals and distinct from our phylogenetically related reptilian ancestors, humans maintain a need for social interactions throughout their life spans. Social separation and isolation for humans, regardless of age, leads to profound disruption in the ability to regulate physiological state and compromises both physical and mental health. This disruption may impact all aspects of development and may be expressed as delays in motor development, growth, and cognition, as well as global health vulnerabilities and atypical social and emotional behaviors. Studies reliably report that various degrees of social abandonment can have disastrous effects on child development. Studies of the Romanian orphans illustrate that caregiving, defined solely by the physical features of food, warmth, and protection without consistent and predictable social engagement opportunities, is insufficient for typical development. For example, in a 3-year follow-up study of Romanian orphans, who had been adopted after living at least 8 months in orphanages, Chisholm (1998) found that the orphans had significantly more behavior problems, insecure attachment, and lower IQ scores than nonadopted or early adopted children. Adoptive parents of these orphans also reported significantly more parenting stress. More recent anatomical studies have revealed that early social and emotional deprivation in many Romanian orphans may lead to functional and structural changes in brain regions, including orbital frontal gyrus, infralimbic prefrontal cortex, medial temporal structures (i.e., amygdala and head of hippocampus), and left uncinate fasciculus (Chugani et al., 2001; Eluvanthingal et al., 2006). Impairment in functions of these brain regions could certainly contribute to lower verbal skills, diminished attention and concentration abilities, impaired impulsivity, conduct problems, and depression frequently reported in these children.

Unlike reptiles and other phylogenetically more ancient vertebrates, birth for mammals is not a transition into independence but an extension of the period of dependence that begins in utero. For humans, maturation does not lead to a total independence from others, but leads to an ability to function independently of other people for short periods. Moreover, humans, as they become more independent of their caregivers, search for appropriate others (e.g., friends, partners, etc.) with whom they may form dyads capable of symbiotic regulation. In fact, individuals, who prefer to use interactions with objects instead of people to regulate physiological state, often receive psychiatric diagnoses (e.g., autism spectrum disorders, borderline personality disorder).

EVOLUTION OF THE AUTONOMIC NERVOUS SYSTEM PREPARES THE HUMAN INFANT FOR SOCIAL BEHAVIOR

It is necessary to understand the phylogenetic origins of mammalian autonomic nervous systems to understand how autonomic state is linked to social behavior. This conceptualization has been described as the polyvagal theory (see chapters 2, 11, and 12; Porges, 2001a, 2007a). The theory was derived from the identification of the two motor branches of the vagus nerve, the Xth cranial nerve, which provides both motor and sensory pathways between brainstem structures and visceral organs. The theory emphasizes not only the phylogenetic shifts in neuroanatomy of the vertebrate autonomic nervous system but also proposes specific, adaptive behaviors that co-occur with these transitions.

As evolutionary forces molded the human nervous system, new structures were added and older structures were modified to allow greater dynamic range and finer control of physiological state and to facilitate emergence of new, adaptive social behaviors. The polyvagal theory, by incorporating an evolutionary approach, provides a strategy to investigate developmental shifts in social behavior from a phylogenetic perspective. The theory provides insights into how developmental shifts in neural regulation of the autonomic nervous system are related to the changing repertoire of adaptive behaviors that, depending on context, either limit or expand expression of social behavior. The theory emphasizes unique features in neural regulation of the autonomic nervous system that distinguish mammals from reptiles and explains how these features serve as a biobehavioral platform for the emergence of face-to-face social behaviors. In addition, the theory provides insights into the biobehavioral mechanisms that are rapidly developing in utero and in the young infant. As the neural mechanisms facilitating self-regulation improve during normal development, the infant's dependence on others to regulate physiological state decreases. This allows social communication to expand beyond the cueing of basic physical survival needs (i.e., warmth, safety, food) and into the realm of prosocial engagements.

The polyvagal theory articulates how each of three phylogenetic stages in the development of the vertebrate autonomic nervous system is associated with a distinct autonomic subsystem that is retained and expressed in mammals. These autonomic subsystems are phylogenetically ordered and behaviorally linked to social communication (e.g., facial expression, vocalization, listening), mobilization (e.g., fight-or-flight behaviors, tantrums, or behavioral meltdowns), and immobilization (e.g., feigning death, vasovagal syncope, and behavioral and physiological shutdown). The product of this phylogeny is a mammalian nervous system with three identifiable circuits that regulate adaptive behaviors and physiological reactions to challenges.

In this phylogenetically organized hierarchy, the newest circuit associated with social communication is used first. If that circuit fails to provide safety, then the older survival-oriented circuits are recruited sequentially. From a developmental perspective, the oldest circuits develop first, and the newest circuit develops last, leaving it the most vulnerable to neural insult and the most sensitive to postpartum experience. The newest circuit becomes only partially available during the last trimester and is expressed at term as the brainstem reflexes that enable the coordination of sucking, swallowing, and breathing. By 6 months postpartum, these brainstem reflexes, which become coordinated with cortical processes, provide a biobehavioral pathway through which reciprocal social engagement behavior can calm and soothe physiological state in both participants of a social dyad (e.g., mother–infant interactions).

DEVELOPMENT OF THE VAGAL BRAKE: CONSEQUENCES FOR POSTPARTUM ADAPTATION AND SOCIAL BEHAVIOR

The mammalian nervous system did not develop solely to survive in dangerous and life-threatening contexts but also to promote social interactions and social bonds in safe environments. To accomplish this adaptive flexibility, a new neural strategy requiring safe environments emerged, while the more primitive neural circuits to regulate defensive strategies were retained. To accommodate both fight-or-flight and social engagement behaviors, the new mammalian vagus evolved to enable rapid, adaptive shifts in autonomic state. The mammalian myelinated vagus functions as an active vagal brake (see chapter 7) in which inhibition and recovery of the vagal tone to the heart can rapidly mobilize or calm an individual. Tonic vagal influences to the sinoatrial node (i.e., the primary cardiac pacemaker) produce a resting heart rate that is substantially lower than the intrinsic rate of the pacemaker alone. When vagal tone, through myelinated vagal pathways, to the pacemaker is high, the vagus acts as a restraint, or brake, limiting the rate at which the heart can beat and functionally calming the individual. When vagal tone to the pacemaker is low, there is little or no inhibition of the pacemaker, and the heart rate increases. The vagal brake construct may be used to describe functional modulation of heart rate by myelinated vagal efferent pathways.

The state of the vagal brake can be quantified as the amplitude of a periodic component in the beat-to-beat heart rate pattern known as respiratory sinus arrhythmia (RSA). RSA is a naturally occurring rhythm in the heart rate pattern that oscillates at approximately the frequency of spontaneous breathing. RSA represents only a portion of beat-to-beat heart rate variability. By quantifying RSA and the relation between RSA and heart rate during various challenges, it is possible to measure the dynamic regulation of the myelinated vagal brake to study the responses of infants and young children to people and to objects (e.g., Bazhenova, Plonskaia, & Porges, 2001).

The human infant is not born with a completely functioning myelinated vagal system. The mammalian vagus is only partially myelinated at birth and continues to develop during the first few months postpartum. Morphological studies demonstrate a rapid developmental increase in the total number of myelinated vagal fibers from 24 weeks through adolescence with the greatest increases observed from approximately 30–32 weeks of gestational age to approximately 6 months postpartum (see Sachis, Armstrong, Becker, & Bryan, 1982). More recent neuroanatomical research suggests that the increase in myelinated fibers may be occurring in the absence of an increase in unmyelinated vagal fibers, since the increase in the number of myelinated vagal fibers is paralleled by a decrease in the ratio of unmyelinated to myelinated vagal fibers (Pereyra, Zhang, Schmidt, & Becker, 1992). A relative increase in myelinated vagal fibers would functionally improve visceral regulation and enable the infant to express better behavioral regulation, which would support spontaneous social engagement behaviors. Based on these studies, preterm infants born before approximately 30 weeks gestational age are likely compromised due to lack of an appropriately functioning mammalian vagus, or vagal brake. Without a functioning mammalian vagus, the preterm has a limited ability to regulate visceral state and is dependent solely on the sympathetic nervous system and on the phylogenetically older unmyelinated vagus to meet physiological needs. This compromised profile of autonomic regulation obligates the preterm infant to rely on the sympathetic nervous system to increase heart rate in response to distress, in order to support tantrums and mobilization behaviors. Preterm infants are also more vulnerable to clinically dangerous hypotensive states and lowered oxygen saturation caused by episodes of bradycardia and apnea (i.e., massive slowing of the heart and cessation of breathing), which may be triggered by ingestive behaviors (e.g., sucking and swallowing) through activity in the more primitive unmyelinated vagus that has already developed.

RSA in the preterm infant follows a maturational trajectory that parallels the reported changes in both number and ratio of myelinated vagal fibers. During the preterm period there is a monotonic increase in RSA from 32 to 37 weeks gestational age (Doussard-Roosevelt, Porges, Scanlon, Alemi, & Scanlon, 1997). Opportunities for skin-to-skin contact (i.e., kangaroo care) between mother and preterm (Feldman & Eidelman, 2003) enhance the development of RSA. Paralleling the enhanced vagal regulation, these authors also reported more rapid improvement in state organization and a more mature neurodevelopmental profile. However, the enhanced development of RSA was only relative to preterm controls not receiving skin-to-skin contact and was still substantially lower than reports of RSA in typically delivered full-terms (see chapter 4).

In longitudinal studies evaluating heart rate and RSA in term infants during the first year postpartum, heart rate reliably slows with age, although RSA changes are less obvious (i.e., Fracasso, Porges, Lamb, & Rosenberg, 1994; Izard et al., 1991). In these studies the effects of development on RSA appear to be maximized during the first 6 months postpartum and taper during the 6–12-month period. Although these developmental trends have been reported and replicated, closer inspection of the data indicates that individual differences in RSA during the first year postpartum are even greater than the developmental shifts.

Based on parallel literatures that describe developmental features in both RSA and the neuroanatomy of the vagus nerve, we may make two inferences: (1) RSA during early infancy reflects the functional outflow of the myelinated vagus, and (2) efficient RSA reactivity and recovery are dependent on both the number of myelinated vagal fibers and the ratio of myelinated to unmyelinated vagal fibers. The literature on young infants supports these assumptions by demonstrating increases in RSA during the last trimester through the first few months postpartum. The second assumption has primarily been tested during feeding when ingestive-vagal reflexes are recruited, although additional research will need to examine reactivity during social challenges during the first few months postpartum (e.g., Bazhenova et al., 2001; Moore & Calkins, 2004; Weinberg & Tronick, 1996).

FEEDING: CHALLENGING AND EXERCISING THE VAGAL BRAKE THROUGH AN INGESTIVE-VAGAL REFLEX

To ingest food properly and efficiently, the newborn must have the neural resources to implement the complex sequence of sucking, swallowing, and breathing. This sequence requires the coordination of the striated muscles of the face, head, and neck with the myelinated vagal regulation of the bronchi and the heart. Unlike the striated muscles of the limbs, striated muscles of the face, head, and neck are regulated by pathways traveling from the brainstem through several cranial nerves. These pathways are known as special visceral efferent pathways, although anatomically, their targets are not considered visceral. These pathways are often called branchiomeric, since they regulate the structures that embryologically emerged from the pharyngeal (branchial or ancient gill) arches. As the infant matures, the special visceral efferent pathways are recruited by corticobulbar pathways and expressed through social engagement behaviors. Autonomic support for these muscles is provided by the myelinated vagus, which can be dynamically monitored by quantifying RSA. This face–heart connection provides the necessary elements for an integrated social engagement system (see later discussion).

Since the structures involved in the neural regulation and coordination of the striated muscles involved in sucking, swallowing, vocalizing, and breathing are all linked to the myelinated vagus, the functioning of these behaviors, and the link between these behaviors and RSA, may provide an early indicator of the functional status of a system that will later be involved in social engagement behaviors.

The status of the face–heart connection can be evaluated by measuring RSA changes during the ingestive behavior of sucking, which requires coordination of the striated muscles of the face with visceral changes in heart rate and breathing. Porges and Lipsitt (1993) monitored the integration of sucking behaviors with heart rate and RSA as infants sucked to obtain sucrose. In response to sucrose, reductions in RSA and corresponding increases in heart rate paralleled increased sucking frequency. When the availability of sucrose was terminated, RSA and heart rate returned to presucrose levels. Moreover, individual differences in baseline RSA were correlated with the magnitude of heart rate reactivity to the gustatory stimulation. These findings illustrate that in the healthy neonate, there is a coordinated ingestive response in which the vagal brake is systematically removed to support the increased metabolic demands of sucking.

Because ingestive-vagal responses can be systematically elicited, a feeding challenge paradigm provides an opportunity in newborns and preterm infants to evaluate the status of coordinated physiological-behavioral sequences that require vagal regulation and control of the striated muscles of the face, head, and neck. Similar to the full-term infants described in the Porges and Lipsitt study, clinically stable low-birthweight preterm infants (near the time of discharge) also decreased RSA and increased heart rate during feeding (Portales et al., 1997). When feeding was terminated, heart rate and RSA returned to prefeeding levels. In a second study, with more clinically compromised infants (Suess et al., 2000), RSA and heart rate were monitored before, during, and after oral or gastric tube bolus feedings in preterm infants at approximately 33–34 weeks postmenstrual age. The preterm neonates were categorized into two groups based on gestational age at birth. The earlier-born group had gestational ages less than 30 weeks, and the later-born group had gestational ages greater than 30 weeks. Consistent with the foregoing studies, RSA decreased in both groups during feeding. However, postfeeding RSA increased toward prefeed levels (i.e., recovered) only in laterborn infants. The results confirmed the assumption that the higher risk group, independent of corrected gestational age, experienced compromised vagal regulation during the feeding paradigm.

The primary characteristics of the feeding response are a withdrawal of vagal control of the heart to increase metabolic activity necessary to ingest food and a postfeeding recovery of vagal tone to foster a calm state and support digestion. Thus, during metabolically demanding ingestive behaviors such as sucking, there is a reduction of myelinated cardiac vagal tone to allow greater mobilization of energy resources. Following these ingestive behaviors, there is a recovery of vagal function to support digestion and calm the infant.

The studies described here indicate that term infants and stable older preterm infants modulate the vagal brake during feeding. This ingestive-vagal reflex might be mediated solely at the brainstem level and might not be sensitive to the increasing number and efficiency of corticobulbar pathways connecting the cortex with the source nucleus of the myelinated vagus, the nucleus ambiguus (NA), which arise during maturation. From an evolutionary perspective, the adaptive consequence of these higher order neuroanatomical changes would enable the older infant to use social cues to regulate the vagal brake. It is possible that through neuroception (see chapter 1), the loving caregiver's facial features and vocal prosody trigger temporal corticolimbic pathways that dampen defensive reactions and recruit the vagal brake to calm. In contrast, the facial and vocal features of a stranger might inhibit the vagal brake to allow mobilizing, protesting, and defensive behaviors.

THE SOCIAL ENGAGEMENT SYSTEM

A face–heart connection evolved in mammals as source nuclei of vagal pathways shifted ventrally from the phylogenetically older dorsal motor nucleus (e.g., unmyelinated vagal pathways) to the NA (e.g., myelinated vagal pathways). This resulted in an anatomical and neurophysiological linkage between neural regulation of the heart via the myelinated vagus and the special visceral efferent pathways that regulate the striated muscles of the face, head, and neck. Together, this linkage, between brainstem motor systems responsible for cardiovascular functions and those necessary for regulating the face, head, and neck, forms an integrated social engagement system.

With increased cortical development, the cortex exhibits greater control over the brainstem via direct (e.g., corticobulbar) and indirect (e.g., corticoreticular) neural pathways originating in the motor cortex and terminating in the source nuclei of the myelinated motor fibers emerging from the brainstem (e.g., specific neural pathways embedded within cranial nerves V, VII, IX, X, and XI). These cranial nerves then extend from their source nuclei to control visceromotor structures (i.e., heart, bronchi) as well as branchiomotor structures (muscles of the face, head, and neck).

Specifically, the social engagement system includes the regulation of the eyelids through the orbicularis oculi (e.g., social gaze and gesture), muscles of facial expression (e.g., emotional expression), middle ear muscles (e.g., extracting human voice from background sounds), muscles of mastication (e.g., ingestion, sucking), laryngeal and pharyngeal muscles (e.g., vocalizing, swallowing, breathing), and muscles of head turning and tilting (e.g., social gesture and orientation). Collectively, these muscles act as filters for social stimuli (i.e., observing others' facial expressions and detecting prosody in human voice), and they allow the expression of motor behaviors necessary for engagement with the social environment.

Based on the polyvagal theory (see chapter 2), the development of the mammalian myelinated vagus is critical in the development of the face–heart connection, which links social behavior and autonomic regulation. Thus, with more optimal vagal regulation, features of more adaptive social behavior emerge. Without a functioning myelinated vagus, social behavior would be compromised, and more primitive defensive strategies, such as fight-or-flight mobilization and tantrums (mediated by the sympathetic nervous system) and shutdown behaviors (mediated by the unmyelinated vagal system) would be more frequently expressed. Clinically, the status of vagal myelination becomes critical for the newborn and the young infant as they attempt to engage and disengage the caregiver and to explore social reciprocity as a mechanism to regulate physiology and behavior.

MODEL: AUTONOMIC STATE PROVIDES A NEURAL PLATFORM FOR SOCIAL BEHAVIOR

The unique features of the autonomic nervous system that support mammalian social behavior start to develop during the last trimester of fetal life. Specifically, myelination of vagal efferent fibers from the NA to the sinoatrial node (i.e., cardiac pacemaker) begins during the last trimester. This process continues during the first few months postpartum and can be monitored by quantifying the amplitude of RSA. Regulation of the myelinated vagus (i.e., vagal brake) provides a mechanism to rapidly increase metabolic output by releasing the brake on the heart's pacemaker (i.e., sinoatrial node). The release of the vagal brake results in an instantaneous increase in heart rate. Subsequently, when the metabolic demands decrease, inhibitory vagal influence on the heart is reinstated, and heart rate instantaneously decreases. The regulation of the vagal brake influences important developmental processes related to survival, including (1) improved reactivity and recovery of the ingestive-vagal reflexes involved during feeding, (2) expanded capacity to self-regulate and calm, and (3) improved abilities to both spontaneously engage others and to be soothed by others. This developmental time line is illustrated in Figure 8.1.

Prematurity, illness, or neglect may dampen the developmental trajectory of the vagal circuit. Atypical maturation of this circuit may be reflected in myelination of the vagus, interneuronal connections in the brainstem that form the face–heart connection, and/or corticobulbar regulation of the brainstem circuits regulating both vagal activity and the striated muscles of the face, head, and neck. The consequences of these delays or disruptions in typical neural maturation would be expressed as lower levels of RSA, less efficient reactivity and recov-

FIGURE 8.1. Developmental timeline relating myelination of the vagus to social behavior.

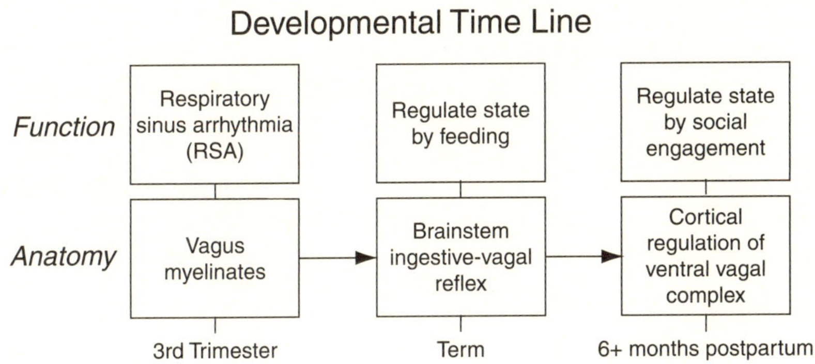

ery of the vagal brake, difficulties in behavioral state regulation, poor affective tone, and diminished abilities for reciprocal social engagement behaviors.

The myelinated vagus is not the sole mediator of autonomic state, in general, or heart rate, specifically. Heart rate is influenced by intrinsic cardiac mechanisms, surrounding thoracic anatomy, the sympathetic nervous system, and the unmyelinated vagus originating in the dorsal nucleus of the vagus. The development of the sympathetic nervous system and the unmyelinated vagal circuit has not been extensively studied in the human fetus and has been assumed to be functioning at term. Within our phylogenetic perspective, we assume that these circuits are functioning at the start of the last trimester. Shortly, we support this assumption with a brief review of the limited literature focusing on studies of the embryological development of the central regulators and peripheral pathways directly influencing heart rate or the contractility of the heart. Although only the development of efferent (motor) fibers is discussed, afferent (sensory) pathways play a vital role in both autonomic function and in providing sufficient input to trigger normal neural development.

The development of the autonomic nervous system in the human fetus mirrors the broader phylogenetic progression already described. The phylogenetically oldest vertebrate autonomic system, which relies on unmyelinated efferent vagal fibers originating from the dorsal motor nucleus of the vagus (DMNX), is also, embryologically, the earliest system to develop in utero. An immature, undifferentiated DMNX first appears in the brainstem at 9 weeks gestation (Cheng, Zhou, Qu, Ashwell, & Paxinos, 2004; Nara, Goto, & Hamano, 1991). Magnocellular subdivisions become visible by 13 weeks, and clear demarcation of DMNX subnuclei, including the lateral cardiomotor subnucleus, occurs by 23 weeks. At 28 weeks, all magnocellular subnuclei are considered essentially mature (Cheng et al., 2004). Some, however, including Nara et al. (1991), believe that there may be some postnatal changes in the DMNX, such as increased nuclear columnar length and volume. Even if present, however, these postnatal changes are not considered to have much functional significance or physiological consequence in the neonate.

The other major component of the parasympathetic, cardioinhibitory ANS is the newest, myelinated vagal system, which originates in the NA. This system, as predicted by the polyvagal theory, develops last in the fetus and continues functional development well into the first postnatal year. Mature neurons appear in the rostral NA by 8 or 9 weeks gestation and fill the nucleus by 12.5 weeks (Brown, 1990). Unlike mature neurons in the lateral subnucleus of the DMNX, however, axons of these mature neurons have not yet reached cardiac tissue to exert cardioinhibitory effects. The functional significance of vagal fibers from the NA depends heavily on myelination, which does not begin until 23 weeks gestation, when nearly mature axon diameter is achieved (Wozniak & O'Rahilly, 1981). Myelination of NA vagal fibers increases linearly from 24 to 40 weeks gestation and, again, continues actively during the first year postpartum (Pereyra et al., 1992; Sachis et al., 1982).

Development of the sympathetic, cardioexcitatory ANS is less well described in the literature. Phylogenetically, this largely catecholaminergic system appears before the mammalian NA vagal system and after the older DMNX vagus. According to the polyvagal theory, then, this system should begin development in the human fetus sometime between the two parasympathetic systems. Anatomically, sympathetic innervation of cardiac tissue is complex and difficult to isolate. Postganglionic cardiomotor nuclei lie mostly within the cardiothoracic and middle cervical ganglia, which lie caudal to the sympathetic superior cervical ganglion. Functionally, sympathetic influence on the heart is also varied. Unlike the two vagal circuits, which exert mostly chronotropic effects (slowing heart rate), sympathetic activity leads to both chronotropic (increasing heart rate) by innervating pacemaker tissue and inotropic (increasing cardiac contractility) by innervating ventricular myocardium. Investigations using fetal heart rate monitoring to infer sympathetic activity provide potential insight into the development of this system. Using continuous 24-hour fetal heart rate monitoring in 28 healthy women, who were 16–28 weeks pregnant, Kintraia, Zarnadze, Kintraia, and Kashakashvili (2005) reported that fetal locomotor activity increased between 16 and 20 weeks gestation. At this stage, increases in activity are accompanied by corresponding increases in heart rate, which returns to normal during "quiet" fetal periods. Since the vagal brake is not functional during this period of fetal development, these increases in heart rate are most likely due to activity in the sympathetic nervous system. Furthermore, the authors interpret an absence of such a coordinated heart rate increase with increased locomotion by 24 weeks gestation as "developmental retardation."

Measurement of RSA can map the development of the myelinated vagus and also enable dynamic monitoring of vagal reactivity and recovery elicited during feeding to quantify the status of ingestive-vagal reflexes. The literature documents that both amplitude of RSA and pattern of RSA responses during feeding are sensitive indices of risk in preterm and term infants. Ingestive-vagal reflexes elicited during feeding provide an opportunity early in development to evaluate a neural circuit that later will be involved in social engagement behaviors. Eliciting these reflexes provide an opportunity to exercise the neural circuits coordinating both the striated muscles of the face and neck and the vagal brake. As the infant develops, the brainstem structures involved in ingestive-vagal reflexes are increasingly recruited by higher brain structures, which regulate the facial and vocal features involved in reciprocal social interactions. Thus, when brainstem ingestive-vagal reflexes are functional, the first year postpartum is characterized by an increase in the efficiency with which corticobulbar pathways recruit and regulate these same brainstem nuclei for the purpose of social engagement. If, during early infancy, ingestive-vagal reflexes are not efficiently working, then there will be difficulties in coordinating sucking, swallowing, and breathing. Problems in regulating these survival-related processes may provide a sensitive prognostic index leading to difficulties not only in social behavior but also in the development of cognitive and language skills that are dependent on appropriate behavioral and physiological state regulation.

Changes in RSA represent a dynamic adjustment of the inhibitory action of the vagus (vagal brake) on the heart. Functionally, the removal of the vagal brake provides a physiological state that promotes vigilance as an intermediary and precautionary psychological process to monitor risk in the environment. The outcome of this assessment includes the induction of different physiological states, either in which social behaviors can proceed, or in which defensive fight-or-flight strategies associated with increased sympathetic excitation are necessary. If defensive behaviors are not necessary to maintain or to negotiate safety, then the rapid vagal regulatory mechanisms that dampen autonomic state are reinstated, allowing the individual to calm and self-soothe. Further support for this interpretation can be seen in the infant data in which suppression of RSA is correlated with maternal reports of longer attention spans and being more easily soothed (Huffman et al., 1998). For example, Huffman et al. (1998) found that 12-week-old infants with higher baseline RSA expressed fewer negative behaviors and were less disrupted by experimental procedures than age-matched infants with lower baseline RSA. Moreover, consistent with the vagal brake concept, the infants who decreased RSA during the laboratory assessment were rated on maternal report temperament scales as having longer attention spans and being more easily soothed.

The regulation of behavioral state is a critical determinant of the range of social behaviors an individual can express. The underlying mechanisms mediating behavioral state are tightly linked to the autonomic nervous system. Investigation of the early maturational changes in vagal regulation of autonomic state unmasks several of the behavioral features that infants exhibit. For example, greater suppression of RSA during challenging situations is related to better state regulation, greater self-soothing, more attentional control, and greater capacity for social engagement (see chapter 7; Calkins, Graziano, & Keane, 2007; DeGangi, DiPietro, Porges, & Greenspan, 1991; Huffman et al., 1998; Stifter & Corey, 2001).

The ability to regulate state follows a developmental trajectory during the early part of life. As the neural circuits involved in state regulation become more available to the developing child, there are parallel opportunities for social engagement behaviors and the development of strong social bonds. Without the dynamic, efficient myelinated vagus, it is difficult to regulate behavioral state and to use the features of the social engagement system (i.e., facial expression, vocal prosody), which at birth are involved in feeding behaviors (i.e., ingestive-vagal reflexes). Developmental limitations in the vagal system, expressed as low level of RSA and difficulties in regulating RSA, may lower thresholds to negative or ambiguous environmental cues with resultant hyperreactivity and severe limitations in the ability to self-soothe and calm.

Social behavior and the capacity to manage challenge are dependent on the neural regulation of physiological state. The neural circuits involved in the regulation of physiological state are modified during gestation and continue during postnatal life. If these circuits are easily available and efficiently functioning, then the laws of learning and the impact of experience can shape behavior. However, if these circuits are not available, either as a function of phase of development or during periods of increased environmental risk, then state regulation is compromised, social skills are not easily learned, and social bonds become difficult to establish. During most of the life span, the vagal brake and the other features of the social engagement system are readily available and provide opportunities for social learning to occur. Without the efficient vagal brake turning off defensive systems and blunting their disruptive manifestations (e.g., fight-or-flight behaviors), prosocial behavior is limited, and opportunities for social learning and social bonding are minimized.

Co-author for this chapter was S. A. Furman.

PART III

SOCIAL COMMUNICATION AND RELATIONSHIPS

CHAPTER 9

Vagal Tone and the Physiological Regulation of Emotion

Because emotions are psychological processes, the experience and regulation of emotion should be functionally dependent on the state of the nervous system. If a major source of emotion variation is dependent on the nervous system, how would this be evaluated? The goal of this chapter is to address this problem by introducing vagal tone as a measurable organismic variable that contributes to individual and developmental differences in the expression and regulation of emotion.

We propose that understanding the mechanisms determining individual and developmental differences in emotion expression and regulation might provide a rationale for identifying subjects who differentially express the ability to regulate emotion. Thus, there is the possibility that individual differences in the nervous system might mediate the expression and regulation of emotion. Most research on the autonomic correlates of emotion has focuses on *sympathetic* activation (e.g., galvanic skin response); here, we attempt to demonstrate that individual differences in *parasympathetic* tone are related to the regulation of emotion by focusing on a construct called *vagal tone*, which reflects the vagal control of the heart.

PHYSIOLOGY AND EMOTION: THE AUTONOMIC NERVOUS SYSTEM

The autonomic nervous system (ANS) regulates homeostatic function and is composed of two subsystems, the parasympathetic (PNS) and the sympathetic (SNS) nervous systems. The PNS and SNS represent neural systems that originate in the brainstem and contribute to the regulation of a variety of target organs, including the eyes; lacrimal, salivary, and sweat glands; blood vessels; heart;

larynx, trachea, bronchi, and lungs; stomach; adrenal glands; kidneys; pancreas; intestines; bladder; and external genitalia. In general, the PNS promotes functions associated with growth and restorative processes. In contrast, the SNS promotes increased metabolic output to deal with challenges from outside the body. However, there are states that require dual excitation (e.g., sexual arousal). Conceptualizations of the ANS by Berntson, Cacioppo, and Quigley (1991a) provide insight into the complex dynamic relation between SNS and PNS processes.

In general, when a visceral organ is innervated by both the SNS and the PNS, the effects are antagonistic. For example, SNS neurons dilate the pupils, accelerate the heart, inhibit intestinal movements, and contract the vesical and rectal sphincters. The PNS neurons constrict the pupils, slow the heart, potentiate peristaltic movement, and relax vesical and rectal sphincters. The PNS deals primarily with anabolic activities concerned with the restoration and conservation of bodily energy and the resting of vital organs. In contrast, stimulation of the SNS prepares the individual for the intense muscular action required to protect and defend in response to external challenges. The SNS quickly mobilizes the existing reserves of the body.

Darwin provides insight into the potential importance of PNS processes in the regulation of emotions. Although Darwin defined emotions as facial expressions, he acknowledged the dynamic relation between parasympathetic structures and central nervous system activity that accompanied the spontaneous expression of emotions. Darwin speculated that there were specific neural pathways that provided the necessary communication between the brain states and the specific pattern of autonomic activity (e.g., heart rate) associated with emotions. In Darwin's formulation, when emotion states occur, the beating of the heart changes instantly, the changes in cardiac activity influences brain activity, and the brainstem structures stimulate the heart via the cranial nerves (i.e., vagus). Although Darwin did not elucidate the neurophysiological mechanisms that translate the initial emotion expression to the heart, this formulation provides us with three important points. First, by emphasizing the afferent feedback from the heart to the brain, Darwin anticipated the views of William James linking autonomic feedback to the experience of emotion. Second, he acknowledged the afferent capacity of the vagus to transmit sensory information from visceral organs independent of the spinal cord and the sympathetics. Third, Darwin's insight regarding the regulatory role of the pneumogastric nerve (renamed the *vagus* at the end of the 19th century) in the expression of emotions anticipates the major theme of this chapter.

Contemporary models of emotion and emotion regulation (i.e., Ekman, Levenson, & Friesen, 1983; Schachter & Singer, 1962), as did their historical antecedents, have focused on the sympathetic nervous system and ignored the vagal system, the primary component of the PNS. Thus, although Darwin speculated about the bidirectional communication between the brain and the heart via the vagus more than 100 years ago, the importance of vagal afferents and efferents in the expression, experience, and regulation of emotion has not been addressed.

VAGAL TONE: BACKGROUND AND DEFINITION

The vagus is the Xth cranial nerve. It originates in the brainstem and projects, independently of the spinal cord, to many organs in the body cavity, including the heart and the digestive system. The vagus is not a single neural pathway but rather a complex bidirectional system with myelinated branches linking the brainstem and various target organs. These neural pathways allow direct and rapid communication between brain structures and specific organs. Because the vagus contains both efferent (i.e., motor) and afferent (i.e., sensory) fibers, it promotes dynamic feedback between brain control centers and the target organs to regulate homeostasis.

The peripheral autonomic nervous system is asymmetrical. The peripheral target organs of the autonomic nervous system are clearly lateralized; for example, the heart is oriented to the left, the stomach is tilted, one lung is larger, and one kidney is higher. The neural wiring of the autonomic nervous system requires asymmetry, and the central regulation via the vagus is lateralized. Although asymmetry of cortical function is well known and has been theorized to contribute to emotion regulation (see Fox, 1994), asymmetrical regulation of autonomic function has been ignored.

The vagus is bilateral, with a left and a right branch. Each branch has two source nuclei, with fibers originating either in the dorsal motor nucleus or in the nucleus ambiguus. Traditional texts in neuroanatomy and neurophysiology (e.g., Truex & Carpenter, 1969; Williams, 1989) have focused on the dorsal motor nucleus of the vagus and neglected both the asymmetry in the vagal pathways and the important functions of the pathways originating from source nuclei in the nucleus ambiguus.

The dorsal motor nucleus is lateralized. Pathways from the left and right dorsal motor nucleus to the stomach have different regulatory functions. The left dorsal motor nucleus innervates the cardiac and body portions of the stomach that promote primarily secretion of gastric fluids (Kalia, 1981; Loewy & Spyer, 1990). The right dorsal motor nucleus innervates the lower portion of the stomach that controls the pyloric sphincter regulating the emptying into the duodenum (Fox & Powley, 1985; Pagani, Norman, & Gillis, 1988).

The nucleus ambiguus is also lateralized. While the right nucleus ambiguus provides the primary vagal input to the sinoatrial (SA) node to regulate atrial rate (Hopkins, 1987) and determine heart rate, the left nucleus ambiguus provides the primary vagal input to the atrioventricular (AV) node to regulate ventricular rate (Thompson, Felsten, Yavorsky, & Natelson, 1987). Given the ipsilateral control of efferent pathways regulating the nucleus ambiguus, characteristics of right-side brain damage are associated with defective right nucleus ambiguus regulation. In this manner, the observed deficits in prosody (e.g., Ross, 1981) and in heart rate changes during attention-demanding tasks (Yokoyama, Jennings, Ackles, Hood, & Boller, 1987) associated with right-side brain damage implicate the right nucleus ambiguus in the regulation of vocal intonation and attention.

Asymmetrical nucleus ambiguus regulation is less clear in other organs, such as the soft palate, the pharynx, and the esophagus.

Functionally, the dorsal motor nucleus is involved with the vegetative functions of digestion and respiration. In contrast, the nucleus ambiguus is more involved with processes associated with motion, emotion, and communication. For example, rapid mobilization of the body may be achieved by regulating heart rate via removal of vagal input to the SA node. Vocal intonation, mediated by vagal connections to the larynx, is intimately related to the processes of emotion and communication. Facial expressions, critical to the expression of emotion and the signaling of information, are related to vagal function. In cats, vagal afferent fibers have direct influences on facial motoneurons (Tanaka & Asahara, 1981). Thus, the vagus originating from the dorsal motor nucleus might be labeled the *vegetative vagus*, in contrast to the emotive or *smart vagus* originating from the nucleus ambiguus. Table 9.1 provides a list of target organs associated with each branch of the vagus.

Sympathetic innervation of the heart is also asymmetrical (Randall & Rohse, 1956). Moreover, lateralized sympathetic input to the heart has been hypothesized to relate to emotion state (Lane & Schwartz, 1987). As with vagal control of the heart and larynx, research has demonstrated that damage to the right hemisphere has greater sympathetic consequences than does left hemisphere damage (Hachinski, Oppenheimer, Wilson, Guiraudon, & Cechetto, 1992).

The central control of the vagus is ipsilateral. Thus, the right vagus originates in either the right dorsal motor nucleus or the right nucleus ambiguus. As noted, the right nucleus ambiguus contains the primary source for the branch of the right vagus that provides input to the SA node. Thus, output from the nucleus ambiguus can be monitored by measuring changes in vagal control of the SA node. The SA node is the primary pacemaker of the heart. Vagal stimulation of the SA node delays the onset of the heartbeat (i.e., slows heart rate), and vagal withdrawal (i.e., a delay or blocking of the neural transmission) shortens the time between heartbeats (i.e., speeds heart rate). Most rapid heart rate changes (i.e., chronotropic mechanisms) are mediated by the vagus. When metabolic de-

TABLE 9.1. Target Organs Associated With the Dorsal Motor Nucleus and the Nucleus Ambiguus

Dorsal Motor Nucleus	Nucleus Ambiguus
Trachea	Heart
Lungs	Soft palate
Stomach	Pharynx
Intestines	Larynx
Pancreas	Esophagus
Colon	Bronchi

mands increase, such as during exercise or fight-or-flight demands, the sympathetic nervous system influences heart rate. Thus, the study of vagal control of the heart might provide an important window on the rapid autonomic changes associated with gradations of emotion state.

VAGAL TONE: POTENTIAL LINK WITH EMOTION

An easily accessible method for evaluating the vagal control of the SA node (i.e., cardiac vagal tone) is to quantify respiratory sinus arrhythmia (RSA). RSA is characterized by a rhythmic increase and decrease in heart rate synchronous with breathing. The heart rate increase is associated with phases of inspiration, when respiratory mechanisms in the brainstem attenuate the vagal efferent action on the heart. The heart rate decrease is associated with phases of expiration, when the vagal efferent influence to the heart is reinstated.

Changes in RSA amplitude in response to sensory, cognitive, and visceral challenges represents a "central command" to regulate vagal efferents originating in the right nucleus ambiguus and terminating in the heart, soft palate, pharynx, larynx, bronchi, and esophagus. These changes in nucleus ambiguus regulation of peripheral autonomic activity support the expression of motion, emotion, and communication by regulating metabolic output (i.e., shifts in heart rate) and organs involved in the production of vocalizations (see chapter 13).

When there are no challenging environmental demands, the autonomic nervous system, through the vagus, services the needs of the internal viscera to enhance growth and restoration. However, in response to environmental demands, homeostatic processes are compromised, and the autonomic nervous system supports increased metabolic output to deal with these external challenges by vagal withdrawal and sympathetic excitation. By mediating the distribution of resources, the central nervous system regulates the strength and latency of autonomic responses to deal with internal and external demands. Perceptions and assumed threats to survival, independent of the actual physical characteristics of the stimulation, may promote a massive withdrawal of parasympathetic tone and a reciprocal excitation of sympathetic tone. These changes promote fight-or-flight behaviors. Less intense environmental demands, often associated with emotion expressions, might be characterized by less withdrawal of parasympathetic tone independent of or in concert with slight increases in sympathetic tone. This trade-off between internal and external needs is monitored and regulated by the central nervous system.

Vagal tone measured via RSA has been documented to be related to affect, attention, and metabolic demands (see later discussion). Although the vagus is bilateral, the right branch originating in the nucleus ambiguus is the primary determinant of RSA. This laterality in the vagus is not a developmental or an individual difference. Rather, the laterality is dependent on the neurophysiology and the neuroanatomy of the mammalian nervous system. In the mammalian nervous system, the right side of the brainstem provides the primary central regulation of homeostasis and physiological reactivity. Thus, right-brainstem structures initiate peripheral physiological states via shifts in vagal tone to facilitate the processes of attention, the expression of emotion, and the initiation of shifts in metabolic output.

THE RIGHT HEMISPHERE: THE REGULATION OF EMOTION

Right hemisphere function, evaluated via electroencephalography (EEG) or disrupted by localized damage, is related to the same cluster of behaviors that has been linked to the vagal tone measure. Research demonstrates that the right hemisphere is implicated in both the expression and the interpretation of emotions (e.g., Bear, 1983; Heilman, Bowers, & Valenstein, 1985; Pimental & Kingsbury, 1989; Tucker, 1981) and in the regulation of attention (e.g., Heilman & Van Den Abell, 1980; Mesulam, 1981; Pimental & Kingsbury, 1989; Voeller, 1986). Research has also linked right hemisphere deficits with aprosody or lack of emotion expression in speech (e.g., Ross, 1981; Ross & Mesulam, 1979; Zurif, 1974) and attenuated autonomic reactivity (e.g., Heilman, Schwartz, & Watson, 1978). Several investigators have argued that the right hemisphere provided the primary control of emotion (for detailed reviews, see Molfese & Segalowitz, 1988; Pimental & Kingsbury, 1989; Silberman & Weingartner, 1986).

EEG research has been used to provide support for laterality theories of emotion. Fox and colleagues (e.g., Dawson, 1994; Fox, 1994; Fox & Davidson, 1984) present a model of emotion expression in which positive (e.g., interest) emotions are associated with the left hemisphere and negative emotions (e.g., disgust or distress) with the right. Asymmetry of hemispheric control of negative and positive affect has also been posited by Tucker (1981). Other laterality theories focus primarily on the role of the right hemisphere in the regulation of negative emotions and fight-or-flight behaviors (for a review, see Silberman & Weingartner, 1986). The data strongly support the relation between right hemisphere EEG activity and the expression of negative emotions in infants, children, and adults; however, research demonstrating the relation between left hemisphere EEG activity and the expression of positive emotions is less conclusive.

In children, right hemisphere dysfunction has been associated with attentional, social, and emotional problems. Voeller (1986) reported data on 16 children with unilateral right hemisphere lesion or dysfunction as assessed by neuropsychological exam and/or CAT scan. Fifteen of these children were extremely distractible and inattentive, meeting the DSM-III criteria for attention deficit disorder; moreover, eight were also hyperactive. Eight children were shy and withdrawn, sharing some of the behavioral characteristics of the inhibited child described by Kagan (1994), and nine expressed atypical emotion expression (i.e., prosody, facial expression, and gesture). Most of these children made little eye contact with others, and virtually all had poor relationship with peers.

In their survey of studies with both normal and lesions subjects, Silberman and Weingartner (1986) suggested that the right hemisphere is superior for recognizing emotional aspects of stimuli. They propose that right hemisphere dominance for emotion regulation reflects a nervous system organization that gives priority to avoidance or defensive mechanisms that have a high survival value. By inference, these avoidance and defensive mechanisms require massive and immediate shifts in autonomic function.

THE RIGHT HEMISPHERE: AUTONOMIC REGULATION AND REACTIVITY

The right side of the brain also plays a special role in the regulation of emotion. Data supporting laterality theories of emotion have been based on studies of electrophysiological recordings from the scalp (e.g., Fox, 1994) and neuropsychological studies of dysfunction in individuals with brain damage (e.g., Silberman & Weingartner, 1986). We propose a convergent approach by emphasizing the right brain's regulation of peripheral autonomic activity.

Asymmetry in the control of the autonomic nervous system has been documented in the previous sections. Because peripheral organs are not symmetrical in shape or placement, it is not surprising that the neural control of the autonomic nervous system is lateralized. For example, the heart is displaced to the left, with the right vagus going to the SA node and the left vagus going to the AV node. Other organs with dual vagal innervation are often tilted (e.g., the stomach and intestines), are located higher on one side (e.g., the kidneys), or are larger on one side (e.g., the lungs).

Emphasis on the asymmetry of autonomic organs has implications for the evolution of central regulatory systems and cortical development. In mammals, the peripheral autonomic organs and brainstem structures are similar across species. Asymmetrical neural control of autonomic processes is characteristic of mammals. However, the process of encephalization differs among mammalian species, with man possessing a uniquely large cerebral cortex. Because the neural control of the vagus is ipsilateral (e.g., the left vagus originates in the left side of the brainstem), the right hemisphere—including the right cortical and subcortical structures—would promote the efficient regulation of autonomic function via the source nuclei in the brainstem. For example, neuroanatomical and electrophysiological studies demonstrate the important regulatory function of the right central nucleus of the amygdala in regulating the right nucleus ambiguus.

We propose that the functional dominance of the right side of the brain in regulating autonomic function has implications for specialization of motor and language dominance on the left side of the brain. The right-side responsibilities of regulating homeostasis and modulating physiological state in response to both internal (i.e., visceral) and external (i.e., environmental) feedback potentially enabled the control of other functions to evolve on the left side of the brain. With greater encephalization, which is characteristic of more cognitive mammalian species such as man, lateralized specialization is more observable.

A sharing of central control of voluntary and emotion-homeostatic processes would enable the individual to express complex voluntary levels of communication and movement via the left side of the brain and more intense emotion-homeostatic processes via the right side of the brain. If these processes are lateralized, they might have a degree of autonomous regulation. Of course, the central nervous system is complex and has, in many instances, both ipsilateral and contralateral communications. This provides a small percentage of individuals with central control of both language and dominant hand motor movement on the right instead of the left side of the brain. However, owing to the asymmetry of the peripheral autonomic organs and the medullary control of the autonomic nervous system, the right side of the brain is always dominant in the regulation of autonomic function and, thus, emotion.

Data from stimulation studies using left and right visual fields (e.g., Hugdahl, Franzon, Andersson, & Walldebo, 1983; Weisz, Szilagyi, Lang, & Adam, 1992) indicate that activation of the right cortex results in larger and more reliable autonomic responses. Additionally, studies of brain-damaged individuals have shown that right hemisphere damage or dysfunction is associated with a severe deficit in the facial, vocal, and autonomic components of the expression of emotions (Pimental & Kingsbury, 1989; Silberman & Weingartner, 1986). Similar asymmetry of the sympathetic nervous system has been reported, with the right stellate ganglion having greater cardiovascular control than the left stellate ganglion (Yanowitz, Preston, & Abildskov, 1966). However, no research has focused on the assessment of cardiac vagal tone in subjects with right hemisphere disorders. Since cardiac vagal tone is neurophysiologically linked to the right hemisphere regulation of autonomic activity, it might index the individual's functional capacity to regulate autonomic function and to express emotion.

THE VAGAL CIRCUIT OF EMOTION REGULATION: A MODEL

The right vagus and, thus, cardiac vagal tone are associated with processes involving the expression and regulation of motion, emotion, and communication. These processes enable individuals to approach and/or withdraw from objects and events in their environment. The regulation of attention, a major substrate for appropriate social behaviors, is included among these processes. Thus, the approach/withdrawal dimension includes movement in psychological as well as physical space. Vagal regulation of the heart modulates metabolic output to physically approach or withdraw; vagal modulation of vocal intonations provides clues indicating whether an individual is safe or dangerous to approach; feedback from our own facial muscles to the vagus and the ability to pay attention to social cues, including another person's facial muscles and verbal commands, allow us to negotiate appropriate approach or withdrawal behaviors.

Consistent with Schneirla (1959), who proposed that all behaviors could be described in terms of approach and withdrawal actions, the dimensions of approach and withdrawal play a central role in our model of the vagal regulation of emotion. Schneirla assumed that stimulus intensities modulated autonomic function to produce sympathetic dominance during high intensities and parasympathetic dominance during low intensities. However, according to our model of emotion regulation, sympathetic modulation is not always necessary, and the vagal system can promote approach or withdrawal behaviors via the right nucleus ambiguus control of heart rate and the intonation of vocalizations.

The vagal circuit of emotion regulation is schematized in Figure 9.1. The circuit focuses on right hemisphere regulation of emotion states via vagal projections from the nucleus ambiguus to the larynx and the SA node of the heart. The vagal control of the right side of the larynx produces changes in vocal intonation associated with the expression of emotions. The vagal control of the SA node produces a cardiovascular state associated with specific emotions and facilitating attention or fight-or-flight behaviors.

Emotion process may originate on a cortical level or may be initiated and/or regulated by afferent feedback from visceral organs. For example, if the emotion were triggered by a psychological process (e.g., perception of a specific stimulus), the following stages may occur: (1) cortical areas stimulate the amygdala; (2) the central nucleus of the amygdala stimulates the nucleus ambiguus; and (3) the right vagus regulates heart rate and vocal intonation by communicating with the SA node and the right side of the larynx. Regulation of the emotion response also may follow a specific path: (1) sensory information regarding the status of vis-

Figure 9.1 Schematization of the vagal circuit of emotion regulation.

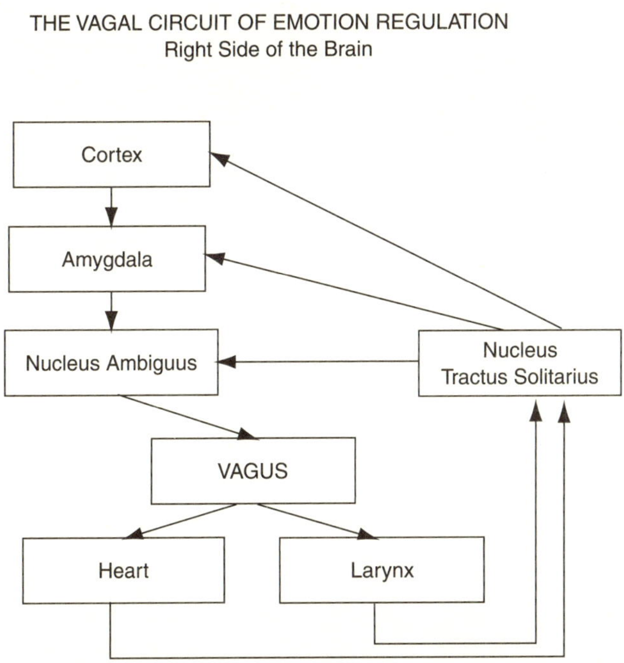

ceral organs stimulates vagal afferents, lateralized vagal afferents stimulate the nucleus tractus solitarius in the brainstem, and projections from the nucleus tractus solitarius stimulate the cortex, amygdala, and/or nucleus ambiguus to regulate the emotion expression; or (2) the emotion state could be initiated by the visceral afferent (e.g., stomach pains) and trigger the cortical, subcortical, brainstem, and autonomic responses associated with emotion.

Interference with transmission on any level of the circuit may result in affective disorders, including emotion regulation problems or severe mood states. Dysfunction in the circuit could be caused by brain damage, neural transmission problems due to drugs, or learned dysfunction. The learning model is based on the demonstrations that classical conditioning and other associative learning paradigms that modify autonomic function are dependent on cortical-autonomic and amygdaloid-autonomic pathways. Thus, autonomic afferents to or from the nucleus ambiguus may be amplified, attenuated, or blocked via neuropathy, drugs, or associative learning to produce different affective states.

The vagal circuit of emotion regulation that we propose makes several important advances in the conceptualization of the physiology of emotion and emotion regulation. It introduces the importance of the vagal system in the physiology of emotion and emphasizes the bidirectional (i.e., afferent feedback) physiological characteristics of the vagus. Furthermore, the vagal circuit is neuroanatomically dependent on right medullary control of autonomic function via the nucleus ambiguus, has a noninvasive window of measurement via the quantification of RSA, explains individual differences due both to defects in neurophysiology and to associative learning, and is consistent with brain damage research. Finally, by emphasizing afferent feedback and communications among various levels of the nervous system, the vagal circuit of emotion regulation provides an explanation for the effectiveness of specific interventions (e.g., nonnutritive sucking, massage, eating, exercise, yoga, and cognitive strategies) in the regulation of emotions.

VAGAL REGULATION AND EMOTION

Interest in vagal tone as a regulatory mechanism in the expression of individual differences in autonomic function is not new. Eppinger and Hess introduced the concept of vagal tone as an individual difference construct in their monograph *Die Vagotonie* (1910). They described a form of autonomic dysfunction for which there was no known anatomical basis: "It is often unsatisfactory for the physician . . . to find that he must be content to make a diagnosis of 'Neurosis'. The symptomatology and the impossibility of establishing any anatomical basis for the disease always remain the most conspicuous points in formulating the diagnosis of a neurosis of an internal organ" (p. 1). The objective of their monograph was to identify a physiological substrate that could explain this anomaly and thus provide the mechanisms for a variety of clinically observed neuroses.

Although Eppinger and Hess were interested in clinical medicine, their case studies described a problem in the regulation of autonomic function that might be intimately related to the regulation of emotion. Their observations are relevant to our interest in the regulation and expression of emotion for four important reasons: first, they alerted us to the importance of the vagal system in mediating physiological and psychological responses; second, they related individual differences in physiology (i.e., vagal tone) to individual differences in behavior (i.e., neuroses); third, they recognized the pharmacological sensitivity of the vagal system to cholinergic agents; and fourth, they brought to the attention of the medical community the commonality of the vagal innervation of various peripheral organs.

In our model of vagal regulation, we adopt a stimulus-organism-response approach. The expression and regulation of emotions are the responses, which are dually determined by the stimulus and the organism. It is not just the stimuli that elicit a response; rather, the response is determined by a complex system of behavioral-physiological responses that involve perception of the stimulus, afferent feedback, and the regulation of approach-withdrawal behaviors via the vagal system. Because of the link between the right vagus and the processes of motion, emotion, and communication, individuals with low vagal tone and/or poor vagal regulation would be expected to exhibit difficulties in regulating emotion state, in appropriately attending to social cues and gestures, and in expressing contingent and appropriate emotions. Thus, the possibility exists that the vagal system may provide a physiological metaphor for the regulation of emotion states. Individual differences in vagal tone may index organismic factors related to the competency of the individual to react physiologically and to self-regulate.

VAGAL TONE RESEARCH

In testing our model of vagal regulation, we have been assessing empirically whether individuals with low vagal tone and/or difficulties in regulating vagal tone have problems with the expression and/or regulation of motion, emotion, and communication. The potential to move, express emotion, and communicate enables an individual to maneuver along a continuum of approach–withdrawal with the environment. Several behaviors are critical to this function, including behavioral reactivity, facial expressivity, and emotion regulation.

If vagal tone mediates the expression and regulation of emotion, developmental shifts in vagal tone might contribute to the observed developmental shifts in affective expression. Research has demonstrated that vagal control of the autonomic nervous system increases developmentally as the nervous system matures. We have reported a relation between gestational age and vagal tone in premature neonates (Porges, 1983) and a monotonic increase in vagal tone from birth through the first 18 days postpartum in rats (Larson & Porges, 1982). In the rat pups, these changes were paralleled by increased organization of behavior, including enhanced state regulation, exploration, and attention. Current longitudinal research with human infants has demonstrated that vagal tone increases monotonically from 3 to 13 months (Izard et al., 1991).

To evaluate whether vagal tone as a construct has properties that may be useful in explaining the expression of emotion and the regulation of affective state, the following sections review research on the relation between vagal tone and variables in the domains of reactivity, the expression of emotion, and self-regulation.

Reactivity

Here we provide theoretical justification and empirical support for the hypothesis that individual differences in vagal tone are related to heart rate and behavioral reactivity in young infants. The core proposition is that vagal tone indexes a dimension of central nervous system organization that disposes an individual to be hypo- or hyperreactive. Thus, subjects with higher levels of vagal tone should have more organized (i.e., consistent) autonomic responses with shorter latency and greater magnitude autonomic responses.

Before 1970, heart rate responses were defined as rapid increases and decreases to discrete stimuli. These response patterns were interpreted as an autonomic correlate of an orienting response (see Graham & Clifton, 1966). Research was not directed at the physiological mechanisms that may mediate individual differences in autonomic reactivity. Observed variations in heart rate response characteristics were assumed to be dependent on both the physical parameters of the stimulus and the subject's previous history with the stimulus. Individual differences that could not be attributed to these two sources were treated as experimental (i.e., measurement) error.

In the early 1970s, our research demonstrated that individual differences in spontaneous base-level heart rate variability were related to heart rate reactivity. These studies stimulated our interest in the vagal mechanisms mediating heart rate variability and in the development of methods to quantify vagal influences on the heart. The first studies (Porges, 1972, 1973) demonstrated, in a sample of college students, that individual differences in heart rate variability assessed during baseline conditions were related to heart rate responses and reaction time performance. These studies were followed by experiments with newborn infants that demonstrated a relation between baseline heart rate variability and the magnitude of heart rate responses to simple visual and auditory stimuli. Newborn infants with higher baseline heart rate variability reacted with larger heart rate responses to the onset and offset of auditory stimuli (Porges, Arnold, & Forbes, 1973) and with shorter latency responses to the onset of an increase in illumination (Porges, Stamps, & Walter, 1974). When the illumination was decreased, only the high heart rate variability subjects responded. Consistent with these findings, only the neonates with higher heart rate variability exhibited a conditioned heart rate response (Stamps & Porges, 1975).

Reports from other studies measuring RSA are consistent with the theme that vagal tone is an index of reactivity. Porter, Porges, and Marshall (1988) demonstrated in a sample of normal newborns that individual differences in RSA were correlated with heart rate reactivity to circumcision. Neonates with higher amplitude RSA exhibited not only larger heart rate accelerations but also lower fundamental cry frequencies in response to the surgical procedures, the latter having been hypothesized to be associated with greater vagal influences (see Lester & Zeskind, 1982). Consistent with these findings, Porter and Porges (1988) demonstrated in premature infants that individual differences in RSA tone are related to the heart rate response during lumbar punctures.

Behavioral reactivity and irritability in response to environmental stimuli assessed with the Neonatal Behavioral Assessment Scale (Brazelton, 1984) are also associated with vagal tone. In a sample of full-term healthy neonates, DiPietro, Larson, and Porges (1987) found that neonates who were breast-fed had higher amplitude RSA, were more reactive, and required more effort to test. DiPietro and Porges (1991) evaluated the relation between RSA and behavioral reactivity to gavage with a sample of preterm neonates. Gavage is a commonly used method to feed premature infants by passing food through a tube inserted into the stomach via the nasal or oral passages. Individual differences in RSA were significantly correlated with behavioral reactivity to the gavage method of feeding.

Similar relations between RSA and reactivity have been reported for older infants. Linnemeyer and Porges (1986) found that 6-month-old infants with higher amplitude RSA were more likely to look longer at novel stimuli, and only those with high-amplitude RSA exhibited significant heart rate reactivity to the visual stimuli. Richards (1985, 1987) reported convergent findings that infants with higher amplitude RSA were less distractible and had larger decelerative heart rate responses to visual stimuli. Huffman et al. (1998) observed that high-amplitude RSA at 3 months of age habituated to novel visual stimuli more rapidly than those with low-amplitude RSA; the former were more likely to suppress RSA during attention-demanding tasks and received a better attention score than the latter.

In summary, vagal tone mediates the behavioral and emotional response of the organism, and the RSA, as an index of vagal tone, provides a measure of behavioral and emotional reactivity. Neonates, infants, children, and adults with higher amplitude RSA exhibit appropriate autonomic reactivity and, in turn, appropriate behavioral, autonomic, and emotional responses to stimulation.

Expression of Emotion

Few studies have investigated individual differences in vagal tone as a mediating variable indexing individual differences in facial expressivity. There are two important reasons for posing this research question. First, both autonomic and facial responses have been theoretically associated with the expression of emotions. Second, measurement of RSA may provide an index of the neural organization necessary for facial expressions—a hypothesis suggested by the nature of the neurophysiological mechanisms that mediate facial expressions and autonomic reactions. Facial expressions and autonomic reactions associated with emotion states are controlled by brainstem structures that are in close proximity (i.e., the source nuclei of the facial nerve and the vagus). Quite often the facial nerve is included as the part of the "vagus complex." Therefore, if expressivity is assumed to be an individual difference determined by the neural tone of the facial nerve, measurement of the neural tone of the vagus might be related to the expressivity of the infant. Thus, vagal tone, monitored during a nonstressed period, might index a neural propensity to produce facial expressions.

Support for this hypothesis comes from studies that have related resting levels of heart rate variability to expressivity. Field, Woodson, Greenberg, and Cohen (1982) reported that newborn infants exhibiting greater resting heart rate variability were more expressive, and Fox and Gelles (1984) found that 3-month-old infants with higher resting heart rate variability displayed a longer duration of interest expressions. Consistent with these findings, Stifter, Fox, and Porges (1989) evaluated the relation between RSA and expressivity in 5-month-old infants and found that infants with higher amplitude RSA displayed more interest, more joy, and more look-away behaviors toward the stranger.

Self-Regulation

Self-regulation is a difficult process to operationalize. Behaviors as diverse as sustained attention, facial expressions, and latency to soothe can be interpreted as regulatory. Several studies have demonstrated the relation between measures of cardiac vagal tone and attention (for a review, see chapter 4). In general, higher vagal tone and proper suppression of vagal tone during an attention-demanding task are related to better performance. More important for the discussion of vagal tone and emotion self-regulation, indices of cardiac vagal tone (e.g., RSA) have also been shown to be related to the ability to self-soothe.

In both full-term and premature newborns, the ability to self-soothe is inversely related to vagal tone as measured by the amplitude of RSA. The higher vagal tone neonates are more irritable and exhibit greater difficulty in self-soothing. However, a subsequent increasing capacity to self-soothe is clearly seen in the high vagal tone neonates. One might speculate that the high vagal tone neonate's reactivity elicits more caregiving from the mother and that, once such an infant becomes physiologically stable, the capacity for self-soothing is consequently enhanced. Thus, the self-regulatory demands might be different for the neonate and for the older infant, and vagal tone might index this propensity to self-regulate under changing developmental demands. Support for this hypothesis comes from a study of 3-month-old infants that found significant relations between amplitude of RSA and soothability (Huffman et al., 1998); high base-level amplitude RSA was correlated with a low soothing score (i.e., little soothing was required) and a high Rothbart soothability score (i.e., distress was easily reduced).

The studies just summarized support the hypothesis that base-level vagal tone measured by the amplitude of RSA is an important determinant of self-regulatory autonomic and behavioral responses. Unfortunately, the relation is more complex, and there are infants with high vagal tone who do not suppress vagal tone under regulatory demands and who show poor emotion regulation (DeGangi, DiPietro, Greenspan, & Porges, 1991; Doussard-Roosevelt, Walker, Portales, Greenspan, & Porges, 1990). According to Greenspan (1991), infants older than 6 months of age who exhibit fussiness, irritability, poor self-calming, intolerance to change, and/or a hyperalert state of arousal are best described as being regulatory disordered.

Preliminary data suggest two important points about infants with regulatory disorders. First, these infants tend to have high vagal tone. Second, these infants tend to exhibit a deficit in the ability to suppress vagal tone during attention-demanding situations. Assessed at 9 months of age, this inability to suppress vagal tone predicts behavior problems at 3 years (see chapter 7) and at 54 months (Dale et al., in press). It appears that these "fussy babies" are hyperreactive not only to environmental stimuli but also to visceral feedback. The relation between higher vagal tone and greater reactivity is supported, but the relation between vagal tone and the ability to self-regulate, assessed via behavior and the suppression of vagal tone during tasks, is not consistent with that observed with normal infants.

CONCLUSIONS

What does vagal tone convey about an individual's ability to regulate and express emotion? To answer this question, we have proposed a model that integrates information regarding lateral brain function with the regulation of the peripheral autonomic nervous system. The model is based on the following observations.

1. The peripheral autonomic nervous system is asymmetrical.
2. The medullary regulation of the autonomic nervous system is also asymmetrical, with structures on the right side exhibiting greater control of physiological responses associated with emotion.
3. The right nucleus ambiguus is a source nucleus of the right vagus, which provides control of the larynx and SA node of the heart and controls vocal intonation and cardiac vagal tone.
4. The right central nucleus of the amygdala has direct influences on the right nucleus ambiguus to promote the laryngeal and cardiovascular responses associated with emotion (e.g., increased pitch of vocalization and increased heart rate).
5. Stimuli that are processed primarily by the right hemisphere produce

greater cardiovascular responses than stimuli processed by the left hemisphere.
6. Damage to the right hemisphere blunts facial expression, vocal intonation, and autonomic reactivity.

Although each of these points has been documented, only recently has an experiment tested the proposed model linking vagal tone to right hemispheric regulation of emotion (Dufey, Hrtado, Fernandez, Manes, & Ibanez, in press). Since RSA is a sensitive measure of the input to the SA node from the right nucleus ambiguus, it provides a noninvasive measure of right hemisphere capacity to process emotion stimuli and to regulate emotional responses. To test this model adequately, it will be necessary to conduct experiments to evaluate measures of vagal tone and vagal reactivity of individuals with known right hemisphere disorders and evaluate covariations between individual differences in vagal tone and vagal reactivity and the expression and interpretation of emotions in non–brain-damaged subjects.

Providing evidence in support of this model, previous studies have addressed the relation between RSA and three dimensions related to the expression and regulation of emotion: reactivity, expressivity, and self-regulation. The literature and our ongoing research permit the following generalizations.

First, independent of developmental stage, RSA as an index of cardiac vagal tone is highly correlated with autonomic reactivity; individuals with higher amplitude RSA consistently exhibit larger and more reliable autonomic responses. Second, the relation between RSA and emotion expressivity appears to be dependent on development. A preliminary study has demonstrated that higher amplitude RSA was associated with greater facial expressivity in 5-month-old infants but failed to establish any such relation in 10-month-old infants. These data suggest that there is a developmental shift in the neurophysiological control of facial expressivity: as infants become older, facial expressivity may become more dependent on higher brain control and less related to individual differences in brainstem function, manifest in the tonic outflow of cranial nerves (see chapter 8).

Third, independent of developmental stage, RSA is correlated with self-regulation. Individuals with high-amplitude RSA consistently suppress RSA or heart rate variability to enhance the intake of information from the environment. Fourth, there is a subset of individuals who have high vagal tone and who do not suppress RSA or heart rate variability during information processing. These individuals appear to have a *regulatory* disorder that is displayed on both behavioral and physiological levels; regulatory disordered infants are often labeled as *fussy* because of their continuous crying and disorganized behaviors, and they have difficulty self-soothing and maintaining a calm state (Dale et al., in press).

Finally, as the infant matures, the range of expressivity increases, the self-regulation of emotion is enhanced, and vagal tone increases; in the course of normal development, the increased myelination and regulation of autonomic function associated with enhanced vagal tone parallels the range and control of emotion states (see chapter 8). Thus, on both developmental and individual difference levels, vagal tone is clearly related to the processes of reactivity, expressivity, and self-regulation.

We introduce vagal tone as a physiological construct that is useful in explaining individual and developmental differences in the expression and regulation of emotion. As an organizing construct, vagal tone is useful in integrating central, autonomic, and psychological components of emotion. Vagal tone, as measured by RSA, may index individual differences in the homeostatic capacity of the autonomic nervous system to foster rapid expression and attenuation of sympathetic reactions. This function is dependent on neural regulation of the reciprocal relation between the antagonistic branches of the autonomic nervous system.

During emotion states, normal homeostatic function is perturbed to express emotions. Initially, sympathetic activity is expressed owing primarily to the withdrawal of the antagonistic vagal tone. Even without discrete sympathetic excitation, the vagal withdrawal will enhance the expression of sympathetic activity when the two systems have antagonistic influences on specific organs. The vagal withdrawal triggers the autonomic correlates of emotions.

If the emotion state is prolonged, the physiological state will be maintained by activation of sympathetic and endocrine systems. Excessive sympathetic activity reflects a deviation from normal homeostatic autonomic function, which then elicits vagal activity to self-regulate and return the autonomic state to homeostasis. In individuals with high vagal tone and appropriate vagal regulation capacities, the autonomic nervous system has the capacity to react (i.e., appropriate reactivity and expressivity) and to return rapidly to homeostasis (i.e., self-regulation and self-soothing).

The relation among the right hemisphere, the right vagus, and the processes involved in the expression and regulation of motion, emotion, and communication makes apparent the relevance of examining RSA in studies of emotion regulation. RSA and RSA regulation in the context of the vagal circuit of emotion regulation that we proposed may provide the physiological measures of the individual's ability to regulate motion, emotion, and communication.

SUMMARY

On the basis of current knowledge of neuroanatomy and our previous research with cardiac vagal tone, we have proposed the vagal circuit of emotion regulation. The vagal circuit of emotion regulation incorporates lateral brain function with the regulation of the peripheral autonomic nervous system in the expression of emotion. The vagus and the vagal circuit do not function independently of other neurophysiological and neuroendocrine systems. Research on brain activity (see Dawson, 1994; Fox, 1994) and research on adrenocortical activity (see

Stansbury & Gunnar, 1994) demonstrate that cortisol levels are related to emotion states and to individual differences similar to those that we have investigated.

The vagal circuit emphasizes not only the vagus but also the lateralization of specific brain structures in emotion regulation. The emphasis of the vagal circuit on right-brainstem structures stimulates several testable hypotheses regarding the function of specific structures in the right brain in emotion regulation. These speculations are consistent with other reports (see Dawson, 1994; Fox, 1994) describing asymmetrical EEG activity during expressed emotions. Moreover, the vagal circuit does not exist independently of the brain structures and peptides systems regulating cortisol (see Stansbury & Gunnar, 1994). Areas in the brainstem (see chapters 12 and 19) regulating vagal activity are also sensitive to the peptides that regulate cortisol (e.g., oxytocin, vasopressin, and corticotropin-releasing hormone).

In this chapter, we have provided information regarding the relation between vagal tone and emotion regulation. A review of research indicates that baseline levels of RSA and RSA reactivity are associated with behavioral measures of reactivity, the expression of emotion, and self-regulation skills. Thus, we propose that cardiac vagal tone (i.e., RSA) can serve as an index of emotion regulation.

Historically, the vagus and other components of the parasympathetic nervous system have not been incorporated in theories of emotion. Recent developments in methodology have enabled us to define and accurately quantify cardiac vagal tone. Theories relating the parasympathetic nervous system to the expression and regulation of emotion are now being tested in several laboratories.

Co-authors for this chapter were J. A. Doussard-Roosevelt and A. K. Maiti.

CHAPTER 10

Emotion: An Evolutionary By-Product of the Neural Regulation of the Autonomic Nervous System

A new theory, the polyvagal theory of emotion, is presented which links the evolution of the autonomic nervous system to affective experience, emotional expression, vocal communication, and contingent social behavior. The polyvagal theory is derived from the well-documented phylogenetic shift in the neural regulation of the autonomic nervous system that expands the capacity of the organism to control metabolic output. The theory emphasizes the phylogenetic dependence of the structure and function of the vagus, the primary nerve of the parasympathetic nervous system. Three phylogenetic stages of neural development are described. The first stage is characterized by a primitive unmyelinated vegetative vagal system that fosters digestion and responds to novelty or threat by reducing cardiac output to protect metabolic resources. Behaviorally, this first stage is associated with immobilization behaviors. The second stage is characterized by a spinal sympathetic nervous system that can increase metabolic output and inhibit the primitive vagal system's influence on the gut to foster mobilization behaviors necessary for "fight or flight." The third stage, which is unique to mammals, is characterized by a myelinated vagal system that can rapidly regulate cardiac output to foster engagement and disengagement with the environment. The myelinated vagus originates in a brainstem area that evolved from the primitive gill arches and in mammals controls facial expression, sucking, swallowing, breathing, and vocalization. It is hypothesized that the mammalian vagal system fosters early mother–infant interactions and serves as the substrate for the development of complex social behaviors. In addition, the mammalian vagal system has an inhibitory effect on sympathetic pathways to the heart and thus promotes calm behavior and prosocial behavior.

The polyvagal theory of emotion proposes that the evolution of the autonomic nervous system provides the organizing principle to interpret the adaptive significance of affective processes. The theory proposes that the evolution of the mammalian autonomic nervous system, specifically the brainstem regulatory centers of the vagus and other related cranial nerves, provides substrates for emotional experiences and affective processes that are necessary for social behavior in mammals. In this context, the evolution of the nervous system limits or expands the ability to express emotions, which in turn may determine proximity, social contact, and the quality of communication. The polyvagal construct has been previously introduced (see chapter 2) to document the neurophysiological and neuroanatomical distinction between the two vagal branches and to propose their unique relation with behavioral strategies. This chapter elaborates on the polyvagal construct and proposes that affective strategies are derivative of the evolutionary process that produced the polyvagal regulation.

There is a consensus that affect is expressed in facial muscles and in organs regulated by the autonomic nervous system. However, with the exception of work by Cannon (1927, 1928), which focused on the sympathetic-adrenal system as the physiological substrate of emotion, the presumed neural regulation of affective state has not been investigated. Even contemporary researchers investigating affective signatures in the autonomic nervous system (Ax, 1953; Ekman, Levenson, & Friesen, 1983; Levenson, Ekman, & Friesen, 1990; Schachter, 1957) have tacitly accepted Cannon's assumption that emotions reflect responses of the sympathetic nervous system.

Unlike the architectural dictum that form (i.e., structure) follows function, *the function of the nervous system* is *derivative of structure*. The flexibility or variability of autonomic nervous system function is totally dependent on the structure. By mapping the phylogenetic development of the structures regulating autonomic function, it is possible to observe the dependence of autonomic reactivity on the evolution of the underlying structure of the nervous system. The phylogenetic approach highlights a shift in brainstem and cranial nerve morphology and function from an oxygen-sensitive system (i.e., the primitive gill arches) to a system that regulates facial muscles, cardiac output, and the vocal apparatus for affective communication.

CANNON'S BLUNDER

Cannon emphasized the idea that emotions were expressions of sympathetic-adrenal excitation. In limiting emotional experiences solely to the mobilization responses associated with sympathetic-adrenal activity, Cannon denied the importance of visceral feelings and neglected the contribution of the parasympathetic nervous system. Cannon's views were not compatible with earlier statements on the importance of visceral feedback and the parasympathetic nervous system. For example, in *The Expression of Emotions in Man and Animals*, Darwin (1872) acknowledged the importance of the bidirectional neural communication between the heart and the brain via the "pneumogastric" nerve. This, the Xth cranial nerve, is now called the vagus nerve and is the major component of the parasympathetic nervous system.

For Darwin, emotional state represented a covariation between facial expression and autonomic tone. However, he did not elucidate the specific neurophysiological mechanisms. Our current knowledge of the neuroanatomy, embryology, and phylogeny of the nervous system was not available to Darwin. At that time, it was not known that vagal fibers originated in several medullary nuclei, that branches of the vagus exerted control over the periphery through different feedback systems, and that the function of the branches of the vagus followed a phylogenetic principle. However, Darwin's statement is important, because it emphasizes afferent feedback from the heart to the brain, independent of the spinal cord and the sympathetic nervous system, as well as the regulatory role of the vagus in the expression of emotions.

The autonomic nervous system is related to visceral state regulation and the regulation of behaviors associated with mobilization or immobilization. For example, sympathetic excitation is clearly linked to mobilization. In vertebrates, the sympathetic nervous system is characterized by a trunk or column of ganglia paralleling the segmentation of the spinal cord. Skeletal motor pathways to the limbs are paralleled by sympathetic fibers to facilitate the metabolically demanding behaviors related to fight or flight. In fact, from Cannon's perspective and to many who followed, the sympathetic nervous system, due to its mobilizing capacity, was the component of the autonomic nervous system associated with emotion. This, however, neglected the autonomic components of affective experiences that were metabolically conservative, including processes such as signaling via facial expressions and vocalizations or specific immobilization responses.

AUTONOMIC DETERMINANTS OF EMOTION

Over the past 100 years we have learned much about the autonomic nervous system, its evolutionary origins, and how it relates to emotion. Initially, we can distinguish among three components of the autonomic nervous system (visceral afferents, sympathetic nervous system, and parasympathetic nervous system) and speculate how each might be related to affective experiences. First, the visceral afferents may be assumed to play a major role in determining "feelings." These mechanisms, which provide us with knowledge of hunger, also may convey a sense of nausea during emotional distress. We frequently hear subjective reports of individuals feeling "sick to their stomach" during periods of severe emotional strain associated with profound negative experiences. Similarly, negative states have been associated with reports of breathlessness or feelings that the heart has stopped. Second, the sympathetic nervous system and adrenal activity are associated with mobilization. Activation of the sympathetic nervous system is usually linked to increased skeletal movement of the major limbs. Thus, consistent with Cannon, the sympathetic nervous system provides the metabolic resources required for fight-or-flight behaviors. The sympathetic nervous system enhances mobilization by increasing cardiac output and decreasing the metabolic demands of the digestive tract by actively inhibiting gastric motility. Third, as proposed by Darwin and Bernard, the parasympathetic nervous system and specifically the vagus are related to emotional state. Few researchers have investigated the link between parasympathetic activity and affective state. However, over the last decade my laboratory has focused on this issue. We documented that cardiac vagal tone, a component of parasympathetic control, is related to affect and affect regulation (see chapter 9; Porges, 1991; Porges & Doussard-Roosevelt, 1997). We presented theoretical models explaining the importance of vagal regulation in the development of appropriate social behavior (see chapter 7). The parasympathetic nervous system is generally associated with fostering growth and restoration (Porges, 1992, 1995). Moreover, knowledge of the polyvagal system allows an appreciation of the importance of the brainstem origin of the specific vagal fibers in the determination of affective and behavioral response strategies (see chapter 7; Porges, Doussard-Roosevelt, Portales, & Suess, 1994).

Researchers and clinicians have had difficulties in the organization or categorization of intensive affective states that appear to have totally different etiologies or behavioral expressions. For example, intense feelings of terror might result in total immobilization or freezing. By contrast, intense feelings of anger or anxiety might be associated with massive mobilization activity. This problem exists, in part, because of a bias toward explanations of affective states defined in terms of either overt behavior such as facial expression (i.e., following Darwin) or sympathetic activity (i.e., following Cannon). The emphasis on sympathetic activity is based on three historical factors. First, theories regarding emotions have minimized or totally neglected the parasympathetic nervous system. Second, Cannon's focus on the sympathetic efferents and mobilization responses associated with fight or flight as the sole domain of autonomic reactivity during emotional states has not been challenged. Third, the database of autonomic correlates of affect, collected to identify autonomic "signatures" of specific affective states, is dominated by measures assumed to be related to sympathetic function (Ax, 1953; Ekman et al., 1983; Levenson et al., 1990; Schachter, 1957).

EVOLUTION OF THE AUTONOMIC NERVOUS SYSTEM: EMERGENT STRUCTURES FOR THE EXPRESSION OF EMOTIONS IN MAN AND ANIMALS

Although there is an acceptance that the autonomic nervous system and the face play a role in emotional expression, there is great uncertainty regarding the autonomic "signature" of specific or discrete emotions. Most researchers evaluating autonomic responses during affective experiences assumed, as Cannon did, that the sympathetic nervous system was the determinant of emotion or at least the primary physiological covariate of emotion. This, of course, neglects the potential role of the parasympathetic nervous system and its neurophysiological affinity to facial structures, including facial muscles, eye movements, pupil dilation, salivation, swallowing, vocalizing, hearing, and breathing. By investigating the evolution of the autonomic nervous system, we may gain insight into the interface between autonomic function and facial expression. In the following sections, the phylogenetic development of the autonomic nervous system will be used as an organizing principle to categorize affective experiences.

The polyvagal theory of emotion is derived from investigations of the evolution of the autonomic nervous system. The theory includes several rules and assumptions.

1. Emotion depends on the communication between the autonomic nervous system and the brain; visceral afferents convey information on physiological state to the brain and are critical to the sensory or psychological experience of emotion, and cranial nerves and the sympathetic nervous system are outputs from the brain that provide somatomotor and visceromotor control of the expression of emotion.
2. Evolution has modified the structures of the autonomic nervous system.
3. Emotional experience and expression are functional derivatives of structural changes in the autonomic nervous system due to evolutionary processes.
4. The mammalian autonomic nervous system retains vestiges of phylogenetically older autonomic nervous systems.
5. The phylogenetic "level" of the autonomic nervous system determines affective states and the range of social behavior.
6. In mammals, the autonomic nervous system response strategy to challenge follows a phylogenetic hierarchy, starting with the newest structures and, when all else fails, reverting to the most primitive structural system.

This chapter focuses on the phylogenetic shift in the neural regulation of the vertebrate heart. The heart has been selected because, in response to environmental challenge, cardiac output must be regulated to mobilize for fight-or-flight behaviors or to immobilize for death-feigning or hiding behaviors. To regulate cardiac output, several efferent structures have evolved. These structures represent two opposing systems: (1) a sympathetic-catecholamine system including chromaffin tissue and spinal sympathetics; and (2) a vagal system (a component of the parasympathetic nervous system) with branches originating in medullary source nuclei (i.e., dorsal motor nucleus of the vagus and nucleus ambiguus). In addition, vertebrates have chromaffin tissue containing high concentrations of catecholamines. Chromaffin tissue is defined as having morphological and histochemical properties similar to those of the adrenal medulla. Classes of vertebrates that do not have an adrenal medulla have relatively more chromaffin tissue, which regulates circulating catecholamines.

Table 10.1 lists the regulatory structures that influence the heart in vertebrates (Morris & Nilsson, 1994; Santer, 1994; Taylor, 1992). Two phylogenetic princi-

TABLE 10.1. Method of Cardiac Control as a Function of Vertebrate Phylogeny

	CHM	DMX	SNS	ADN	NA
Cyclostomes					
Myxinoids	x+				
Lamproids	x+	x+			
Elasmobranchs	x+	x–			
Teleosts	x+	x–	x+		
Amphibians	x+	x–	x+		
Reptiles	x+	x–	x+	x+	
Mammals	x+	x–	x+	x+	x–

Abbreviations: CHM = chromaffin tissue; DMX = vagal pathways originating in the dorsal motor nucleus of the vagus; SNS = spinal sympathetic nervous system; ADN = adrenal medulla; NA = vagal pathways originating in the nucleus ambiguus; + = increases cardiac output; – = decreases cardiac output.

ples can be extracted from Table 10.1. First, there is a phylogenetic pattern in the regulation of the heart from endocrine communication, to unmyelinated nerves, and finally to myelinated nerves. Second, there is a development of opposing neural mechanisms of excitation and inhibition to provide rapid regulation of graded metabolic output.

In the most primitive fish, the cyclostomes, the neural control of the heart is very primitive. Some cyclostomes such as the myxinoids (hagfish) use circulating catecholamines from chromaffin tissue to provide the sole excitatory influences on the heart. Other cyclostomes such as the lampetroids (lampreys) have a cardiac vagus. However, in contrast to all other vertebrates that have a cardioinhibitory vagus that acts via postganglionic muscarinic cholinoceptors, the cyclostome vagal innervation is excitatory and acts via nicotinic cholinoceptors. One striking feature of the cyclostome heart is the location of chromaffin tissue within the heart that stores large quantities of epinephrine and norepinephrine. As in other vertebrates, the circulating catecholamines produced by the chromaffin tissue stimulate beta-adrenergic receptors in the heart. Thus, the cyclostomes appear to have only excitatory mechanisms to regulate the heart.

The elasmobranchs (cartilaginous fish) are the first vertebrates to have a cardioinhibitory vagus. The vagus in these fish is inhibitory and the cholinoceptors on the heart are muscarinic as they are in other vertebrates. The cardioinhibitory vagus is functional in the elasmobranchs as a response to hypoxia. In conditions of hypoxia, metabolic output is adjusted by reducing heart rate. This modification of neural regulation may provide a mechanism to enable the elasmobranchs to increase their territorial range, by providing a neural mechanism that adjusts metabolic output to deal with changes in water temperature and oxygen availability. However, unlike more evolutionarily advanced fish or tetrapods, elasmobranchs do not have direct sympathetic input to the heart. Instead, cardiac acceleration and increases in contractility are mediated via beta-adrenergic receptors stimulated by circulating catecholamines released from chromaffin tissue. Thus, because activation of metabolic output is driven by circulating catecholamines and not by direct neural innervation, once the excitatory system is triggered, the ability to self-soothe or calm is limited.

In vertebrates with sympathetic and vagal neural innervation, vagal influences to the sinoatrial node inhibit or dampen the sympathetic influence and promote rapid decreases in metabolic output (Vanhoutte & Levy, 1979) that enable almost instantaneous shifts in behavioral state. As a whole, the teleosts may be considered phylogenetically the first class of vertebrates with both sympathetic and parasympathetic neural control of the heart, with innervation similar to that found in tetrapods. This enables rapid transitory changes in metabolic output, permitting changes from mobilization to immobilization. These are observed as "darting" and "freezing" behaviors. Amphibians, similar to the teleosts, have dual innervation of the heart via systems with direct neural components from the spinal cord via the sympathetic chain, producing increases in heart rate and contractility, and direct neural pathways from the brainstem via the vagus, producing cardioinhibitory actions.

True adrenal glands, in which a distinct medulla is formed of chromaffin tissue, are only present in birds, reptiles, and mammals (Santer, 1994). Neural regulation by the spinal sympathetics of the adrenal medulla provides a neural mechanism for rapid and controlled release of epinephrine and norepinephrine to stimulate cardiovascular function. In teleosts, chromaffin tissue is primarily related to parts of the cardiovascular system, but chromaffin tissue is also associated with the kidney. However, in amphibians, chromaffin tissue is primarily associated with the kidney, and substantial aggregations of chromaffin cells are located along the sympathetic chain ganglia. Thus, we can observe a phylogenetic shift in the location of chromaffin tissue and the concurrent evolution of a distinct adrenal medulla near the kidney.

In mammals, the morphology of the vagus changes (see chapter 2). Unlike that of all other vertebrates with cardioinhibitory vagi, the mammalian vagus contains two branches. One branch originates in the dorsal motor nucleus of the vagus and provides primary neural regulation of subdiaphragmatic organs, such as the digestive tract. However, at the level of the heart, the dorsal motor nucleus of the vagus does not play a major role in normal dynamic regulation of cardiac output. Rather, during embryological development in mammals, cells from the dorsal motor nucleus of the vagus migrate ventrally and laterally to the nucleus ambiguus (Schwaber, 1986) where they form the cell bodies for visceromotor myelinated axons that provide potent inhibition of the sinoatrial node, the pacemaker for the heart.

By transitory down-regulation of the cardioinhibitory vagal tone to the heart (i.e., removal of the vagal brake), mammals are capable of rapid increases in cardiac output without activating the sympathetic-adrenal system. By engaging this system rather than the sympathetic-adrenal system, mammals have the opportunity to rapidly increase metabolic output for immediate mobilization. Under prolonged challenge, the sympathetic system also may be activated. However, by rapidly reengaging the vagal system, mammals can inhibit sympathetic input on the heart (Vanhoutte & Levy, 1979) and rapidly decrease metabolic output to self-soothe and calm.

PHYLOGENETIC DEVELOPMENT OF THE AUTONOMIC NERVOUS SYSTEM: AN ORGANIZING PRINCIPLE FOR HUMAN EMOTION

Inspection of Table 10.1, which summarizes the primary regulatory structures of the heart in vertebrates, provides a basis for speculation on the behavioral repertoire of various classes of vertebrates. These speculations support the premise that the phylogenetic development of the autonomic nervous system provides an organizing principle for affective experiences and determines the limits on social behavior and, therefore, the possibility of affiliation. Phylogenetic development generally results in increased neural control of the heart via mechanisms that can rapidly increase or decrease metabolic output. This phylogenetic course results in greater central nervous system regulation of behavior, especially behaviors to engage and disengage with environmental challenges.

To further focus on the impact of phylogenetic development of the neural regulation of the autonomic nervous system, we can observe five phylogenetically dependent response systems: (1) a *chemical excitatory system* via the catecholamine-rich chromaffin tissue to increase cardiac output and to support mobilization; (2) an *inhibitory vagal system* via the dorsal motor nucleus of the vagus to reduce cardiac output when metabolic resources are scarce and to support immobilization in response to danger; (3) a *spinal sympathetic nervous system* to provide neural excitation to promote rapid mobilization for behaviors associated with fight or flight; (4) a neurally regulated *adrenal medulla system* to provide more direct control over the release of circulating catecholamines to support mobilization for the prolonged metabolic requirements of fight-or-flight behaviors; and (5) the specialization of the *mammalian vagal system* into a "tonic" inhibitory system that allows graded withdrawal of the vagal brake, which can promote transitory mobilization and the expression of sympathetic tone without requiring sympathetic or adrenal activation. With this new vagal system, transitory incursions into the environment can be initiated without the severe biological price of either metabolic shutdown, via primitive vagal inhibition, or metabolic excitation, via sympathetic-adrenal activation.

The five phylogenetically dependent response systems are associated with three neuroanatomical constructs related to affective experience and expression: (1) dorsal vagal complex (DVC), (2) sympathetic nervous system (SNS), and (3) ventral vagal complex (VVC). Each of these three neural constructs is linked to a specific emotion subsystem observable in humans. Each emotion subsystem is manifested via differentiated motor output from the central nervous system to

TABLE 10.2. Physiological Functions Associated With Each Subsystem of the Autonomic Nervous System

	VVC	SNS	DVC
Heart rate	+/–	+	–
Bronchi	+/–	+	–
Gastrointestinal		–	+
Vasoconstriction		+	
Sweat		+	
Adrenal medulla		+	
Vocalization	+/–		
Facial muscles	+/–		

Abbreviations: VVC = ventral vagal complex; SNS = sympathetic nervous system; DVC = dorsal vagal complex. DVC slows heart rate, constricts bronchi, and stimulates gastrointestinal function. SNS increases heart rate, dilates bronchi, inhibits gastrointestinal function, promotes vasoconstriction, increases sweating, and activates catecholamine release from the adrenal medulla. Depending on the degree of neural tone, VVC either slows or speeds heart rate, constricts or dilates bronchi, lowers or raises vocalization pitch, and increases or decreases facial expressivity.

perform specific adaptive functions: to immobilize and to conserve metabolic resources, to mobilize in order to obtain metabolic resources, or to signal with minimal energy expense. The constituent responses associated with each subsystem are listed in Table 10.2.

THE DORSAL VAGAL COMPLEX: A VESTIGIAL IMMOBILIZATION SYSTEM

The DVC is primarily associated with digestive, taste, and hypoxic responses in mammals. It includes the nucleus tractus solitarius (NTS) and the interneuronal communication between the NTS and the dorsal motor nucleus of the vagus (DMX). The efferents for the DVC originate in the DMX, and primary vagal afferents terminate in the NTS. The DVC provides primary neural control of subdiaphragmatic visceral organs. It provides low tonic influences on the heart and bronchi. This low tonic influence is the vestige from the reptilian vagal control of the heart and lung. In contrast to reptiles, mammals have a great demand for oxygen and are vulnerable to any depletion in oxygen resources. The metabolic demand for mammals is approximately five times greater than that for reptiles of equivalent body weight (Else & Hulbert, 1981). Thus, reptilian dependence on this system provides a shutdown of metabolic activity to conserve resources during diving or death feigning. The DVC provides inhibitory input to the sinoatrial node of the heart via unmyelinated fibers and thus is less tightly controlled than the myelinated fibers from the VVC. Hypoxia or perceived loss of oxygen resources appears to be the main stimulus that triggers the DVC. Once triggered, severe bradycardia and apnea are observed, often in the presence of defecation. This response strategy is observed in the hypoxic human fetus. Although adaptive for the reptile, hypoxic triggering of this system may be lethal for mammals. In addition, it is important to note that the DVC has beneficial functions in humans. Under most normal conditions, the DVC maintains tone to the gut and promotes digestive processes. However, if up-regulated, the DVC contributes to pathophysiological conditions, including the formation of ulcers via excess gastric secretion and colitis. Research supports the importance of the unmyelinated vagal fibers in bradycardia (Daly, 1991) and suggests the possibility that massive bradycardia may be determined by the unmyelinated vagal fibers associated with the DVC recruiting myelinated vagal fibers to maximize the final vagal surge on the heart (Jones, Wang, & Jordan, 1995).

THE SYMPATHETIC NERVOUS SYSTEM: ADAPTIVE MOBILIZATION SYSTEM FOR FIGHT-OR-FLIGHT BEHAVIORS

The SNS is primarily a system of mobilization. It prepares the body for emergency by increasing cardiac output, stimulating sweat glands to protect and lubricate the skin, and inhibiting the metabolically costly gastrointestinal tract. The evolution of the sympathetic nervous system follows the segmentation of the spinal cord, with cell bodies of the preganglionic sympathetic motor neurons located in the lateral horn of the spinal cord. The sympathetic nervous system has long been associated with emotion. The label "sympathetic" reflects the historical identity of this system as a nervous system "with feelings" and contrasts it with the parasympathetic nervous system, a label that reflects a nervous system that "guards against feelings."

THE VENTRAL VAGAL COMPLEX: THE MAMMALIAN SIGNALING SYSTEM FOR MOTION, EMOTION, AND COMMUNICATION

The primary efferent fibers of the VVC originate in the nucleus ambiguus. The primary afferent fibers of the VVC terminate in the source nuclei of the facial and trigeminal nerves. The VVC has primary control of supradiaphragmatic visceral organs including the larynx, pharynx, bronchi, esophagus, and heart. Motor pathways from the VVC to visceromotor organs (e.g., heart and bronchi) and somatomotor structures (e.g., larynx, pharynx, and esophagus) are myelinated to provide tight control and speed in responding. In mammals, visceromotor fibers to the heart express high levels of tonic control and are capable of rapid shifts in cardioinhibitory tone to provide dynamic changes in metabolic output to match environmental challenges. This rapid regulation characterizes the qualities of the mammalian vagal brake that enable rapid engagement and disengagement in the environment without mobilizing the SNS.

A major characteristic of the VVC is that the neural fibers regulating somatomotor structures are derived from the branchial or primitive gill arches that evolved to form cranial nerves V, VII, IX, X, and XI. Somatomotor fibers originating in these cranial nerves control the branchiomeric muscles including facial muscles, muscles of mastication, neck muscles, larynx, pharynx, esophagus, and middle ear muscles. Visceromotor efferent fibers control salivary and lacrimal glands as well as the heart and bronchi. The primary afferents to the VVC come from facial and oral afferents traveling through the facial and trigeminal nerves and the visceral afferents, terminating in the NTS. The VVC is involved in the control and coordination of sucking, swallowing, and vocalizing with breathing.

EVOLUTION AND DISSOLUTION: HIERARCHICAL RESPONSE STRATEGY

The evolution of the autonomic nervous system provides substrates for the emergence of three emotion systems. This phylogenetic adjustment of the autonomic nervous system represents an exaptation (see Crews, 1997) of structures to express emotions that initially evolved in primitive vertebrates to extract oxygen from water, to oxygenate and transport blood, and to adjust metabolic output to match resources. The polyvagal theory of emotion is based on a phylogenetic model. The polyvagal theory of emotion proposes a hierarchical response strategy to challenge, with the most recent modifications employed first and the most primitive last. This phylogenetic strategy can be observed in our day-to-day interactions. Our social behavior follows a strategy that focuses initially on communication via facial expressions and vocalizations. The strategy has low metabolic demand and, if appropriately interpreted, results in contingent social interactions via verbal–facial mechanisms. Often, hand gestures and head movements contribute to increase the mammalian repertoire of communication-related behavior. An important characteristic of these prosocial behaviors is their low metabolic demand and the rapid contingent "switching" of transitory engagement to transitory disengagement strategies (i.e., speaking then switching to listening).

This phylogenetically based hierarchical response strategy is consistent with the concept of dissolution proposed by Jackson (1958) to explain diseases of the nervous system. Jackson proposed that "the higher nervous arrangements inhibit (or control) the lower, and thus, when the higher are suddenly rendered functionless, the lower rise in activity." This is observed in the polyvagal theory of emotion, not in terms of disease but in terms of response strategies to differential challenges to survival. The VVC with its mechanisms of "signaling" and "communication" provides the initial response to the environment. The VVC inhibits, at the level of the heart, the strong mobilization responses of the SNS. Withdrawal of VVC, consistent with Jackson's model, results in a "disinhibition" of the sympathetic control of the heart. Similarly, withdrawal of sympathetic tone results in a "disinhibition" of the DVC control of the gastrointestinal tract and a vulnerability of the bronchi and heart. There are several clinical consequences to unopposed DVC control, including defecation, due to relaxation of the sphincter muscles and increased motility of the digestive tract; apnea, due to constriction of the bronchi; and bradycardia, due to stimulation of the sinoatrial node. Thus, when all else fails, the nervous system elects a metabolically conservative course that is adaptive for primitive vertebrates but lethal to mammals. Consistent with the Jacksonian principle of dissolution, specific psychopathologies defined by affective dysfunction may be associated with autonomic correlates consistent with the three phylogenetic levels of autonomic regulation. The three levels do not function in an all-or-none fashion; rather, they exhibit gradations of control determined by both visceral feedback and higher brain structures.

UNVEILING DARWIN

Contemporary research and theory on emotion owes much to Darwin and his volume, *The Expression of Emotions in Man and Animals* (1872). Through careful and astute observations of facial expressions, Darwin insightfully interpreted emotional expressions within an evolutionary model of adaptation and natural selection. However, Darwin's knowledge of neurophysiology and neuroanatomy was limited. In contrast to Darwin's creative insights into the adaptive function of facial expression, his understanding of underlying physiological mechanisms and the linkage between facial muscles and emotion was synthetic and derivative. He repeatedly referenced the 1844 edition of *Anatomy and Philosophy of Expressions*, written by Sir Charles Bell, for physiological explanations of facial expression. As further support for the importance of facial muscles in emotional expressions, Darwin incorporated the work of Duchenne in his text. Duchenne conducted experiments by electrically stimulating the face of humans. Electrical stimulation of selected facial muscles provided expressions that were readily perceived as different emotional states.

In contrast to the polyvagal theory of emotion, which uses evolution of the autonomic nervous system as the primary organizing principle for the expression and experience of affect, Darwin's writings did not emphasize the importance of the nervous system as a structure involved in the evolution of emotion. Rather, he focused on affect as a functional system that responded to the determinants of evolution to produce the facial and vocal expressions of human emotion. Darwin neglected the importance of treating the nervous system as a structure that is vulnerable to the pressures of evolution. A choice between investigating affect as a functional behavioral system or investigating the structural determinants of affect (i.e., nervous system) was clearly made by researchers who followed Darwin. This research tradition followed the observational approach of organizing facial expression into affective categories. Although the physiological correlates of affect and facial expression were investigated (Ekman et al., 1983; Levenson et al., 1990; Stifter, Fox, & Porges, 1989). these investigations were made on a psychophysiological or correlative level and did not emphasize specific neural regulatory processes.

Consistent with the observational approach, Tomkins (1962, 1963) developed a theory of affect that emphasized the importance of the face not only as a structure of communication but also as a structure of self-feedback. Following Tomkins (1962, 1963), Ekman (1978) and Izard (1979) developed detailed coding systems for facial affect and have used these methods to study individual differences, developmental shifts, and the cross-cultural consistency of human facial expression,

Several contemporary theories of emotion have focused on facial expressions in a manner similar to that initially presented by Darwin. Rather than incorporating knowledge of neural regulation of the face or the evolution of neural regulation of autonomic function, researchers and theorists have attempted to organize information in terms of the functional significance of sequences or patterns of facial expressions. This difficult task, modeled on Darwin, often becomes bogged down in semantics, philosophical inconsistencies, and circularity. Darwin in his descriptions of emotions speculated and provided hypothetical examples of natural selection contributing to the uniqueness of species-specific affective response patterns. However, the terms selected to characterize specific emotions often vary from culture to culture. Tomkins and later Ekman and Izard promoted the description of affective experiences in terms of the specific facial muscles or groups of muscles involved in the facial expression. However, they then used subjective reports to label these facial expressions.

We may "unveil" Darwin by investigating the neural regulation that underlies facial expression. Facial expressions are controlled by cranial nerves. Motor pathways from the trigeminal nerve (V) control the muscles of mastication with branches to the temporalis, masseter, medial, and lateral pterygoid muscles. Motor pathways from the facial nerve (VII) control the muscles of facial expression, including zygomaticus, frontalis, orbicularis oculi, elevators, orbicularis oris, depressors, and platysma. The nucleus ambiguus serves as the source of cell bodies for motor pathways traveling through several cranial nerves, including the glossopharyngeal (IX), vagus (X), and accessory nerves (XI). Pathways from the glossopharyngeal nerve regulate pharyngeal muscles. Pathways from the vagus regulate the muscles of the pharynx and larynx, and pathways of the accessory nerve control the neck muscles, allowing rotation and tilting of the head. These cranial nerves are derivative from primitive gill arches (Gibbins, 1994; Langley, 1921) and may be collectively described as the ventral vagal complex. Thus, the evolutionary origins (i.e., primitive gill arches) of the somatomotor pathways traveling through these cranial nerves provide us with an organizing principle to understand affective expressions. In addition to the described neural regulation of somatomotor structures, these branchiomeric (i.e., derived from the primitive arches) cranial nerves also regulate the visceromotor processes associated with salivation, tearing, breathing, and heart rate.

Other cranial nerves contribute to the expression of emotions. The hypoglossal nerve (XII) innervates the muscles of the tongue. The trochlear (IV), abducens (VI), and oculomotor (III) nerves innervate muscles to provide movements of the eyes and eyelids. Thus, the facial expressions observed by Darwin, detailed by Tomkins, and coded by Ekman and Izard are a direct reflection of the regulation of the face by the cranial nerves.

VOODOO OR VAGUS DEATH? THE TEST OF THE POLYVAGAL THEORY

The polyvagal theory of emotion provides a theoretical framework to interpret the phenomenon of voodoo or fright death described by Cannon (1957) and Richter (1957). Cannon believed that extreme emotional stress, regardless of the specific behavioral manifestation, could be explained in terms of degree of sympathetic-adrenal excitation. In 1942, Cannon described a phenomenon known as voodoo death. Voodoo death was assumed to be directly attributable to emotional stress. Being wed to a sympathicoadrenal model of emotional experience (as just described), Cannon assumed that voodoo death would be the consequence of the state of shock produced by the continuous outpouring of epinephrine via excitation of the sympathetic nervous system. According to the Cannon model, the victim would be expected to breathe very rapidly and have a rapid pulse. The heart would beat fast and gradually lead to a state of constant contraction and, ultimately, to death in systole. Because his speculations were not empirically based, he offered the following challenge to test his model of voodoo death: "If in the future, however, any observer has opportunity to see an instance of 'voodoo death,' it is to be hoped that he will conduct the simpler tests before the victim's last gasp."

Richter responded to Cannon's challenge with an animal model. Rats were prestressed and placed in a closed turbulent water tank, and the latency to drowning was recorded. Most domestic laboratory rats lasted for several hours, whereas unexpectedly all of the wild rats died within 15 minutes. In fact, several wild rats dove to the bottom and, without coming to the surface, died. To test Cannon's hypothesis that stress-induced sudden death was sympathetic, Richter monitored heart rate and determined whether the heart was in systole or diastole after death. He assumed, on the basis of Cannon's speculations, that tachycardia would precede death and that at death the heart would be in a state of systole, reflecting the potent effects of sympathetic excitation on the pacemaker and the myocardium. However, Richter's data contradicted the Cannon model. Heart rate slowed prior to death, and at death the heart was engorged with blood, reflecting a state of diastole. Richter interpreted the data as demonstrating that the rats died a "vagus" death, the result of overstimulation of the parasympathetic system rather than the sympathicoadrenal system. However, Richter provided no physiological explanation except the speculation that the lethal vagal effect was related to a psychological state of "hopelessness."

The immediate and reliable death of the wild rats in Richter's experiment may represent a more global immobilization strategy. Sudden prolonged immobility or feigned death is an adaptive response exhibited by many mammalian species. Hofer (1970) demonstrated that several rodent species, when threatened, exhibited prolonged immobility accompanied by very slow heart rate. For some of the rodents, heart rate during immobility was less than 50% of the basal rate. During prolonged immobility, respiration became so shallow that it was difficult to observe, although the rate greatly accelerated. Although physiologically similar, Hofer distinguished between prolonged immobility and feigned death. The onset of feigned death was sudden with an apparent motor collapse during active struggling. Similar to Richter, Hofer interpreted this fear-induced slowing of heart rate as a vagal phenomenon. In support of this interpretation, he noted that of the four species that exhibited prolonged immobility, 71% of the subjects had cardiac arrhythmias of vagal origin; in contrast, in the two species that did not exhibit immobility behaviors, only 17% exhibited cardiac arrhythmias of vagal origin.

The polyvagal theory of emotion places Richter's and Hofer's observations in perspective. Following the Jacksonian principle of dissolution, the rodents would exhibit the following sequence of response strategies: (1) removal of VVC tone, (2) increase in sympathetic tone, and (3) a surge in DVC tone. The more docile domestic rats in Richter's experiment apparently progressed from removal of VVC tone, to increased sympathetic tone, and then death from exhaustion. However, the profile of the wild rats was different. Being totally unaccustomed to enclosure, handling, and also having their vibrissae cut, a mobilization strategy driven by increased sympathetic tone was not functional. Instead, these rats reverted to their most primitive system to conserve metabolic resources via DVC. This strategy promoted an immobilization response characterized by reduced motor activity, apnea, and bradycardia. Unfortunately, this mode of responding, although adaptive for reptiles, is lethal for mammals. Similarly, the onset of feigned death, as described by Hofer, illustrates the sudden and rapid transition from an unsuccessful strategy of struggling requiring massive sympathetic activation to the metabolically conservative immobilized state mimicking death associated with the DVC.

These data suggest that the vagus contributes to severe emotional states and may be related to emotional states of "immobilization" such as extreme terror. Application of the polyvagal approach enables the dissection of vagal processes into three strategic programs: (1) when tone of the VVC is high, the ability to communicate via facial expressions, vocalizations, and gestures exists; (2) when tone of the VVC is low, the sympathetic nervous system is unopposed and easily expressed to support mobilization such as fight-or-flight behaviors; and (3) when tone from DVC is high, immobilization and potentially life-threatening bradycardia, apnea, and cardiac arrhythmias occur.

CONCLUSION

Three important scientific propositions provide the basis for this theory. First, Darwin provided the concept of evolution and the processes that contribute to phylogenetic variation. Second, Jackson provided the concept of dissolution as a viable explanation for diseases of brain function. And, third, MacLean (1990) provided the concept that the human brain retains structures associated with phylogenetically more primitive organisms.

The polyvagal theory of emotion focuses on the evolution of the neural and neurochemical regulation of structures involved in the expression and experience of emotion as a theme to organize emotional experience and to understand the role of emotion in social behavior. Over 100 years ago Jackson, intrigued with Darwin's model of evolution, elaborated on how evolution in reverse, termed "dissolution," might be related to disease. According to Jackson, higher nervous system structures inhibit or control lower structures or systems and "thus, when the higher are suddenly rendered functionless, the lower rise in activity." The polyvagal theory of emotion follows this Jacksonian principle.

CHAPTER 11

Love: An Emergent Property of the Mammalian Autonomic Nervous System

There is no fear in love; but perfect love casteth out fear. —1 John 4:18

Love has had a variety of expressions. Foremost in our culture is the love between individuals of different genders. The products of this love are observed in terms of children, of cooperative and shared responsibilities to survive, of the transmitting of culture, and of pleasure and ecstasy. Although we assume that love is a unique human emotion, several neurobiological processes involved in the experience and expression of love are shared with other mammals. The phylogenetic origins of these processes reflect their antecedent adaptive function. In mammals, these processes have evolved into an integrated neurobehavioral system, which promotes proximity, reproduction, and physical safety. Central to the neural mediation of these processes is the autonomic nervous system. The focus of this chapter is to describe how the autonomic nervous system is involved in the processes associated with feelings of love and behaviors linked to reproduction. The chapter proposes a hypothetical model, which speculates that the phylogenetic changes in the autonomic nervous system are related to the emergence of two components of love: an appetitive phase associated with courting and seductive behaviors and a consummatory phase associate with passionate sexual behaviors and the establishment of enduring pair-bonds. According to this model, courting and seduction are dependent on phylogenetically newer structures. For example, the cortex, via corticobulbar pathways, regulates facial expressions and vocalizations to express availability to a prospective mate. In contrast, passionate visceral feelings are dependent on phylogenetically older structures, such as the hypothalamus and medulla, which involve phylogenetically more recent neuropeptides (oxytocin and vasopressin).

EVOLUTION AND DISSOLUTION: A HIERARCHICAL RESPONSE STRATEGY DURING MATE SELECTION

The evolution of the autonomic nervous system provides substrates for the emergence of the three emotion subsystems described above. Although reminiscent of the triune brain proposed by MacLean (1990), the polyvagal theory emphasizes that even the phylogenetically more primitive structures have changed in structure and function. This phylogenetic adjustment of the autonomic nervous system represents an exaptation (i.e. a shift in the function) of structures to express emotions. The ancient gill arches that characterize primitive vertebrates evolved into structures that convey emotional state via facial expressions, gestures and vocal communication.

The polyvagal theory emphasizes the phylogenetic changes in the autonomic nervous system. Specifically, as mammals evolved, the vagal regulation of the viscera was maintained by two vagal pathways. The second vagal circuit has myelinated efferent pathways and originates in the nucleus ambiguus, a nucleus ventral to the dorsal motor nucleus of the vagus. The ventral vagal circuit is described as the ventral vagal complex (VVC). The dorsal vagal circuit is shared with most other vertebrates and is described as the dorsal vagal complex (DVC). These two vagal circuits in concert with the sympathetic nervous system (SNS) form a hierarchical system regulating visceral organs. The polyvagal theory proposes a hierarchical response strategy to environmental challenges, with the most recent modifications employed first (i.e., VVC) and the most primitive (i.e., DVC) last. However, the response strategy is not all-or-none and may include transitional blends between the boundaries of the three emotion subsystems. These transitional blends may be determined by both visceral feedback and higher brain structures (including vasopressinergic and oxytocinergic pathways that communicate between the hypothalamus and the medullary source nuclei of the vagus). Thus, the neurophysiological substrate of specific states and behaviors may incorporate activation of more than one emotion subsystem. For example, sexual arousal, with features of facial and vocal expressiveness in concert with facial flush, sweating and tachycardia, may reflect a blend defined by the activation of the VVC and the SNS.

The proposed hierarchical response strategy provides a model for the exploration of human social behavior. This phylogenetic strategy can be observed in human mating strategies. Our mating behavior is usually initiated by communication via facial expressions and vocalizations, a strategy with low metabolic cost. If appropriately used, communication will determine availability, induce proximity and promote reproductive behavior. Or, the strategy will determine unavailability, induce social distance, and promote a search for another prospective mate. An important feature of this mate selection strategy is that it limits vulnerability and risk by allowing participants to rapidly switch between engagement and disengagement behaviors (i.e., speaking then switching to listening; moving toward then rapidly retreating).

This phylogenetically based hierarchical response strategy is consistent with the concept of dissolution proposed by John Hughlings Jackson (1958) to explain diseases of the nervous system. Jackson proposed that "the higher nervous arrangements inhibit (or control) the lower, and thus, when the higher are suddenly rendered functionless, the lower rise in activity." The polyvagal theory (see chapter 10) proposed dissolution, not in response to disease or brain trauma, but as a response strategy to differential challenges. The VVC with its mechanisms for signaling and communication provides the initial response to the environment. The VVC inhibits, at the level of the heart, the strong mobilization responses of the SNS. Withdrawal of the VVC, consistent with Jacksonian principles, results in a disinhibition of the sympathetic control of the heart. Similarly, withdrawal of sympathetic tone results in a disinhibition of the DVC control of the gastrointestinal tract and a vulnerability of the bronchi and heart. There are several clinical consequences to unopposed DVC control including defecation, due to a relaxation of the sphincter muscles and increased motility of the digestive tract; apnea, due to constriction of the bronchi; and bradycardia, due to stimulation of the sinoatrial node. Thus, when all else fails, the nervous system elects a metabolically conservative course that is adaptive for primitive vertebrates, but may be lethal for mammals. Consistent with the Jacksonian principle of dissolution, specific psychopathologies defined by affective dysfunction may be associated with autonomic correlates consistent with the three phylogenetic levels of autonomic regulation.

THE SOCIAL ENGAGEMENT SYSTEM: AN EMERGENT PROPERTY OF THE VENTRAL VAGAL COMPLEX

Phylogenetically, the VVC is the most recent neurophysiological affect system. The VVC is composed of a somatomotor component consisting of the special visceral efferents and a visceromotor component consisting of the myelinated vagal pathways from the nucleus ambiguus to the sinoatrial node of the heart and the bronchi. As illustrated in Figure 11.1, the special visceral efferents and the vagal brake collectively constitute an emergent social engagement system. The somatomotor components of the VVC contribute to the regulation of behaviors involved in exploration of the social environment (e.g., looking, listening, ingesting) and behaviors involved in acknowledging social contact (e.g., facial expressions, head gestures, and vocalizations). More specifically, the somatomotor components of the VVC are involved in head turning (via cranial nerve XI), vocalizations (IX, X), facial expression (VII, V), the filtering of low frequency sounds via the middle ear muscles to extract human voice from backgrounds sounds (VII) and mastication (V). The visceromotor components of the VVC contribute to the rapid modulation of vagal (X) control of the heart and the bronchi (X), which provides metabolic resources to engage and disengage in a social setting.

Three important features define the social engagement system. First, the efferent pathways that regulate the social engagement system originate in medul-

FIGURE 11.1. The social engagement system: social communication is determined by the cortical regulation of medullary nuclei via corticobulbar pathways. The social engagement system consists of a somatomotor component (special visceral efferent pathways that regulate the muscles of head) and a visceromotor component (the vagal brake that regulates the heart and bronchi).

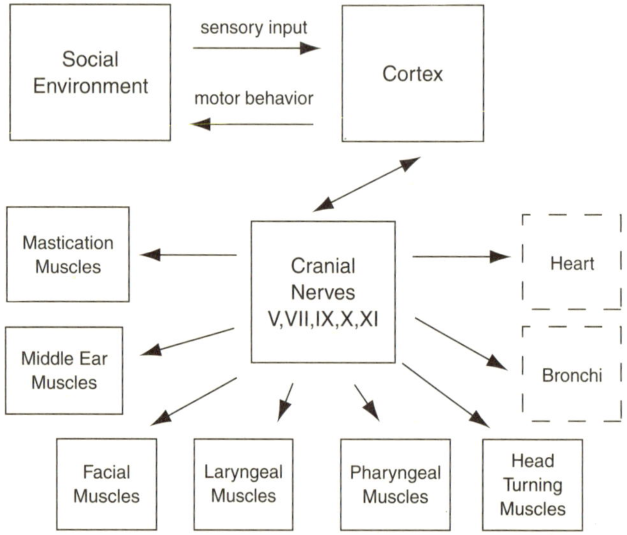

lary structures (i.e., nucleus of cranial nerve V, nucleus of cranial nerve VII, nucleus ambiguus). Second, corticobulbar pathways, which originate in frontal cortex (i.e., upper motor neurons), enable the possibility of efficient cortical regulation of these medullary source nuclei (i.e., lower motor neurons). Third, on the medullary level, the structures that regulate the efferent regulation of social communication behaviors neuroanatomically communicate with structures that regulate ingestion (e.g., sucking, swallowing, salivation) and cardiac output. Thus, modulation of the vagal brake may either promote calming and self-soothing states (i.e., attenuate the influence of the sympathetic influence on the heart) or support mobilization (i.e., potentiate the sympathetic influence on the heart).

Mammals have a unique vagal system that includes myelinated fibers that regulate heart rate. The mammalian vagus functions as an active vagal brake (see chapter 7) in which rapid inhibition and disinhibition of the vagal tone to the heart can change cardiac output to promote immediate engagement and disengagement with objects and individuals. Thus, the autonomic components, coincident with social interactions, may be mediated by changes in vagal tone to the heart, rather than the assumed changes in sympathetic arousal. Consistent with the polyvagal theory, difficulties in regulating the vagal brake may result in the phylogenetically older systems (i.e., neural regulation of the adrenal and the

SNS) being recruited to regulate metabolic output to deal with environmental challenges. Consistent with the polyvagal theory, during states of mobilization, characterized by classic "fight–flight" behaviors and sympathetic excitation, both the vagal brake and the behavioral components of the social engagement system are not easily accessible.

The functional impact of the mammalian vagus on the heart produces a heart rate pattern known as respiratory sinus arrhythmia (RSA). RSA is the rhythmic increase and decrease in heart rate observed at the frequency of spontaneous breathing. Because the brainstem nuclei that regulate the mammalian vagus are neuroanatomically and neurophysiologically linked to the brainstem source nuclei of the special visceral efferents that regulate facial expression, monitoring dynamic changes in RSA and heart rate (i.e., the vagal brake) provides an efficient and noninvasive method of assessing the status of the social engagement system.

COURTING AND SEDUCTION: SPECIALIZED FUNCTIONS OF THE SOCIAL ENGAGEMENT SYSTEM

Seduction and courting behaviors convey an invitation to reduce physical and psychological distance. Primates express this invitation via cortical regulation of the brainstem source nuclei of the VVC that control facial expressions, head movements, and vocalizations. Mammalian social behaviors appear to be an emergent property of the cortical regulation of the VVC and the peripheral structures identified in Figure 11.1. Courting and other behaviors of social engagement require direct cortical modulation of the medullary source nuclei of the VVC. This cortical regulation of the brainstem inhibits protective and defensive response strategies that are dependent on subcortical structures (e.g., amygdala, hypothalamus). However, courting and other expressions of social behavior are not independent of neurophysiological state. When the brainstem is under subcortical control, such as in states associated with fight-or-flight behaviors, cardiac output is increased by activation of the SNS to support the mobilization behaviors necessary to avoid or to respond to potential conflict. During these states, cortical modulation of the visceromotor control of the heart (i.e., the vagal brake) would substantially reduce cardiac output and compromise the effectiveness of the adaptive fight-or-flight behaviors. Thus, cortical regulation of the VVC requires the setting to be perceived as safe. The perception of safety, or at least the lack of fight-or-flight responses, would provide a neurophysiological state in which cortical regulation of medullary nuclei could promote proximity and increase the probability of reproductive behaviors.

Love and the Polyvagal Theory

Based on the polyvagal theory, one would expect a neurobehavioral model of love to contain three phases, one representing each of the three emotion subsystems already described in chapter 10. The first two phases are easily identified. The first phase would be associated with the social engagement system, which would systematically signal and engage a prospective mate, and the regulation of vagal brake, which would modulate the metabolic resources necessary to carry out the behaviors. The first system would function only during periods of perceived safety. The second phase would be associated with mobilization and would provide the energy, via sympathetic excitation, to defend and to facilitate proximity for reproductive behaviors when separated. However, a third phase associated with immobilization is more difficult to conceptualize within the polyvagal theory. Although sexual behaviors often incorporate a state of immobilization, immobilization during coitus is not consistent with the state of fear predicted by the polyvagal theory. In addition, the initial description of the polyvagal theory made no statement regarding experiences of pleasure and ecstasy associated with sexual behavior. Therefore, to provide a neurophysiological explanation of love, the configuration of the polyvagal theory requires modification.

Love Without Fear: Hypothalamic Regulation of the DVC

The third emotional subsystem of the polyvagal theory assumes that immobilization is adaptive only in response to danger. A state of fear would be inconsistent with the acknowledged behavioral states associated with seduction and passion. However, for many mammals, behavioral immobilization of the female is required for intromission. This active inhibition of motor activity optimally occurs in humans, not in a state of terror or fear but in a state defined by safety and trust of the mate. If trust and safety do not characterize the period of copulation, intercourse may be painful and produce tissue damage. Alternatively, if a faulty sense of safety is perceived, both male and female may be vulnerable to predation.

How do mammals immobilize without fear? And what are the physiological mechanisms underlying the mating rituals that allow behavioral immobilization without the physiological consequences of fear-induced shutdown responses?

Although the polyvagal theory has emphasized the potentially lethal shutdown behaviors associated with massive surges from the dorsal motor nucleus of the vagus, the DVC is involved in other functions. The DVC, with motor fibers originating in the dorsal motor nucleus of the vagus and afferent fibers terminating in the nucleus of the solitary tract and area postrema, has been assumed to be involved primarily in homeostatic functions (Leslie, 1985). The DVC promotes anabolic activities related to the restoration and conservation of bodily energy and the resting of vital organs. The DVC regulates digestion by modulating digestive polypeptides and gastric motility (Rogers & Hermann, 1992). In addition, Uvnas-Moberg (1989, 1994) has proposed a parallel between DVC regulation of gastrointestinal hormones and the regulation of visceral states including stress, hunger, and satiety. Without external challenges, the DVC optimizes the function of the internal viscera. In contrast, by increasing metabolic output to deal directly with external challenges, the SNS attempts to optimize the organism's relationship with the environment. Thus, increases in ambient temperature, noise, pain, and pyrogenic agents produce not only increased sympathetic activity but an active inhibition of DVC actions on the gut (Uvnas-Moberg, 1987).

Paraventricular Nucleus and the DVC

The paraventricular nucleus of the hypothalamus is an important regulator of the DVC. Neural communication between the paraventricular nucleus and the DVC is involved in responses that are not only homeostatic but protective and defensive (e.g., nausea and vomiting, conditioned taste aversion, behavioral defense) (Lawes, 1990). Communication between the paraventricular nucleus and the DVC changes with experience and thus may exhibit a type of learning or memory. Associations may be established rapidly between environmental features or experiences and visceromotor responses. Perhaps, as in conditioned taste aversion, this memory is expressed as a learned association between a specific environmental feature and nausea. Once the association is made, subsequent exposure to the environmental feature may result in immediate nausea and defensive avoidance behaviors. These speculations regarding the changing communication between the paraventricular nucleus and the DVC with experience are consistent with general theories of aversion learning (Garcia, Lasiter, Bermudez-Rattoni, & Deems, 1985).

The paraventricular nucleus regulation of the DVC evolved in phylogenetically older vertebrates in which escape and avoidance behaviors contributed to the maintenance of visceral homeostasis (Lawes, 1990). Because the early vertebrates lacked an elaborate nervous system to control their viscera, behavior was a primary mechanism for the maintenance of homeostasis (e.g., moving to regulate thermoregulatory and oxygen requirements). As the nervous system evolved, an autonomic nervous system and neuroendocrine mechanisms emerged and displaced the need to use behavior to regulate internal state. The neural and neuroendocrine regulation of internal state allowed behavioral processes to be directed toward environmental challenges. However, the brain structures, specifically the paraventricular nucleus, that governed the homeostatically driven behaviors in the phylogenetically older species, evolved into the structures responsible for regulating internal homeostatic functions in the phylogenetically newer species (Leslie, Reynolds, & Lawes, 1992).

The role of the paraventricular nucleus in the regulation of the DVC in modern vertebrates retains phylogenetically older functions and continues to respond to threatening situations by contributing to visceral and endocrine responses. However, this phylogenetic organization results in vulnerabilities, because perceived challenges to survival, whether or not truly life-threatening, may elicit visceral and endocrine reactions that compromise normal physiological function.

The phylogenetic emphasis of the polyvagal theory emphasizes that defense and avoidance behaviors have a vagal component manifested through the DVC.

For example, a physiological shutdown mediated by the DVC would support avoidance behaviors such as death feigning or freezing. However, the evolution of hypothalamic regulation of the DVC provides response alternatives. Specifically, in mammals, the paraventricular nucleus produces two neuropeptides, oxytocin and vasopressin, that differentially communicate with the sensory and motor portions of the DVC. Using the push-pull perfusion technique, Landgraf et al. (1990) demonstrated that both oxytocin and vasopressin are released in the DVC. Binding sites for vasopressin are prevalent in the sensory component, but are not represented in the motor component (Fuxe et al., 1994). In contrast, oxytocin appears to provide a primary pathway from the paraventricular nucleus to the dorsal motor nucleus of the vagus with oxytocin injections into the DVC mimicking the vagal responses normally observed immediately following feeding (Rogers & Hermann, 1992). Direct pathways from the nucleus of the solitary tract to the paraventricular nucleus provide a potential source of feedback for hypothalamic influences on visceromotor functions (Sawchenko & Swanson, 1982). The communication between the DVC and the paraventricular nucleus appears to modulate specific visceromotor reflexes involving cardiovascular (Nissen, Cunningham, & Renaud, 1993) and gastrointestinal systems (Bray, 1985).

Oxytocin and Vasopressin

Oxytocin and vasopressin are synthesized primarily in the paraventricular and supraoptic nuclei of the hypothalamus and released centrally via parvocellular neurons and systemically via magnocellular neurons (Swanson & Sawchenko, 1977). The central and systemic effects of these neuropeptides are different. Central release of oxytocin regulates the output of the dorsal motor nucleus of the vagus, usually maintaining output within levels optimal to support homeostasis. Peripheral release of oxytocin is related to milk ejection, uterine contractions, and ejaculation (Arletti, Benelli, & Bertolini, 1992; Wakerley, Clarke, & Summerlee, 1994). Central release of vasopressin appears to modulate afferent feedback from the viscera and to shift set points, independent of sensitivity, for vagal reflexes such as the baroreceptor reflex (Michelini, 1994). The raising of the baroreceptor set point would, by increasing cardiac output, potentiate fight-or-flight behaviors and allow sympathetic excitation of the heart to be unopposed by homeostatic vagal reflexes. Thus, central levels of oxytocin have been assumed to be associated with vagal processes and central levels of vasopressin have been assumed to be associated with sympathetic processes (Uvnas-Moberg, 1997).

Because the peripheral influences of oxytocin and vasopressin function through feedback, primarily via the sensory component of the DVC, the effects are less clear and may be level-dependent. For example, it is possible that peripheral vasopressin, by stimulating vagal afferents, may trigger massive vagal responses via the dorsal motor nucleus of the vagus. In support of this speculation, it is known that in humans, peripheral vasopressin, and not oxytocin, is related to the nausea experienced during motion sickness (Koch, Summy-Long, Bingaman, Sperry, & Stern, 1990). In addition, systemic vasopressin may induce a baroreceptor-mediated withdrawal of sympathetic tone, which is observed in increases in baroreceptor-elicited bradycardia and a fall in plasma concentration of norepinephrine (Buwalda, Koolhaas, & Bohus, 1992; Michelini, 1994).

Under certain conditions, such as during periods of perceived safety, small increases in peripheral vasopressin might trigger parvocellular release of both oxytocin and vasopressin. Potentially, this could occur via stimulation of either peripheral vagal afferents or vasopressinergic receptors in the area postrema. This stimulation would initiate communication between the paraventricular nucleus and both the sensory and motor nuclei of the DVC. The simultaneous central release of oxytocin and vasopressin would activate both vagal and sympathetic activity. This unique physiological state might characterize sexual arousal and would support intimate behaviors. Since vestibular stimulation elicits systemic vasopressin release (Koch et al., 1990), the perception of motion or environments that move might elicit visceral states vulnerable for intimacy. This could explain the selection of porch swings, trains, boats, planes, water beds, or even rollercoasters as preferred arenas for eliciting and experiencing passionate love.

Oxytocin may be part of a complex response profile related to the perception of the environment as safe. Consistent with this view, Uvnas-Moberg (1997) and Carter and Altemus (1997) propose that oxytocin promotes states resistant to stress (i.e., antistress). In contrast, vasopressin may be part of a complex response profile related to the perception that the environment is challenging or dangerous. In fact, central vasopressin could potentiate mobilization responses via sympathetic excitation, while high levels of systemic vasopressin may potentiate a physiological shutdown associated with fear (e.g., bradycardia) via feedback to the dorsal motor nucleus and inhibition of sympathetic outflow (Ferguson & Lowes, 1994). In addition, lesions of vagal afferents, which functionally block the visceral input to the sensory component of the DVC (areas sensitive to vasopressin), attenuate or abolish specific conditioned taste aversions (Andrews & Lawes, 1992).

Based on the polyvagal theory, the mammalian or smart vagus, with myelinated motor fibers originating in the nucleus ambiguus, provides a system for voluntary engagement with the environment with special features associated with the prosocial behaviors of communication. Paralleling this evolutionary shift in the vagus is a mammalian modification of the hypothalamic regulation of the DVC via both oxytocin and vasopressin. The advent of specific receptors for oxytocin and vasopressin increases the range of adaptive functions involving the DVC. In mammals, the dorsal motor nucleus of the vagus, the motor component of the DVC, is sensitive to oxytocin and insensitive to vasopressin. In contrast, the sensory components of the DVC, the nucleus of the solitary tract and area postrema, are most sensitive to vasopressin. Although the nucleus of the solitary tract has receptors for oxytocin (Landgraf et al. 1990), the area postrema may not be directly influenced by oxytocin (Carpenter, 1990). The differential sensitivity of specific components of the DVC to these two neuropeptides (the differential effects of central and systemic release on visceral function and a potential level dependency) results in a wider range of response options and the co-opting of the primitive vagal system to support avoidance (death feigning, vomiting), engagement (e.g., nursing, feeding) and copulation.

Conditioned Love: Physiological Mechanisms Involved in the Learning and Memory of Intimacy

Classical conditioning provides a potential neurophysiological process to associate gastrointestinal responses with specific sensory events. Classical conditioning may incorporate oxytocinergic and vasopressinergic pathways connecting the paraventricular nucleus with the dorsal motor vagal complex. Garcia et al. (1985), in presenting a general theory of aversion learning, speculated that two specialized coping systems evolved in mammals. The first coping system includes behaviors to protect oneself from predatory attack. This system employs instrumental mobilization behaviors, including active approach and avoidance behaviors. The second coping system deals with protecting the gut from toxic foods and includes the hedonic appraisal of visceral stimulation during eating and copulation. The second system produces rapidly conditioned and difficult-to-extinguish gustatory–visceral associations. Garcia and colleagues speculated that to approach a receptive mate is a product of the first system and to find a sexually satisfying mate more desirable is a product of the second system. This distinction between approach behaviors and conditioned visceral feelings is convergent with the proposed neurobiological theory of love, which distinguishes between seduction and conditioned or passionate love.

Consistent with the hypothesis that a conditioned association between positive visceral feelings and the mate are a product of copulation, Carter and colleagues (Carter, Devries, & Getz, 1995; Carter et al., 1997) have shown that sexual interactions, probably mediated through oxytocin and/or vasopressin, can facilitate pair-bonding. Oxytocin has been associated with positive states, such as physical proximity, touching, prosocial behavior, and the ingestion of food (Carter et al., 1997; Uvnas-Moberg, 1997). Oxytocin also has been implicated in the cephalic phase of digestion. The cephalic phase, the initial digestive phase, is stimulated by psychological factors such as sight, smell, taste, or associations with food before food enters the stomach. The cephalic phase is characterized by increased gastric secretion and reduced gastric motility, providing a receptive environment for the passage of food and allowing the gastric secretions to more efficiently aid in digestion of food in the stomach (Rogers & Hermann, 1992).

Oxytocin and vasopressin are related to other learned responses. For example, intracerebroventricular injection of oxytocin attenuates passive avoidance (Kovacs & Telegdy, 1982), whereas vasopressin enhances passive avoidance (De Wied, 1971). Although these findings may be paradigm-dependent, there is consistent evidence that central levels of both neuropeptides are involved in learning social cues and in the development of partner preferences (Carter, 1998;

Engelmann, Wotjak, Neumann, Ludwig, & Landgraf, 1996). In addition, it is well known that the oxytocin released during milk ejection can be conditioned (Wakerley et al., 1994). Likewise, it is plausible that the oxytocin released during coitus could be conditioned and associated with specific social cues. Thus, engagements between pair-bonded mates would trigger a release of oxytocin, which might decrease the latency for subsequent sexual encounters.

Communication Between the Paraventricular Nucleus and the DVC: A Mammalian System for Love and Fear

The neural and neuropeptide communication between the paraventricular nucleus and the DVC, with its involvement in both emotional and learned associations, may provide the physiological mechanism that enables mammals to respond reliably to both fear-related and safety-related environmental cues. Thus, this communication, through the partitioned roles of two related peptides, vasopressin and oxytocin, may promote several classes of behavior. First, the oxytocinergic pathways from the paraventricular nucleus to the dorsal motor nucleus of the vagus appear to co-opt the ancient immobilization fear system that characterizes reptiles. By blunting the shutdown fear response mediated by the dorsal motor nucleus of the vagus, oxytocin modulates vagal function to promote homeostasis and shifts the function of the visceral organs to support progenitive behavior and experiences of passion. Second, in the absence of central oxytocin communication with the dorsal motor nucleus of the vagus, increases in systemic vasopressin would facilitate a fear-induced avoidance, consistent with phylogenetic origins, as a shutdown response system. Third, central vasopressin would facilitate mobilization via sympathetic excitation. Fourth, small increases in systemic vasopressin may trigger a coexcitation of central oxytocin and vasopressin coincident with the peripheral coexcitation of vagal and sympathetic activity characteristic of sexual arousal.

Consistent with the literature on visceral (i.e., vagal) conditioning and pair-bonding (Carter et al., 1997), the oxytocinergic communication between the paraventricular nucleus and the dorsal motor nucleus of the vagus, may provide a neurophysiological mechanism to explain how specific progenitive behaviors including proximity with a mate would be linked with positive visceral feelings. The conditioning process would be facilitated by both systemic vasopressin, which could trigger sexual arousal, and central oxytocin, which could modulate vagal responses. The conditioning process may provide a plausible mechanism to explain other classes of behavior including parent–child bonding, friendships, and the visceral reactions to the loss of a loved one either through death or violation of vows of love. For example, grief and unrequited love, often characterized by potent unpleasant visceral responses, may be mediated by increases in systemic vasopressin, which can trigger vagal responses (e.g., nausea and syncope), which are no longer protected or modulated within the homeostatic range by oxytocin. Vasopressin and oxytocin may work in concert in other behavioral states. For example, during sexual or nursing behaviors, peripheral oxytocin release may enable the visceral organs to be responsive and pliable, while central oxytocin and/or vasopressin release may result in a modulation or an attenuation of painful tactile stimulation, such as that reported following electrical stimulation of the solitary tract (Ren, Randich, & Gebhart, 1990; Uvnas-Moberg, 1998).

Additional neuroanatomical structures may be involved in the establishment of intimacy. The amygdala appears to play a major role in the retention of fear-related or aversive associations (Davis, 1992; LaBar & LeDoux, 1996; LeDoux, Iwata, Cicchetti, & Reis, 1988). For example, lesions of the central nucleus of the amygdala attenuate the conditioned bradycardia, independent of the conditioned corneoretinal potential (Gentile, Jarrell, Teich, McCabe, & Schneiderman, 1986) or the magnitude of the heart rate orienting response (Kapp, Frysinger, Gallagher, & Haselton, 1979). This research demonstrates a role for the amygdala in the retention of negative affective states. However, the role of the amygdala in the retention of positive affective states with prosocial consequences, such as a hypothesized conditioned love, has not been investigated.

Immobilization Without Fear: The Importance of Perceived Safety

By incorporating the influence of the neuropeptides oxytocin and vasopressin on the DVC, the polyvagal theory can be used to explain two classes of immobilization behaviors: one associated with fear and the other with passion. Mammals require a perception of safety to digest food efficiently, to sleep, and to reproduce. During perceived threat or fear, these processes are inhibited. The paraventricular regulation of the DVC provides a plausible mechanism for a central switching circuit that determines whether specific DVC processes are fostered or inhibited. Thus, the neuropeptide modulation of the DVC may contribute to two important processes: first, the determination of whether immobilization is due to fear or security; second, a specific conditioned association with each behavioral state. Similar to other conditioned vagal responses (e.g., taste aversion), the learned associations with either fear or security may be easily established and very difficult to extinguish.

The oxytocinergic pathways from the paraventricular nucleus to the dorsal motor nucleus of the vagus modulate the neural stimulation of organs of fear, digestion, and elimination to foster reproduction, feelings of safety, visceral sensations of pleasure and ecstasy and the conditioning of visceral associations with the mate. In contrast, the vasopressinergic pathways from the paraventricular nucleus to the nucleus of the solitary tract and area postrema may inhibit processes associated with digestion, elimination, and reproduction, thereby facilitating fight-or-flight (mobilization) behaviors. Other neural pathways from the hypothalamus to the DVC may promote either primitive avoidance behaviors (such as freezing and death feigning) or the more phylogenetically advanced flight-or-fight behaviors associated with the SNS. In addition, pathways from the amygdala may modulate the communication between the hypothalamus and the DVC (Lawes, 1990) and contribute to specific fear-associated behaviors (LeDoux et al., 1988; Rosen, Hamerman, Sitcoske, Glowa, & Schulkin, 1996).

Mammalian neuropeptides modulate autonomic functions during love-related behaviors. The polyvagal theory emphasizes the phylogenetically more recent vagal pathways that originate in the nucleus ambiguus. The nucleus ambiguus vagal pathways are involved in the voluntary behaviors required for social engagement, including the general category of seduction. However, the visceral experience of ecstasy, diffuse visceral pleasure, and analgesia are related to the phylogenetically older DVC. The DVC, according to the polyvagal theory is associated with an immobilization fear system. However, the mammalian neuropeptide oxytocin, which is released from the paraventricular nucleus of the hypothalamus, provides a neurophysiological mechanism to co-opt the function of the DVC. Oxytocin may modify the function of the DVC from an immobilization fear system to an immobilization passion or love system. Oxytocin, although stimulating vagal activity (e.g., DVC), appears to limit vagal activity to a functional range that protects the organism from experiencing massive vagal surges that would shut down physiological homeostasis.

Seduction or Rape?

The autonomic nervous system is involved in several aspects of human mating behavior. First, as discussed, the autonomic nervous system can support seduction (behaviors of engagement). The mammalian or smart vagus with its somatomotor regulation of facial expressions and vocalizations provides the neural regulatory structures for this phase of social engagement. Second, by an inhibition of the vagal system and an excitation of the SNS, cardiac output can be increased to support behavioral mobilization including active withdrawal from unwelcomed engagements, fighting behavior to protect the mate, and approach behaviors to reduce distance from the mate. Third, the phylogenetically older DVC (visceral or vegetative vagus) contributes to behavioral immobilization by initiating a primitive shutdown of physiological systems. This form of immobilization is usually in response to fear when there is no option to mobilize. Fourth, by co-opting the DVC, the neuropeptides from the paraventricular nucleus can promote sexual arousal, immobilization without fear, copulatory behavior, positive visceral experiences, and conditioned associations with the mating partner.

A physiological shutdown response profile may characterize the female during rape, an unwelcomed and physiologically dangerous event. This physiological shutdown, due to a massive surge from the dorsal motor nucleus of the vagus, may be associated with or conditioned to specific events or individuals. This classically conditioned response may require only a single trial to be learned and may exhibit great resistance to extinction. For example, following the rape, sexual encounters, even with a desired partner, may elicit a vagal syncope. Or the raped woman may become anxious about sexual encounters and physiologically mobilized via sympathetic excitation to escape. An important aspect of the immobilization phase is that it may follow the well-documented laws of conditioning visceral responses mediated by the DVC (e.g., nausea and vomiting) used to explain conditioned taste aversion (Garcia et al., 1985). A similar response profile may characterize individuals who fear death and believe that they are unable to escape, such as the description of hopelessness (Richter, 1957) and perhaps, clinical disorders such as post-traumatic stress disorder.

Seduction provides a prosocial vehicle for mate selection. Appropriate mate selection, in turn, changes the visceral and psychological experiences associated with female immobilization from fear to passion, which is required for intromission. Seduction allows intimacy to occur without trauma. When the female perceives the male as providing security, an immobilization love system is initiated. This immobilized love system is physiologically and psychologically incompatible with the immobilized fear system. Although both immobilization response patterns share common physiological substrates, the response profiles are different. The immobilized fear system results in a physiological shutdown and a functional inhibition of social behavior and sexual receptivity and responsivity of the genitalia. The immobilization fear system, when initiated, attempts to turn off behavior and consciousness by lowering heart rate and blood pressure, which may produce syncope. In contrast, the immobilization love system heightens sexual arousal in response to genital stimulation, lubricates genital tissue, maintains blood pressure, and raises pain thresholds. The immobilization love system co-opts the paraventricular communication with the DVC and modifies immobilization from a fear-related psychologically dissociative and physiologically compromised state to a love-related psychologically ecstatic and reproductively available state.

By co-opting the communication between the paraventricular nucleus and the DVC, an immobilized love circuit fosters reproductive behaviors. Reproductive behaviors occurring during states of immobilized love promote enduring associations between the mate and the ecstatic experiences. The development of these associations appears to follow the laws of visceral conditioning, since they are easy to establish and result in relatively permanent bonds (Carter et al., 1997). Love may be a classically conditioned response with enduring resistance to extinction. Perhaps species differences in monogamy (Carter et al., 1995; Dewsbury, 1987) might be related to differences in the capacity to recruit the paraventricular control over the DVC in prosocial associative learning paradigms. If this is true, the selective nature of the seduction phase and the fight-or-flight behaviors of the mobilization phase may become a functional barrier to this associative vulnerability. Thus, when we are careful about whom we allow ourselves and our children to be physically close to and to have sexual activities with, we are respecting our vulnerability to the conditioning that characterizes passionate love.

How does our nervous system organize these unique and important behaviors? As illustrated in Figure 11.1, the social engagement system and the vagal brake provide neurobiologically based constructs to describe mechanisms of seduction. Modulation of the social engagement system enables symbolic approach behaviors (e.g., facial expressions, head tilt, and vocalizations), and modulation of the vagal brake provides metabolic support for the behavioral mobilization necessary to engage a prospective mate physically. However, if there is a mismatch between the expectations of the prospective mating partners, mobilization may occur to ensure an increase in physical distance. This mobilization response requires sympathetic excitation and a withdrawal of the vagal brake (the smart vagus). If physical escape is not available, the vegetative vagus (DVC) may become activated to provide a primitive avoidance strategy characterized by a physiological shutdown and a possible loss of consciousness due to compromised homeostatic regulation (e.g., decreased blood pressure).

Successful mating and bonding are the product of a different sequence. In this sequence, seduction is successful and proximity between the prospective mating partners is reduced. Mobilization is restricted to the physical activities associated with the preparation to copulate and copulation. Finally, to ease intromission for the female and the postcoitus recovery for the male, an immobilization system is stimulated. This immobilization system is confined to situations of perceived security. Because states of immobilization for mammals are periods of vulnerability, this type of immobilization occurs only in a safe environment with mutual trust as a defining feature. Thus, an important feature of the love experience is not mediated by physical attractiveness, but is driven by trust and security.

As illustrated in Figure 11.2, hypothalamic–DVC regulation is flexible. Higher brain structures determine whether the hypothalamic–DVC communication results in an immobilized fear response or an immobilized love response. The amygdala may play a major role in determining which hypothalamic–DVC circuit is recruited. If Pavlovian conditioning provides a plausible metaphor for the enduring nature of a conditioned love (Garcia et al., 1985), then the amygdala may be involved in maintaining these learned associations.

The proposed model attempts to integrate the role of neuropeptides (i.e., oxytocin and vasopressin) with the autonomic nervous system. As illustrated in Figure 11.2, the perceptual mechanisms of higher brain structures determine if a situation is dangerous or safe. During perceived fear, there are two options. The organism may mobilize and express fight-or-flight behaviors. Or, if the first option is not available, the organism may immobilize. Immobilization results in a behavioral shutdown, death feigning, and a loss of consciousness. The effect of vasopressin released centrally via the parvocellular neurons, communicating between the hypothalamus and the sensory portion of the DVC (nucleus of solitary tract and area postrema), inhibits feedback from the viscera and promotes sympathetic activation and increased mobilization. However, vasopressin released systemically via the magnocellular neurons originating in the hypothalamus stimulates visceral afferents and promotes feedback to the DVC, which may result in the massive vagal surge associated with physiological shutdown.

FIGURE 11.2. Neural and neuropeptide regulation of the dorsal motor nucleus of the vagus: fear or love? Higher brain structures including the amygdala and cortex influence hypothalamic–dorsal vagal complex (DVC) communication. The DVC includes sensory nuclei in the nucleus of the solitary tract (NTS) and area postrema (AP) and motor nuclei in the dorsal motor nucleus of the vagus (DMX). During perceived danger, when mobilization is adaptive, central vasopressinergic pathways (AVP) communicate between the hypothalamus and both NTS and AP to change the set-point of vagal reflexes to facilitate sympathetic excitation. Immobilized fear occurs when fight-or-flight behaviors are not an option. Immobilized fear is fostered by vagal surges from DMX to visceral organs, which are potentiated by systemic AVP. Systemic AVP triggers increased DMX output by stimulating visceral afferents via NTS and AP. During perceived safety, oxytocin (OXT) is released centrally and systemically to foster an immobilized love response pattern. Central OXT limits DMX output to a functional range protecting homeostasis and systemic OXT stimulates visceral organs. Small increases in systemic AVP might, either via vagal afferents or direct stimulation of vasopressinergic receptors in AP, trigger central AVP and OXT and promote sexual arousal.

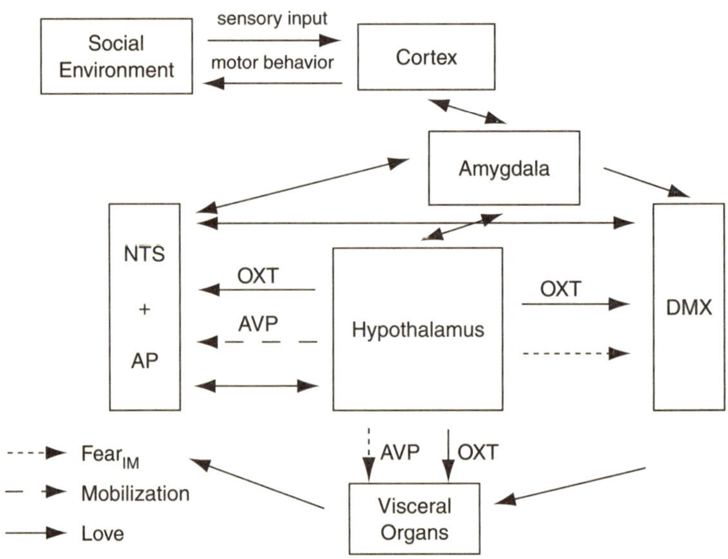

In contrast, perceived security changes the immobilization system, which originally evolved to cope with fear, to a system that promotes reproduction and provides heightened sensory experiences that are psychologically reinforcing. Perceived security enables the hypothalamic release of oxytocin centrally to modulate the vagal discharge that can stimulate the viscera and systemically to foster reproduction and heightened sensory feedback. Enhanced sensory feedback provides a positive visceral state that acts as a reinforcer to enhance the conditioned association between the mate and reproductive availability. In addition, sensory feedback acts as a modulator of pain (Komisaruk & Whipple, 1995), which allows areas of the body to experience sensations that would have been perceived as painful in other situations. The positive visceral feelings lead to experiences of pleasure, ecstasy, and the less well-defined emotional states that we associate with love. Thus, via the influence of oxytocin on the autonomic nervous system, organs of fear and vigilance become organs of pleasure, nurturance, and reproduction. Oxytocin, a hormone unique to mammals, co-opts ancient structures changing a fear-induced shutdown system in to a receptive and ecstatic reproductive system. In addition, as stated, there is the possibility that low levels of peripheral vasopressin, perhaps elicited by gentle vestibular stimulation in an environment perceived as safe (e.g., the porch swing or a sailboat) triggers central release of oxytocin.

Of course, the violation of trust changes the context, and a mate that once conveyed a sense of safety would now convey cues of danger. Thus, violation of trust might result in mobilized fight-or-flight behaviors, or the shutdown behavior associated with immobilized fear. In addition, unrequited love or the loss of a loved one might result in syncope or visceral feelings associated with nausea, characteristic of vagal activation due to systemic vasopressin release, without the protective or modulated influence of oxytocin.

The Monogamy Switch and the Biological Prenuptial

Love, as an emotional and motivational process, may have evolved to maximize the adaptive benefits associated with reproduction and safety. However, to achieve these benefits, individuals need to negotiate the relative costs of coping with two potent risks: (1) the vulnerability to predation; and (2) the vulnerability of the nervous system to develop enduring social bonds following the mating sequence. The first risk is obvious. The environment is competitive and often hostile. To survive, coalitions must be developed. Prominent among these coalitions is the social bond between mating partners. The second risk acknowledges that our nervous system may be stimulated to form enduring social bonds with an inappropriate mate. The articulation of the second risk is new to science. Rather, the second risk has been the focus of gender-specific myths and cultural expectations regarding chastity, promiscuity, and marriage. In contemporary culture, monogamy is the focal point around which seduction and sexual encounters are expected to revolve. However, not all sexual and love experiences lead to monogamous relationships. Although the partitioning of the love experience into two sequential components (seduction and a conditioned or enduring passionate love) assumes a monogamous end point, many individuals may focus on seduction and opt for relationships that are not monogamous.

Conditioned love with its enduring social bond might require a prerequisite neurophysiological state that might be conceptualized as a monogamy switch. Once a decision is made to become monogamous with a selected mate, the individual may immobilize without fear and the nervous system becomes vulnerable to conditioned love. Alternatively, to protect oneself from monogamy, the monogamy switch may be disabled by mobilization strategies, even during sexual encounters. Mobilization strategies engage SNS mechanisms, which are inhibitory of the conditioning processes associated with DVC mechanisms. For example, promiscuous sexual activity need not lead to enduring bonds, if the sexual activity were physically active and both sexual partners limited periods of immobilization. This strategy would limit oxytocin release, while experiencing the activation of sexual arousal. Illicit affairs fit this model, especially if the sexual activity is brief, intense, and under the threat of discovery.

The risks or vulnerabilities to states of conditioned love have been described in gender-specific myths, which promote female chastity and female vulnerability to first love in contrast to male promiscuity. Underlying these myths may be an implicit understanding of the monogamy switch, a neurophysiological mechanism that promotes pair-bonding or conditioned love. For example, female immobilization without fear might heighten a vulnerability to a conditioned or learned love. Thus, the male, who conquers the female's fears and gives her a sense of safety and security, not only is allowed to copulate with her, but in return she may be permanently bonded to him. Possibly, this gender bias might have evolved because copulatory behavior in mammals requires only the female to immobilize, but to immobilize outside the realm of fear. In contrast, the male tends to be more mobilized in the sexual act; only following ejaculation does the male become immobilized and at physical risk from the environment. It is this mobilization that may protect the male from a conditioned love. Perhaps, if the male, following copulation, remained immobilized or slept in the presence of the female, he would be as vulnerable as the female to conditioned love. Cultural and self-imposed prohibitions of spending the night together, even following sex, might reflect an implicit biological awareness of this phenomenon.

The potential gender differences in conditioned love vulnerability may result in an unstated but assumed biological prenuptial. The biological prenuptial reflects the interactive negotiations between prospective mating partners in which the male requests exclusive copulatory rights of the female's reproductive organs and the female requests that the male ensure her security and safety needs before activating the monogamy switch. Violation of the biological prenuptial occurs when the male physically abuses the female or when the female copulates with another male. The valence of these two violations appears to be gender specific. In support of this hypothesis, Buss, Larsen, Westen, and Semmelroth (1992) reported that men are more distressed by their mate's sexual infidelity, while women are more distressed by their mate's emotional infidelity. Violations of the biological prenuptial are destructive to the love bond and result in a lack of trust and security for both genders. This gender-biased prenuptial is so rooted in our history that it finds its way into our marriage vows and religious tenants, which have been used to support monogamy.

CONCLUSION

The evolution of the neural and hormonal regulation of the autonomic nervous system provides a framework to interpret mammalian love as an adaptive process that facilitates reproduction in a rapidly changing and challenging environment. The development of love and intimacy consists of several sequential processes with adaptive functions that promote safety and progenitive behavior. Love, as a neurophysiological construct, not only promotes reproduction but also provides a pair-bond to promote safety in the challenging environment. Within this adaptive context, love may have evolved functionally as a temporal shortcut to bypass the slow, often tedious, and potentially unsuccessful processes of communication and social engagement to foster physical proximity and to promote intimacy and reproductive behaviors.

CHAPTER 12

Social Engagement and Attachment: A Phylogenetic Perspective

As the scientific knowledge of neuroanatomy and neurophysiology expands, there is a growing interest in the role neural processes play in the development of normal social behavior and in the expression of the atypical social behaviors that may provide the roots of mental illness in children. Recent advances in neuroscience have enabled researchers to study nervous system function and structure in the intact living individual. Now neuronal function can be studied, and the structural hypotheses derived from animal models and postmortem histology can be challenged and explained. These new methods of assaying neural structure and function, coupled with the breakthroughs in molecular genetics, are providing new tools and models, which can be integrated with existing strategies that effectively monitor dynamic neural function by time sampling neuroendocrine and autonomic parameters.

DEFINING SOCIAL BEHAVIOR: THE GREAT CONCEPTUAL DIVIDE

An objective of this chapter is to build bridges among researchers who study the development of social behavior with both animal models and clinical populations. As a preliminary premise, it is assumed that both cohorts share the same objective of generating knowledge related to the mechanisms of normal and atypical social behavior that could be translated into clinical practice. The contrasts between the research strategies and methods of the two cohorts may force a reevaluation of this assumption.

Animal models often emphasize the role of a specific neural system, neurotransmitter, neuropeptide, hormone, or brain structure as a regulator of social behavior. In contrast, clinical research often focuses on studying aberrant psychological processes in clinical populations. When neurophysiological systems are studied with clinical populations, the research designs focus on establishing correlations with the disorders and, in general, preclude the possibility of distinguishing whether the physiological correlates are causes or effects of the disorder.

Although the two research strategies often use similar terms, the terms may reflect different domains of social behavior. Animal models tend to focus on the establishment of pair-bonds and generate paradigms to evaluate the strength of these bonds. In contrast, research with children, investigating normal and atypical social behavior, tends to focus on the behaviors that reduce social and physical distance between individuals. For example, the terminology associated with measuring and defining social behavior differs when contrasting the compromised social engagement strategies expressed by an institutionalized child with the ability to establish pair-bonds by a vole.

A final perplexing part of the conceptual divide relates to the translation of neuroscience principles and research findings into clinical practice. The clinician is the third limb of this triad. Paradoxically, although the link between social behavior and mental illness in children emerged directly from clinical observations, the features and dimensions of social behavior studied in both animal models and in laboratory studies of normal and atypical children often deviates from the features that clinicians use to define the pathology. Clinical researchers who conduct studies of social behavior are interested in either how outlier behaviors overlap with features of clinical diagnoses or how behavioral, psychological, and physiological parameters differentiate the clinical population from normal subjects. Often the parameters of interest or, at least, those that distinguish the clinical group from normal subjects focus on processes that do not have an obvious relation to the behaviors observed in clinical settings or used to define the pathology (e.g., cortisol).

Most research in psychopathology accepts the validity of clinical assessment and diagnostic systems (e.g., DSM-IV) as inclusion criteria and then attempts to demonstrate that deficits in psychological processes and/or atypical neurophysiological response patterns underlie the disorder. The research on processes and mechanisms, whether obtained from clinical populations or by studying animal models assumed to express behaviors similar to the clinical populations, does not easily enter the clinical realm and inform clinical assessment. Similarly, other than global diagnoses and quantitative information from standardized assessment instruments, little information from clinical observations regarding the specific features of behavior that have triggered the clinician's concern easily enters the research environment. Thus, the construct of social behavior is treated differently by researchers testing animal models, researchers studying normal social behavior, researchers studying the psychological and neurophysiological mechanisms and processes underlying a clinical diagnosis, and clinicians who diagnose and treat social behavior problems in children. Missing in this mix of metaphors, worldviews, paradigms, and diagnostic models is a shared agenda to translate research findings into practice (i.e., assessment and treatment) and to use clinical information to inform the theoretical models being tested.

SOCIAL BEHAVIOR AND ATTACHMENT

Several researchers who study the development of social behavior in children have focused on the construct of attachment. Several of these researchers conduct studies derived from the observations of Bowlby (1982) and the paradigm building research of Ainsworth et al. (1972) Much of the current research on human attachment is based on the Ainsworth typology, which applies a paradigm assessing infant responses to separation. Clinicians and researchers in developmental psychopathology assume that the Ainsworth classification system and recent derivatives (Cassidy & Shaver, 1999) will provide insights into the psychological mechanisms of specific disorders. In fact, diagnostic categories now include disorders such as reactive attachment disorder (RAD).

The traditional attachment schema derived from the Bowlby theory constitutes only a small part of social behavior. Moreover, traditional attachment theory by focusing on mother–infant relations does not include other putative attachment behaviors that are observed in the enduring bonds between peers, siblings, and mates. Missing from the traditional attachment theories is an articulation of the mechanisms mediating engagement between the individuals bonding or forming attachments.

SOCIAL ENGAGEMENT: THE PREAMBLE OF A SOCIAL BOND

To develop a social bond, individuals have to be in close proximity. This is true for the models focusing on both mother–infant attachment and the strong bonds associated with social monogamy. Both models test the strength and features of the relationship through separation paradigms. There are, of course, major differences between the contexts in which mother–infant attachment and the social bonds of reproductive partners are established and tested. One specific difference is the contrast in mobility between the mother–infant and reproductive partner dyads. In the mother–infant dyad there is an imbalance, with the infant having limited abilities to move toward or away from the mother. However, in the reproductive partner dyad, there is a balance between the behavioral repertoires of the two adults.

Although proximity is critical to the establishment of social bonds, proximity is totally caused by the ability to navigate across physical distance via voluntary behavior. If social bonds were dependent on voluntary motor behaviors, then the newborn infant would be greatly disadvantaged because the neural regulation of the spinal motor pathways are immature at birth and take several years to fully develop. However, in mammals not all muscles are driven by corticospinal pathways. Unlike the striated muscles of trunk and limbs, corticobulbar pathways regulate the striated muscles of the face and head. The corticobulbar pathways are sufficiently developed at birth to be available to the full-term infant to signal caregiver (e.g., vocalizations, grimace) and to engage the social (e.g., gaze, smile) and nutrient (e.g., sucking) aspects of the world. These motor pathways originate in the brainstem and regulate muscles through the branches of five cranial nerves (V, VII, IX, X, XI). Thus, the neural regulation of muscles that provide important elements of social cueing are available to facilitate the social interaction with the caregiver and function collectively as an integrated social engagement system (Porges, 2001a).

The muscles of the face and head influence both the expression and receptivity of social cues and can effectively reduce or increase social distance. Behaviorally this is observed as facial expressions, eye gaze, vocalizations, and head orientation. Neural regulation of these muscles can reduce social distance by making eye contact, expressing prosody in voice, displaying contingent facial expressions, and modulating the middle ear muscles to improve the extraction of human voice from background sounds. Alternatively, by reducing the muscle tone to these muscles, the eyelids droop, prosody is lost, positive and contingent facial expressions are diminished, the ability to extract human voice from background sounds is compromised, and the awareness of the social engagement behaviors of others may be lost. Thus, the neural regulation of the striated muscles of the face and head function both as an active social engagement system that reduces psychological distance and as a filter that can influence the perception of the engagement behaviors of others.

Special visceral efferent pathways mediate the neural regulation of the striated muscles of the face and head. Special visceral pathways emerge from three nuclei in the brainstem (nucleus of the trigeminal nerve, nucleus of the facial nerve, and nucleus ambiguus) and provide motor pathways that are contained within five cranial nerves (i.e., trigeminal, facial, hypoglossal, vagus, accessory). These pathways regulate structures that evolved from the ancient gill arches. From both clinical and research perspectives, the striated muscles of the face and head provide potent information regarding the behavioral dimensions used to express as well as to evaluate the strength of attachment or the stress to the social bond. For example, facial expressivity and prosody of vocalizations have been used as clinical indicators as well as quantifiable responses of separation distress (Newman, 1988).

THE SOCIAL ENGAGEMENT SYSTEM: PHYLOGENIC ORIGINS OF BEHAVIORAL AND AUTONOMIC COMPONENTS

The phylogenic origin of the behaviors associated with the social engagement system is intertwined with the phylogeny of the autonomic nervous system. As the striated muscles, via special visceral efferent pathways, evolved into a behavioral system that regulated social engagement behaviors, there was a profound shift in neural regulation of the autonomic nervous system. Phylogenetically, these changes in both somatomotor and visceromotor regulation are observed in the transition from reptiles to mammals. As the muscles of the face and head evolved into an ingestion (i.e., nursing) and social engagement system, a new component of the autonomic nervous system (i.e., a myelinated vagus) evolved that was regulated by a brainstem nucleus, which was also involved in the regulation of the striated muscles of the face and head (i.e., nucleus ambiguus). This convergence of neural mechanisms resulted in an integrated social engagement system with a synergism between behavioral and visceral features of social engagement. Thus, activation of the somatomotor component would trigger visceral changes that would support social engagement, while modulation of visceral state would either promote or impede social engagement behaviors. For example, stimulation of visceral states that would promote mobilization (i.e., fight-or-flight behaviors) would impede the ability to express social engagement behaviors, whereas increased activity through the myelinated vagus would promote the social engagement behaviors associated with a calm visceral state.

We can infer the specific neural mechanisms related to the effectiveness that feeding and rocking have on promoting calm behavioral and visceral states. Specifically, both the ingestive behaviors associated with feeding and the passive rocking of an infant promote calmness by influencing the myelinated vagus. Feeding activates the muscles of mastication via trigeminal efferent pathways, which, in turn, provide afferent feedback input to the nucleus ambiguus (i.e., the source nucleus of the myelinated vagus). Rocking provides an efficient and direct influence on the vagus by stimulating vagal afferent pathways via the baroreceptors. Moreover, activation of the social engagement system dampens the neural circuits including the limbic structures that support fight, flight, or freeze behaviors.

POLYVAGAL THEORY: THREE NEURAL CIRCUITS REGULATING REACTIVITY

Evolutionary forces have molded both human physiology and behavior. Via evolutionary processes, the mammalian nervous system has emerged with specific neural and behavioral features that react to challenge to maintain visceral homeostasis. These reactions change physiological state and, in mammals, limit sensory awareness, motor behaviors, and cognitive activity. To survive, mammals must determine friend from foe, evaluate whether the environment is safe, and communicate with their social unit. These survival-related behaviors are associated with specific neurobehavioral states that limit the extent to which a mammal can be physically approached and whether the mammal can communicate or establish new coalitions.

Through stages of phylogeny, mammals and especially primates have evolved a functional neural organization that regulates visceral state to support social behavior. The polyvagal theory (see chapters 2, 10, 11; Porges, 2001a) emphasizes the phylogenetic origins of brain structures that regulate social and defensive behaviors, domains compromised in individuals with autism and several psychiatric disorders. The polyvagal theory proposes that the evolution of the mammalian autonomic nervous system provides the neurophysiological substrates for the emotional experiences and affective processes that are major components of social behavior. The theory proposes that physiological state limits the range of behavior and psychological experience. In this context, the evolution of the nervous system determines the range of emotional expression, quality of communication, and the ability to regulate bodily and behavioral state. The polyvagal theory links the evolution of the autonomic nervous system to affective experience, emotional expression, facial gestures, vocal communication, and contingent social behavior. Thus, the theory provides a plausible explanation of several social, emotional, and communication behaviors and disorders.

The Social Engagement System

The polyvagal theory provides an explicit neurobiological model of how difficulties in spontaneous social behavior are linked to both facial expressivity and the regulation of visceral state, and, alternatively, how social behavior may serve as a regulator of physiological activity. The theory proposes a possible mechanism to explain how these difficulties might form a core domain of several psychiatric profiles. Relevant to this focus on psychiatric disorders are the specific deficits associated with several diagnoses in both the somatomotor (e.g., poor gaze, low facial affect, lack of prosody, difficulties in mastication) and visceromotor (difficulties in autonomic regulation resulting in cardiopulmonary and digestive problems) of the social engagement system. For example, clinicians and researchers have documented these deficits in individuals with autistic spectrum disorders. Deficits in the social engagement system would compromise spontaneous social behavior and social awareness and affect expressivity, prosody, and language development. In contrast, interventions that improve the neural regulation of the social engagement system hypothetically would enhance spontaneous social behavior, state and affect regulation, reduce stereotypical behaviors, and improve language skills.

Embryologically, components of several cranial nerves known as special visceral efferent pathways develop together to form the neural substrate of a social engagement system (see chapter 11). This system, as illustrated in Figure 3.1, p. 56, provides the neural structures involved in social and emotional behaviors. The social engagement system has a control component in the cortex (i.e., upper motor neurons) that regulates brainstem nuclei (i.e., lower motor neurons) to control eyelid opening (e.g., looking), facial muscles (e.g., emotional expression), middle ear muscles (e.g., extracting human voice from background noise), muscles of mastication (e.g., ingestion), laryngeal and pharyngeal muscles (e.g., vocalization and language), and head-turning muscles (e.g., social gesture and orientation). Collectively, these muscles function as filters that limit social stimuli (e.g., observing facial features and listening to human voice) and determinants of engagement with the social environment. The neural control of these muscles determines social experiences. In addition, the source nuclei (i.e., lower motor neurons) of these nerves, which are located in the brainstem, communicate directly with an inhibitory neural system that slows heart rate, lowers blood pressure, and actively reduces arousal to promote calm states consistent with the metabolic demands of growth and restoration of our neurophysiological systems. Direct corticobulbar pathways reflect the influence of frontal areas of the cortex (i.e., upper motor neurons) on the regulation of this system. Moreover, afferent feedback through the vagus to medullary areas (e.g., nucleus of the solitary tract) influences forebrain areas that are assumed to be involved in several psychiatric disorders. In addition, the anatomical structures involved in the social engagement system have neurophysiological interactions with the hypothalamic-pituitary-adrenal (HPA) axis, the neuropeptides of oxytocin and vasopressin, and the immune system (Porges, 2001a).

The study of comparative anatomy, evolutionary biology, and embryology may provide important hints regarding the functional relation between the neural control of facial muscles and emergent psychological experiences and behavior. The nerves that control the muscles of the face and head share several common features. Pathways from five cranial nerves control the muscles of the face and head. Collectively, these pathways are labeled as special visceral efferent. Special visceral efferent nerves innervate striated muscles, which regulate the structures derived during embryology from the ancient gill arches (Truex & Carpenter, 1969). The special visceral efferent pathways regulate the muscles of mastication (e.g., ingestion), muscles of the middle ear (e.g., listening to human voice), muscles of the face (e.g., emotional expression), muscles of larynx and pharynx (e.g., prosody and intonation), and muscles controlling head tilt and turning (e.g., gesture). In fact, a neural pathway involved in the regulation of the eyelids also tenses the stapedius muscle in the middle ear, which facilitates hearing human voice. Thus, the neural mechanisms for making eye contact are shared with those needed to listen to human voice. As a cluster, the difficulties in gaze, extraction of human voice, facial expression, head gesture, and prosody are common features of individuals with autism.

Disorders of the Social Engagement System: Maladaptive or Adaptive Behavioral Strategies?

Individuals with several psychiatric and behavioral disorders have difficulties in establishing and maintaining relations. Several clinical diagnostic categories include features associated with difficulties both in expressing social behavior and in reading social cues (i.e., social awareness). These features are observed in individuals with a variety of primary psychiatric diagnoses including autism, social anxiety, post-traumatic stress disorder, and RAD.

Although a compromised social engagement system results in "maladaptive" social behavior, do these asocial behavioral strategies have "adaptive" features?

The phylogeny of the vertebrate autonomic nervous system serves as a guide (i.e., polyvagal theory) to understand these adaptive features. Phylogenetically, the vertebrate autonomic nervous system follows three general stages of development. Each stage supports a different category of behavior with only the phylogenetically most recent innovation (i.e., myelinated vagus) supporting social engagement behaviors. Because the neural regulation of the myelinated vagus is integrated into the social engagement system, when the social engagement system is compromised the effects are both behavioral and autonomic. The resultant changes in autonomic state support a range of adaptive defensive behaviors. Specifically, the compromised social engagement system is associated, neurophysiologically, with a change in autonomic regulation characterized by a reduction in the influence of the myelinated vagus (i.e., ventral vagal complex including nucleus ambiguus) on the heart. The removal of the regulatory influence of the ventral vagal complex on the heart potentiates the expression of the two phylogenetically older neural systems (i.e., sympathetic nervous system, dorsal vagal complex including dorsal nucleus of the vagus). These two older neural systems foster mobilization behaviors of fight or flight via the sympathetic nervous system or immobilization behaviors of death feigning, freezing, and behavioral shutdown via the dorsal vagal complex.

Neuroception: A Nervous System Evaluation of Risk

Regardless of the model of attachment or its dependence on cognitive, affective, behavioral, or biological constructs, the critical features that determine the valence of the interaction are related to perceived safety. Thus, the perception of safety is the turning point in the development of relationships for most mammals. The perception of safety determines whether the behavior will be prosocial (i.e., social engagement) or defensive. If the context and the other individual are perceived as safe, then the candidates for the social bond may inhibit the adaptive primitive neurobiological reactions of defense to allow the expression of social engagement. However, how are the adaptive neurobiological systems for defense functionally subdued to insure that attachment and the formation of social bonds will be the products of appropriate social engagement?

Before a social bond can occur, both individuals have to perceive each other as safe. What mediates the individual's ability to engage? Why would an infant look and coo at a caregiver, but avert gaze and cry as a stranger approached? Why would a gentle embrace be experienced as pleasurable when expressed by a lover and be experienced as assault when expressed by a stranger? Mammals have adaptive neurobehavioral systems for both defensive and social engagement behaviors. However, what enables engagement behaviors to occur, while disenabling the mechanisms of defense? The polyvagal theory with its focus on the phylogeny of the vertebrate autonomic nervous system provides a perspective to identify and to understand the plausible mechanisms that enable mammals to functionally switch between positive social engagement and defensive behavioral strategies. To effectively switch from defensive to social engagement strategies, the mammalian nervous system needs to perform two important processes: (1) assess risk, and (2) if the environment is perceived as safe, inhibit the more primitive limbic structures that control fight, flight, or freeze behaviors.

The nervous system, through the processing of sensory information from the environment, continuously evaluates risk. Because the neural evaluation of risk does not require conscious awareness, the term *neuroception* (see chapter 1) is introduced to emphasize the neural circuits that function as a safety-threat detection system capable of distinguishing among situations that are safe, dangerous, or life-threatening. Because of the phylogenetic heritage of mammals, neuroception can operate without cognitive awareness via relatively primitive mechanisms that are dependent on subcortical structures (e.g., limbic). As a product of evolution, new neural systems evolved in mammals that involved cortical regulation of subcortical structures and, in many instances, co-opted the defense functions of the primitive structures to support other functions including those related to reproductive behavior and pair bonding (see chapter 11).

Based on the relative risk of the environment, both social engagement and defense behaviors may be interpreted as either adaptive or maladaptive. For example, the inhibition of defense systems by the social engagement system would be adaptive and appropriate only in a safe environment. From a clinical perspective, it would be the inability to inhibit defense systems in safe environments (e.g., anxiety disorders, RAD) or the inability to activate defense systems in risk environments (e.g., Williams syndrome) that might contribute to the defining features of psychopathology. Thus, an invalid neuroception of safety or danger might contribute to maladaptive physiological reactivity and the expression of the defensive behaviors associated with specific psychiatric disorders.

There is a common feature between the invalid neuroception that identifies risk when no risk is there and McEwen's concept of "allostatic load" (McEwen & Wingfield, 2003). The physiological reaction to a valid risk, although metabolically costly, is adaptive. Thus, the increased metabolic activity necessary to support the mobilization behaviors of fight or flight are adaptive in the short term, but costly to the organism if maintained. The duration of the response is an important feature that distinguishes between adaptive and maladaptive reactions. The complex mammalian nervous system evolved with a great dependence on oxygen and, unlike the reptile, can survive only for short periods without oxygen. Thus, breath holding for mammals is adaptive only for short periods. In contrast, apnea is adaptive for reptiles, who because of their limited needs for oxygen can inhibit breathing for long periods, whereas apnea is potentially lethal for mammals (Porges et al., 2003). Similarly, temporal features, in part, determine the construct of allostatic load. McEwen describes chronic stress or allostatic state as a physiological response that, although having adaptive functions in the short term, can be damaging if used for long periods when it is no longer needed (i.e., invalid neuroception). This cost of adaptation or "maladaptation" McEwen refers to as allostatic load.

Safety Trumps Fear

In safe environments, autonomic state is adaptively regulated to dampen sympathetic activation and to protect the oxygen-dependent central nervous system from the metabolically conservative reactions of the dorsal vagal complex. However, how does the nervous system know when the environment is safe, dangerous, or life-threatening and what neural mechanisms evaluate risk in the environment?

New technologies, such as functional magnetic resonance imaging, have identified specific neural structures that are involved in detecting risk. The temporal lobe is of particular interest in expanding the construct of neuroception and in identifying neural mechanisms that modulate the expression of adaptive defensive behaviors and autonomic states. Functional imaging techniques document that areas of the temporal cortex, fusiform gyrus (FG), and superior temporal sulcus (STS) are involved in detecting features such as movements, vocalizations, and faces, which contribute to an individual being perceived as safe or trustworthy (Adolphs, 2002; Winston, Strange, O'Doherty, & Dolan, 2002). Slight changes in these stimuli can pose threat or signal endearment. Connectivity between these areas of the temporal cortex and the amygdala suggests a top-down control in the processing of facial features that could actively inhibit activity of the structures involved in the expression of defensive strategies (Pessoa, McKenna, Gutierrez, & Ungerleider, 2002).

Neuroanatomical and neurophysiological research with animals provides additional information regarding the modulation and inhibition of defensive behaviors via well-defined connections between the amygdala and the periaqueductal gray (PAG). The PAG is a heterogenous midbrain structure that consists of gray matter surrounding the cerebral aqueduct that connects the third and fourth ventricles. Studies have identified areas of the PAG that are organized to regulate flight, fight, or freeze behaviors and the autonomic states that support these behaviors (Keay & Bandler, 2001). Stimulating rostrally within the lateral and dorsolateral PAG produces confrontational defensive behaviors (i.e., fight), while stimulating caudally within the lateral PAG and dorsolateral PAG produces escape behaviors (i.e., flight). Autonomic shifts such as increases in heart rate and blood pressure parallel these behaviors. In contrast, stimulation in the region of the PAG ventrolateral to the aqueduct (vlPAG) evokes a passive reaction of immobility, a decrease in blood pressure, and a slowing of heart rate. Interestingly, excitation of the vlPAG evokes an opioid-mediated analgesia that might adaptively raise pain thresholds. In addition, there is evidence of a functional connection between the central nucleus of the amygdala and the vlPAG that modulates both antinociception and immobilization (Leite-Panissi, Coimbra, & Menescal-De-Oliveira, 2003). Consistent with the polyvagal theory, the vlPAG communicates with dorsal vagal complex, whereas the lPAG and dlPAG communicate with the sympathetic nervous system.

In the absence of threat, inhibitory projections from the FG and STS to the amygdala would be available to actively inhibit the limbic defense systems. This inhibition would provide an opportunity for social behavior to occur. Thus, the appearance of a friend or mate would subdue the limbic activation with the biobehavioral consequences of allowing proximity, physical contact, and other social engagement behaviors. In contrast, during situations in which the appraisal of risk is high, the amygdala and various areas of the PAG are activated. The amygdala and PAG only share connections through the central nucleus (Rizvi, Ennis, Behbehani, & Shipley, 1991).

The detection of safety subdues the adaptive defensive systems dependent on limbic structures. Thus, providing a plausible model of how a neural detection of environmental risk (i.e., neuroception) would modulate behavior and physiological state to support adaptive behaviors in response to safe, dangerous, and life-threatening environments. Conceptually, the process of detecting safety is inclusive of the detection of risk. Thus, the neural circuits that mediate the more primitive defense systems have through the processes of evolution been co-opted to support the social behavior necessary for mammalian survival. These behaviors include social engagement and the behaviors associated with social bonding (e.g., reproductive behaviors and nursing).

Co-opting the Immobilization Defense System for Reproductive Behaviors, Nursing, and the Formation of Social Bonds

Immobilization as a defense system is phylogenetically old and is associated with reduced metabolic demands and increased pain threshold. In reptiles, because of their limited need for oxygen, immobilization is a very effective defense strategy. In contrast, because mammals have a great need for oxygen, the inhibition of movement coupled with a shift in autonomic state to support the immobilization behavior (i.e., apnea and bradycardia) can be lethal (Hofer, 1970; Richter, 1957). However, several aspects of mammalian social behavior require immobilization, but immobilization without fear. Immobilization without fear is accomplished by co-opting the structures that regulate immobilization and pain thresholds to serve a broad range of social needs, including reproduction, nursing, and pair-bonding. By focusing on the area of the PAG that coordinates freezing behavior, we can see how a primitive immobilization defense system has been modified through evolution to serve the intimate social needs of mammals. In addition, when we study the vlPAG we find that it is rich in receptors for oxytocin, a neuropeptide associated with parturition, nursing, and the establishment of pair-bonds (Carter, 1998; Insel & Young, 2001).

Overlapping with the area of the PAG that organizes immobility (i.e., vlPAG) are areas that when stimulated produce lordosis and kyphosis. The lordosis reflex is a hormone-dependent behavior displayed by female rodents and other mammalian species during mating. In most mammals, lordosis involves the female immobilizing in a crouching posture with her hind end available to the male for copulation. Neural tracing studies have demonstrated that the vlPAG is part of the neural circuit involved in regulating lordosis (Daniels, Miselis, & Flanagan, 1999). Kyphosis is an upright crouching posture that is accompanied by inhibition of limb movements. This posture is stimulated by nipple attachment and provides an opportunity for the dam to feed simultaneously a large litter. When dams initiate a nursing bout, behavioral state shifts immediately from high activity to immobility (Stern, 1997). When the caudal portion of the vlPAG is lesioned, there are important consequences: (1) kyphotic nursing decreases, (2) litter weight gains decrease, and (3) the lesioned rats are more aggressive and more frequently attack strange males (Lonstein & Stern, 1998).

Test of the Model

The processes of attachment and the formation of social bonds require appropriate social engagement strategies. In the preceding sections, elements of a preliminary model that links social engagement to attachment and the formation of social bonds are presented. The model is expanded from the polyvagal theory and emphasizes the following points: (1) there are well-defined neural circuits to support social engagement behaviors and the defensive strategies of fight, flight, or freeze; (2) without being dependent on conscious awareness, the nervous system evaluates risk in the environment and regulates the expression of adaptive behavior to match the neuroception of a safe, dangerous, or life-threatening environment; (3) social engagement behaviors and the benefits of the physiological states associated with social support require a neuroception of safety; (4) social behaviors associated with nursing, reproduction, and the formation of strong pair bonds require immobilization without fear; and (5) immobilization without fear is mediated by a co-opting of the neural circuit regulating defensive freezing behaviors through the involvement of oxytocin, a neuropeptide involved in the formation of social bonds (Carter & Keverne, 2002; Winslow & Insel, 2002).

Figures 12.1, 12.2, and 12.3 illustrate the role that neuroception plays in determining the neural circuits recruited to regulate social engagement and fight, flight, or freeze behaviors. Each figure illustrates a different environment context (i.e., safe, dangerous, life threat). Figure 12.1 illustrates the assumed neural circuits involved in promoting social engagement behaviors in a safe context. The detection of safe or trustworthy features derived from face, voice, and movement activate a neural circuit that projects from the temporal cortex (i.e., FG, STS) to the central nucleus of the amygdala to inhibit defensive limbic functions (see Figures 12.2 and 12.3). This circuit disenables the limbic defense systems that organize and regulate fight, flight, or freeze behaviors and enables the corticobulbar pathways that regulate the social engagement behaviors (see Figure 3.1, p. 56). Figure 12.2 illustrates the neural circuits involved in a response to a neuroception of danger. In response to danger, the limbic defense circuits function to adaptively protect the individual. The specificity of the defense strategy, whether confrontational or avoidant (i.e., fight or flight), is regulated by the PAG. To support these mobilization behaviors, the sympathetic nervous system is acti-

FIGURE 12.1. Neural structures and pathways involved in a neuroception of safety.

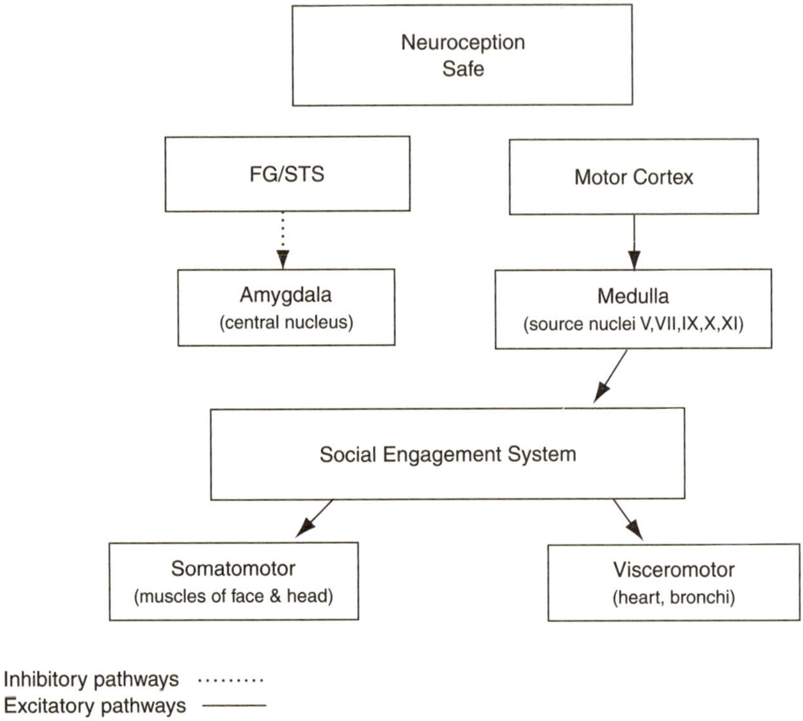

vated and dominates autonomic state. Figure 12.3 illustrates the neural circuits involved in response to life threat. In response to life threat, the mammalian nervous system promotes immobilization or freezing behavior. Freezing, as a defense strategy, is coordinated by the PAG. To inhibit metabolic activity during immobilization, autonomic state is under the control of the dorsal vagal complex. As proposed by the polyvagal theory, the autonomic reactions during each adaptive behavioral strategy is hierarchically organized after the phylogeny of both the changes in the vertebrate autonomic nervous system and changes in the behavioral repertoire from immobilization to mobilization to social engagement.

The ability to evaluate whether the environment is safe or if a person is trustworthy is difficult for individuals with a variety of psychiatric diagnoses. Current research suggests that the areas in the temporal cortex (i.e., FG, STS), which are assumed to inhibit limbic defense reactions, are not activated in clinical populations that have difficulties with social engagement behaviors (e.g., autism, schizophrenia). Moreover, individuals with other psychiatric disorders, such as anxiety disorders and depression, which have as diagnostic features compromised social

FIGURE 12.2. Neural structures and pathways involved in a neuroception of danger.

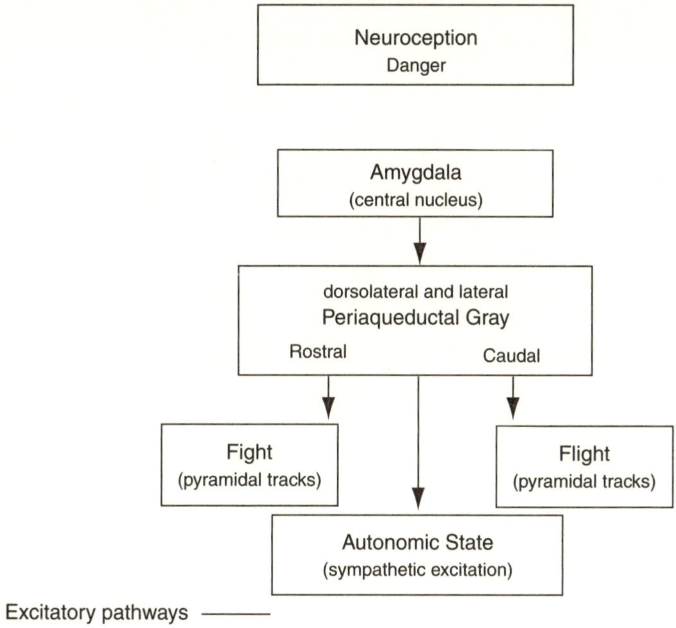

behavior, have difficulties in regulating visceral state (e.g., less vagal regulation of the heart) and supporting social engagement behaviors (e.g., reduced facial expressiveness and motor control of the striated muscles of the face and head). Thus, from a theoretical perspective, a potential root of several psychiatric disorders might be linked to an inability to detect safety in the environment and trustworthiness from interactions and, thus, the inability to express appropriate social engagement behaviors.

The study of attachment disorders such as RAD provides an intriguing test of the critical role of neuroception in mediating appropriate attachment and social behavior. RAD is described in both the DSM-IV (American Psychiatric Association, 1994) and the ICD-10 (World Health Organization, 1992) psychiatric diagnostic manuals. RAD comprises two clinical patterns (i.e., inhibited and uninhibited subtypes). The inhibited subtype is characterized by an emotionally withdrawn, unresponsive pattern in which there is an absence of attachment behaviors. The disinhibited subtype is characterized by indiscriminate attachment, which often is directed at strangers. These patterns have been described in institutionalized and maltreated children (Zeanah, 2000). From a neuroception perspective, in both subtypes, the evaluation of the risk in the environment is not accurate.

FIGURE 12.3. Neural structures and pathways involved in a neuroception of life threat.

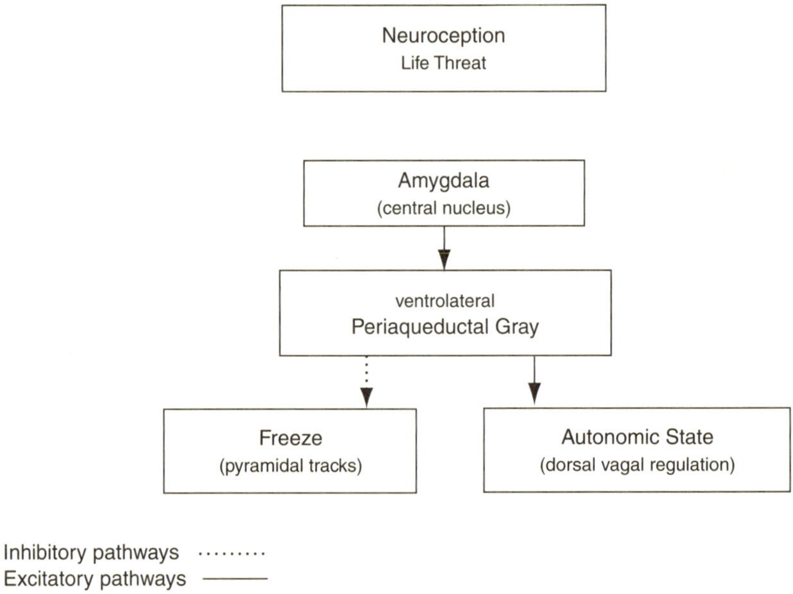

Recent research on the outcomes of children raised in institutions in Romania has stimulated interest in RAD and in developing intervention strategies to remediate these devastating disturbances in social development. If an accurate neuroception of the environment is necessary for normal social behavior, then what features in the environment might potentiate normal social development? A recent study of Romanian toddlers (Smyke, Dumitrescu, & Zeanah, 2002) provides insight into the process. In this study, indices of RAD were evaluated in children as a function of the number of different caregivers. Two groups of institutionalized children were evaluated and contrasted with children who were never institutionalized. One group consisted of the standard institution unit in which 20 different caregivers worked rotating shifts with approximately 3 caregivers for 30 children on each shift. A second group consisted of a pilot unit in which the number of children were reduced to approximately 10, and the pool of caregivers was reduced to 4. If neuroception of safety is necessary to promote appropriate social behavior, then familiarity of caregiver would be critical. By having familiar caregivers, the child's detection of the caregiver's face, voice, and movements (the features that define a safe and trustworthy person) should trigger the inhibitory pathways to disenable the limbic defense system and foster the behaviors expressed by the social engagement system. In support of this model, the study demonstrated a monotonic relation between the number of different caregivers that a child had contact with and the indices of RAD. On all measures, the standard unit children were more likely to have higher indices of RAD, and on some measures the pilot group did not differ from the children who were never institutionalized. Thus, once we understand the contextual and social features that inhibit the neural circuits that mediate defensive behavioral strategies, we can optimize the developmental consequences of the neural circuits that promotes social engagement behaviors.

CHAPTER 13

The Polyvagal Hypothesis: Common Mechanisms Mediating Autonomic Regulation, Vocalizations, and Listening

Vocalizations are an intricate component of the complex biobehavioral repertoire of mammals. Since vocalizations are involved in coordinating behaviors for mammals that are both prosocial and survival-oriented, the predominance of research on mammalian vocalizations has focused on describing the adaptive functions of specific vocal features. In contrast, there is a paucity of research investigating the neurophysiological linkage between autonomic regulation and both the production of vocalizations and the processing of acoustic information. This chapter applies hypotheses and principles derived from the polyvagal theory (see chapter 2; Porges, 2001a, 2007a) to interpret mammalian vocalizations. The theory emphasizes the parallel phylogenetic shift in both the neural regulation of the autonomic nervous system and the evolutionary emergence of an integrated social engagement system that includes features optimizing conspecific vocal communication. The chapter presents the polyvagal hypothesis as a new way to interpret the adaptive functions of mammalian vocalizations. The chapter emphasizes neural mechanisms involved in social communication, including the reciprocal relationship between production and reception of vocalizations.

THE POLYVAGAL THEORY: THREE PHYLOGENETIC RESPONSE SYSTEMS

The polyvagal theory (see chapter 2; Porges, 2001a, 2007a) links parallel phylogenetic changes in the neural regulation of the autonomic nervous system with adaptive behaviors. The theory emphasizes the phylogenetic shift in the features of the vagus, the primary parasympathetic cranial nerve involved in regulating visceral state. The theory is named polyvagal, since only in mammals does the vagus contain two distinct efferent pathways. In addition to an unmyelinated pathway originating in the dorsal motor nucleus of the vagus shared with other vertebrates (i.e., reptilians, amphibians, teleosts, and elasmobrachs), mammals have a myelinated pathway originating in the nucleus ambiguus, and this circuit communicates in the brainstem with source nuclei regulating the striated muscles of the face and head that are involved in several of the features of social communication (e.g., facial expression, vocalizations, listening).

The polyvagal theory provides a physiological basis to link uniquely mammalian anatomical and physiological circuits involved in visceral state regulation to both the expressive and receptive domains of social communication. The development of these features reflects the phylogenetic distinction between reptiles and mammals, and includes a cluster of behaviors dependent on the function of structures that phylogenetically emerged with mammals. These changes include detached middle ear bones, the advent of a diaphragm, and a myelinated vagal system regulating supradiaphragmatic organs that is distinct from an unmyelinated vagal system regulating subdiaphragmatic organs. The classic definition of mammals focuses on the observation of mammary glands and hair. However, the fossil record, since it cannot be explored through these features, relies on the identification of detached middle ear bones as the defining feature of mammals. Coincident with the separation of the middle ear bones, other phylogenetic transitions resulted in brainstem areas regulating the vagus becoming intertwined with the areas regulating the striated muscles of the face and head. The result of this transition was a dynamic social engagement system with social communication features (e.g., facial expression, head movements, vocalizations, and listening) interacting with visceral state regulation.

The polyvagal theory articulates how each of three phylogenetic stages of the development of the vertebrate autonomic nervous system is associated with a distinct autonomic subsystem that is retained and expressed in mammals. These autonomic subsystems are phylogenetically ordered and behaviorally linked to social communication (e.g., facial expression, vocalization, listening), mobilization (e.g., fight-or-flight behaviors), and immobilization (e.g., feigning death, vasovagal syncope, and behavioral suppression). Social communication (i.e., social engagement system, see later discussion) involves the myelinated vagus, which serves to foster calm behavioral states by inhibiting the sympathetic influences to the heart and dampening the hypothalamic–pituitary axis (HPA) (e.g., Bueno et al., 1989). The mobilization system is dependent on the functioning of the sympathetic nervous system. The most phylogenetically primitive component, the immobilization system, is dependent on the unmyelinated vagus, which is shared with most vertebrates. With increased neural complexity due to phylogenetic development, the organism's behavioral and affective repertoire is enriched. The three circuits can be conceptualized as dynamically adjusting to provide adaptive responses to safe, dangerous, and life-threatening events and contexts.

Unlike reptiles, the mammalian nervous system did not evolve solely to survive in dangerous and life-threatening contexts, but it evolved to promote social interactions and social bonds in safe environments. To accomplish this adaptive flexibility, the mammalian nervous system evolved a new neural strategy for safe environments, while retaining two more primitive neural circuits to regulate defensive strategies (i.e., fight-or-flight and death-feigning behaviors). It is important to note that social behavior, social communication, and visceral homeostasis are incompatible with the neurophysiological states and behaviors promoted by the two neural circuits that support defense strategies. Thus, via evolution, the mammalian nervous system retains three neural circuits, which are in a phylogenetically organized hierarchy. In this hierarchy of adaptive responses, the newest circuit associated with social communication is used first, and if that circuit fails to provide safety, the older survival-oriented circuits are recruited sequentially.

By investigating the phylogeny of the regulation of the vertebrate heart (see chapters 2 and 10; Morris & Nilsson, 1994; Taylor, Jordan, & Coote, 1999), four principles can be extracted that provide a basis for speculation regarding emergent behaviors and social communication. These principles lead to testable hypotheses relating the specific neural mechanisms supporting social engagement, fight-or-flight, and death-feigning behaviors.

1. There is a phylogenetic shift in the regulation of the heart from endocrine communication, to unmyelinated nerves, and finally to myelinated nerves.
2. There is a development of opposing neural mechanisms of excitation and inhibition to provide rapid regulation of graded metabolic output.
3. A face–heart connection evolved as the brainstem source nuclei of vagal pathways shifted ventrally from the older dorsal motor nucleus to the nucleus ambiguus. This resulted in an anatomical and neurophysiological linkage between the neural regulation of the heart via the myelinated vagus and the special visceral efferent pathways that regulate the striated muscles of the face and head, forming an integrated social engagement system (see Figure 3.1, p. 56) (for more details see chapter 12; Porges, 2001a, 2007a).
4. With increased cortical development, the cortex exhibits greater control over the brainstem via direct (e.g., corticobulbar) and indirect (e.g., corticoreticular) neural pathways originating in motor cortex and terminating in the source nuclei of the myelinated motor nerves emerging from the brainstem (e.g., specific neural pathways embedded within cranial nerves V, VII, IX, X, and XI), controlling visceromotor structures (i.e., heart, bronchi) and somatomotor structures (muscles of the face and head).

THE SOCIAL ENGAGEMENT SYSTEM

The study of comparative anatomy, evolutionary biology, and embryology provide important hints regarding the functional relationship between the neural control of the striated muscles of the face and head and emergent behaviors, including facial expressions, head movements and vocalizations. The nerves that control the muscles of the face and head share several common features. Pathways from five cranial nerves control the muscles of the face and head. Collectively, these pathways are labeled as special visceral efferent. Special visceral efferent nerves innervate striated muscles, which regulate the structures derived during embryology from the ancient gill arches (Truex & Carpenter, 1969). The special visceral efferent pathways regulate the muscles of mastication (e.g., ingestion), muscles of the middle ear (e.g., listening to conspecific vocalizations), muscles of the face (e.g., emotional expression), muscles of the larynx and pharynx (e.g., prosody and intonation), and muscles controlling head tilt and turning (e.g., gesture). In fact, the neural pathway that enables the eyelids to be closed in a graded manner (i.e., winking) in humans is also involved in tensing the stapedius muscle in the middle ear to facilitate hearing the human voice (Djupesland, 1976).

The source nuclei of the circuits regulating the striated muscles of the face and head interact in the brainstem with the source nucleus of the myelinated vagus, forming an integrated social engagement system. This system (as illustrated in Figure 3.1, p. 56) provides the neural structures involved in social and emotional behaviors. The social engagement system has a control component in the cortex (i.e., upper motor neurons) that regulates brainstem nuclei (i.e., lower motor neurons) to control eyelid opening (e.g., looking), facial muscles (e.g., emotional expression), middle ear muscles (e.g., extracting vocalizations from background noise), muscles of mastication (e.g., ingestion), laryngeal and pharyngeal muscles (e.g., vocalization), and head-turning muscles (e.g., social gesture and orientation). Collectively, these muscles function as filters that limit social stimuli (e.g., observing facial features and listening to vocalizations) and determine engagement with the social environment. The neural control of these muscles determines social experiences by changing facial features (especially in humans and other primates), modulating laryngeal and pharyngeal muscles to regulate intonation of vocalizations, and coordinating both facial and vocal motor tone with respiratory actions (see also Smotherman, Schwartz, & Metzner, 2010). In addition, the frequency of breathing is encoded into the phrasing of vocalizations and may convey urgency by expressing short phrases associated with short exhalations (i.e., rapid breathing) or convey calmness by expressing long phrases associated with long exhalations (i.e., slow breathing).

The source nuclei (i.e., lower motor neurons) of the special visceral efferent pathways are located in the brainstem and communicate with the source nuclei of the mammalian myelinated vagus, which functions as a neural pathway inhibiting visceral functions (e.g., slowing heart rate, lowering blood pressure, etc.) to actively reduce arousal to promote calm states consistent with the metabolic demands of growth and restoration. Direct corticobulbar pathways reflect the influence of frontal areas of the cortex (i.e., upper motor neurons) on the regulation of this system. Moreover, afferent feedback, through the sensory vagus to medullary areas (e.g., nucleus of the solitary tract) influences forebrain areas and regulates states of arousal and alertness. In addition, the anatomical structures involved in the social engagement system have neurophysiological interactions with the HPA, the neuropeptides of oxytocin and vasopressin, and the immune system (for overview, see Porges, 2001a).

PHYLOGENY OF THE MIDDLE EAR

As vertebrates evolved from reptiles to mammals, the structures at the end of the mandible (i.e., jaw bone) that define components in the middle ear became detached (Luo, 2007; Luo, Crompton, & Sun, 2001; Rowe, 1996; Wang, Hu, Meng, & Li, 2001) and formed the small bones (auditory ossicles) of the middle ear. For humans and other mammals, sound in the environment impinges on the eardrum and is transduced from the eardrum to the inner ear via the ossicles in the middle ear. Bárány (1938) argued that the main purpose of the ossicular chain in land mammals was to reduce the effect of low-frequency sounds via bone conduction. In addition to the filtering imposed by bone separation, further attenuation can be achieved when the stapedius muscle (stabilizing stapes and innervated via a branch of the facial nerve) and the tensor tympani muscle (innervated via a branch of the trigeminal nerve) are contracted. Tension reduces the compliance of the ossicular chain and dampens the amplitude of the low-frequency acoustic stimulation from the environment reaching the inner ear. This process is similar to tightening the skin on a kettledrum. When the skin is tightened, the pitch of the drum is higher. When the ossicular chain is tightened, similar to the stretched skin, the movement of the eardrum is reduced and only higher frequencies bouncing against the eardrum are transmitted to the inner ear and to the auditory processing areas of the brain. The impact of these muscles on the perceived acoustic environment is to markedly attenuate low-frequency sounds, which facilitates the extraction of sounds in a higher frequency band associated with human voice and other mammalian vocalizations.

The detachment of the middle ear bones from the mandible was paralleled by two phylogenetic shifts: (1) the jawbone no longer restricted the cranium to expand and fostered the cortical development that characterizes modern mammals (Rowe, 1996); and (2) the mammalian middle ear enabled low-amplitude relatively high-frequency airborne sounds (i.e., sounds in the frequency of vocalizations) to be heard, even when the acoustic environment was dominated by low-frequency sounds.

The evolution of the mammalian middle ear enabled mammals to communicate in a frequency band that could not be detected by reptiles that, due to a dependence on bone conduction, were able to hear predominantly lower frequencies. This ability to hear low-amplitude, high-frequency airborne sounds in an acoustic environment dominated by loud low-frequency sounds is accomplished when the middle ear muscles are tensed to create rigidity along the ossicular chain. This mechanism unmasks the high-frequency sounds associated with mammalian vocalizations from background sounds. Without stiffening the ossicular chain, mammals would lose this advantage, and the soft airborne sounds of vocalizations would be easily lost in the acoustic background (see Borg & Counter, 1989). In fact, individuals who can voluntarily contract middle ear muscles exhibit an attenuation of approximately 30 dB at frequencies below 500 Hz, while there is no or minimal attenuation at frequencies above 1,000 Hz (see Kryter, 1985).

The earliest mammals were small, and vocal communication outside the acoustic range of their predominant predators (i.e., reptiles) was crucial to survival. The physics of the middle ear resulted in a specific range of frequencies requiring a lower sound pressure level to be detected. In small mammals, this frequency band was noticeably higher than the frequency band that large reptiles, due to a dependency on bone conduction, could easily detect. However, as mammals evolved, selective pressure resulted in larger mammals surviving. The size of the middle ear's structures increased with increased body size and the resonant frequency of the middle ear became lower. Thus, with large mammals (e.g., elephants and whales) the frequencies enhanced by middle ear structures foster infrasound communication with wavelengths that can travel over long distances and overlap with the lower frequencies that reptiles detect via bone conduction.

IMPACT OF MIDDLE EAR STRUCTURES ON SENSITIVITY TO CONSPECIFIC VOCALIZATIONS

The perception of sound is not equal at all frequencies. We hear sounds at low frequencies as if they were softer than their actual physical energy. In contrast, humans are relatively accurate in estimating the acoustic energy of frequencies associated with voice. This phenomenon initially reported as the Fletcher–Munson equal loudness contours (Fletcher & Munson, 1933), illustrated how human perception attenuated the "loudness" of low-frequency sounds. As measurement technologies improved, researchers refined the perceived loudness contours, and sound meters were modified to include a scale known as dB(A), which adjusted for the perceived differences in loudness as a function of frequency (i.e., the acoustic energy of lower frequencies had to be greatly increased to be perceived at the equivalent loudness of higher frequencies). This contrasts to sound pressure level, which describes the physical energy of the signal and does not apply any perceptually based weighting to the frequencies that constitute the acoustic stimulation.

The perceptual process of detecting conspecific vocalizations in background noise, illustrates the antimasking function of the middle ear muscles (attenuating the sounds at low frequencies). In addition to the antimasking function of the middle ear muscles, the middle ear structures act as a natural amplifier and contribute to the advantage in detecting conspecific vocalizations. Amplification occurs when the acoustic energy of vocalizations is characterized by a frequency band that overlaps with the resonance frequencies of the middle ear structures.

Thus, due to the selective active antimasking by the middle ear muscles and the passive amplification by the middle ear structures, there are species-specific equal loudness contours. As a general rule, conspecific vocalizations occupy this frequency band of perceptual advantage.

Dammeijer, Dijk, Chenault, Manni, and Mameren (2007) evaluated the effect of noise exposure on the stapedius muscle in the rat. Their data suggest that even in the absence of loud noise the stapedius is active, with contraction observed at sound pressure levels much lower than those needed to elicit the acoustic reflex threshold (Pilz, Ostwald, Kreiter, & Schnitzler, 1997). In addition, the data were consistent with the assumed purpose of the stapedius in unmasking high-frequency signals by attenuating low-frequency, low-level constant noise in everyday life (Pang & Guinan, 1997). The middle ear muscles are composed primarily of relatively small fast-twitch fibers (deJong, Kingma, Wirtz, Berge, & Marres, 1988). Since the muscles are characterized, at least in the rat, by relatively high anaerobic, glycolytic, and aerobic oxidative enzyme activity, there is a natural resistance to fatigue. In addition, the numerous motor end plates, in combination with the numerous axon bundles, are indicative of small motor units and support the assumption that the middle ear muscles are able to perform finely graded contractions. In our laboratory, we are demonstrating a similar intensity-tuned function of the middle ear muscles in humans.

The antimasking role of the middle ear muscles in auditory processing is especially relevant when considering the impact of low-frequency background sounds on cochlear mechanisms. Standing waves from pure tone stimuli occupy larger regions of the basilar membrane as the intensity increases, reducing the sensitivity of cochlear filtering for intense stimuli. This process is observed in the flattening of the equal loudness profile. Thus, by attenuating low-frequency sound waves, even below the level of the acoustic reflex threshold, the graded contractions of the middle ear muscles would improve the frequency sensitivity and selectivity mediated by the outer hair cells in the frequency band of mammalian vocalizations.

The physics of the middle ear structures impose other filter characteristics. Although the stiffening of the ossicular chain functions as a high-pass filter by contracting the middle ear muscles and dampening the influence of low-frequency sounds on the inner ear, the physical characteristics of the ossicular chain also influence the acoustic energy reaching the inner ear. Ossicle inertia determines the highest frequencies that can pass through the middle ear (Hemilä et al., 1995). The high-frequency limit is inversely proportional to the ossicular mass. Although, in general, larger mammals have greater ossicular mass, there are instances of larger mammals being able to detect higher frequencies due to adaptive shifts in ossicle mass to facilitate the detection of sounds associated with predator, prey, and cohort. For example, cats have excellent sensitivity at very high frequencies and may benefit from hearing high-frequency sounds produced by small rodents (Forsman & Malmquist, 1988; Rosenzweig & Amon, 1955).

THE FREQUENCY BAND OF PERCEPTUAL ADVANTAGE

In very small mammals, the middle ear and inner ear structures can convey acoustic information in a range well above the audible sounds that humans can reliably detect. The upper frequency limit for audible sounds in humans is approximately 20,000 Hz. Thus, 20,000 Hz is often used to delineate audible from ultrasound in the acoustic spectrum. However, the terminology is misleading, since acoustic stimuli characterized as ultrasonic are within the "audible" range of several mammalian species.

When audiograms of mammals are plotted on a logarithmic x-axis (for review see Fay, 1988), the lowest threshold is observed in a band of frequencies functionally defined by the high pass of the middle ear muscles and the low-pass features of the combined effect of olivary–cochlear mechanisms and the inertia of the ossicular chain. This frequency band of perceptual advantage (i.e., lower thresholds to hear) is specific to each mammalian species with the smaller mammals, in general, having an advantage to hear higher frequencies. However, since low-frequency sounds dominate most acoustic environments, this frequency band of perceptual advantage is optimized only when lower frequencies do not overwhelm the acoustic apparatus. Thus, the importance of contracting the middle ear muscles is to reduce acoustic energy in the lower frequencies. In general, it is within this frequency band of perceptual advantage that mammalian species produce most of their relevant conspecific vocalizations. For example, with the human, although the generally accepted frequencies for human hearing are between 20 and 20,000 Hz, the human frequency band of perceptual advantage includes a band of frequencies from approximately 500 Hz to about 4,000 Hz. Within these frequencies, the second and third formant in both male and female human speech always occur, and in many cases so does the first formant. This select band, which conveys the information of human voice, is functionally amplified by the antimasking mechanisms of the middle ear muscles that dampen low-frequency activity and olivary–cochlear mechanisms that dampen high-frequency activity. Similar mechanisms in the rat provide a frequency band of perceptual advantage from approximately 5 kHz to 50 kHz (see Bjork, Nevalainen, Hakumaki, & Voipio, 1999).

Auditory information can be weighted within this frequency band to improve the extraction of human speech. Two such methods are known as the "index of articulation" (Kryter, 1962) and the more recent "speech intelligibility index" (American National Standards Institute, 1997). These indices emphasize the relative importance of specific frequencies in conveying speech-related information embedded in human vocalizations. In the normal ear, acoustic energy within the primary frequencies of these indices is not attenuated, as it passes through the middle ear structures to the inner ear. The frequency band defining the index of articulation is similar to the frequency band that composers have historically selected to express melodies. It is also the frequency band that mothers have used to calm their infants by singing lullabies. Modulation of the acoustic energy within the frequencies of human voice that characterize music, similar to vocal prosody, will recruit and modulate the neural regulation of the middle ear muscles, functionally calm the behavioral and physiological state by increasing vagal regulation of the heart, and promote more spontaneous social engagement behaviors. Vocal music duplicates the effect of vocal prosody and triggers neural mechanisms that regulate the entire social engagement system with the resultant changes in facial affect and autonomic state. Basically, we start to look and feel better when we listen to melodies.

The auditory system is capable of compressing the range of acoustic stimuli. Much of this compression occurs at the periphery. For example, stapedius muscle contraction reduces sound transmission at low frequencies. Zwislocki (2002), stated that: "placement of stimulus compression in the auditory periphery must have been an important evolutionary adaptation through which the remaining system can operate within a biologically more easily achievable range" (p. 14601). As Zwislocki suggests, by compressing the energy of loud low-frequency sounds, the inner ear and higher brain structures can process the higher frequency content of the acoustic signal in the range of vocalizations. From an engineering point of view, placing a mechanism to compress the nonlinearity at the periphery of a system reduces the dynamic range required of the remaining parts of the system. This compression mechanism would function as an automatic gain control to filter the acoustic energy at frequencies lower than the vocalizations and would allow higher brain structures to extract meaning and syntax by processing the acoustic energy in this narrower frequency range.

Although humans and other mammals can vocalize outside the frequency band of perceptual advantage, the within-species social communication is usually characterized by frequency modulated vocalizations within this frequency band. In contrast, danger and pain signals may be shrill cries (i.e., high pitch with diminished frequency modulation) at the upper edge of this frequency band. In addition, aggressive signaling may push vocalizations to lower frequencies outside this band (e.g., the roar of a lion). This preference to vocalize in a social context within the frequencies most easily detected by conspecifics has clear adaptive features, but it also creates challenges. In particular, the frequencies of these vocalizations are dependent on the processing of airborne acoustic energy and are above the frequencies easily conveyed through bone conduction. The higher frequencies of airborne mammalian vocalizations (audible and ultrasound) are characterized by very short wavelengths that dissipate rapidly with distance from the source. In contrast, low frequencies have long wavelengths that travel over long distances.

The short wavelength of mammalian vocalizations evolved with convergent mechanisms to aid in adaptive social engagement behaviors (see Porges, 2007a). For many mammals, including humans, facial expressivity and behavioral gestures (e.g., use of the hands by primates) are coordinated with the shifts in prosody (intonation) to reduce ambiguity of the acoustic message (Corballis, 2003).

Thus, the signals of distress and danger often require concordant facial cues and hand gestures (see also Eberl, 2010). Areas in the temporal cortex are sensitive to this cross-modal binding of auditory–visual inputs during vocalizations. Congruent speech-related visual input activates supra-additive multisensory neurons in the superior temporal cortex. In contrast, reduced activation in these areas has been reported during tasks requiring the integration of auditory and visual language inputs in schizophrenics, a disorder frequently associated with auditory hallucinations (Surguladze et al., 2001). Functionally, the simultaneous observation of facial and head movements, while listening to human vocalizations, improves speech intelligibility (e.g., McGurk & MacDonald, 1976; Munhall, Jones, Callan, Kuratate, & Vatikiotis-Bateson, 2004) and has been reported to increase the ability to extract speech from background sounds by approximately 10–20 dB (Chen & Rao, 1998; Sumby & Polack, 1954).

One of the consequences of depending on high frequencies for social communication is that infants cannot stray far from the protection of their mother. In many small mammalian species (e.g., rats, mice) the predominance of ultrasound vocalizations by infants further restricts the distance that the caregiver can move from the litter. In rats, the frequencies used to communicate change developmentally. As rat pups develop and express exploratory behaviors, vocalizations shift from infantile ultrasound to adult type communication, which may also include audible sounds (Takahashi, 1992). As the rat pups mature, well-organized mobilization behaviors support exploration, and the pups extend the distance they explore from the mother. Paralleling this shift toward adult vocalizations are increases in the neural regulation of the larynx and pharynx, structures involved in the production and articulation of vocalizations, with a parallel increase in the neural regulation of the heart via the myelinated vagus (Larson & Porges, 1982).

ADAPTIVE COST FOR ACTIVE LISTENING TO VOCALIZATIONS

There may be a cost for actively dampening the sensitivity to low-frequency sounds and engaging the neural mechanisms involved in listening to the frequency band of perceptual advantage. Listening to the frequency band of perceptual advantage requires the neural implementation of an active filter that reduces the acoustic information at low frequencies that can reach the brain. Since the sounds associated with predators, especially the movements of larger animals, are characterized by low-frequency sounds, engaging in this active "listening" process has maladaptive consequences by reducing the ability to detect predators. Thus, the advantage of listening to conspecific vocalization also comes at a cost. In the "wild" the potential cost of social communication is reduction of predator detection. The adaptive consequence of this vulnerability is to restrict or to limit listening to vocalizations within the frequency band of perceptual advantage (an important component of social engagement and social communication) primarily in safe environments such as nests and burrows.

THE SOCIAL ENGAGEMENT SYSTEM AND THE POLYVAGAL "VOCALIZATION" HYPOTHESIS

As proposed by the polyvagal theory, the functioning and development of the striated muscles of the face and head involved in listening and in production of vocalizations parallel the maturation of the myelinated vagus (see Larson & Porges, 1982). This developmental covergence, among several neural circuits that constitute an integrated functional social engagement system (see Figure 3.1, p. 56), results in facilitating several adaptive behaviors, including: (1) an improved ability to regulate physiological state via myelinated vagal pathways (i.e., vagal brake) to both self-soothe and maintain calm states, as well as to mobilize by withdrawing the vagal brake to explore, forage, and defend; (2) increased neural regulation of the larynx and pharynx to promote conspecific vocalizations in the frequency band of perceptual advantage for the species to selectively signal peers and caregivers with a vocal mechanism that produces vocalizations with the highest adaptive value; and (3) improved thermoregulatory activity that reduces the need for the caregiver, as the autonomic nervous system matures.

The polyvagal theory emphasizes a phylogenetic parallel in the changing neural regulation of the autonomic nervous system and the neural regulation of the striated muscles of the face and head. This point is relevant to the study of mammalian vocalizations, since the striated muscles of the face and head are involved in both the detection of vocalizations (during listening) and in the production of these sounds through the coordination of the laryngeal and pharyngeal muscles with respiratory mechanisms.

The convergent phylogenetic changes in the neural regulation of the structures involved in the production and detection of mammalian vocalizations leads to the polyvagal hypothesis. Specifically, only mammals have a diaphragm to coordinate vocalizations with respiratory effort and volume. Consistent with the dependence on the mammalian diaphragm is the uniquely mammalian distinction between the two branches of the vagus: one dealing with supradiaphragmatic organs and the other dealing with subdiaphragmatic organs. The neural regulation of the subdiaphragmatic vagus is involved in abdominal breathing, while the neural regulation of supradiaphragmatic vagus is coordinated with the laryngeal and pharyngeal muscles that shape the acoustic features and provide facial expressions consistent with prosodic features of vocalizations. Moreover, slow exhalation, the respiratory process associated with expressive social vocalizations, enhances the impact of the myelinated vagus on the heart, promoting calm states.

The polyvagal hypothesis proposes that acoustic characteristics of vocalization not only serve to communicate to conspecifics relevant features in the environment, but also reflect the physiological state of the producer of the vocalizations. Mammals, but not reptiles or other phylogenetic antecedents to mammals, have a myelinated vagus, a diaphragm, detached middle ears, and neural circuits in the brainstem linking and coordinating the regulation of the myelinated vagus with the regulation of the striated muscles of the face and head. Specifically, engagement of this circuit conveys and expresses states of calmness and safety and would be associated with greater vagal influences to the heart and lungs to promote calmer physiological states, increased neural tone to the middle ear muscles to optimize listening in the frequency band of perceptual advantage, and increased neural tone to the laryngeal and pharyngeal muscles to shift the acoustic energy of vocalizations to lower frequencies and increased frequency modulation within the band of perceptual advantage. In contrast, retraction of this circuit conveys and expresses states of danger and distress, and would be associated with faster heart rate and breathing and higher pitched vocalizations. Thus, in humans the features of vocal prosody are expressed during social interactions and reduced during both mental and physical illness. Similarly, the vocalizations of small mammals may have a parallel to human prosody. Rats, while playing or experiencing more positive affective states, modulate their ultrasonic vocalizations across a range of frequencies within the rat's band of perceptual advantage, while vocalizations communicating negative states such as danger are characterized by vocalizations at a relatively constant frequency through a different neural mechanism (e.g., Brudzynski, 2007).

Consistent with the polyvagal hypothesis, medically compromised human infants have a high-pitched cry with little frequency modulation that is articulated in short bursts (Lester & Zeskin, 1982; Porter, Porges, & Marshall, 1988). Intonations of infant cries are regulated by neural tone, via source nuclei in the nucleus ambiguus, to the laryngeal muscles and the heart. In the physiologically stressed infant, decreased neural tone theoretically reduces the inhibitory effect on the heart and bronchi and the contraction of laryngeal muscles, thus producing dramatic increases in both heart rate and respiration rate and the fundamental frequency of the cry.

Porter and colleagues (1988) reported a convergence between withdrawal of cardiac vagal tone (i.e., measured by respiratory sinus arrhythmia and mediated via the myelinated vagal pathways originating in the nucleus ambiguus) and the shift in fundamental frequency of newborn pain cries in response to circumcision. Cardiac vagal tone was significantly reduced during the severe stress of circumcision, and these reductions were paralleled by significant increases in the pitch of the infants' cries. These results document the important role that the social engagement system has in signaling and responding to "stress" and pain, and provide a demonstration that the vocalizations convey information regarding visceral and emotional state.

SUMMARY

The polyvagal theory emphasizes the phylogenetic shifts in the neural regulation of the autonomic nervous system and how this evolutionary shift in neural regulation converged with the regulation of the middle ear muscles to facilitate mammalian vocal communication. The theory emphasizes the different neural circuits that support defensive behaviors (i.e., fight-or-flight and freeze) and social interactions. According to the theory, during defensive states, when the middle ear muscles are not contracted, acoustic stimuli are prioritized by intensity and during safe social engagement states, acoustic stimuli are prioritized by pitch. During safe states, hearing of the frequencies associated with conspecific vocalizations is selectively being amplified, while other frequencies are attenuated. During the defensive states, the loud, low-frequency sounds signaling a predator could be more easily detected, and the soft, higher frequencies of conspecific vocalizations are lost in background sounds. During social engagement behaviors, an integrated social engagement system regulates a shift in autonomic state to dampen sympathetic activity and to increase parasympathetic tone, while simultaneously increasing the neural tone to the striated muscles of the face and head (i.e., facial expressions, increased "emotional" cueing of the eyes associated with increased eye contact, increased prosody, and enhanced listening by contracting the middle ear muscles). During social interactions, the stiffening of the ossicular chain actively changes the transfer function of the middle ear, and functionally dampens low-frequency sounds and improves the ability to extract conspecific vocalizations. However, the selectivity to listen to conspecific vocalizations comes at a cost, and the detection of lower acoustic frequencies generated by predators becomes more difficult. Thus, the identification and construction of safe contexts (e.g., burrows, nests, or houses) plays an important role in enabling the social engagement system to promote prosocial behavior.

Co-author for this chapter was G. F. Lewis.

PART IV

THERAPEUTIC AND CLINICAL PERSPECTIVES

CHAPTER 14

The Vagus: A Mediator of Behavioral and Physiological Features Associated With Autism

The vagus nerve, as a system, provides a rich organizing principle to investigate several of the behavioral, psychological, and physiologic features associated with a diagnosis of autism. The vagus is not only a cranial nerve meandering through the periphery, but also an important bidirectional conduit carrying specialized motor and sensory signals that are part of a larger integrated feedback system that includes brain structures involved in the regulation of visceral state and affect. The premise of this chapter is that several features of autism become more understandable if a more integrated model of the nervous system is applied in which the vagus is a critical component.

THE VAGUS AND AFFECT REGULATION

The relation between affect and vagal afferent activity is not a recent idea. Darwin (1872) noted in *The Expression of Emotions in Man and Animals* the importance of the bidirectional neural communication between the heart and the brain via the "pneumogastric" nerve, now known as the vagus nerve.

Current research emphasizes the importance of the vagal afferents in the regulation of visceral state, mood, and affect. Studies have demonstrated that stimulation of vagal afferents regulate brain structures involved in epilepsy (Boon et al., 2001), depression (George et al., 2000), and even repetitive self-destructive behaviors often associated with autism (Murphy, Wheless, & Schmoll, 2000).

POLYVAGAL THEORY: THREE NEURAL CIRCUITS REGULATING REACTIVITY

Through stages of phylogeny, mammals, and especially primates, have evolved a functional neural organization that regulates visceral state to support social behavior. The polyvagal theory (see chapters 2, 10, and 11; Porges, 2001a) emphasizes the phylogenetic origins of brain structures that regulate social and defensive behaviors, domains compromised in individuals with autism. The polyvagal theory proposes that the evolution of the mammalian autonomic nervous system provides the neurophysiologic substrates for the emotional experiences and affective processes that are major components of social behavior. The theory proposes that physiologic state limits the range of behavior and psychological experience. In this context, the evolution of the nervous system determines the range of emotional expression, quality of communication, and the ability to regulate bodily and behavioral state. The polyvagal theory links the evolution of the autonomic nervous system to affective experience, emotional expression, facial gestures, vocal communication, and contingent social behavior. Thus, the theory provides a plausible explanation of several social, emotional, and communication behaviors and disorders associated with autism.

The polyvagal construct was introduced to emphasize and document the neurophysiologic and neuroanatomical distinction between two branches of the vagus and to propose that each vagal branch is associated with a different adaptive behavioral strategy. The theory proposes that the different branches are related to unique, adaptive behavioral strategies and articulates three phylogenetic stages of the development of the mammalian autonomic nervous system. These stages reflect the emergence of three distinct subsystems, which are phylogenetically ordered and behaviorally linked to social communication (e.g., facial expression, vocalization, listening), mobilization (e.g., fight-or-flight behaviors), and immobilization (e.g., feigning death, vasovagal syncope, and behavioral shutdown). The mobilization system is dependent on the functioning of the sympathetic nervous system. The most phylogenetically primitive component, the immobilization system, is dependent on the unmyelinated or "vegetative" vagus, which is shared with most vertebrates. With increased neural complexity due to phylogenetic development, the organism's behavioral and affective repertoire is enriched (see Table 14.1).

The theory emphasizes the functional aspect of neural control of both the striated muscles of the face and the smooth muscles of the viscera, because their functions rely on common brainstem structures. It does not make any assumptions regarding structural damage to either the vagal systems or the brain structures that regulate brainstem structures associated with the vagal systems. Thus, although the compromised brainstem features described by Rodier and colleagues (1996) are consistent with the predictions of the polyvagal theory, the theory emphasizes functional deficits and does not necessarily assume structural damage.

By investigating the phylogeny of the regulation of the vertebrate heart (Morris & Nilsson, 1994), three principles can be extracted. First, there is a phylogenetic shift in the regulation of the heart from endocrine communication, to unmyelinated nerves, and finally to myelinated nerves. Second, there is a development of opposing neural mechanisms of excitation and inhibition to provide

TABLE 14.1. The Three Phylogenetic Stages of the Neural Control of the Heart Proposed by the Polyvagal Theory

Phylo-genetic Stage	ANS Component	Behavioral Function	Lower Motor Neurons
III	Myelinated vagus	Social communication, self-soothing and calming, inhibit sympathetic-adrenal influences	Nucleus ambiguus
II	Sympathetic-adrenal	Mobilization (active avoidance, inhibit dorsal vagal influences)	Spinal cord
I	Unmyelinated vagus	Immobilization (death feigning, passive avoidance)	Dorsal motor nucleus of the vagus

rapid regulation of graded metabolic output. Third, with increased cortical development, the cortex exhibits greater control over the brainstem via direct (e.g., corticobulbar) and indirect (e.g., corticoreticular) neural pathways originating in the motor cortex and terminating in the source nuclei of the myelinated motor nerves emerging from the brainstem (e.g., specific neural pathways embedded within cranial nerves V, VII, IX, X, and XI), controlling visceromotor structures (i.e., heart, bronchi, thymus) and somatomotor structures (muscles of the face and head).

These phylogenetic principles provide a basis for speculations regarding the behavioral and physiologic responses associated with autism. With this new vagal system, transitory incursions into the environment or withdrawals from a potential predator can be initiated without the severe biologic cost associated with sympathetic-adrenal activation. Paralleling this change in neural control of the heart is an enhanced neural control of the face, larynx, and pharynx that enables complex facial gestures and vocalizations associated with social communication. This phylogenetic course results in greater central nervous system regulation of physiologic state that supports behaviors needed to engage and disengage with environmental challenges.

THE VAGAL BRAKE

Due to the tonic vagal influences to the sinoatrial node (i.e., the heart's pacemaker), resting heart rate is substantially lower than the intrinsic rate of the pacemaker. When the vagal tone to the pacemaker is high, the vagus acts as a brake on the rate at which the heart is beating (see chapter 7). When vagal tone to the pacemaker is low, there is little or no inhibition of the pacemaker. Thus, neurophysiologically, the vagal brake provides a mechanism to rapidly switch between physiologic states that either support social communication or mobilization. Functionally, the vagal brake, by modulating visceral state, enables the individual to rapidly engage and disengage with objects and other individuals and to promote self-soothing behaviors and calm behavioral states. These behaviors are obviously compromised in autism. Is it possible that autism is associated with a deficit in the vagal brake and an inability to switch between neurobiologic states that foster either defensive or social behaviors?

The polyvagal theory provides an explicit neurobiologic model of how difficulties in spontaneous social behavior are linked to both facial expressivity and the regulation of visceral state. The theory proposes a possible mechanism to explain how these difficulties might form a core domain of several psychiatric profiles. Relevant to autism are the specific deficits in both the somatomotor (e.g., poor gaze, low facial affect, lack of prosody, difficulties in mastication) and visceromotor (e.g., difficulties in autonomic regulation resulting in cardiopulmonary and digestive problems) areas of the social engagement system. Deficits in the social engagement system compromise spontaneous social behavior, social awareness, affect expressivity, prosody, and language development. In contrast, interventions that improve the neural regulation of the social engagement system hypothetically should enhance spontaneous social behavior and state and affect regulation, reduce stereotypical behaviors, and improve language skills.

During the development of the human embryo, components of several cranial nerves, known as special visceral efferent pathways, develop together to form the neural substrate of a social engagement system (see chapter 11). This system, as illustrated in Figure 3.1, p. 56, provides the neural structures involved in social and emotional behaviors. The social engagement system has a control component in the cortex (i.e., upper motor neurons) that regulates brainstem nuclei (i.e., lower motor neurons) to control eyelid opening (e.g., looking), facial muscles (e.g., emotional expression), middle ear muscles (e.g., extracting the human voice from background noise), muscles of mastication (e.g., ingestion), laryngeal and pharyngeal muscles (e.g., vocalization and language), and head-turning muscles (e.g., social gesture, orientation). Collectively, these muscles function as filters that limit social stimuli (e.g., observing facial features, listening to the human voice) and determinants of engagement with the social environment. The neural control of these muscles determines social experiences. In addition, the source nuclei (i.e., lower motor neurons) of these nerves, which are located in the brainstem, communicate directly with an inhibitory neural system that slows heart rate, lowers blood pressure, and actively reduces arousal to promote calm states consistent with the metabolic demands of growth and restoration of human neurophysiologic systems.

Direct corticobulbar pathways reflect the influence of frontal areas of the cortex (i.e., upper motor neurons) on the regulation of this system. Moreover, afferent feedback through the vagus to medullary areas (e.g., the nucleus of the solitary tract, which is the source nucleus of the afferent vagus) influences forebrain areas that are assumed to be involved in several psychiatric disorders. In addition, the anatomical structures involved in the social engagement system have neurophysiologic interactions with the hypothalamic-pituitary-adrenal (HPA) axis, the neuropeptides of oxytocin and vasopressin, and the immune system (Porges, 2001a). As a cluster, the difficulties with gaze, extraction of the human voice, facial expression, head gesture, prosody, and state regulation are common features of individuals with autism. For example, the neural pathway that raises the eyelids also tenses the stapedius muscle in the middle ear, which facilitates hearing the human voice (Borg & Counter, 1989). Thus, the neural mechanisms for making eye contact are shared with those needed to listen to the human voice.

Studies have demonstrated that the neural regulation of middle ear muscles, a necessary mechanism to extract human voice from loud low-frequency background noise, is defective in individuals with language delays, learning disabilities, and autistic spectrum disorders (Smith et al., 1988; Thomas et al., 1985). Middle ear infection (i.e., otitis media) may result in a total inability to elicit the "reflexive" contraction of the stapedius muscles (Yagi & Nakatani, 1987). Disorders that influence the neural function of the facial nerve (i.e., Bell's palsy) not only influence the stapedius reflex (Ardic, Topaloglu, Oncel, Ardic, & Uguz, 1997) but also affect the patient's ability to discriminate speech (Wormald et al., 1995). Thus, the observed difficulties that many autistic individuals have in extracting the human voice from background sounds may be dependent on the same neural system that is involved in facial expression.

PREDICTIONS BASED ON POLYVAGAL THEORY

Observations of the behaviors and physiologic response of autistic individuals suggest that they have great difficulties in recruiting the neural circuit that regulates the social engagement system. It appears that autism is associated with autonomic states that remove the individual from direct social contact by supporting the adaptive defensive strategies of mobilization (i.e., fight-or-flight behaviors) or immobilization (i.e., shutdown). Behaviorally, the retraction of the neural regulation of the social engagement system is expressed as limited use and regulation of the muscles of the face and head. The functional consequences limit facial expressions and head gestures, compromise the ability to extract the human voice from background sounds, and reduce prosody.

Neurophysiologically, because the vagus is integrated into several feedback systems involving both peripheral and central structures, depression or dysregulation of the vagus might be manifested on several levels. First, it may compromise the regulation of visceral organs, such as the gut, heart, and pancreas. Second, because the vagus is involved in the modulation of pain and the regulation of cytokines and the HPA axis, there may be regulational disorders in those systems. Third, because the brainstem areas regulating the myelinated vagal system provide both output and input to feedback systems involving other brain structures, the vagal system may provide a portal to assess and stimulate higher neural processes. Although there is a limited scientific literature evaluating the role of the vagus in autism, the plausibility of these predictions are reviewed in this chapter and discussed within the context of the current literature, which includes studies with other clinical populations and animal preparations.

VAGAL REGULATION OF HEART RATE AND HEART RATE VARIABILITY

Because vagal efferent pathways to the heart are cardioinhibitory, changes in vagal tone can influence the metrics used to monitor heart rate and heart rate variability. In general, greater cardiac vagal tone produces slower heart rate and regulates the transitory changes in heart rate in response to stimulation. The myelinated vagal efferents that synapse on the sinoatrial node have a respiratory rhythm. This rhythmic increase and decrease in cardioinhibitory activity through the vagus produces a cardiac rate rhythm known as respiratory sinus arrhythmia (RSA). The greater the cardioinhibitory influence through the vagus, the greater the rhythmic increases and decreases in this heart rate pattern. Thus, the amplitude of RSA provides a sensitive index of the influence of the myelinated vagus has on the heart. The rapid changes in heart rate in response to specific stimuli are primarily under vagal control. The characteristic heart rate pattern to stimulus changes—an immediate deceleration followed by either a continued deceleration or an acceleration—is primarily due to dynamic increases or decreases in cardioinhibitory activity through the myelinated vagus. The literature suggests that autism is associated with reliable differences in the amplitude of RSA and the transitory heart rate response pattern to various stimuli and task demands.

An early publication by Hutt, Rorresst, and Richer (1975) reported that normal children suppressed RSA more than autistic children did. Similarly, Althaus et al. (1999) found that children with a pervasive developmental disorder not otherwise specified (PDD-NOS) did not suppress RSA. Consistent with these findings, an early study of children diagnosed with schizophrenia (Piggott et al., 1973) identified significant differences in respiration and in the covariation between respiration and heart rate. The schizophrenic children had significantly faster and more shallow breathing patterns, a pattern consistent with reduced vagal efferent activity.

Other studies report that autistic children have dampened transitory heart rate responses to a variety of stimulation. Zahn, Rumsey, and Van Kammen (1987) reported unusually small deceleratory heart rate responses to auditory stimulation. Palkovitz and Wiesenfeld (1980) reported dampened heart rate responses to socially relevant speech, nonsense phrases, and a 500 Hz tone. Corona et al. (1998) reported that the heart rate of children with autism did not change across conditions.

VAGAL NERVE STIMULATION

Although not currently being used to treat autism, vagal nerve stimulation has been effective in treating epilepsy and depression. Vagal nerve stimulation is based on the assumption that stimulation of vagal afferents has a direct effect on the regulation of higher brain structures. The source nucleus of the vagal afferents is the nucleus of the solitary tract. This medullary nucleus plays an important role in the regulation of behavioral state, respiration, and blood pressure, and in conveying information to higher brain structures. The nucleus of the solitary tract relays the incoming sensory information via three primary pathways: (1) feedback to regulate the periphery, (2) direct projections to the reticular formation in the medulla, and (3) ascending projections to the forebrain, primarily through the parabrachial nucleus and the locus ceruleus. The parabrachial nucleus and the locus ceruleus send direct connections to all levels of the forebrain (e.g., hypothalamus, amygdala, the thalamic regions that control the insula and orbitofrontal and prefrontal cortices), areas that have been implicated in neuropsychiatric disorders. Thus, vagal afferent stimulation has direct input to both the lower motor neurons in the brainstem and the upper motor neurons in the cortex that regulate the social engagement system. Recent reviews provide a detailed description of the neurophysiologic basis for the intervention (George et al., 2000) and provide an explanation of the neural mechanisms involved in treating depression with vagal nerve stimulation (Marangell et al., 2002). Missing from these explanations is an acknowledgment of the communication between vagal afferents and the source nuclei of the nerves that regulate striated muscles of the face and head (i.e., special visceral efferent pathways), which collectively form the motor part of the social engagement system. It is this interaction that is emphasized in the polyvagal theory (Porges, 2001a).

Extrapolating from the vagal nerve stimulation model, one might speculate that other forms of vagal stimulation might have beneficial effects. Behaviorally, one of the most potent strategies for vagal stimulation is to stimulate the peripheral baroreceptors that regulate blood pressure. Rocking and swinging, in which the position of the head is changed relative to the position of the heart, will stimulate the baroreceptors and engage this feedback loop. This suggests that the frequently observed rocking and swinging behaviors in autistic individuals may reflect a naturally occurring biobehavioral strategy to stimulate and to regulate a vagal system that is not efficiently functioning.

One publication reported that vagal nerve stimulation reduced autistic-like behaviors (Murphy et al., 2000). In this study, vagal stimulation was administered to six patients with hypothalamic hamartoma, a congenital brain malformation that is associated with medically refractory epilepsy and injurious autistic behavior. Four of the six patients had autistic behaviors that included poor communication, ritualisms, compulsions, no social skills, and injury to self and others. The authors report that during vagal nerve stimulation, all four showed impressive improvements in behavior. In one subject, the behavioral improvements were immediately reversed when the vagal nerve stimulation was temporarily discontinued without worsening of seizure frequency.

VAGAL REGULATION OF THE GUT

Due to the high prevalence of gastrointestinal symptoms in individuals with autism (Horvath & Perman, 2002; Wakefield et al., 2002), there has been an interest in a possible link between gut and brain as a determinant of autism. This interest was stimulated by reports from parents who indicated that the administration of intravenous secretin reduced autistic symptoms. However, there has been no evidence for the efficacy of secretin when it was administered in a randomized, placebo-controlled, double-blind clinical trial (Owley et al., 2001).

Current research suggests that the prevalence of gastrointestinal symptoms represents an unsolved problem in autism. However, if we conceptualize the problem from a "vagal" perspective, we can identify the vagus as a primary regulator of the gut, with vagal afferents providing important information to brain structures. Support for this argument comes from animal studies in which it has been demonstrated that the vagus is involved in the regulation of secretin (Li, Chang, & Chey, 1998; Lu & Owyang, 1995). Thus given the compromised behavioral components of the social engagement system, it is not surprising to find that the vagal regulation of gastrointestinal processes is also compromised in autistic individuals.

Additional information regarding the role that vagal afferents from the gut have in modulating sensory experiences comes from research on eating disorders. Research suggests that vagal afferents are involved not only in regulating satiety via vagovagal reflexes but also in regulating nociceptive sensations via solitary-spinal pathways. Faris et al. (2000) and Raymond, Eckert, et al. (1999) have proposed that vagal afferent activation by binge eating and vomiting also activates the descending pain inhibitory pathway, resulting in an elevated pain threshold. Similarly they have reported elevated pain thresholds in anorexia nervosa subjects (Raymond, Faris, et al., 1999). Their research has led to administering ondansetron as an intervention for bulimia nervosa (Faris et al., 2000). Ondansetron is marketed for the prevention of vagally mediated emesis caused by cancer chemotherapeutic agents.

THE VAGUS AND THE IMMUNE SYSTEM

The subdiaphragmatic vagal afferents may be conceptualized as providing a targeted signal to the central structures that regulate immune function. Other researchers have linked the vagal efferent pathways to immune function. Bulloch and Pomerantz (1984) described motor pathways via the vagus to the thymus. The link between the vagal regulation of immune function and the polyvagal theory is not clear. However, it might be plausible to speculate that the neural mediation of the myelinated vagus may, via direct influence on thymus and direct inhibition of the sympathetic nervous system, trigger a physiologic state that would promote immune function. Likewise, mobilization strategies, resulting in a withdrawal of vagal tone to the heart, increased sympathetic tone, and the release of cortisol, have been associated with suppressed immune function. More relevant to the expression of psychiatric disturbances is the finding that the afferent vagus mediates behavioral depression, but not fever, in response to peripheral immune signals following abdominal inflammation (Konsman et al., 2000).

Consistent with this model, it has been reported that autism spectrum disorder patients with developmental regression express excessive innate immune responses (Jyonouchi, Sun, & Le, 2001).

VAGAL REGULATION OF THE HPA AXIS

The vagus is involved in the regulation of the HPA axis. Vagal afferents exhibit an inhibitory influence on HPA axis and reduce cortisol secretion (e.g., Bueno et al., 1989; Miao et al., 1997). Studies (Cacioppo et al., 1995; Gunnar et al., 1995) have demonstrated a covariation between increases in cortisol and decreases in cardiac vagal tone (i.e., the amplitude of RSA). Thus, there appears to be a coordinated response that functions to promote metabolic activity and mobilization behaviors by withdrawing the vagal tone through the myelinated vagus and increasing both sympathetic activity and activation of the HPA axis.

Several studies have reported that the regulation of the HPA axis is dysfunctional in autistic children. Poorly developing autistic children were more likely to have an abnormal diurnal rhythm and an abnormal response on the dexamethasone suppression test than less severe cases (Hoshino et al., 1987). The results suggest that the negative feedback mechanism of the HPA axis may be disturbed in autistic children, especially in poorly developing individuals. Similarly, Jensen, Realmuto, and Garfinkel (1985) reported that most of the autistic patients studied failed to suppress cortisol with the dexamethasone test. Consistent with these reports, Jansen et al. (2000) reported the PDD-NOS children had a diminished cortisol response to physical stress.

THE VAGAL SYSTEM AS AN ORGANIZING PRINCIPLE

In this chapter, I have illustrated how the vagus is involved in the expression of several disparate symptoms associated with autism. Consistent with the polyvagal theory, the symptom clusters are associated with components of the vagal system. First, there are the behavioral characteristics linked to the neural regulation of the striated muscles of the face via special visceral efferent pathways (i.e., the somatomotor component of the social engagement system). Second, autism is associated with dysfunctional regulation of target organs (e.g., heart, gut) regulated by vagal efferent pathways (i.e., the visceromotor component of the social engagement system). Third, the vagal afferents exert a powerful regulatory influence on several systems—including visceral and tactile pain thresholds, the HPA axis, and the immune system—that are dysfunctional in autism. Fourth, the nucleus of the solitary tract (the source nucleus of the afferent vagus) influences areas of the forebrain that have been speculated to be compromised in autism.

CHAPTER 15

Borderline Personality Disorder and Emotion Regulation

The concept of a "borderline personality disorder" dates back to the early 1800s, when clinicians were unsure of the diagnosis of patients who displayed a combination of neurotic and psychotic symptoms. Since clinicians viewed these patients as being on the "border" between neurotic and psychotic, the borderline personality disorder (BPD) evolved as a diagnostic category and was listed as an Axis II diagnosis in 1980, with the publication of DSM-III (Hodges, 2003). The current DSM-IV-TR emphasizes that patients with BPD express symptoms that include affective instability, intense and tumultuous relationships, difficulty controlling anger, impulsivity, suicidal tendencies, and self-mutilation (American Psychiatric Association [APA], 2000; Rothschild, Haslam, Cleland, & Zimmerman, 2003). This cluster of symptoms indicates that BPD is associated with difficulty in regulating emotions, behavioral states, and relationships. BPD is a severe mental disorder that is more prevalent in women and is believed to impact approximately 2% of the population (APA, 2000; Hodges, 2003; Swartz, Blazer, George, & Winfield, 1990; Torgersen, Kringlen, & Cramer, 2001) and approximately 20% of the hospitalized psychiatric patients (Zanarini & Grankenbrug, 2001).

Because BPD is associated with problems in regulating emotions and responding appropriately to daily life events, BPD has been linked to a wide variety of poor outcomes including job-related problems (Zweig-Frank & Paris, 2002), dysfunction in developing strong personal relationships (Daley, Burge, & Hammen, 2000), social maladjustment, and reduced academic achievement (Bagge et al., 2004). Due to the breadth and severity of these frequently observed problems, BPD has been difficult to treat effectively (Hoffman, Buteau, Hooley, Fruzzetti, & Bruce, 2003).

The high correlation reported between BPD and past sexual abuse and family dysfunction (Weaver & Clum, 1993) has led to the developmental hypothesis that BPD may develop as a result of traumatic experiences early in life. Other adverse events, such as abandonment or fear of abandonment and lack of a secure emotional attachment with a caregiver, often accompany BPD (Benjamin, 1996; Gunderson, 1996). Furthermore, BPD is highly comorbid with other mood and anxiety disorders (Hodges, 2003; Skodol, Gunderson, et al., 2002; Weaver & Clum, 1993).

Despite the prevalence and severity of BPD, few studies have investigated the underlying neurological and physiological mechanisms of the disorder (e.g., Schmahl et al., 2004). Coccaro and Kavoussi (1991) suggested that an improved understanding of the neurological and physiological mechanisms mediating the clinical symptoms of BPD might lead to the development of more effective treatments. During the past decade, research has begun to identify specific neurobiological features that differentiate between BPD and controls. These features might provide clues to the mechanisms mediating the difficulties in emotion regulation experienced by individuals diagnosed with BPD.

Since impulse control is a characteristic deficit associated with BPD, dysfunction of the prefrontal cortex has been hypothesized to be a mediator of BPD. This speculation is based on observations of increased impulsivity following brain damage in prefrontal areas (Blair & Cipolott, 2000). Consistent with this hypothesis, individuals with BPD perform poorer on a go/no-go task, a test of impulse control assumed to evaluate prefrontal function (Völlm et al., 2004). In addition, volumetric studies applying imaging techniques have found smaller frontal lobes in BPD participants (Lyoo, Han, & Cho, 1998).

Imaging has also identified in individuals with BPD anomalies in limbic structures implicated in emotion regulation, such as smaller hippocampal and amygdala volumes (Tebartz van Elst et al., 2003). Volumetric reductions, especially in the hippocampus, are thought to be caused by the excessive stress that BPD patients experience (Schmahl, Vermetten, Elzinga, & Bremner, 2003). Because the hippocampus and the amygdala are involved in the processing of and responding to emotional stimuli (Anderson & Phelps, 2000; Nolte, 1993), a consequence of volumetric reductions might be related to the difficulties in emotion regulation that BPD individuals experience.

Other neurophysiological systems mediating processes such as emotion regulation, impulsivity, and aggressive behavior have been studied. Abnormalities in serotonin, a neurotransmitter linked to aggression, impulsivity, and suicidal behavior (Coccaro, 1989) have been reported in individuals diagnosed with BPD (Hansenne et al., 2002; New & Siever, 2002; Paris et al., 2004; Skodol, Siever, et al., 2002). BPD may be associated with a hyperresponsiveness of the hypothalamic-pituitary-adrenal (HPA) system (Rinne et al., 2002), a system implicated in stress responses, anxiety, and emotional reactivity. These findings provide limited evidence that a dysfunction in systems involved in controlling reactivity and emotion accompanies BPD.

Because several features of BPD are related to difficulties in regulating behavioral state and emotional reactivity, measurement of the autonomic nervous system might provide a portal into understanding the neural mechanisms of this disorder. Thus, it might be hypothesized that: (a) the sympathetic component of the autonomic nervous system, which supports fight-or-flight behaviors, would be hyperaroused; and (b) the parasympathetic component, which supports calm visceral states and social engagement behaviors, would be depressed. Previous research (for detailed review, see Herpertz, Kunert, Schwenger, & Sass, 1999; Schmahl et al., 2004) contrasted physiological responses regulated by the sympathetic nervous system in individuals with BPD and controls. Herpertz et al. (1999) monitored heart rate, skin conductance, and startle responses in a paradigm varying the emotional valence (pleasant, neutral, and unpleasant) and intensity of visual stimuli. Schmahl et al. (2004) measured heart rate, skin conductance, and blood pressure in response to reminders of personal experiences of severe stress (i.e., abandonment, trauma). Neither study found evidence of sympathetic hyperarousal associated with a diagnosis of BPD. However, both studies did not monitor the parasympathetic component of the autonomic nervous system or expose BPD participants to dynamically changing emotional stimuli (e.g., film clips).

The phylogenetic model of the autonomic nervous system described in the polyvagal theory (see chapters 2, 10, and 12; Porges, 2001a), provides an innovative theoretical framework to study the potential involvement of the parasympathetic nervous system in BPD. The theory focuses on the role that autonomic state plays in mediating both prosocial and defensive behaviors. The theory emphasizes an integrated social engagement system that regulates the muscles of the face and head involved in social engagement behaviors (e.g., gaze, expression, prosody, and gesture) and a component of the parasympathetic nervous system, the myelinated vagal pathways to the heart that calm visceral state and dampen sympathetic and HPA activity. The polyvagal theory emphasizes how neural circuits involved in the regulation of autonomic state evolved to support various adaptive biobehavioral responses to challenges. The theory proposes that autonomic reactions to challenges follow a phylogenetically ordered hierarchy with three distinct adaptive biobehavioral strategies. Each biobehavioral strategy reflects a specialized neurophysiological substrate that evolved to maximize adaptive strategies in safe, dangerous, or life-threatening contexts. Within this model the nervous system, through a process of "neuroception," is continuously evaluating risk and safety in the environment. Neuroception is not a conscious process; rather, it occurs via unconscious subcortical systems that functionally trigger one of these three adaptive neural circuits. Therefore, based on the polyvagal theory, difficulties in emotional regulation that are associated with a diagnosis of BPD could be interpreted as a behavioral expression of a physiological state that has evolved to support defensive strategies in dangerous and life-threatening situations. According to the polyvagal theory, the myelinated vagus, which phylogenetically evolved with mammals, is critical for two reasons: to inhibit defensive limbic circuits, and to establish social bonds (see chapter 12).

Phylogenetically, as mammals expressed special visceral efferent pathways to regulate the striated muscles of the face and head (e.g., facial expressions, head gesture), there was a parallel shift in the neural regulation of the heart from an unmyelinated to a myelinated vagus. This new myelinated (i.e., mammalian) vagus actively inhibits the sympathetic nervous system's influence on the heart and dampens HPA axis activity (Porges, 2001a). The mammalian vagus functions as an active vagal brake (see chapter 7) to maintain calm states in social contexts. However, when risk is detected, the vagal brake can be rapidly withdrawn to support defensive mobilization behaviors. Thus, BPD might be associated with difficulties in regulating the vagal brake in social settings.

The mammalian heart is characterized by a relatively strong vagal influence, via the myelinated pathways, on the heart's pacemaker (i.e., sinoatrial node). Functionally, the impact of the vagal brake produces a baseline or resting heart rate substantially lower than the intrinsic rate of the pacemaker. When the vagal brake is removed, heart rate can approximate the intrinsic rate of the pacemaker without recruiting sympathetic influences. When cardiac vagal tone via the myelinated vagus is high, the vagus acts as a restraint or brake limiting the rate the heart is beating. When vagal tone to the pacemaker is low, there is little or no inhibition of the pacemaker. Thus, the vagal brake may be used as a construct to describe the functional modulation of heart rate by the myelinated vagal efferent pathways.

The vagal brake provides a neural mechanism to change visceral states by slowing or speeding heart rate. Neurophysiologically, the influence of the vagal brake is reduced or removed to support the metabolic requirements for mobilization (e.g., fight-or-flight behaviors) and maintained or increased to support social engagement behaviors. The amplitude of respiratory sinus arrhythmia (RSA) indexes the state of the vagal brake. RSA is a natural rhythm in the heart rate pattern at approximately the frequency of spontaneous breathing. The amplitude of RSA provides a sensitive index of the impact that the myelinated vagus has on the heart (see chapter 2). By quantifying RSA during various challenges, it is possible to measure the dynamic regulation of the vagal brake.

It was hypothesized that the BPD participants, unlike typically behaving individuals, will have difficulties maintaining the vagal brake in social contexts. Thus, in response to social stimuli, BPD participants should rapidly shift from a calm state (i.e., high-amplitude RSA) to a state of agitation (i.e., low-amplitude RSA). To test this hypothesis, we contrasted the regulation of the vagal brake by measuring the amplitude of RSA in participants with BPD and controls during the presentation of film clips assumed to reflect emotional content. In addition, the experiment, by requiring an interaction between the participant and the experimenter, provides a secondary context related to social interactions.

METHOD

Participants

Participants (all female) consisted of 9 borderline personality disorder (BPD) patients and 11 controls between the ages of 18 and 45. Only females were recruited, since females represent the majority of individuals diagnosed with BPD and to remove gender as a possible source of variance in the neurophysiological regulation of autonomic state. The groups were equivalent in education level and age. BPD participants were referred to the study by clinicians in the Washington, DC, area. The BPD participants were identified and screened to eliminate comorbid diagnoses by National Institute of Mental Health clinical researchers at St. Elizabeth's Hospital (Washington, DC). The control group consisted of volunteers who were recruited from lists maintained by the National Institutes of Health. Both groups were free of drug and alcohol abuse and were not current users of prescription or illicit drugs. The diagnosis of BPD, based on DSM-IV criteria (APA, 1994), was confirmed by the Structured Clinical Interview for DSM-III-R (Spitzer, Williams, Gibbon, & First, 1990, 1992) and the Diagnostic Interview for Borderlines (Gunderson, Kolb, & Austin, 1981). The BPD participants were tested at St. Elizabeth's Hospital. The BPD participants, while participating in the study, were off medication and as a precautionary procedure were in residence at the hospital. Controls were free of psychiatric or neurological disorders. The control participants were not in residence at the hospital and were tested either at the hospital or at the Developmental Assessment Laboratory (University of Maryland, College Park) in similar testing environments.

Procedure

Following informed consent, participants were seated in a quiet room facing a television screen. To monitor electrocardiography (ECG), from which the heart period and RSA were derived, three disposable Ag–AgCl electrodes were placed on the participant's chest, connected to an ECG amplifier, and output to a Vagal Tone Monitor-II (Delta-Biometrics). After the initial baseline period, participants were instructed to watch three 10-min film clips. Each film clip was followed by questions specific to the film clip just viewed. Physiological data were collected during each of the four 10-min segments (i.e., baseline, film clip 1, film clip 2, film clip 3). To facilitate the measurement of a stable indicator of autonomic state in response to the specific emotional content of each film clip and to allow for a transition in physiological state due to the onset of each film clip, the last 5 minutes of data within each of the four conditions were analyzed. The experiment lasted approximately 1 hour. Heart period and RSA were collected for the baseline and film clip conditions. Participants were instructed to minimize their movements during the experiment. The experimenter remained in the room with the participant during the experimental procedures, since BPD is associated with an inability to tolerate being alone (see Gunderson, 1996). While in the experimental room, the experimenter ran the equipment and asked questions about each film clip.

Film clips 1 and 3 were selected to elicit a strong emotional response. Film clip 1 was a conflict scene with the mother in *Frances*, and film clip 3 was a conflict scene with the father in *The Great Santini*. In contrast to these two conflict scenes, film clip 2 was selected to be a neutral scene from *A Handful of Dust*. Participants rated the film clips on a Likert scale ranging from 0 (not arousing) to 10 (extremely arousing). Participants' ratings confirmed the assumed emotional content of each film sequence. The first conflict scene had a mean rating of 7.25 and the second conflict scene had a mean rating of 9.15. In contrast, the neutral scene had a mean rating of 1.75. The conflict scenes were rated as significantly more arousing than the neutral scene ($p < .001$). There were no significant differences in ratings between groups.

Data Quantification

The Vagal Tone Monitor detected the peak of the R-wave with 1-msec accuracy, timed sequential heart periods to the nearest ms (Riniolo & Porges, 1997), and stored the heart periods in files for offline analyses of RSA and heart period. The data files of sequential heart periods (i.e., R–R intervals in msec) were input into MXedit (version 2.21) software (Delta-Biometrics) in order to edit outlier data produced by movement and digitizing error. Editing consisted of integer addition or division of sequential values.

RSA estimates were calculated using the following procedures (Porges, 1985): (a) the heart period time series were converted to time-based data by resampling at successive 500-msec intervals; (b) a 21-point moving cubic polynomial filter was stepped through the time-sampled series to produce a smoothed template series; (c) the template series was subtracted from the original series to produce a residual time series; (d) the residual time series was processed by a digital bandpass filter with 25 coefficients to extract the variance in the frequency band of 0.12–0.40 Hz (i.e., the frequency of spontaneous breathing for adults); and (e) the bandpassed variance was transformed to its natural logarithm and used to quantify RSA. Data from our laboratory (Denver, Reed, & Porges, 2007) demonstrate that this methodology accurately captures the heart rate variability associated with spontaneous breathing. Denver et al. (2007) report a correlation of 0.99 between the frequency observed in the heart rate and respiration spectra. Moreover, the amplitude of the heart rate periodicity derived from spectral analysis was correlated 0.99 with the values derived from the MXedit analysis. These procedures result in a sensitive, noninvasive marker of the influence of the myelinated vagal fibers on the heart (see chapter 2; Porges, 2001a).

Analyses

Group (Borderline, Control) by Condition (Baseline, Film 1, Film 2, Film 3) analyses of variance (ANOVA) were used to identify statistical effects for RSA and heart period. Data from one participant during the baseline condition were lost due to technical error. Data from this participant were analyzed during the experimental conditions. Heart period was calculated as the time interval in msec between successive R-waves of the ECG. The metric for the current analyses represents the average R–R interval in msec for each condition. To evaluate the vagal contribution to heart period changes during each of the film clips, correlations between the changes from baseline in heart period and RSA were calculated. High correlations would illustrate that the changes in both variables were mediated by a common mechanism (i.e., vagal regulation of the heart). If the heart period change is totally dependent on vagal regulation, the correlation with RSA should approach 1.0. In contrast, low correlations would suggest that heart period is not tightly regulated by the vagus and would be mediated by other mechanisms.

RESULTS

Across all conditions there was a significant group effect for RSA, $F(1,77) = 7.16$, $p < .05$. The control group had significantly higher RSA than the BPD group. This main effect was functionally determined by the group trajectories during the experiment and statistically represented in the group × condition interaction, $F(3,51) = 3.62$, $p < .05$. As illustrated in Figure 15.1a, the trajectory of RSA during the experimental session differed between the groups. The values for RSA were similar for the two groups during baseline. However, over the course of the experiment, the control participants exhibited an increase in RSA, and the BPD participants exhibited a decrease in RSA. These distinct patterns reflect different neural strategies. The BPD participants exhibited a vagal withdrawal, which would support the increased metabolic demands of fight-or-flight behaviors. The control participants exhibited an increase in vagal influences to heart, which would support social engagement behaviors. As illustrated in Figure 15.1b, there was a significant group × condition interaction for heart period, $F(3,51) = 6.49$, $p < .05$. The heart period response pattern during the experiment confirms the observed group specific shifts in cardiac vagal tone. The BPD group progressively exhibited shorter heart periods (i.e., faster heart rate), while the control group exhibited longer heart periods (i.e., slower heart rate). Simple effects tests (see Table 15.1) confirm that at the end of the experiment, group differences were pronounced for both variables. Consistent with the RSA data, across conditions there was a group effect for heart period, $F(1,77) = 14.2$, $p < .05$.

The vagal contribution to heart period changes during the experiment was estimated by correlating the change from baseline in heart period with change

FIGURE 15.1. Means (± SE) for respiratory sinus arrhythmia in ln msec^2 units (a) and heart period in msec (b) across test conditions.

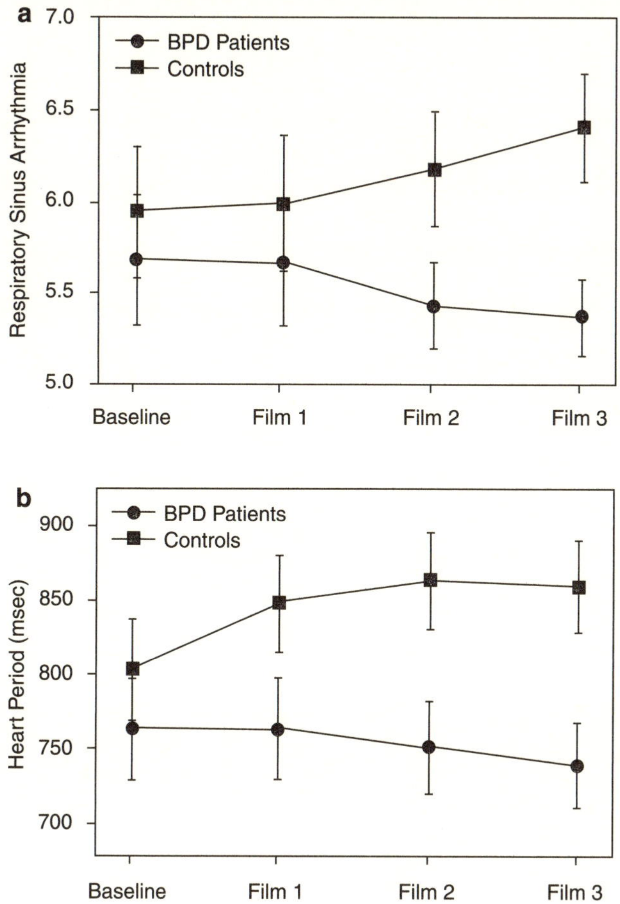

from baseline in RSA. Correlations were calculated within each group to evaluate whether the observed heart period change from baseline to a specific film clip were under vagal control. As illustrated in Figure 15.2, the relations between changes in RSA and heart period are significantly correlated only for the control group. Thus, the changes in heart period are strongly linked to an increase in the vagal control of the heart, but only in the control group. In the BPD group, although there is a consistent vagal withdrawal, the changes in RSA are not sufficient to account for the changes in heart period. These findings demonstrate that BPD participants have poor vagal regulation and the changes in heart period may be due, in addition, to other influences such as sympathetic activation.

TABLE 15.1. Simple Effects for ANOVA

	BPD Patients (n = 9)	Controls (n = 11)	t-value	df	p-value
Respiratory sinus arrhythmia (ln msec^2)					
Baseline	5.69[a] (1.0)	5.96 (1.2)	–0.520	17	.6098
Film 1	5.67 (1.1)	6.00 (1.2)	–0.636	18	.5329
Film 2	5.44 (0.72)	6.19 (1.1)	–1.81	18	.0867
Film 3	5.38 (0.64)	6.42 (0.98)	–2.74	18	.0134[b]
Heart period (msec)					
Baseline	762 (123)	803 (114)	–0.748	17	.4645
Film 1	763 (103)	848 (121)	–1.66	18	.1134
Film 2	751 (94)	863 (109)	–2.43	18	.0256[b]
Film 3	739 (86)	859 (103)	–2.78	18	.0123[b]

[a] Means (and standard deviations).
[b] Statistically significant at $p < .05$.

DISCUSSION

Previous investigations of the autonomic nervous system of BPD participants focused on indices of the sympathetic nervous system. These studies did not identify differences between BPD and controls (Herpertz et al., 1999; Schmahl et al., 2004). In contrast, by focusing on the parasympathetic limb of the autonomic nervous system, the current study provides the first report of unique characteristics of autonomic regulation associated with a diagnosis of BPD.

Based on the limited literature studying the psychophysiology of post-traumatic stress disorder (e.g., Sahar, Shalev, & Porges, 2001), we assumed that BPD patients and controls would have similar levels of RSA during baseline. This assumption was confirmed. By challenging the participants with film clips of both high (clips 1 and 3) and low (clip 2) emotional content, the experiment was designed to elicit a withdrawal of the vagal brake (i.e., lower RSA and shorter heart period) in both groups during high-emotion stimuli with an expectation that the vagal brake would be reinstated (i.e., increases in RSA and heart period) during the low-emotion stimulus. However, we anticipated that the BPD participants, due to their sensitivity to affective stimuli and difficulty in state regulation, would exhibit an exaggerated withdrawal of the vagal brake (i.e., lower RSA and shorter heart period). Interestingly, we found that neither group exhibited a film clip–related response. Instead as illustrated in Figure 15.1a and b, the control group exhibited a trajectory of increasing vagal influences on the heart across the entire duration of the experiment, while the BPD group exhibited decreasing vagal influences on the heart.

At the start of the experiment, vagal influences on the heart were similar in both groups. However, as the experiment progressed, there was an intriguing divergence between the groups. The polyvagal theory provides two insights into the adaptive nature of the physiological state for each group as the experiment

FIGURE 15.2. Correlations of change from baseline in heart period and change from baseline in RSA from film clips 1, 2, and 3; $^{*}p < .05$.

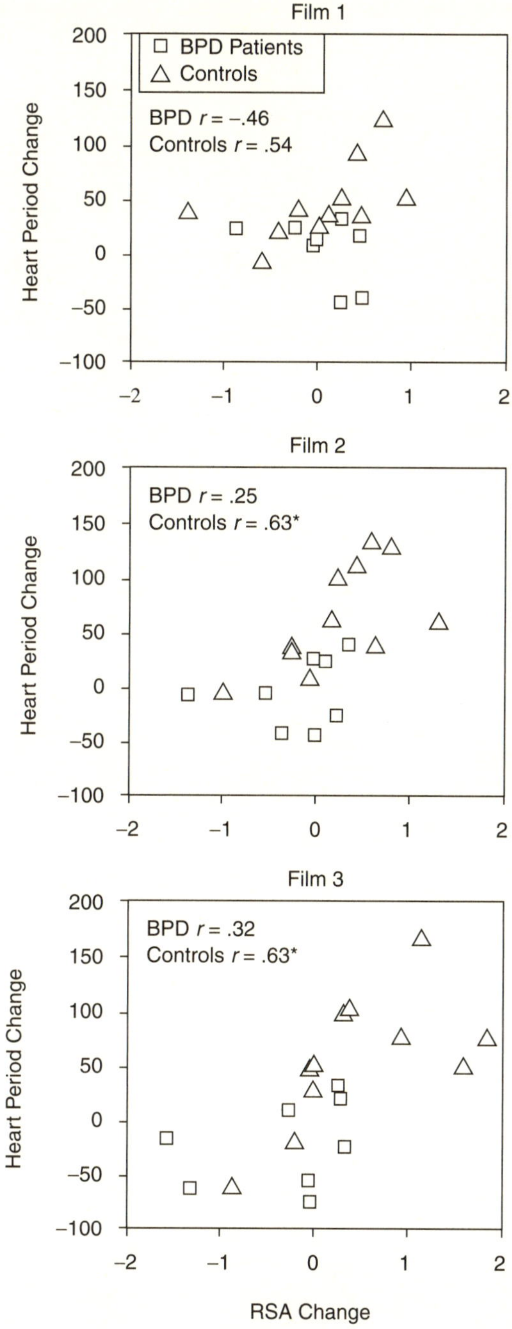

progressed. First, the polyvagal theory emphasizes that the physiological state that characterizes each group at the end of the experiment supports different classes of behavior. For the BPD group, the physiological state, characterized by a vagal withdrawal, would support the mobilization behaviors of fight or flight. In contrast, for the control group, the physiological state, characterized by increased vagal influence on the heart, would support spontaneous social engagement behaviors. Interestingly, embedded in the diagnosis of BPD are features related to compromised social engagement behaviors, including a hyperreactivity or emotional dysregulation during social interactions. Thus, although the experimental conditions provided the same context and task demands for all participants, the BPD group reacted with a visceral state to promote defensive behaviors, while the control group reacted with a visceral state to promote increased spontaneous social engagement behaviors. Second, the polyvagal theory (see chapter 1) proposes a mechanism (i.e., neuroception) that triggers defense strategies. Based on the clinical features of BPD, social interactions with a stranger (i.e., the experimenter) might provide a social stimulus that would trigger the nervous system and elicit a physiological state supporting fight-or-flight behaviors. However, the film clips in this experiment, with their depictions of social interactions, might have contributed to the need to mobilize. It would be interesting to see whether in the absence of a person in the experimental room, the physiological states of the two groups would still diverge during the film clips. Perhaps the physiological states of both groups would have been more similar and more stable throughout the experiment in the absence of the experimenter. Under these conditions, the BPD participants might not detect risk and elicit a defensive strategy and the control participants would not detect the cues from the experimenter to trigger spontaneous social engagement behaviors.

The correlations between RSA and heart period provide additional support for the hypothesis that in individuals without psychiatric disturbances, there is a strong link between vagal regulation and the control of heart period. In previous research, we have reported that this covariation is compromised in other psychiatric disorders that have difficulties in regulating behavior (Sahar et al., 2001; Umhau et al., 2002). The lack of correlation between RSA and heart period for the BPD group is consistent with these studies.

It is possible that the neuroception of the environment provides an invalid indicator of risk for individuals with BPD. Thus, rather than being calm in the presence of another "nonthreatening" human, the autonomic nervous system is regulated to a state that supports fight or flight and not a state that would support spontaneous social engagement. If invalid neuroception related to social stimuli accurately describes individuals with BPD, it may partially explain why BPD patients have a variety of poor outcomes, especially related to social relationships and emotional instability in real-world situations.

This study has provided the first documented evidence of autonomic nervous system differences between controls and individuals diagnosed with BPD. Thus, it offers a theoretical framework to explain the emotional reactivity that is linked to BPD. The study, however, has several limitations, including small sample size, isolated experimental manipulation, and no measures of test–retest reliability. However, this investigation into the autonomic response profile of BPD patients may lead to additional research to confirm our hypotheses relating autonomic state and neuroception in a variety of other social challenges. Thus, monitoring RSA during social challenges may provide a measurable index of neuroception in BPD and provide a method to delineate the features in the social environment that would trigger autonomic states that support and promote defensive behaviors.

Co-authors for this chapter were M. A. Austin and T. C. Riniolo.

CHAPTER 16

Abuse History Is Related to Autonomic Regulation

Many individuals experience abuse, either in childhood or adulthood, and those who experience childhood abuse are more likely to experience adult abuse (e.g., Desai, Arias, Thompson, & Basile, 2002). Women are extremely vulnerable to victimization (Bremner & Vermetten, 2001), and the abuse is also more likely to occur by those closest to the victim. As in child abuse, the various types of adult abuse (e.g., domestic violence, sexual abuse, and emotional abuse) may occur in combination. Given the great overlap, it is difficult to investigate the effects of a particular type of child or adult abuse. Research suggests that history of childhood sexual abuse, an experience which occurs in about 16% of women, is the most common cause of post-traumatic stress disorder (PTSD) in women (Bremner & Vermetten, 2001).

It is important to note that women may experience abuse, including sexual abuse, without the severe debilitating features of PTSD. These women may present with symptoms that may or may not be consistent with other psychiatric diagnoses. Victims of abuse may develop mood disorders (e.g., Zavaschi et al., 2006), including depression (e.g., Schuck & Widom, 2001). The depressive symptoms may be related to self-esteem issues common in victims of abuse (e.g., Arata, Langhinrichsen-Rohling, Bowers, & O'Farrill Swails, 2005). Victims of abuse may also employ maladaptive coping mechanisms, which may be related to paying inordinate attention to internal stimuli and distorting environmental cues (Rothschild, 2000). These maladaptive coping strategies may initially be functional but, in the long term, result in detrimental consequences such as substance abuse, eating disorders, and suicide (Doyle, 2001).

Little is known about the effects of abuse on the victim's bodily responses to stressful events. Studies investigating the influence of abuse on the autonomic nervous system have generally focused on participants with chronic PTSD. The results of these studies have been inconsistent (Buckley & Kaloupek, 2001). For example, reported differences in baseline heart rate might not reflect a reliable difference in autonomic state but may be influenced by other psychologically related factors, including the laboratory setting, the experimental paradigm, and the psychological state (e.g., anticipatory anxiety) in which the participant was tested (Prims, Kaloupek, & Keane, 1995). In addition, supporting the idea that PTSD is associated with a sympathetic overdrive (Blanchard, 1990) studies have reported heightened physiological reactivity to stimuli related to traumatic events (e.g., Elsesser, Sartoy, & Tackenberg, 2004). Thus, assessment of cardiovascular regulation variables during both baseline and following a stressor may provide useful information in determining whether trauma history impacts on the physiological response strategies available to react and to calm in normal nonthreatening situations.

Even if the abuse does not result in PTSD, it may impact on day-to-day experiences and influence the development of social relationships. A history of abuse may "tune" the nervous system to be cautious and prepared for defensive fight-or-flight behaviors, even when real danger does not exist. Since the metabolic demands of exercise require a physiological adjustment that mimics physiological states associated with flight-or-fight behaviors, it is possible that abuse history may influence the neural circuits involved in calming following exercise. By monitoring heart rate patterns in response to mild exercise, it may be possible to evaluate an individual's ability to self-regulate and to promote a calm state following exercise.

The quantification of respiratory sinus arrhythmia (RSA) provides an opportunity to dynamically monitor the changing vagal regulation of the heart (see chapter 2) during recovery from exercise. Vagal regulation of the heart is associated with self-regulated behaviors. Optimally, during challenges demanding mobilization there is a rapid withdrawal of the vagal inhibition on the heart to raise heart rate to support the increased metabolic demands, and immediately following exercise there is a recovery of vagal tone to foster calm states. This rapid regulation of the vagus in support of social engagement behaviors has been labeled the vagal brake (see chapter 7).

Deficits in vagal regulation are present in perpetrators of violent abuse (Umhau et al., 2002) and are related to a variety of psychiatric disorders such as PTSD (Sack, Hopper, & Lamprecht, 2004; Sahar, Shalev, & Porges, 2001), generalized anxiety disorder (McLeod, Hoehn-Saric, Porges, Kowalski, & Clark, 2000), and depression (Rottenberg, Solomon, Gross, & Gotlib, 2005). There is an extensive literature demonstrating that vagal regulation of the heart, both in terms of level of cardiac vagal tone and the efficient regulation of the vagal brake, is related to processes such as emotional reactivity, social engagement, and reactions to stress.

Victims of abuse have state regulation difficulties with a bias toward behavioral states that are self-protective. This potential vulnerability to be defensive may result in difficulties in feeling safe with others and in developing trusting social relationships. A self-awareness of difficulties in regulating state, especially staying calm in the presence of others, may lead individuals to seek alternative strategies, such as yoga. Yoga exercises may help reduce symptoms of depression and anxiety, increase a sense of self-efficacy (Lee, Mancuso, & Charlson, 2004), and improve regulation of the autonomic nervous system (Sovik, 2000). Thus, individuals, who practice yoga, may be exercising their autonomic nervous system in an attempt to normalize an abuse-related damage to their ability to self-regulate.

Practitioners of yoga classes served as a forum to recruit participants for the current study. We hypothesized that women with a history of abuse, but without a diagnosis of PTSD, would exhibit greater physiological coping difficulties characterized by lower RSA and less RSA recovery following mild exercise. Additionally, we hypothesized that abuse history would be related to a greater use of dysfunctional coping strategies, increased mood disturbances, and lower self-concept.

METHOD

The analyses are based on 49 female participants, who were recruited from a local yoga studio. Forty-five participants described themselves as Caucasian, one as Hispanic, and three as multiracial. The majority (69.4%) were in a committed relationship, and approximately half (46%) reported having children. Most (96%) had college and graduate education. These participants were between 17 and 66 years of age. No participant reported PTSD, although diagnoses of depression ($n = 7$) and anxiety disorders ($n = 4$) were present.

Heart rate data were collected while the participant sat quietly for 5 minutes prior to and for 5 minutes following riding a stationary bike at her own pace for 1 mile.

RESULTS

Reported Abuse History

Reported abuse history is displayed in Table 16.1. Twenty-two participants did not report a history of abuse, 27 participants reported child abuse and/or adult abuse. Chi-square analysis indicated a significantly higher incidence of a mental health diagnosis in the abuse group, $\chi^2(1, N = 49) = 6.23, p < .05$. Specifically, 9 of the 11 participants who reported a current mental health diagnosis also reported a history of abuse. Frequency of yoga practice was not related to the physiological response pattern or abuse history.

TABLE 16.1. Reported History of Abuse: Number and Percent

Child abuse	21 (42.9%)	Adult abuse	18 (36.7%)
Emotional abuse	16 (32.7%)	Emotional abuse	14 (28.6%)
Physical abuse	10 (20.4%)	Physical abuse	5 (10.2%)
Sexual abuse	9 (18.4%)	Sexual abuse	3 (6.1%)
Neglect	7 (14.3%)	Intimate partner violence	5 (10.2%)

Impact of Abuse History on Autonomic Regulation and Psychological Well-Being

To examine the potential impact of abuse history on autonomic state regulation, repeated measures analyses of variance were used to evaluate the pattern from pre- to post exercise for both RSA and heart rate. For these analyses, the participants were separated into two groups according to abuse history. A no-abuse-history group consisted of 22 participants and an abuse-history group consisted of 27 participants.

Heart rate was sensitive to the exercise challenge, but not related to abuse history. Heart rate significantly increased post exercise, regardless of abuse history, $F(1, 47) = 76.17$, $p < .001$. In contrast to the heart rate analyses, RSA was related to abuse history. Since age was significantly correlated with the pre-exercise level of RSA, $r(49) = -.53$, $p < .001$, an analysis of covariance was conducted to remove the influence of age on RSA level and RSA reactivity. When age was covaried, abuse history influenced level of RSA, $F(1, 46) = 4.63$, $p < .05$, and interacted with the reactivity to exercise, $F(1, 46) = 4.06$, $p = .05$. As illustrated in Figure 16.1 participants who reported abuse history had lower RSA and following exercise RSA did not recovery to pre-exercise levels.

In addition, abuse history was related to dysfunctional coping, $F(1, 47) = 4.67$, $p < .05$, and total self-concept, $F(1, 47) = 9.24$, $p < .01$. Women with an abuse history reported using more dysfunctional coping strategies. Women with an abuse history also reported having significantly lower self-concept.

To determine whether recency of abuse influenced the response profiles, participants were partitioned into three groups: no abuse ($n = 22$), child abuse only ($n = 9$), and adult abuse with or without child abuse ($n = 18$). Analyses with age being covaried indicated that pre-exercise level of RSA was significantly related to abuse group with the group reporting adult abuse having the lowest RSA, $F(2, 45) = 3.33$, $p = .05$. Moreover, the group experiencing adult abuse not only had lower levels of RSA but also exhibited the least recovery.

A cumulative abuse index was generated by assigning a 0 to the no-abuse group ($n = 22$), a 1 to the child-abuse-only group ($n = 9$), a 2 to the adult-only group ($n = 6$), and a 3 to those reporting child and adult abuse ($n = 12$). Although the categorization is only via self-report, the higher the self-reported in-

FIGURE 16.1. RSA reactivity to exercise as a function of abuse history.

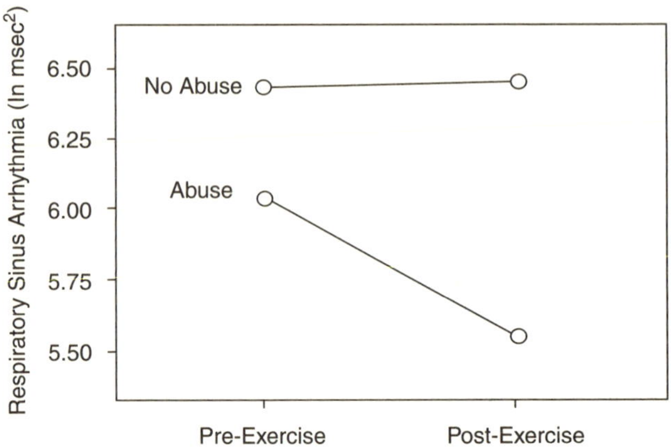

dex of abuse, the greater the decrease in RSA, but not heart rate, following exercise, $r(49) = .34$, $p < .05$. This relationship remained when partial correlations removed the influence of baseline RSA on the change scores, $r(49) = .41$, $p < .01$. Thus the two indices of autonomic regulation, baseline RSA and RSA reactivity, were independently related to abuse history.

DISCUSSION

The current study investigated the potential impact of abuse history in women without a diagnosis of PTSD. Although more than half of the participants reported abuse either in childhood or adulthood, no participant reported a diagnosis of PTSD. This high percentage of reported abuse is larger than would be expected based on normative data (e.g., Administration on Children Youth and Families Children's Bureau, 2006). Several of the women reporting a history of abuse were experienced practitioners in yoga. It is possible that the yoga training might have helped improve their ability to self-regulate, to dampen physiological reactivity, and to feel more comfortable in their bodies.

We hypothesized that a history of abuse would "tune" the autonomic nervous system to facilitate defensive mobilization strategies of fight-or-flight behaviors and would compromise physiological recovery following mild exercise (i.e., low RSA and poor RSA recovery). This hypothesis was supported. Women who experienced abuse had lower RSA prior to mild exercise and poorer RSA recovery following mild exercise. These findings suggest that women with an abuse history are less able to recruit the calming influence of the vagal "brake" after exercise. Although these findings are consistent with the findings of Sack et al. (2004), who observed decreased RSA in response to traumatic reminders, our findings are unique since our experimental manipulation was not related to trauma or abuse.

The human autonomic nervous system evolved to rapidly and efficiently shift between physiological states that facilitate either social engagement or mobilization. The myelinated vagus provides a mechanism to rapidly adjust physiological state to behavioral demands. This vagal circuit is uniquely mammalian and evolved to dampen defensive systems. The myelinated vagal circuit allows us (and other mammals) selectively to down-regulate defensive systems when engaged by "safe" individuals and to remove this "brake" to promote the necessary fight-or-flight behaviors when engaged by "dangerous" individuals. Functionally, the vagal input to the heart results in the base-level heart rate being substantially lower than the intrinsic rhythm of the heart's pacemaker. When vagal influences are reduced to the pacemaker, the heart immediately beats faster. Thus, it appears that abuse history, even in individuals who appear to be functioning well, may lower the tonic influence of the vagal brake and limit the ability of the myelinated vagal circuit to rapidly recover and to support a calm physiological state.

The relationship between abuse history and an inability to rapidly engage neural regulation of the vagus to support calm physiological states is consistent with clinical impressions that abused individuals are more likely to exhibit asocial reactions such as fight-or-flight behaviors in response to stress, and to have difficulties shifting from a mobilized state to a state of calmness. These findings are consistent with research indicating that poor vagal modulation may be related to psychological dysfunction, including greater social anxiety (Movius & Allen, 2005) and poorer recovery from depression for depressed individuals (Rottenberg et al., 2005).

The impact of abuse history on mood disturbances and self-concept was also investigated. Women who participate in yoga may self-select due to a self-awareness of their difficulties in regulating state, especially staying calm in the presence of others, and may use yoga as a coping skill to regulate state. Consistent with these predictions, individuals with an abuse history had lower self-concept. Moreover, when considering total abuse, there appeared to be a graded relation between cumulative abuse experiences and both self-concept and mood disturbances. These findings are consistent with research suggesting that victims of abuse may also develop self-esteem issues (e.g., Arata et al., 2005) and mood disorders (e.g., Zavaschi et al., 2006) including depression (e.g., Schuck & Widom, 2001).

The findings that abuse history is related to autonomic regulation are consistent with the polyvagal theory (see chapter 2; Porges, 2001a, 2007a). The theory focuses on the adaptive functions of autonomic reactivity and describes how each of three phylogenetic stages in the development of the vertebrate autonomic nervous system is associated with a distinct autonomic subsystem that is retained and expressed in humans.

Abuse experiences challenge adaptive survival mechanisms. According to the polyvagal theory, the adaptive consequence is to react to features in the environment conservatively, by becoming hypervigilant and more sensitive to predators. Hypothetically, abuse experiences would "retune" the autonomic nervous system. Functionally, abuse history would dampen the ability to express socially "trusting" behaviors and facilitate more vigilant states to prepare for fight-or-flight behaviors. By measuring RSA in this study, an index of the functioning of the vagal brake was dynamically evaluated. Since the vagal brake supports trusting interactions and social engagement behaviors, it was hypothesized that abuse history would compromise the efficiency of this circuit. The data support the hypothesis and demonstrate that the individuals with abuse history who were tested in the current study had depressed cardiac vagal tone and a compromised ability to recruit and reinstate the vagal brake to self-soothe following the transitory physiological state disruption due to mild exercise. Thus, what appears to be a maladaptive inability to re-engage the vagal brake may have emerged from an adaptive response to potential abusive threats by promoting hypervigilance for danger and facilitating an immediate execution of fight-or-flight behaviors.

It has been speculated that PTSD may be a consequence of triggering the unmyelinated vagus as a primitive defense system, often in inescapable contexts, when mobilization defensive strategies cannot be employed (see Porges, 2007a). In this state, a lower brainstem system, more frequently employed by reptiles, is regulating peripheral physiology. This system reduces oxygenated blood flow to the brain and leads to fainting and experiences of dissociation. It is possible that a lower threshold to mobilize and a hypervigilance for danger might have potential survival consequences in this situation. Thus, from an adaptive perspective, the lower threshold to mobilize would protect the individual from recruiting this primitive shutdown circuit.

In the current study, we did not evaluate individuals with PTSD. However, it is possible that individuals with a history of PTSD, may react to the exercise challenge similar to our individuals with an abuse history. Thus, it is possible that individuals with a history of PTSD may have a lower threshold to remove the vagal brake and to employ fight-or-flight defensive strategies.

The study provides a plausible explanation of the mechanisms mediating fight-or-flight reactions clinically observed in clients with histories of abuse. It underscores the importance of demystifying personal experiences and understanding that the consequences of abuse are multidimensional and impacting both psychological and physiological domains. Trauma not only may retune perceptions of others, making it more difficult to feel safe with others, but also may retune the neural circuits by lowering the threshold to react defensively. These changes affect are ability to socially engage, which may lead to dysfunctional coping strategies, lower self-concept, and greater mood disturbance symptoms.

Therefore, assessments and interventions may need to incorporate a multidimensional conceptualization of trauma and abuse in which a retuning of autonomic regulation is a key feature. Within this model, treatments might apply clinical strategies that would enable the client to move from a fight-or-flight state to a physiological state associated with safety and social engagement (e.g., Ogden, Minton, & Pain, 2006). If treatments are unable to shift the client to a calmer physiological state, then access to the psychological mechanisms and processes that have been the bases of psychotherapy may not be efficiently available (see chapter 3).

Co-authors for this chapter were L. P. Dale, L. E. Carroll, G. Galen, J. A. Hayes, and K. W. Webb.

CHAPTER 17

Music Therapy, Trauma, and the Polyvagal Theory

Music is a documented feature of civilizations. Cultures have incorporated music into the educational process, religious and tribal rituals, and patriotic expressions. Vocal music, through both lyrics and melody, has been used both as a contemporary vehicle and an archival mechanism to transmit important cultural, moral, spiritual, and historical events and values. Music has been used to calm, to enable feelings of safety, to build a sense of community, and to reduce the social distance between people.

Music is an important component of the human experience. Music is intertwined with emotion, affect regulation, interpersonal social behavior, and other psychological processes related to personal responses to environmental, interpersonal, and intrapersonal challenges. Types of music have been uniquely associated with distinct feelings, experiences, and social interactions. These psychological processes shape our sense of self, contribute to our abilities to form relationships, and determine whether we feel safe in various contexts or with specific people. Although these processes can be objectively observed and subjectively described, they represent a complex interplay between our psychological experience and our physiology.

This chapter provides a novel insight into the traditions of music as a therapy aiding physical and mental health. More than listening to music, singing, or playing a musical instrument, music therapy involves the dynamic interactions among three features: (1) therapist, (2) client, and (3) music. In the following pages, the polyvagal theory is used to present a plausible model to explain how and why music therapy is helpful in supporting physical health and in enhancing function during compromised states associated with mental and physical illness, including the consequences of trauma. The polyvagal theory provides a strategy to understand the mechanisms and processes that enable music and music therapy to improve social engagement behaviors and to facilitate the regulation of bodily and behavioral states. The theory further provides insights that bridge music therapy to the nervous system and to health outcomes, and is used to deconstruct music therapy into two components: (1) the interpersonal relationship between therapist and client, and (2) the acoustic features of music used in the therapeutic setting as it pertains to clinical treatment.

THE POLYVAGAL THEORY

Our nervous system functions as a sentry by continuously evaluating risk in the environment. Through neural surveillance mechanisms (i.e., neuroception), our brain identifies features of risk or safety (see chapter 1). Many of the features of risk and safety are not learned, but are hard-wired into our nervous system and reflect adaptive strategies associated with our phylogenetic history. The way we react to the specific acoustic frequency bands that constitute music is determined by the same neural circuits that we use to evaluate risk in our environment. For example, low-frequency sounds elicit a sense of danger associated with an approaching predator. In "Peter and the Wolf," Prokofiev exploits this biological feature by conveying impending and predictable danger with the low-frequency sounds of the kettledrums.

Due to our phylogenetic history, the rumble of low-frequency sounds shifts our attention from social interactions to potential dangers in the environment. This reaction is shared with other vertebrates, including reptiles and amphibians. In contrast, high-pitched screams from another mammal (not just our children, but also our dogs and cats) elicit a sense of urgent concern or empathy as a response to the perceived pain or injury of a targeted other. In humans, high-frequency screams shift our attention from the social group or object of focus to the specific individual who is screaming. Music in the frequency band of human voice, however, elicits visceral and emotional states that are associated with neither impending doom nor a sense of urgency. As such, music in the frequency band of human voice is often used melodically in compositions to convey the functional and metaphorical "voice" of the composer. Thus, the orchestral instruments, which duplicate the human vocal range (e.g., violins, flutes, clarinets, trumpets, oboes, and French horns), are used to express the composer's emotional narrative.

Specific acoustic frequency bands in the environment elicit a variety of emotional experiences that are paralleled by adaptive physiological states. Each of these physiological states is functionally an adaptive state that influences affect regulation, social engagement behaviors, and our ability to communicate. We experience these states with feelings of safety, danger, or ultimate demise (i.e., life threat). Physiological state is an implicit component of the subjective experience of listening to or producing music. Music not only changes our emotive state but also elicits changes in our physiology that parallel the feelings of anxiety, fear, panic, and pain. For example, while listening to certain melodies, we relax, slow our heart rate, and smile. However, while listening to other music we may start to imagine danger and visualize marching off to war or protecting our loved ones. The feelings of danger will change our facial expression and increase our heart rate.

As Oliver Sacks (2007) discussed in *Musicophilia*, music appears to be part of the human experience, yet no brain area or circuit has been identified to explain or represent music. From a polyvagal perspective, this question is viewed differently. Rather than seeking specificity in the neural regulation required to process and to express music, this perspective points to the convergence and similarity between the neural mechanisms required to process music and the neural mechanisms required to process features of social engagement behaviors and risk in the environment. Furthermore, this convergence between physiological state and music-related emotional experience is neurophysiologically determined and explained by the polyvagal theory (see chapters 2, 10, 11, and 12; Porges, 2001a, 2007a). As this discussion progresses, the polyvagal theory (see chapter 2) is used as an organizing principle to explain how music, especially music expressed via music therapy, can recruit the neural mechanisms that integrate facial muscles and visceral state, and consequently promote restorative affective states and prosocial behavior.

In order to illustrate this link fully, it is important to briefly review the origins of the polyvagal theory. The polyvagal theory emerged from the study of the evolution of the vertebrate autonomic nervous system (ANS), and is based on the functions of the ANS that automatically regulate several major organs, including the heart, the lungs, and the gut. Circuits in the brain dynamically regulate the ANS. This regulation is bidirectional; the brain and its neural sentries continuously monitor body state, and body state dynamically influences brain function. Moreover, the neural regulation of the ANS is linked to the neural regulation of the muscles of the face and head, which signal to others our emotional state. These muscles of the face and head are involved both in actively listening to (i.e., the modulation of our middle ear muscles) and in producing of music whether by singing (i.e., the modulation of the laryngeal and pharyngeal muscles) or by playing a wind instrument (i.e., the modulation of the facial and oral muscles supporting an embouchure). Polyvagal theory assumes that many of our social behaviors and vulnerabilities to emotional disorders are "hard-wired" into our nervous system. Based on this theory, it is possible to understand various aspects of mental health, including trauma responses, and to develop treatment techniques that can help individuals communicate better and relate better to others.

This theoretical perspective is particularly important in understanding the mechanisms underlying music therapy, which require both the processing of acoustic stimuli and face-to-face social interactions within the therapeutic setting. Thus, the polyvagal theory provides insights into the beneficial effects of music therapy, since it provides an understanding of the neural control of structures involved in the two features of music therapy: (1) social interactions between the client and the therapist, and (2) listening and expressing music. The neural mechanisms recruited by these features of music therapy are described in further detail later in this chapter.

The Biobehavioral Quest for Safety, Survival, and a Painless Death

The polyvagal theory proposes that the evolution of the mammalian ANS provides the neurophysiological substrates for affective processes and stress responses. The theory proposes that physiological state limits the range of adaptive behaviors and psychological experiences. Thus, the evolution of the nervous system determines the range of emotional expression, quality of communication, and the ability to regulate body and behavioral state, including the expression and recovery of stress-related responses. Relevant to adaptive social and emotional behaviors, these phylogenetic principles illustrate the emergence of a brain-face-heart circuit and provide a basis not only for investigating the relation between several features of mental health and autonomic regulation, but also for deconstructing how music and music therapy can support mental and physical health.

The investigation of human phylogenetic history identifies changes in neural regulation that occurred as vertebrates evolved from jawless fish to humans and other mammals. Phylogenetic development resulted in humans having an increased neural control of the heart via a myelinated vagal system. The evolution of the myelinated vagus was paralleled by an enhanced neural control of the face, larynx, and pharynx. This integrated face–heart system enabled complex facial gestures and vocalizations associated with social communication to influence physiological states. The face–heart system can cue others of safety and danger via facial expressions or vocalization, while promoting transitory mobilization by increasing heart rate. Removing the myelinated vagal inhibition from the heart physiologically supports this biobehavioral process of mobilization. These mechanisms provide us with an understanding of how a warm smile simultaneously reflects a calm state and triggers calmness and a sense of safety and benevolence in the observer. In contrast, an angry face reflects a mobilized state and triggers a matching defensive state in the observer. Vocalizations, in addition to facial expression, can reflect and trigger bodily states. Similar to the relationship between smiling and calmness just described, the melodic patterns of vocalizations, which are not typically shrill or booming, provide convergent cues to the observer that indicate a relative sense of safety. However, the lower pitch associated with a booming voice will often startle and/or frighten the observer, while the high pitch of a shrill voice will generally evoke anxiety and fear.

THE SOCIAL ENGAGEMENT SYSTEM

The social engagement system regulates facial muscles, including the sphincter muscles around the eyes that promote social gaze and emotional expressivity; middle ear muscles that enable human voice to be extracted from background sounds; muscles of mastication that are involved in ingestion; laryngeal and pharyngeal muscles that are used in sucking, swallowing, vocalizing, and breathing; and muscles of head that enhance social gesture and orientation, such as turning and tilting. Collectively, these muscles act as filters of social stimuli and determinants of engagement with the social environment. It is interesting to note that the neural pathways regulating the orbicularis oculi, a sphincter muscle around the eye involved in expressive displays, also are involved in the dynamic regulation of the stapedius muscle in the middle ear (Djupesland, 1976). Thus, the neural mechanisms for emotional cueing via eye contact are shared with those needed to listen to human voice.

As a cluster, difficulties in behaviors associated with the social engagement system (e.g., avoidant gaze, nonresponsiveness to human voice, reduced facial affect and diminished vocal prosody, and atypical or lack of head gesture) are common features of individuals with autism, post-traumatic stress disorder, and other psychiatric disorders. This information leads the astute clinician to infer difficulties in both social engagement behaviors and physiological state regulation from facial expressions and vocal prosody. Several psychiatric disorders have deficits in both the somatomotor (e.g., poor gaze, low facial affect, lack of prosody, difficulties in mastication) and visceromotor (difficulties in autonomic regulation including cardiopulmonary and digestive problems) components of the social engagement system. Deficits in the social engagement system compromise spontaneous social behavior, social awareness, affect expressivity, prosody, and language development.

Human responses to trauma are devastating and compromise subsequent social behavior and emotion regulation. Understanding the mechanisms underlying the mammalian hard-wired response to life threat may demystify these debilitating consequences. From this neurophysiological perspective, a variety of clinical features, including severely compromised social behavior and difficulties in emotion regulation, are predictable. An understanding of the mechanisms mediating these atypical behaviors in response to trauma is helpful to the client, the family, and the therapist in developing supportive and restorative contexts and treatments.

Functionally, our nervous system is continuously evaluating risk in the environment through an unconscious process of neuroception (see chapter 1). Specific features in the environment trigger physiological states associated with feelings of safety, danger, or ultimate demise. The human nervous system evolved efficiently to shift between conditions of safety and danger. We easily adjust and calm following situations requiring fight-or-flight maneuvers. We use social interactions with attuned and contingent facial expressions, intonation of our voice (i.e., prosody), and gaze to calm and be calmed. However, in contrast to challenges of danger, reactions to life threat are not easily remediated. Attempts to socially engage a traumatized individual, rather than calming, may result in defensive strategies of rage and anger. Life threat triggers a very ancient neural circuit that severely limits social engagement behaviors and may distort neuroception, resulting in a false detection of risk. Thus, treatment of trauma requires a new model distinct from the traditional psychotherapeutic strategies of face-to-face dialog in order to trigger the calm states associated with the social engagement system. Music and music therapy strategies may provide an alternate portal to the social engagement system and avoid the initial face-to-face interactions that may be misinterpreted as threat by a traumatized individual.

HOW MUSIC AND PROSODIC VOCALIZATIONS TRIGGER THE SOCIAL ENGAGEMENT SYSTEM

As vertebrates evolved from reptiles to mammals, the structures at the end of the mandible (i.e., jaw bone) that define the middle ear bones became detached (Luo, Crompton, & Sun, 2001; Rowe, 1996; Wang, Hu, Meng, & Li, 2001). For humans and other mammals, sound in the environment impinges on the eardrum and is transduced from the eardrum to the inner ear via the small bones in the middle ear known as ossicles. When the stapedius (regulated by a branch of the facial nerve) and the tensor tympani (regulated by a branch of the trigeminal nerve) muscles are innervated, the ossicular chain becomes more rigid and dampens the amplitude of the low-frequency acoustic stimulation from the environment reaching the inner ear. This process is similar to tightening the skin on a kettledrum. When the skin is tightened, the pitch of the drum is higher. When the ossicular chain is tightened, similar to the stretched skin, only higher frequencies bouncing against the eardrum are transmitted to the inner ear and to the auditory processing areas of the brain. This functional relation is described and illustrated in a *Scientific American* article by Borg and Counter (1989).

The evolution of the human middle ear enabled low-amplitude, relatively high-frequency airborne sounds matching the frequency of the human voice to be heard, even when the acoustic environment was dominated by low-frequency sounds, such as sounds made by large predators. Detached middle ear bones were a phylogenetic innovation that enabled mammals to communicate in a frequency band that could not be detected by reptiles. Reptiles have difficulties in hearing higher frequencies, since their hearing is dependent on bone conduction.

Studies have demonstrated that this critical neural regulation of middle ear muscles, a necessary mechanism to extract the soft sounds of human voice from the loud sounds of low-frequency background noise, is defective in individuals with language delays, learning disabilities, and autistic spectrum disorders (Thomas, McMurry, & Pillsbury, 1985). Additionally, middle ear infection (i.e., otitis media) may result in a total inability to elicit the *reflexive* contraction of the stapedius muscles (Yagi & Nakatani, 1987). Disorders that influence the neural function of the facial nerve (i.e., Bell's palsy) not only influence the stapedius reflex (Ardic, Topaloglu, Oncel, Ardic, & Uguz, 1997), but may also affect the patient's ability to discriminate speech (Wormald, Rogers, & Gatehouse, 1995). The observed difficulties that individuals with a variety of physical and mental disorders have in extracting human voice from background sounds may be dependent on the same neural system that regulates facial expression. Thus, deficits in the social engagement system would compromise the expression of emotion, as well as social awareness and language development.

MUSIC THERAPY, TRAUMA, AND THE SOCIAL ENGAGEMENT SYSTEM

The frequency content of melodies in most musical compositions duplicates the frequency band of human voice. Functionally, acoustic properties of melodies, typically encompassing middle C and the two octaves above middle C, easily pass through the middle ear structures regardless of the neural tone to the middle ear muscles. Once the frequencies pass through the middle ear, they trigger a neural feedback mechanism to tense the ossicle chain. Vocal music duplicates the effect of vocal prosody and triggers neural mechanisms that regulate the entire social engagement system with the resultant changes in facial affect and autonomic state. Basically, we start to look and feel better when we listen to melodies. Thus, while social engagement is a common goal in music therapy practice, incorporating the polyvagal theory provides a plausible scientific justification for how music therapy may provide opportunities to exercise the social engagement system.

Consistent with the parallel between music and social communication, the same frequency band that characterizes melodies defines, in human voice, the frequency band in which all information (i.e., verbal content) is communicated. When this frequency band is weighted to enhance the understanding of voice, it is known as the "index of articulation" (Kryter, 1962) and more recently as the "speech intelligibility index" (American National Standards Institute, 1997). These indices emphasize the relative importance of specific frequencies in conveying the information embedded in human speech. In the normal ear, acoustic energy within the primary frequencies of these indices is not attenuated as it passes through the middle ear structures to the inner ear. The frequency band defining the index of articulation is similar to the frequency band that composers have historically selected to express melodies. It is also the frequency band that mothers have used to calm their infants by singing lullabies.

Trauma can turn off the social engagement system. Attempts to engage a person with a trauma history, rather that eliciting spontaneous social behavior, may trigger defensive and aggressive behaviors. From a clinical perspective, traumatized individuals often present features of gaze aversion and flat facial affect. If we were to monitor the physiological state of these individuals, we would observe an ANS that is poised to fight or flee (i.e., high heart rate and low vagal regulation of the heart). The traumatic experience functionally retunes neuroception to conservatively detect risk when there is no risk. Most therapeutic strategies attempt to engage with direct face-to-face eye contact. Working with traumatized individuals creates a great challenge to therapists, since the normal social engagement behaviors of the therapist may trigger fear and reactive defensive strategies. Music therapy provides a special portal to reengage the social engagement system that does not require an initial face-to-face interaction. Music can be used to stimulate the social engagement system without requiring face-to-face reciprocity. Since melodic music contains acoustic properties similar to vocal prosody, music may be used to recruit the social engagement system by challenging and modulating the neural regulation of the middle ear muscles. If the social engagement system is effectively recruited, positive facial expressions will emerge, eye gaze will spontaneously be directed at the therapist, and the traumatized individual will shift to a more calm and positive physiological state.

CONCLUSION

Based on the polyvagal theory, elements of music therapy can be deconstructed into biobehavioral processes that stimulate the social engagement system. When the social engagement system is stimulated, the client responds both behaviorally and physiologically. First, the observable features of social engagement become more spontaneous and contingent as the face and voice become more expressive. Second, there is a change in physiological state regulation that is expressed through increased behavioral regulation and calmness. The improved state regulation is mediated by the myelinated vagus, which directly promotes health, growth, and restoration. However for some clients, especially those who have been traumatized, face-to-face interactions can be threatening and may not elicit a neuroception of safety. In these circumstances, the social engagement system can potentially be activated through vocal prosody or music while minimizing direct face-to-face interactions.

From a polyvagal perspective, music therapy can be deconstructed into two integrated processes. As illustrated in Figure 17.1, the therapeutic environment often invites face-to-face interaction between the therapist and the client. This face-to-face interaction, if effective, will trigger the client's neuroception of safety. Second, the frequency band associated with melodies functionally duplicates the frequency band conveying information in the human voice. The human nervous system evolved to be very selective of these frequencies. Music, especially vocal music, produces melodies by modulating these frequencies. This process engages and exercises the neural regulation of the social engagement system with the positive effects of improved socioemotional behaviors and enhanced physiological state. Interestingly, the phrasing of music is also an important component of this process. The phrasing of music, especially when singing or playing a wind instrument, results in short inhalations and extended durations

FIGURE 17.1. Deconstructing music therapy: A polyvagal perspective.

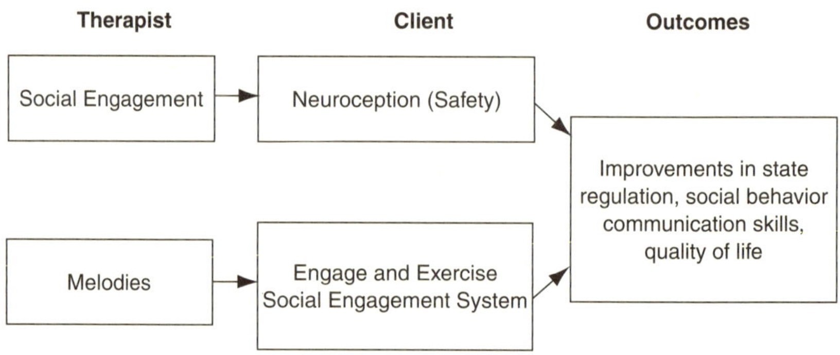

of exhalations. Physiologically, breathing "gates" the influence of the myelinated vagus on the heart. Functionally, when we inhale, the influence of the vagus is attenuated and heart rate increases. In contrast, when we exhale, the influence of the vagus is increased and heart rate decreases. This simple mechanical change in breathing increases the calming impact and health benefits of the myelinated vagus on our body. Thus, music therapy by engaging and exercising the social engagement system may promote positive outcomes improving several features related to quality of life.

PART V

SOCIAL BEHAVIOR AND HEALTH

CHAPTER 18

Reciprocal Influences Between Body and Brain in the Perception and Expression of Affect

Emotions, affect regulation, and interpersonal social behavior are psychological processes that describe basic human experiences in response to events, environmental challenges, and people. These processes shape our sense of self, contribute to our abilities to form relationships, and determine whether we feel safe in various contexts or with specific people. Although these processes can be objectively observed and subjectively described, they represent a complex interplay between our psychological experience and our physiological regulation. These psychological–physiological interactions are dependent on the dynamic bidirectional communication between peripheral organs and the central nervous system connecting the brain with these organs. For example, the neural circuits, providing a bidirectional communication between the brain and heart, can trigger either a rapid increase in heart rate to support protective fight-or-flight behaviors or a rapid decrease in heart rate to support social interactions. Peripheral physiological reactions can be initiated by the brain detecting features of danger in the environment, and alternatively, changes in peripheral physiological state can influence the brain and alter our perceptions of the world. Thus, affect and interpersonal social behavior are more accurately described as biobehavioral than psychological processes, since our physiological state can profoundly influence the quality of these psychological processes and our feelings can, in turn, determine dynamic changes in our physiology.

Our nervous system functions as a sentry by continuously evaluating risk in the environment. Through neural surveillance mechanisms (i.e., neuroception), our brain identifies features of risk or safety. Many of the features of risk and safety are not learned, but are hard-wired into our nervous system and reflect adaptive strategies associated with our phylogenetic history. For example, low-frequency sounds elicit in mammals a sense of danger associated with an approaching predator. This reaction is shared with other vertebrates, including reptiles and amphibians. Due to our phylogenetic history, the rumble of low-frequency sounds shifts our attention from social interactions to potential dangers in the environment. In contrast, high-pitched screams from another mammal (not just our children, but also our dogs and cats) elicit a sense of urgent concern or empathy for another who may be feeling pain or being injured. With humans, high-frequency screams shift our attention to the specific individual who is screaming. Through exposure and associative learning, we can link these features with other events. Specific features in the environment recruit physiological states differentially associated with feelings of safety, danger, or ultimate demise (i.e., life threat). Each of these states is characterized by a specific set of capacities for affect regulation and social engagement and communication (see chapter 12).

Current research in affective neuroscience focuses on brain structures and neural circuits related to specific motivational and emotional processes (e.g., Panksepp, 1998). These important discoveries emphasize cortical and subcortical structures in the emergence of the complex affective repertoire of humans and their contribution to social relationships (e.g., Schore, 1994, 2003; Siegel, 2007). However, underlying these contributions are details of an important and often overlooked neurobiological substrate, the neural circuits mediating the reciprocal communication between body states and brainstem structures, which impact on the availability of these affective circuits. These underlying circuits not only promote feelings (e.g., Damasio, 1999), but also form a bidirectional circuit (e.g., Darwin, 1872) that enables mental and psychological processes to influence body state and body state to color and, at times, to distort our perception of the world. Thus, the study of affective processes, especially in their prosocial and healing roles, requires an understanding of the neural circuits both between higher brain structures and the brainstem and between the brainstem and the visceral organs (e.g., the heart) mediated through the autonomic nervous system. All affective or emotional states are dependent on lower brain regulation of the visceral state and the important visceral, tactile, and nociceptive cues that travel to the brain from the periphery. Moreover, there are distinct visceral regulatory states that foster different domains of behavior. These states do not preclude the important bidirectional information from higher brain structures.

This chapter emphasizes the neural regulation of observable facial movements and concurrent subjective visceral experiences that characterize the expressions, feelings, and perceptions of emotion and affective state. The chapter uses the polyvagal theory (see chapters 2, 10, 11, and 12; Porges, 2001a, 2007a) as an organizing principle to explain the role of visceral state in the accessibility of prosocial emotions and restorative affective states. The polyvagal theory is an attempt to reorganize our conceptualization of the autonomic nervous system with a focus on the specific neural circuits involved in regulating visceral organs for specific adaptive functions related to affect, emotions, and social communication behaviors.

The polyvagal theory interprets social interactions and emotion as biobehavioral processes. Thus, the theory is particularly important for psychotherapists, who focus on the social interaction within the therapeutic setting and forgo pharmacological interventions. By treating the social interaction as a biobehavioral process, it is possible to conceptualize a therapeutic treatment that relies not on pharmacological manipulations but on the profound positive impact of social interactions and interpersonal behaviors on the neural regulation of body state and behavior. By exploring these bidirectional biobehavioral processes, psychotherapeutic treatments may change the neural regulation of physiological state, which in turn will support further benefits from interpersonal interactions.

EMOTION, MOTION, AND VISCERAL STATE: FEATURES OF MENTAL HEALTH

Regardless of the operational, and often arbitrary, distinction between emotion and affect or between emotional expressions and feelings, the measurement of physiological state (e.g., autonomic, endocrine, and muscle activity) needs to be embraced in affective neuroscience, particularly if there is to be a functional dialogue with experiential clinicians. In most cases physiological state has been conceptualized as a correlate or a consequence of higher brain structures (e.g., cortex) presumed to be driving emotion and affect. However, it would be naive not to explore the connections and potential bidirectional influences between peripheral physiological state and the brain circuits related to affective processes.

Physiological state is an implicit component of the subjective experiences associated with specific psychological constructs such as anxiety, fear, panic, and pain. The convergence between physiological state and emotional experience is neurophysiologically determined, since the metabolic requirements necessary to modulate the muscles of the face and body require supporting changes in autonomic state. All emotional and affective states require specific physiological shifts to facilitate their expression and to reach their implicit goals (e.g., fight, flight, freeze, proximity, etc.).

Through the study of phylogenetic shifts in the vertebrate autonomic nervous system, it is possible to link the different expressive features of emotion in humans with the phylogenetic transitions in visceral regulation observed in vertebrates. Physiological monitoring provides an important portal to monitor these reactions, since some affective responses are often not observable in overt behavior. For example, the convergence between the neural mechanism mediating autonomic state and facial expressions phylogenetically occurs in the transition from reptiles to mammals (see chapter 2; Porges, 2007a).

There is a rich history of research linking the neural regulation of face and viscera (e.g., heart) with brain circuits. Gellhorn (1964) elaborated on how proprioceptive discharges from facial muscles influence brain function and promote changes in visceral state. Thus, providing an example of the bidirectionality between peripheral and central structures and providing a neurophysiological basis for the assumed relation between facial expression and body feelings. Even earlier, Darwin (1872) acknowledged the important and often neglected bidirectional relation between the brain and the heart.

Although Hess was awarded the Nobel Prize in Physiology or Medicine in 1949 for his work emphasizing the importance of the central regulation of visceral state,* journals in contemporary affective neuroscience (e.g., *Nature Neuroscience*) and psychiatry (e.g., *Biological Psychiatry*) express a disconnect between subjective affective experience and visceral state regulation. Contemporary affective neuroscience with the aids of both imaging techniques and neurochemistry has focused on brain structures contributing to various neural circuits involved in adaptive behaviors with apparent motivational objectives.

Panksepp (1998) organizes affective experiences into seven neural-based motivational systems that include seeking, rage, fear, lust, care, panic, and play. However, missing from these functionally adaptive motivational circuits is the role that neural regulation of visceral state plays in potentiating or dampening these circuits. For example, if an individual is in a physiological state characterized by vagal withdrawal and high sympathetic excitation, body feelings of a fast pounding heartbeat are experienced and the threshold to react aggressively is low. In contrast, when in a physiological state characterized by an engaged myelinated vagus, sympathetic and hypothalamic-pituitary-adrenal axis reactivity are dampened. The physiological state is experienced as "calm." Intrusive stimuli that previously would have triggered aggressive behaviors when the vagal activity is withdrawn will now result in a dampened reaction. Accompanying this change in physiological state are options to further dampen reactivity through social interactions.

Most proponents of affective neuroscience embrace a science of parallelism

*In 1949 W. Hess was awarded the Nobel Prize in Physiology or Medicine (http://nobelprize.org/nobel_prizes/medicine/laureates/1949/hess-lecture.html). His Nobel lecture was titled "The Central Control of Activity of Internal Organs." In his lecture, he acknowledged the importance of the prevailing model of the autonomic nervous system, which emphasized the paired-antagonistic innervations of the internal organs and the definition of sympathetic and parasympathetic functions. However, he went well beyond this conceptualization to emphasize the importance of central structures in the regulation of visceral state by describing his studies that demonstrated the influence of the hypothalamus on the autonomic nervous system. By emphasizing the central mechanisms that mediate the dynamic regulation of peripheral organs, Hess anticipated the need for methodologies and technologies to continuously monitor the neural circuits involving both defined brain structures and peripheral nerves in the regulation of visceral function and state and to move from the prevailing conceptualization of the autonomic nervous system as a peripheral system. Hess's lecture (1) emphasized the importance of feedback circuits linking peripheral organs to brain structures and the bidirectionality of these feedback circuits, and (2) acknowledged that although much can be learned about neural structures and functions via traditional experimental paradigms (e.g., neural blockade, surgery, electrical stimulation), dynamic feedback circuits, that is, the moment-to-moment dynamic shifts in the system, cannot be adequately studied through these paradigms.

that links either observable emotional expressions or subjective experiences with a "neural" specificity that is concretized and assumed to be validated by imaging studies that identify activation of brain areas or blockade studies interfering with appropriate functioning of these circuits. Thus, to many neuroscientists, affect resides solely in the brain and does not require inputs or outputs linking the body to the brain. Missing from this research agenda and theoretical explanation is an appreciation of the necessary contributions of both the sensory inputs from the periphery influencing central circuits and the motor outputs in the periphery driven by the central circuits. Focusing on the central circuits, without studying the sensory and motor contributions from the periphery, is like studying the behavior of a thermostat independent of information regarding both ambient temperature and the capacities of the heating, ventilation, and air conditioning components.

Hess in his Nobel speech articulates an awareness of the complex features of a system. From his perspective, although the components of a feedback circuit might be identified and studied independently, the functioning of independent parts will not explain how the system, as a whole, functions dynamically during moment-to-moment challenges. This limitation was, in part, dependent on the methodologies available to study neurophysiology that required pharmacological, surgical, or electrical manipulations to block or stimulate "global" branches of the autonomic nervous system that either shared a specific neurotransmitter (e.g., acetylcholine, epinephrine) or an easily identifiable nerve (e.g., vagus) that could be cut or stimulated.

Within the field of mental health, there is a similar acceptance of a disease model without a focus on the intervening feedback circuits that mediate the features of the disorder. Within the medical discipline of psychiatry, anxiety and depression are defined by clinical features and not by a measurable physiological substrate. The prevalent strategies in mental health research that use neurophysiological variables (e.g., imaging, autonomic measures) are not directed at defining anxiety or depression, but use neurophysiological variables as correlates of a clinical diagnosis.

The value of taking a different perspective can be illustrated with the construct of anxiety. If anxiety were viewed as dependent on a shift in autonomic state in which an individual's physiological state is dominated by the sympathetic nervous system, new clinical research strategies might emerge that focus on characterizing how states of anxiety and a vulnerability to being anxious would be potentiated or dampened by different autonomic states. Treatments would then be developed either to (1) dampen sympathetic tone or (2) enable the individual to move into environments or shift contexts that are less likely to trigger the increased reactivity associated with higher sympathetic excitation. Unfortunately, most researchers in psychiatry and psychology express little interest in the mapping autonomic regulation as a "vulnerability" dimension for various psychiatric disorders and behavioral problems, although visceral features are often symptoms of the disorders they are treating.

Clinical disciplines rarely acknowledge the proximal functions of visceral state. Clinicians seldom monitor the expression of vagal withdrawal or sympathetic excitation in their patients. Such a shift in autonomic state would be manifested in several physical and psychiatric symptoms including flat affect, difficulties in auditory processing, hyperacusis, tachycardia, and constipation. In addition, conventional models of mental disorders neglect the role of neurophysiological mechanisms dynamically interacting with contextual cues in the environment. In contrast, these disciplines have embraced distal constructs related to the functions of receptors within the brain that lead almost reflexively to drug treatment, while generally failing to recognize the important role of visceral state and visceral afferent feedback on the global functioning of the brain. This strategy is far from parsimonious and does not take into account either the phylogeny of the mammalian nervous system or the intervening neurophysiological and biobehavioral systems along a continuum from genes to behavior. Rather, these disciplines have assumed that clusters of observable behaviors or subjective experiences are linked parsimoniously and directly to neurochemical levels in specific brain circuits. Thus, this strategy misses the important potential of psychological and behavioral interventions (including changes in environment) that would be therapeutic by directly influencing physiological state without necessitating pharmacological treatments.

STATE REGULATION AND THE AUTONOMIC NERVOUS SYSTEM: A HISTORICAL PERSPECTIVE

Researchers for more than a century have measured autonomic variables (e.g., heart rate, palmar sweat gland activity) as indicators of emotional state related to perceived stress (e.g., fear, mental effort, workload, and anxiety). Historically, arousal theories (e.g., Berlyne, 1960; Darrow, 1943; Gray, 1971) provided scientists who study brain–behavior relations with a model that assumed that activation of peripheral physiological measures regulated by the sympathetic branch of the autonomic nervous system were sensitive indicators of brain "arousal" or "activation." This view was based on a rudimentary understanding of the autonomic nervous system in which changes in easily measured peripheral organs (e.g., sweat glands, heart) were assumed to be accurate indicators of how the brain was processing emotional stimuli. Usually, emotional states were associated with fight-or-flight behaviors and the sympathetic-adrenal system (e.g., increases in heart rate, sweat gland activity, and circulating catecholamines) as initially described by Cannon (1929b). Based on Selye (1936, 1956), emotional states were also associated with increased activity of the HPA axis (e.g., increases in cortisol). From a psychological level, arousal theories emphasized fight-or-flight behaviors and neglected or minimized the importance of both prosocial affective states that facilitated social interaction and also the defensive strategy of immobilization (e.g., fainting, death feigning).

An acceptance of a unitary arousal system is assumed in several research domains, including investigations of sleep, deception, sexual behavior, and anxiety. Moreover, it led to research on cortical "arousal" and the use of electroencephalography, single photon emission computed tomography, functional magnetic resonance imaging, and other imaging technologies that accepted the arousal construct with little interest in the distinction between activation of neural pathways that were excitatory or inhibitory. This resulted in difficulties in establishing whether "activation" represents the turning on or the turning off of a specific neural structure. From a physiological level, arousal theories emphasize an assumed continuity between central cortical activation and peripheral arousal marked by increases in the activity of the sympathetic nervous system and the adrenal hormones. However, arousal theories have neglected both the importance of the parasympathetic branch of the autonomic nervous system and the bidirectional communication between brain structures and visceral organs.

The continuity between brain and peripheral arousal created a research environment that neglected several important factors, including an understanding of the brain structures that regulate autonomic function; how these structures evolved from the most primitive vertebrates to mammals; how the autonomic nervous system interacts with the immune system, the hypothalamic-pituitary-adrenal axis, and the neuropeptides oxytocin and vasopressin; and the coevolution of stress and coping strategies with the increasing complexity of the autonomic nervous system. Missing from this dialog is a discussion of the role of the parasympathetic nervous system and especially the vagus (the Xth cranial nerve) with its bidirectional portal between the brain and specific visceral organs such as the heart.

THE POLYVAGAL THEORY: A PRIMER

The polyvagal theory (see chapter 2) emerged from the study of the evolution of the vertebrate autonomic nervous system. The theory assumes that many of our social behaviors and vulnerabilities to emotional disorders are "hard-wired" into our nervous system. Based on the theory, it is possible to understand various aspects of mental health and to develop treatment techniques that can help people communicate better and relate better to others. The term "polyvagal" combines "poly," meaning "many," and "vagal," which refers to the important nerve called the "vagus." To understand the theory, we need to investigate features of the vagus nerve, a primary component of the autonomic nervous system. The vagus nerve exits the brainstem and has branches that regulate several organs, including the heart. The theory proposes that there are two branches of the vagus that are related to different behavioral strategies, one related to social interactions in safe environments and the other related to adaptive responses to life threat.

Historically, the autonomic nervous system has been broken into two opposing components, one labeled sympathetic and the other parasympathetic. This organizational model was used to describe the function of the autonomic nervous system in the late 1800s and the early 1900s. In the 1920s this paired-antagonism model was formalized (Langley, 1921). This model characterized the function of the autonomic nervous system as a constant battle between the sympathetic nervous system associated with fight-or-flight behaviors and the parasympathetic nervous system associated with growth, health, and restoration. Because most organs of the body, such as the heart, the lungs, and the gut, have innervations from both sympathetic and parasympathetic components, the paired-antagonism model evolved into "balance theories." Balance theories attempted to link "tonic" imbalances to both physical and mental health. For example, a sympathetic dominance might be related to symptoms of anxiety, hyperactivity, or impulsivity, while a parasympathetic dominance might be related to symptoms of depression or lethargy. In addition to the tonic features of autonomic state, the paired-antagonism model also was assumed to explain the reactive features of the autonomic nervous system. This dependence on the construct of "autonomic balance" is still prevalent in textbooks, although there has been an intervening century in which neurophysiology has documented a second vagal pathway involved in regulating autonomic function. Unfortunately, this new knowledge of the second vagal pathway has not permeated the teaching of physiology, which still is dominated by descriptions of the paired antagonism between the sympathetic and parasympathetic components of the autonomic nervous system.

The primary parasympathetic influence to peripheral organs is conveyed through the vagus, a cranial nerve that exits the brain and innervates the gastrointestinal tract, respiratory tract, heart, and abdominal viscera. The vagus can be conceptualized as a tube or conduit containing several sensory and motor fibers originating or terminating in different areas of the brainstem. For example, the primary vagal motor pathways that regulate the lower gut originate in the dorsal nucleus of the vagus, the primary vagal motor pathways that regulate the heart and the lungs originate in the nucleus ambiguus, and the vagal pathways sending sensory information from the gut terminate in the nucleus of the solitary tract.

The polyvagal theory proposes that the autonomic nervous system reacts to real-world challenges in a predictable hierarchical manner that parallels, in reverse, the phylogenetic history of the autonomic nervous system in vertebrates. In other words, if we study the evolutionary path of how the autonomic nervous system unfolded in vertebrates (i.e., from ancient jawless fish to bony fish, amphibians, reptiles, and mammals), we learn not only that there is an increase in the growth and complexity of the cortex (the outer layer of the cerebrum), but also that there is a change in composition and function of the autonomic nervous system. In mammals, the autonomic nervous system functions as a hierarchical system that parallels phylogenetic states in reverse and not as the balance between sympathetic and parasympathetic components.

The phylogenetic changes in the autonomic nervous system (including changes in neural pathways and brainstem areas regulating the peripheral organs) determine how the autonomic nervous system reacts to challenges. In humans and other mammals, the hierarchy is composed of three neural circuits with the newer circuits having the capacity to override the older circuits. Under most challenges in our environment, we initially react with our newest system (i.e., myelinated vagus). If that circuit does not satisfy our biobehavioral quest for safety, an older circuit spontaneously reacts (i.e., sympathetic nervous system). Finally, if the former strategies are unsuccessful, as our last option we reflexively trigger the oldest circuit (i.e., unmyelinated vagus). Functionally, in humans the older vagal circuit is involved in adaptive reactions characterized by immobilization and decrease in metabolic resources, while the newer vagal circuit is involved in regulating calm states that promote both spontaneous social engagement and health, growth, and restoration. Along the phylogenetic hierarchy, between the two vagal circuits is the sympathetic nervous system that supports fight-or-flight behaviors.

THE POLYVAGAL THEORY: A BIOBEHAVIORAL QUEST FOR SAFETY

To survive, mammals must determine friend from foe, when an environment is safe, and communicate to their social unit. These survival-related behaviors limit the extent to which a mammal can be physically approached, whether vocalizations will be understood, and whether coalitions can be established. Moreover, these behavioral strategies, which are used to navigate through the "stress of life," form the bedrock on which social behaviors and higher cognitive processes can be developed and expressed. Thus, learning and other expansive mental processes must be structured, manipulated, and studied within the context of how the environment fosters or ameliorates stress-related physiological states.

The polyvagal theory proposes that the evolution of the mammalian autonomic nervous system provides the neurophysiological substrates for affective processes and stress responses. The theory proposes that physiological state limits the range of adaptive behaviors and psychological experiences. Thus, the evolution of the nervous system determines the range of emotional expression, quality of communication, and the ability to regulate body and behavioral state, including the expression and recovery of stress-related responses. Relevant to adaptive social and emotional behaviors, these phylogenetic principles illustrate the emergence of a brain-face-heart circuit and provide a basis for investigating the relation between several features of mental health and autonomic regulation.

Via evolutionary processes, the mammalian nervous system has emerged with specific features that react to challenge to maintain visceral homeostasis. In general, the domains of homeostasis, which have been monitored, have focused on the visceral systems involved in cardiovascular, digestive, reproductive, and immune functions. For example, studies have evaluated how long it takes heart rate to recover following a challenge to a prestress level. Adaptive coping requires minimizing the magnitude and duration of this deviation, whether the deviation is observed in raising heart rate, blood pressure, cortisol, or disrupting digestion.

By investigating the phylogeny of the regulation of the vertebrate heart (e.g.,

Morris & Nilsson, 1994), three principles can be extracted. First, there is a phylogenetic shift in the regulation of the heart from endocrine communication, to unmyelinated nerves, and finally to myelinated nerves. Second, there is a development of opposing neural mechanisms of excitation and inhibition to provide rapid regulation of graded metabolic output. Third, with increased cortical development, the cortex exhibits greater control over the brainstem via direct (e.g., corticobulbar) and indirect (e.g., corticoreticular) neural pathways originating in motor cortex and terminating in the source nuclei of the myelinated motor nerves emerging from the brainstem (e.g., specific neural pathways embedded within cranial nerves V, VII, IX, X, XI), controlling visceromotor structures (i.e., heart, bronchi, thymus) and somatomotor structures (muscles of the face and head) that results in a neural circuit that functions to facilitate social behavior and to maintain calm behavioral states.

These phylogenetic principles illustrate the emergence of a brain-face-heart circuit and provide a basis for investigating the relation between several features of mental health and autonomic regulation. In general, phylogenetic development results in increased neural control of the heart via the myelinated mammalian vagal system that is paralleled by an increase in the neural regulation of the facial muscles. This integrated system can "cue" others of safety and danger, while promoting transitory mobilization and the expression of sympathetic tone without requiring sympathetic or adrenal activation (i.e., raising heart rate by removing the myelinated vagal inhibition from the heart). Functionally, this phylogenetic progression provides a system that can respond rapidly (i.e., via myelinated pathways), selectively regulate the magnitude (i.e., via opposing inhibitory and excitatory circuits) and specificity of the features (e.g., via regulating the linkage between autonomic reactivity with facial muscles) of the reaction. With this new vagal system, transitory incursions into the environment or withdrawals from a potential predator can be initiated without the severe biological cost of the metabolic excitation associated with sympathetic-adrenal activation. Paralleling this change in neural control of the heart is an enhanced neural control of the face, larynx, and pharynx that enables complex facial gestures and vocalizations associated with social communication. This phylogenetic course results in greater central nervous system regulation of behavior, especially behaviors needed to engage and to disengage rapidly with environmental challenges. These phylogenetic shifts, which promote a greater bidirectional communication between brain and viscera, provide opportunities for mental processes, including voluntary behavior, to impact on body state. Thus, a greater understanding of the circuit mediating these interactions might lead to functional models of intervention that would both calm visceral state and promote more prosocial interactions. Consistent with this trend, new research and clinical programs are emerging. For example, Cleveland Clinic has created the Bakken Heart-Brain Institute and hosts an annual Heart-Brain Institute Summit to bring "together researchers, clinicians and others to stimulate greater collaboration and understanding of the heart–brain link and to positively impact research, education, and patient care."

THREE PHYLOGENETICALLY DEFINED AUTONOMIC CIRCUITS SUPPORT ADAPTIVE BEHAVIORS

The polyvagal theory (see chapters 2, 3, 10, 11, and 12; Porges, 2001a, 2007a) emphasizes and documents the neurophysiological and neuroanatomical distinction between the two branches of the vagus (i.e., Xth cranial nerve) and proposes that each vagal branch is associated with a different adaptive behavioral and physiological response strategy to stressful events. The theory describes three phylogenetic stages of the development of the mammalian autonomic nervous system. These stages reflect the emergence of three distinct subsystems, which are phylogenetically ordered and behaviorally linked to social engagement, mobilization, and immobilization. The phylogenetic orientation focuses our interest on the parasympathetic neural structures and neurobehavioral systems that we share with or have adapted from our phylogenetic ancestry. With increased neural complexity, due to phylogenetic development, the organism's behavioral and affective repertoire is enriched.

The polyvagal theory emphasizes the phylogenetic origins of brain structures that regulate social and defensive behaviors. For example, prosocial behaviors cue others that the environment is safe. Safe environments signal the individual to dispense with the hypervigilance required to detect danger and allows this precautionary strategy to be replaced with social interactions that further calm and lead to close proximity and physical contact. The prototypical prosocial behaviors in mammals are related to nursing, reproduction, interactive play, and being able to be calm in the presence of another. In contrast, defensive behaviors could be categorized into two domains: one related to mobilization including fight-or-flight behaviors and the other related to immobilization and death feigning that might be associated with dissociative psychological states. Within this dichotomy of defensive strategies, freezing behavior that requires increased muscle tension in the absence of movement, such as stalking or vigilance behaviors, is categorized within mobilization. In contrast, immobilization is associated with a decrease in muscle tension and often with fainting and other features of decreased metabolic activity. From a health perspective, the prosocial behaviors trigger neurophysiological circuits that not only support affect regulation and social interactions but also promote health, growth, and restoration.

Relevant to adaptive social and emotional behaviors, the polyvagal theory makes the following assumptions.

1. Evolution has modified the structures of the autonomic nervous system.
2. The mammalian autonomic nervous system retains vestiges of phylogenetically older autonomic nervous systems.
3. Emotional regulation and social behavior are functional derivatives of structural changes in the autonomic nervous system due to evolutionary processes.
4. In mammals, the autonomic nervous system response strategy to challenge

follows a phylogenetic hierarchy, starting with the newest structures and, when all else fails, reverting to the most primitive structural system.

5. The phylogenetic stage of the autonomic nervous system determines the behavioral, physiological, and affective features of reactivity to people and objects in the environment.

The phylogenetic orientation focuses our interest on the parasympathetic neural structures and neurobehavioral systems that we share with or have adapted from our phylogenetic ancestry. First, there are three response systems proposed in the polyvagal theory: (1) cranial nerves to regulate the face and to mediate calm autonomic and behavioral states, (2) sympathetic-adrenal system to increase metabolic output, and (3) an inhibitory vagal system to decrease metabolic output and promote immobilization and defecation. These three response strategies are the products of distinct neurophysiological systems. Second, these distinct neurophysiological systems represent a phylogenetically dependent hierarchy with the use of cranial nerves to regulate facial expression emerging in mammals (well developed in primates), the sympathetic-adrenal system shared with other vertebrates including reptiles, and the inhibitory vagal system shared with more primitive vertebrates, including amphibians, bony fish, and cartilaginous fish (see chapters 10 and 11). The three systems represent different phylogenetic stages of neural development. This phylogenetic development starts with a primitive behavioral inhibition system, progresses to a fight-or-flight system, and, in humans (and other primates), culminates in a complex facial gesture and vocalization system. Thus, from a phylogenetic perspective, the nervous system of vertebrates evolved to support a greater range of behaviors and physiological states, including states that we often associate with social engagement behaviors.

HOW THE "MAMMALIAN" AUTONOMIC NERVOUS SYSTEM FOSTERS PROSOCIAL BEHAVIORS VIA A VAGAL BRAKE

The mammalian vagus (i.e., myelinated efferent pathways) functions as an active vagal brake (see chapter 7) in which rapid inhibition and disinhibition of vagal tone to the heart can support behavioral mobilization or self-soothe and calm an individual. When the vagal tone to the pacemaker is high, the vagus acts as a restraint or brake limiting heart rate. When vagal tone to the pacemaker is low, there is little or no inhibition of the pacemaker. Due to vagal influences to the sinoatrial node (i.e., the heart's pacemaker), resting heart rate is substantially lower than the intrinsic rate of the pacemaker. Neurophysiologically the vagal brake provides a mechanism to support the metabolic requirements for mobilization and communication behaviors; functionally, the vagal brake, by modulating visceral state, enables the individual to rapidly engage and disengage with objects and other individuals and to promote self-soothing behaviors and calm behavioral states. Thus, withdrawal of the vagal brake is associated with adaptive states of mobilization and a reinstatement of the vagal brake with calm behavioral recovery. In mammals, the primary vagal inhibitory pathways occur through the myelinated vagus originating in the nucleus ambiguus.

By transitory down-regulation of the cardioinhibitory vagal tone to the heart (i.e., removing the vagal brake), the mammal is capable of rapid increases in cardiac output without activating the sympathetic-adrenal system. This enables the ability to rapidly shift states from calm engagement to precautionary states of vagal withdrawal that rapidly increase cardiac output to support movements. But unlike the sympathetic-adrenal strategy, which is slow to initiate and slower to dampen, re-engaging the vagal brake instantaneously down-regulates cardiac output to produce a calm physiological state (Vanhoutte & Levy, 1979). By withdrawing the vagal brake, rather than stimulating the sympathetic-adrenal system, mammals have an opportunity to rapidly increase metabolic output for immediate, but limited mobilization. If the duration and intensity of mobilization is increased, the sympathetic nervous system is activated.

A withdrawal of the vagal brake will facilitate the recruitment of other neural mechanisms (e.g., excitation of sympathetic or the unmyelinated vagal pathways) and neural chemical mechanisms (e.g., stimulation of the hypothalamic-pituitary-adrenal axis) to regulate physiological state. Thus, consistent with the polyvagal theory, if the vagal brake is not functioning or will not serve the survival needs of the organism, then the phylogenetically "older" systems (e.g., the sympathetic-adrenal system or unmyelinated vagus originating in the dorsal motor nucleus of the vagus) will be recruited to regulate metabolic output to deal with environmental challenges. For example, if the vagal brake is not functioning, there is the potential for greater dependence on the sympathetic excitation of the cardiovascular system. This dependence on sympathetic excitation to regulate cardiac output may create health risks (e.g., hypertension) and lead to difficulties in modulating behavioral state (i.e., rage, panic, aggression). Consistent with assumptions of the polyvagal theory, the vagal brake contributes to the modulation of cardiac output by decreasing or increasing the inhibitory vagal control of the heart to influence rate and thereby adjust metabolic resources to support either mobilization or social engagement behaviors.

THE SOCIAL ENGAGEMENT SYSTEM

As mammals evolved from more primitive vertebrates, a new circuit emerged to detect and to express signals of safety in the environment (e.g., to distinguish and to emit facial expressions and intonation of vocalizations) and to rapidly calm and turn off the defensive systems (i.e., via the myelinated vagus) to foster proximity and social behavior. This recent neural circuit can be conceptualized as a social engagement system. The Social Engagement System involves pathways traveling through several cranial nerves (i.e., V, VII, IX, X, and XI) that regulate the expression, detection, and subjective experiences of affect and emotion. Neuroanatomically, this includes special visceral efferent pathways regulating the striated muscles of the face and head (i.e., special visceral efferent) and the myelinated vagal fibers regulating the heart and lungs (see chapters 11 and 12; Porges, 2001a).

The social engagement system is an integrated system with both a somatomotor component regulating the striated muscles of the face and a visceromotor component regulating the heart via a myelinated vagus. The system is capable of dampening activation of the sympathetic nervous system and hypothalamic-pituitary-adrenal axis activity. By calming the viscera and regulating facial muscles, this system enables and promotes positive social interactions in safe contexts.

The somatomotor component includes the neural structures involved in social and emotional behaviors. Special visceral efferent nerves innervate striated muscles, which regulate the structures derived during embryology from the ancient gill arches (Truex & Carpenter, 1969). The social engagement system has a control component in the cortex (i.e., upper motor neurons) that regulates brainstem nuclei (i.e., lower motor neurons) to control eyelid opening (e.g., looking), facial muscles (e.g., emotional expression), middle ear muscles (e.g., extracting human voice from background noise), muscles of mastication (e.g., ingestion), laryngeal and pharyngeal muscles (e.g., prosody of vocalizations), and head-turning muscles (e.g., social gesture and orientation). Collectively, these muscles function as neural gatekeepers detecting and expressing features of safety (e.g., prosody, facial expression, head gestures, eye gaze) that cue others of intention and control social engagement with the environment.

The phylogenic origin of the behaviors associated with the social engagement system is intertwined with the phylogeny of the autonomic nervous system. As the muscles of the face and head emerged as social engagement structures, a new component of the autonomic nervous system (i.e., a myelinated vagus) evolved that was regulated by nucleus ambiguus, a medullary nucleus ventral to the dorsal motor nucleus of the vagus. This convergence of neural mechanisms produced an integrated social engagement system with synergistic behavioral and visceral components as well as interactions among ingestion, state regulation, and social engagement processes. As a cluster, difficulties in gaze, extraction of human voice, facial expression, head gesture, and prosody are common features of individuals with autism and other psychiatric disorders in which the social engagement system is compromised. Thus, we infer from the functioning of the face and the prosody of the voice, difficulties in both social engagement behaviors and physiological state regulation.

There are interneuronal connections between the source nuclei (i.e., lower motor neurons) of special visceral efferent pathways and the source nucleus of the myelinated vagus. These neurophysiological circuits provide an inhibitory pathway to slow heart rate and lower blood pressure, which, by actively reducing autonomic arousal, promote the calm states necessary to express social engagement behaviors and to support health, growth, and restoration. The brainstem source nuclei of this system are influenced by higher brain structures and by visceral afferents. Direct corticobulbar pathways reflect the influence of frontal areas of the cortex (i.e., upper motor neurons) on the medullary source nuclei of this system. Moreover, feedback through the afferent vagus (e.g., tractus solitarius) to medullary areas (e.g., nucleus of the solitary tract) influences both the source nuclei of this system and the forebrain areas that are assumed to be involved in several psychiatric disorders (e.g., Craig, 2005; Thayer & Lane, 2000). In addition, the anatomical structures involved in the social engagement system have neurophysiological interactions with the hypothalamic-pituitary-adrenal axis, the social neuropeptides (e.g., oxytocin and vasopressin), and the immune system (see chapter 19; Carter, 1998; Porges 2001b).

Afferents from the target organs of the social engagement system, including the muscles of the face and head, provide potent afferent input to the source nuclei regulating both the visceral and somatic components of the social engagement system. Thus, activation of the behavioral component (e.g., listening, ingesting, looking) could trigger visceral changes that would support social engagement, while modulation of visceral state, depending on whether there is an increase or decrease in the influence of the myelinated vagal efferents on the sinoatrial node (i.e., increasing or decreasing the influence of the vagal brake) would either promote or impede social engagement behaviors. For example, stimulation of visceral states that would promote mobilization (i.e., fight-or-flight behaviors) would impede the ability to express social engagement behaviors.

Relevant to psychiatric disorders are the specific deficits in both the somatomotor (e.g., poor gaze, low facial affect, lack of prosody, difficulties in mastication) and visceromotor (difficulties in autonomic regulation resulting in cardiopulmonary and digestive problems) components of the social engagement system. For example, clinicians and researchers have documented these deficits in individuals with autism. Thus, deficits in the social engagement system would compromise spontaneous social behavior, social awareness, affect expressivity, prosody, and language development. In contrast, interventions that improve the neural regulation of the social engagement system, hypothetically would enhance spontaneous social behavior, state and affect regulation, reduce stereotypical behaviors, and improve vocal communication (i.e., including enhancing both prosody in expressive speech and the ability extract human voice from background sounds). This is more than a plausible hypothesis. We not only have demonstrated relations between vagal regulation of the heart and social engagement behaviors, but have demonstrated in preliminary studies that is possible to improve social engagement behaviors in autistic individuals by engaging the neural regulation of the social engagement system (i.e., stimulating the neural regulation of the middle ear muscles with exaggerated prosodic acoustic stimulation), thus providing an empirical basis to understand the interpersonal social features, such as prosody and facial expressivity, that characterize individuals who effectively calm and sooth others.

DISORDERS OF THE SOCIAL ENGAGEMENT SYSTEM: MALADAPTIVE OR ADAPTIVE BEHAVIORAL STRATEGIES?

Several psychiatric and behavioral disorders are characterized as having difficulties in establishing and maintaining relationships. Diagnostic features often include features associated with difficulties both in expressing social behavior and in reading social cues (i.e., social awareness). These features are observed in a variety of psychiatric diagnoses, including autism, social anxiety, and posttraumatic stress disorder. From a psychopathology orientation, these clinical disorders have different etiologies and features. However, from a "polyvagal" perspective, they share a core component. This core component is characterized by a depressed social engagement system with the consequences of poor affect regulation, poor affect recognition, and poor physiological state regulation. Although a compromised social engagement system results in "maladaptive" social behavior, do these asocial behavioral strategies have "adaptive" features? The phylogeny of the vertebrate autonomic nervous system serves as a guide to understand these adaptive features.

Through the lens of the polyvagal theory, the vertebrate autonomic nervous system follows three general stages of phylogenetic development. In the mammalian autonomic nervous system the structures and circuits representing each of the stages remain, but have been co-opted for various adaptive functions. The neural circuit associated with each stage supports a different category of behavior with the phylogenetically most recent innovation (i.e., the myelinated vagus) capable of supporting high levels of social engagement behavior. Since the neural regulation of the "new" mammalian myelinated vagus (i.e., ventral vagus) is integrated into the social engagement system, when the social engagement system is compromised, the effects are both behavioral and autonomic. The resultant changes in autonomic state compromise spontaneous social engagement behaviors and minimize states of calmness, but support a range of adaptive defensive behaviors. Specifically, the compromised social engagement system (see Figure 3.1, p. 56) is associated, neurophysiologically, with a change in autonomic regulation characterized by a reduction in the influence of the myelinated vagus on the heart resulting in difficulties in behavioral state regulation and with a loss of neural regulation to the muscles of the face mediating the flat affective expression often observed in several clinical disorders. The removal of the regulatory influence of the myelinated vagus on the heart potentiates (i.e., disinhibits) the expression of the two phylogenetically older neural systems (i.e., sympathetic nervous system, unmyelinated vagus). These two older neural systems foster mobilization behaviors of fight or flight, via the sympathetic nervous system, or immobilization behaviors of death feigning, freezing, and behavioral shutdown via the unmyelinated vagus. Thus, withdrawal of the myelinated vagal circuit provides access to the more primitive adaptive defensive systems at a cost. If the removal is prolonged, there is an increased risk for both physical (e.g., risk for cardiovascular disorders) and mental (e.g., anxiety disorders, depression) illness as the protective antistress and self-soothing features of the myelinated vagus and the associated prosocial features of the social engagement system are lost.

NEUROCEPTION: CONTEXTUAL CUEING OF ADAPTIVE AND MALADAPTIVE PHYSIOLOGICAL STATES

To effectively switch from defensive to social engagement strategies, the mammalian nervous system needs to perform two important adaptive tasks: (1) assess risk, and (2) if the environment is perceived as safe, inhibit the more primitive limbic structures that control fight, flight, or freeze behaviors. In other words, any intervention that has the potential for increasing an organism's experience of safety has the potential of recruiting the evolutionarily more advanced neural circuits that support the prosocial behaviors of the social engagement system.

The nervous system, through the processing of sensory information from the environment and from the viscera, continuously evaluates risk. Since the neural evaluation of risk does not require conscious awareness and may involve subcortical limbic structures (e.g., Morris, Ohman, & Dolan, 1999), the term *neuroception* (see chapter 1) was introduced to emphasize a neural process, distinct from perception, that is capable of distinguishing environmental (and visceral) features that are safe, dangerous, or life-threatening. In safe environments, autonomic state is adaptively regulated to dampen sympathetic activation and to protect the oxygen-dependent central nervous system, and especially the cortex, from the metabolically conservative reactions of the dorsal vagal complex. However, how does the nervous system know when the environment is safe, dangerous, or life-threatening and what neural mechanisms evaluate this risk?

Neuroception might involve feature detectors involving the temporal cortex (see later discussion), since the temporal cortex responds to familiar voice and faces and hand movements and can influence limbic reactivity. Thus, the neuroception of familiar individuals and individuals with appropriately prosodic voices and warm expressive faces translates into a social interaction promoting a sense of safety. In most individuals (i.e., without a psychiatric disorder or neuropathology) the nervous system evaluates risk and matches neurophysiological state with the actual risk of the environment. When the environment is appraised as being safe, the defensive limbic structures are inhibited enabling social engagement and calm visceral states to emerge. In contrast, some individuals experience a mismatch and the nervous system appraises the environment as being dangerous, even when it is safe. This mismatch results in physiological states that support fight, flight, or freeze behaviors, but not social engagement behaviors. According to the theory, social communication can be expressed efficiently through the social engagement system, only when these defensive circuits are inhibited. Neuroception represents a neural process that enables humans to engage in social behaviors by distinguishing safe from dangerous contexts. Neuroception is proposed as a plausible mechanism mediating both the expression and the disruption of positive social behavior, emotion regulation, and visceral homeostasis.

New technologies, such as functional magnetic resonance imaging, have identified specific neural structures that are involved in detecting risk. The temporal lobe is of particular interest in expanding the construct of neuroception and in identifying neural mechanisms that, by detecting and evaluating risk, modulate the expression of adaptive defensive behaviors and autonomic states. Functional imaging techniques document the involvement of the temporal cortex, fusiform gyrus, and superior temporal sulcus in the evaluation of biological movement and intention including the detection of features such as movements, vocalizations, and faces, which contribute to an individual being perceived as safe or trustworthy (Adolphs, 2002; Winston, Strange, O'Doherty, & Dolan, 2002). Slight changes in these stimuli can be appraised as posing threat or alternatively signally endearment. Connectivity between these areas of the temporal cortex and the amygdala suggests a top-down control in the processing of facial features that could inhibit activity of the structures involved in the expression of defensive strategies (Pessoa, McKenna, Gutierrez, & Ungerleider, 2002).

Based on the relative risk of the environment, both social engagement and defense behaviors may be interpreted as either adaptive or maladaptive. For example, the inhibition of defense systems by the social engagement system would be adaptive and appropriate only in a safe environment. From a clinical perspective it would be the inability to inhibit defense systems in safe environments (e.g., anxiety disorders, post-traumatic stress disorder, reactive attachment disorder) or the inability to activate defense systems in risk environments (e.g., Williams syndrome, a genetic disorder with a behavioral repertoire characterized by engaging without detecting or respecting the emotional state of others) that might contribute to the defining features of psychopathology. Thus, an invalid neuroception of safety or danger might contribute to maladaptive physiological reactivity and the expression of the defensive behaviors associated with specific psychiatric disorders that include in their diagnostic criteria a social deficit (e.g., autism, social anxiety, Williams syndrome) or fear (e.g., various phobias, obsessive-compulsive disorder) (Leckman et al., 1997). However, in most individuals neuroception accurately reflects risk, and there is a consistency between the cognitive awareness of risk and the visceral response to risk.

The features of risk in the environment do not solely drive neuroception. Afferent feedback from the viscera provides a major mediator of the accessibility of prosocial circuits associated with social engagement behaviors. For example, the polyvagal theory predicts that states of mobilization would compromise our ability to detect positive social cues. Functionally, visceral states color our perception of objects and others. Thus, the same features of a person engaging another may result in range of outcomes, depending on the physiological state of the target individual. If the person being engaged is in a state in which the social engagement system is easily accessible, the reciprocal prosocial interactions are likely to occur. However, if the individual is in a state of mobilization, the same engaging response might be responded to with the asocial features of withdrawal or aggression. In such a state, it might be very difficult to dampen the mobilization circuit and enable the social engagement system to come back online.

The insula may be involved in the mediation of neuroception, since it has been proposed as a brain structure involved in conveying the diffuse feedback from the viscera into cognitive awareness. Functional imaging experiments have demonstrated that the insula has an important role in pain experience and the experience of several emotions, including anger, fear, disgust, happiness, and sadness. Critchley, Wiens, Rothstein, Ohman, and Dolan (2004) propose that internal body states are represented in the insula and contribute to subjective feeling states and have demonstrated that activity in the insula correlated with interoceptive accuracy.

CO-OPTING THE IMMOBILIZATION DEFENSE SYSTEM FOR REPRODUCTIVE BEHAVIORS, NURSING, AND THE FORMATION OF SOCIAL BONDS

Immobilization as a defense system is phylogenetically old and is associated with reduced metabolic demands and increased pain threshold. In reptiles, with a larger tolerance for reductions in oxygen, immobilization is a very effective defense strategy. In contrast, since mammals have a great need for oxygen, the inhibition of movement coupled with a shift in autonomic state to support the immobilization behavior (i.e., apnea and bradycardia) can be lethal (Hofer, 1970; Richter, 1957) such that death feigning can lead to death. In humans, fainting or dissociating in anticipation of death or painful injury reflects a less extreme form of this response.

However, several aspects of mammalian social behavior require immobilization, but do so in the absence of life threat. In these contexts an immobilization without fear is required. Immobilization without fear is accomplished by coopting the structures that regulate immobilization in response to life threat to serve a broad range of social needs, including reproduction, nursing, and pairbonding. The area of the periaqueductal gray that coordinates immobility as a primitive defense system has been modified in mammals to serve their intimate social needs. In addition, it has been reported that the ventral lateral portion of the periaqueductal gray is rich in receptors for oxytocin, a neuropeptide associated with parturition, nursing, and the establishment of pair-bonds (Carter, 1998; Insel & Young 2001).

CO-OPTING THE MOBILIZATION DEFENSE SYSTEM FOR PLAY

Often the playful "rough and tumble" behaviors observed in mammals are interpreted as preliminary exercises to develop adaptive defensive and aggressive behaviors. However, play is also inherently motivating and provides a unique and positive experience (Panksepp, 1998). Play, at least rough and tumble play, is characterized by mobilization. Thus, play shares with the defensive fight-or-flight behaviors a neurophysiological substrate that functionally increases metabolic output by increasing sympathetic excitation. Concurrent with the sympathetic excitation is a withdrawal of the myelinated vagal pathways that characterize the vagal brake. Just as the primitive mechanisms mediating immobilization in response to life threat can be co-opted to support loving and nutrient processes, so can mobilization mechanisms be involved occur to facilitate both defensive flight-or-fight behaviors and pleasurable "play."

How is play distinguished from aggressive behavior? More important, are there "neuroceptive" processes that either dampen or potentiate aggressive retaliation? If we observe play, we can reliably observe cues lead to either aggression or calming. Frequently play leads to acts that are painful and potentially aggressive. For example, often a playmate is injured. This may occur with various mammalian species. When dogs play, they may bite too hard and elicit a painful cry in the playmate. When a human is playing with a dog, the dog might accidentally hit in a vulnerable and tender place like the nose. When humans play a sport such as basketball, an individual may be hit with an elbow to the face. How are these situations diffused? What processes enable anger to be contained and play to be resumed?

Access to the social engagement system can transform potential aggression to play. The social engagement system cues others that the "intentionality" of the behavior is benign. For example, a fight is likely to occur if the individual who accidentally hits another in the face while playing basketball walks away without diffusing the tension through a face-to-face expression of concern. Similarly, play will not continue if dogs playing do not make face-to-face engagements after an accidental, but hurtful bite. Consistent with the importance of the social engagement system in the process of play, autism is associated with noninteractive (i.e., parallel) play. Thus, access to the social engagement system is critical in defining mobilization as play and not aggression. Team sports, which are prevalent in our culture, involve mobilization strategies that require face-to-face interactions to signal intentionality and share a common feature of integrating the social engagement system with mobilization.

Jogging and other forms of exercise also result in a physiological state similar to team sports or rough and tumble play. However, unlike exercise, a "polyvagal" definition of play requires reciprocal interactions and a constant awareness of the actions of others. Play is different than fight-or-flight behaviors. Although fight-or-flight behaviors often require an awareness of others, they do not require reciprocal interactions and an ability to restrain mobilizations. Play recruits another circuit that enables aggressive and defensive behaviors to be contained. The rapid recruitment of the social engagement system results in an immediate face-to-face evaluation of whether there is intentionality in the event that provoked the painful response. Areas of the cortex, such as superior temporal sulcus, provide a plausible location for this neuroceptive process. The superior temporal sulcus has been proposed to be an area of the brain that evaluates biological movement and intentionality. Thus, familiar voices, calming gestures, and appropriate facial expression can rapidly diffuse a possible physical conflict. Even the dogs that whimpers after being hit on the nose or bit on the leg while playing will rapidly make a face-to-face engagement and wait for a gesture that will provide the reassurance that the event was not intentional.

How does the social engagement system calm us down and keep us from expressing inappropriate aggressive acts? First, there are inhibitory pathways from the temporal cortex that dampen the limbic reactivity associated with defensive behaviors. Second, as Gellhorn (1964) noted almost 50 years ago, facial muscle activity influences the brain structures that regulate visceral state. This is frequently observed in humans of all ages from the very young infants who use sucking behaviors to calm to older individuals who use conversation, listening, smiling, and ingesting to calm. Consistent with and in contrast to these strategies of defusing conflict, walking away or turning the head away from the conflict can trigger a violent reaction.

By investigating the unique physiological mechanisms involved in play, we uncover the unique properties of reciprocal interactions that may define play and distinguish it from exercise and other solitary behaviors. Play requires turn taking in expressive motor movements and reciprocal receptive inhibition of activity. This is also observed in talking and listening, in throwing and catching, and in hiding and seeking. When there is mutual activity and contact, such as in rough and tumble play, there are more opportunities for cues to be mistaken and aggressive behaviors to unfold. However, if face-to-face engagement occurs rapidly with the appropriate features of concern and empathy, then the physiological state that was driven by the physical contact is evaluated for intentionality and diffused with the appropriate cues exchanged between two social engagement systems involved in the face-to-face exchange. Although play may share some of the neural mechanisms involved in fight-or-flight behaviors, unlike solitary exercise, play requires dynamic neural regulation of state to ensure safe interactions. Thus, both sympathetic activation to increase metabolic output to support motor activity and the vagal brake to restrain mobilization and to support the function of the social engagement system are recruited to maintain a mutual playful activity. Another adaptive process involves the coactivation of sympathetic excitatory and vagal inhibitory processes. This process is associated with sexual arousal, another vulnerable state that evolutionarily requires face-to-face interactions to evaluate intentionality of physical contact to determine whether the behaviors are caring or hurtful.

SUMMARY STATEMENTS

The polyvagal theory is an attempt to reorganize our conceptualization of the autonomic nervous system with a focus on the specific neural circuits involved in regulating visceral organs for specific adaptive functions, including the domains of affect, emotions, and goal-directed behaviors. The theory identifies specific variables that can be used to dynamically evaluate the changing neural regulation of specific adaptive circuits. Implicit in the theoretical model are four prominent features that impact directly on the development of testable hypotheses: (1) the role specific brain structures and neural circuits have in regulating autonomic state, (2) the justification of developing methods that can distinguish and track the dynamic vagal output to target organs through the myelinated vagus originating in the nucleus ambiguus and the unmyelinated vagus originating in the dorsal motor nucleus, (3) the role visceral afferents and sensory feature detectors have on the switching among the neural circuits regulating autonomic state, and (4) the relation between the regulation of visceral organs and the regulation of the striated muscles of the face and head involved in social engagement behaviors including affect recognition and emotional expression.

The polyvagal theory suggests that affective and emotional states are dependent on lower brain regulation of the visceral state and the important visceral, tactile, and nocioceptive cues that travel between the brain and the periphery. Through the lens of the polyvagal theory, specific bodily states foster different domains of behavior. Specifically, the neural regulation of five physiological states has been described and each state has been linked with a specific biologically based behavioral repertoire.

1. Social engagement: a state dependent on a well-defined social engagement system. This system promotes positive social interactions, reduces psychological distance, and promotes a sense of safety between people.
2. Mobilization—fight-or-flight: This state supports fight-or-flight behaviors and requires an increase in metabolic output.
3. Play: a blend of the above. Play is a hybrid state requiring features from both states of mobilization and social engagement.
4. Immobilization—life threat: This state is associated with life threat and is characterized by a reduction of metabolic output and shutdown behaviors. This primitive neural circuit works fine for reptiles but is potentially lethal in mammals.
5. Immobilization without fear: This state is associated with prosocial and positive states that require a reduction of movement without the massive reduction of metabolic resources. This circuit recruits pathways from the immobilization circuit and is used during nursing, childbirth, and reproductive behaviors and digestive and restorative processes.

Functionally, these five states color our perception of objects and others. Thus, the same features of a person engaging another may result in range of outcomes, if the target individual is in a different physiological state. If the person being engaged is in a state in which the social engagement system is easily accessible, the reciprocal prosocial interactions are likely to occur. If the individual is in a state of mobilization, the same engaging response might be responded to with the asocial features of withdrawal or aggression. This stimulus-organism-response (S-O-R) model is reminiscent of Woodworth (1928), who postulated an S-O-R model with an active organism intervening between stimulus and response. In the Woodworth model, processes internal to the organism mediated the effects of stimuli on behavior. Within the polyvagal theory, neuroception is an S-O-R model. Within this context, autonomic state is an intervening process that contributes to the transformation from the external physical stimulus to the complex internal cognitive-affective processes that determine the quality of the interpersonal interaction.

The five states described provide a good fit with the underlying physiological states required to successfully express the seven neural-based systems described by Panksepp (1998). Moreover, the polyvagal perspective, with its emphasis on phylogenetic shifts in visceral regulation, provides a unique insight into the use of psychological constructs. For example, the polyvagal theory will lead to three different visceral phenotypes for the emotion of fear. One type is characterized by mobilization strategies consistent with the features of fight-or-flight behaviors. A second type is characterized by immobilization (e.g., death feigning), a biobehavioral state that, due to metabolic depression, can potentially be lethal for a mammal. In humans this might be observed as fainting, defecating, and/or dissociating. A third type is more cognitive and involves a transitory depression of the social engagement system as a precautionary response to evaluate intentionality behaviors. If behavior is detected as dangerous, then the sympathetic nervous system is activated to support the fight-or-flight mobilization behaviors. All three are "fear" responses, but they have different behavioral topographies and different underlying neurophysiological substrates. Thus, the understanding of affective experiences and the strategy of organizing of these experiences into psychological constructs such as "emotions" may be informed by understanding the covariation between the specific phylogenetic shifts in the neural regulation of the viscera and the adaptive nature of these various affective states in phylogenetically older vertebrates

CONCLUDING COMMENTS

To optimize strategies studying the bridge between nervous system function and both clinical disorders and affective experiences, affective neuroscience will need to incorporate methodologies and to test hypotheses dependent on our expanding knowledge of neurophysiology and the central structures involved in both appraisal of context (i.e., neuroception) and neural regulation of visceral state. These questions have motivated previous (e.g., Cannon, Darwin, James, Gellhorn, Hess) and contemporary researchers (e.g., Critchley, 2005; Ekman, Levenson, & Friesen, 1983; Thayer & Lane, 2000) attempting to bridge the gap between visceral states and the subjective labels of affective experiences (i.e., emotions). To close this gap, new methodologies are necessary that are capable of evaluating dynamic changes in and interactions among various physiological (e.g., respiration, heart rate, blood pressure, vasomotor tone, and motor activity) variables in a changing context. In response to these needs, the polyvagal theory was developed.

The polyvagal theory provides a perspective to demystify features of clinical disorders. The theory provides principles to organize previously assumed disparate symptoms observed in several psychiatric disorders (i.e., a compromise in the function of the social engagement system). Moreover, by explaining features of disorders from an adaptive perspective, interventions may be designed that trigger the neural circuits that will promote spontaneous social engagement behaviors and dampen the expression of defensive strategies that disrupt social interactions.

CHAPTER 19

Neurobiology and Evolution: Mechanisms, Mediators, and Adaptive Consequences of Caregiving

DEFINING FEATURES OF CAREGIVING

Caregiving includes providing food, protection, or other resources. However, caregiving also may extend beyond these physical elements to include social support to fulfill needs for affiliation and perceived safety. Most mammals, including humans and rodents, are altricial at birth and caregiving is necessary to compensate for the infant's undeveloped motor and autonomic nervous systems. Due to an immature corticospinal motor system, the infant is incapable of independently obtaining food or protecting from a predator. Due to an immature autonomic nervous system, the infant is incapable of independently thermoregulating to maintain a necessary body temperature to survive. Thus, the mature nervous system of the caregiver becomes intertwined with the undeveloped nervous system of the infant to create a model of "symbiotic regulation." The caregiver becomes part of a complex feedback system supporting the biological and behavioral needs of the infant. Within this model of symbiotic regulation, the caregiver is not solely giving to the infant. The behaviors of the infant also trigger specific physiological processes (e.g., neural and endocrine feedback circuits) that help establish strong bonds, provide emotional comfort for the caretaker, stimulate neural pathways, and support the health of the caregiver.

Through the process of maturation, motor and autonomic systems change. As the infant matures, there is a transition from a dependence on the caregiver for the regulation of biobehavioral processes to a greater degree of self-regulation. However, throughout the life span most mammals will continue to be dependent on others to maintain optimal well-being and state regulation (Hrdy, 2008). In some (but not all) mammalian species, caregiving is based on or induces selective and reinforcing emotional social relationships and bonds (see chapter 11;

Carter. 1998). When enduring bonds are present, devastating reactions to separation or loss are to be expected (Bowlby, 1988).

Caregiving may or may not be reciprocal. However, reciprocity and the spontaneous reversal of the roles of giving and receiving are positive features of strong relationships and are the optimal features of symbiotic regulation. Conversely, a lack of reciprocity often signals distressed and vulnerable relationships. The inability of an individual to enter and to maintain reciprocal social relations is a feature of several psychiatric disorders (Teicher et al., 2003).

When a mammalian mother initially interacts with her offspring, usually she has just given birth and must provide milk to nurture the newborn. The onset of maternal caregiving is normally closely associated with birth and lactation. The physical events of birth and lactation provide endocrine windows of opportunity for the establishment of strong social bonds. Thus, the hormones of birth and lactation are plausible candidates to explain the beneficial effects of caregiving (Carter, 1998; Numan, 2007).

THE EVOLUTION OF A CAREGIVING SYSTEM: THE TRANSITION FROM "SELF-REGULATION" TO "OTHER REGULATION"

Evolutionary theories attempting to explain between- and within-species variation in social behavior tend to focus on ultimate causes and assumed selection pressures. These theories are based on ancient historical events and are limited to the fossil record. Thus, it is difficult to test evolutionary theories within the context of the expressed behavior or physiology of contemporary animals. However, a phylogenetic perspective that investigates the biological and behavioral shifts from reptiles to mammals illustrates several neurobiological features underlying sociality. For example, most behaviors associated with caregiving and prosociality in humans are uniquely mammalian and are not evident in reptiles. Differences among mammalian species, individual variation, and developmental changes in social contact and caregiving are common. Analyses of these variations provide experiments of nature, which cast a new light on the neurobiology of sociality.

In part, the phylogenetic transition from reptiles to mammals appears to be a shift from an organism capable of "self-regulation" to an organism that is dependent at certain points in development on "other regulation." It is within this phylogenetic transition, in which regulation by "other" becomes adaptive, that the neurobiology of sociality emerges. The defining features of the "other" in the mammalian model of regulation often have survival consequences that may involve various dimensions of support, including warmth, food, and protection. For most mammals, and especially humans, a developmental increase in self-regulation capacity parallels the development of specific features of the nervous system. With physical maturation, neural pathways from the cortex to the brainstem exhibit a greater efficiency in regulating the autonomic nervous system and enable the maintenance of physiological homeostasis in both safe and dangerous situations (Porges, 2001a). These maturational changes provide greater abilities to self-regulate and to reduce dependence on others.

THE PHYLOGENY OF MAMMALIAN SOCIAL ENGAGEMENT AND COMMUNICATION SYSTEMS

The mammalian autonomic nervous system retains three neural circuits, which are expressed in a phylogenetically organized hierarchy (Table 19.1). In this

TABLE 19.1. Polyvagal Theory: Phylogenetic Stages of Neural Control

Autonomic Nervous System Component	Origin of Motor Neurons	Behavioral Functions	Autonomic Functions
Myelinated vagus (*ventral vagal complex*)	Nucleus ambiguus (NA)	Social engagement and caregiving. Expressed as a coordinated face–heart connection and observed as enhanced regulation of the striated muscles of the face and head and increased calming of the viscera including an active dampening of sympathetic-adrenal functions and reducing fear. The enhanced regulation of facial muscles result in greater prosody, improved listening, and greater emotional expressivity.	Neuroprotection. Stabilization of autonomic processes, including respiratory sinus arrhythmia (RSA), which protects the heart and enhances oxygenation of the brain. By regulating state and calming the individual, these functions of the autonomic nervous system permit sociality and provide resources necessary for symbiotic and reciprocal social interactions.
Sympathetic-adrenal system (*sympathetic nervous system*)	Spinal cord	Mobilization. Active adaptations including flight-or-fight responses.	Activation. Increased heart rate, release of glucocorticoids and catecholamines. Production of energy, including glucose, and conversion of norepinephrine to epinephrine.
Unmyelinated vagus (*dorsal vagal complex*)	Dorsal nucleus of the vagus (DMX)	Immobilization. Passive adaptations including death feigning and loss of consciousness.	Conservation. Prevalence of bradycardia (slowing the heart) and apnea (cessation of breathing). Reduced energy production.

hierarchy of adaptive responses, the newest circuit, associated with social communication, is used first. If the newest circuit fails to provide safety, older survival-oriented circuits are recruited sequentially. It is important to note that social behavior, social communication, and visceral homeostasis are largely incompatible with neurophysiological states and behaviors that are regulated by circuits that support the defense strategies of both flight or fight and immobilization. Inhibition of systems, which are in general defensive or protective, is necessary to initiate social engagement and to allow positive social behaviors. Conversely, positive social behaviors may be inhibited during prolonged periods of adversity. However, systems that support sociality also may be protective against the costly or destructive effects of chronic fear or stress (Porges, 2001a, 2007b).

THE POLYVAGAL THEORY

Often overlooked, but especially critical to social and emotional behavior, is the autonomic nervous system (see chapter 2). The central nervous system cannot function without the support of visceral organs supplying oxygen and energy. The autonomic nervous system, via bidirectional pathways, regulates the viscera and conveys information upward to the hypothalamus, amygdala, and neocortex. Sensory information from the viscera contributes to what humans experience as "emotion" or "emotional states." These emotional states, in turn, are components of a "motivational" system that stimulates social engagement and allows sociality to be experienced as reinforcing. Often these emotional and motivational states involve other brain systems, including those that rely on dopamine and endogenous opioids.

Of particular importance to mammalian social behavior is the parasympathetic component of the autonomic nervous system. The evolution of this system in mammals permitted the emergence of complex social interactions and social communication. Embedded in the brainstem and associated cranial nerves are conserved and evolved elements that are essential for modern mammalian physiology and behavior (see chapters 2, 11, and 12; Porges, 2001a, 2007b). The vagus (Xth cranial) nerve is of special relevance, because it transmits and integrates complex bidirectional communication between the brain and peripheral organs involved in cardiovascular, respiratory, digestive, and immune functions. Critical to understanding mammalian sociality is knowledge of the origins of the neuranatomical pathways of the social engagement system, linking visceral state regulation and emotion to both the expressive and receptive domains of social communication.

In mammals, but not reptiles, the vagus nerve has two distinct efferent (motor) pathways with separate brainstem source nuclei (Table 19.1; see also Figure 3.1, p. 56). In addition, approximately 80% of vagal fibers are afferent pathways, transmitting sensory input from the viscera to the brainstem.

The evolution of the polyvagal system parallels the phylogenetic distinction between reptiles and mammals and includes a cluster of behaviors dependent on the function of structures that phylogenetically emerged first in mammals. These changes include detached middle ear bones, the advent of a diaphragm, and the myelinated vagal system regulating supradiaphragmatic organs. The latter vagal system is distinct from the unmyelinated vagus, which primarily regulates subdiaphragmatic organs. However, branches of both myelinated and unmyelinated vagus do reach the heart, where they coordinate the need for oxygen with the behavioral demands of a rapidly changing physical and social environment.

The phylogeny of the mammalian nervous system offers important clues to social behavior. In the transition from aquatic to terrestrial life, ancient gill (branchial) arches were co-opted to form the face and head, resulting in the modern versions of these structures, which included new or additional functions. Changes also were necessary in the muscles and nerves associated with the branchial arches. Taken together in modern mammals, including humans, these systems permit social engagement and social communication, including sucking, swallowing, facial expressions, and the production and receipt of airborne vocalizations.

Brainstem structures that regulate the efferent (motor) branch of the vagus have two source nuclei. The *unmyelinated* component of the vagus, which permits slowing of heart rate, originates in the dorsal motor nucleus of the vagus and provides the efferent component of the dorsal vagal complex. The unmyelinated vagus is shared by mammals with other vertebrates (i.e., reptiles, amphibians, teleosts, and elasmobrachs). The dorsal motor nucleus of the vagus is the source nucleus for the unmyelinated vagus, which carries neural impulses to and is capable of slowing heart rate. The more modern branch originates in the nucleus ambiguus of the ventral vagal complex and is *myelinated*, allowing rapid interaction between the brain and viscera. The myelinated vagus stabilizes cardiovascular function and is responsible for respiratory sinus arrhythmia (RSA), a rhythmic component of the heart rate pattern with a periodicity similar to spontaneous breathing. RSA is an index of the dynamic influence of the myelinated vagus on the heart. The ventral vagal complex also contains source nuclei for other facial nerves as well as autonomic functions. When RSA is withdrawn (reduced myelinated vagal tone), heart rate quickly accelerates. Thus, emotional states and social communication can be coordinated with visceral demands (see chapter 2).

Information from the myelinated vagus, measured by quantifying RSA, is cardioprotective and directly implicated in cortical oxygenation. RSA, due to its sensitivity to the influence of ventral vagal fibers on the heart is often used as an index of health and resilience in humans. The comparatively modern processes that supplied oxygen to the large primate cortex allowed the emergence of higher levels of cognitive functions. Such processes may be at the core of the uniqueness of human cognition. Furthermore, the myelinated vagus is associated in the brainstem with cranial nerves that innervate the face and head (see chapter 3). Thus, the myelinated vagal functions are coordinated with the neural regulation of the larynx and pharynx to coordinate sucking, swallowing, and breathing with vocalizations. The muscles of the human face, especially of the upper face involved in subtle emotional expressions, have projections from this system, which may be particularly important in social communication (see chapter 13).

THE NEUROANATOMY OF SOCIAL COGNITION

The expanding mammalian cortex set the stage for human cognition, speech, and more elaborate forms of caregiving beyond the maternal–infant interaction. Several features of anatomy that emerged concurrently with the expanding cortex provided the mechanisms necessary for mammalian social communication.

The classic definition of Mammalia focuses on the occurrence of mammary glands and hair. However, the fossil record relies on the identification of middle ear bones detached from the jawbone as the defining feature of Mammalia. The tiny middle ear bones form an ossicular chain that transmits sound vibrations from the ear drum to the inner ear. As the middle ear muscles tense or relax the middle ear structures change the frequency band that is transmitted to the inner ear. In safe environments, when there is no risk and defensive systems are down regulated, the ossicular chain is relatively tense. This state of stiffness in the ossicular chain enables mammals to process sounds in a frequency range that is higher than that available to reptiles. Thus, mammalian acoustic communication usually occurs at frequencies that cannot be heard by reptiles. The anatomical separation of the middle ear bones from the jawbone allows airborne auditory communication (see chapter 13). Concurrently, phylogenetic transitions in brainstem areas regulating the vagus are physically and functionally intertwined with the brainstem areas regulating the striated muscles of the face and head. The result of this transition is the emergence of a dynamic social engagement system with social communication features (e.g., head movements, production of vocalizations, and a selective ability to hear conspecific vocal communication).

In support of this new mammalian anatomy, a myelinated vagus emerged. The myelinated vagus could inhibit the sympathetic nervous system and the hypothalamic-pituitary-adrenal axis. This feature of the autonomic nervous system allowed mammals to inhibit mobilization and experience calm behavioral states. In this context it was possible for animals to engage in high levels of social interaction.

The phylogenetic transition from reptiles to mammals also resulted in a face–heart connection in which the striated muscles of the face and head were regulated in the same brainstem areas that evoked the calming influence of the myelinated vagus. The striated muscles of the face and head are involved in social cueing (e.g., facial expressions, vocalizations, listening, head gesture, etc.). These systems serve as "trigger" stimuli to the feature detectors in the nervous system that detect risk and safety in the environment (see discussion on neuroception). However, the expanded mammalian cortex also demands high levels of oxygen. Oxygenation of the cortex in mammals is accomplished in part through the same adaptations of the autonomic nervous system that permit elaborate forms of reciprocal sociality. These systems, including terrestrial lungs and a four-chamber heart, which support the oxygenation of the neocortex are also regulated in part by the myelinated branch of the vagus nerve.

This synergism of neural mechanisms in mammals allows for symbiotic regulation of behavior and the elaboration of reciprocal caregiving. These same systems provide setting conditions during which social behaviors can have a significant impact on cognition and health. In the human nervous system specific features of person-to-person interactions are innate triggers of adaptive biobehavioral systems, which in turn can support health and healing. In the absence of social interactions or under conditions of social adversity various forms of maladaptive behaviors and illness may be expressed.

NEUROCEPTION AND THE SOCIAL MANAGEMENT OF THREAT AND DANGER

The integrated functions of the myelinated vagus permit the expression of positive emotions and social communication. However, the nervous system also is constantly assessing risk in the environment through a process of "neuroception" (see chapter 1), during which specific neural circuits are triggered that may support defensive strategies of fight-or-flight or alternatively shutdown.

The mammalian nervous system has retained two primitive defensive neural circuits for either active or passive coping that can be called on in the presence of threat or danger. The fight-or-flight system allows mobilization and active coping. This system is supported by the sympathoadrenal systems, including the release of catecholamines and glucocorticoids, which increase available energy. However, active avoidance is not the only mechanism through which mammals may deal with threat or danger. Under some conditions, such as inescapable danger or other forms of extreme stress, mobilization strategies may be inhibited. This alternate defensive strategy is characterized by passive coping and immobility. Under more severe conditions many systems may be shut down, including those dependent on the neocortex. In these circumstances animals may show death-feigning and "helpless" behaviors.

The unmyelinated vagus tends to slow the heart, consistent with a reptilian adaptive strategy of freezing and conserving energy in the face of danger. However, mammals, with their large cortex, cannot maintain alertness without relatively high concentrations of oxygen. Thus, a prolonged slowing of heart rate could lead to unconsciousness and eventually death. Neurophysiological mechanisms exist for protecting the heart and brain from shutting down. As described shortly, the release of peptide hormones are among these neural mechanisms.

SOCIAL ENGAGEMENT SYSTEM

Critical to human social behavior are pathways from the five cranial nerves that control the muscles of the face and head. Collectively, these motor pathways are labeled as *special visceral efferents*. The special visceral efferent pathways regulate the muscles of mastication (e.g., ingestion), muscles of the middle ear (e.g., listening to vocalizations), muscles of the face (e.g., emotional expression), muscles of larynx and pharynx (e.g., vocal prosody and intonation), and muscles controlling head tilt and turning (e.g., gesture). The source nuclei of the circuits regulating the striated muscles of the face and head interact in the brainstem with the source nucleus of the myelinated vagus (i.e., nucleus ambiguus); together these form an integrated social engagement system. This system provides the neural structures involved in the expression of social and emotional behaviors and the feelings associated with these behaviors.

MAMMALIAN SOCIAL COMMUNICATION AND THE EVOLUTION OF SOCIAL COGNITION

Positive forms of communication, usually including speech and other vocalizations, are typically components of successful caregiving. Vocalizations also convey information regarding physiological state. For example, infant cries are indicators of health state and also can elicit caregiving. The coordinated regulation of social communication and visceral systems helps explain the relationship between positive social experiences and health.

Shared neural pathways underlie social communication and visceral functions, such as the regulation of the cardiovascular, digestive, and immune systems. For example, through the myelinated vagus, the brainstem regulates vocal communication (i.e., pathways controlling breath and the muscles of the larynx and pharynx) as well as heart rate. Thus, both heart rate, expressed in RSA, and the acoustic features of vocalizations, expressed in prosody, are parallel outputs of the integrated social engagement system.

A depressed social engagement system is characterized by low variability in both heart rate (i.e., low-amplitude RSA through the myelinated vagus) and vocal intonations (i.e., lack of prosody). Human voices that lack prosody fail to attract or interest others and are perceived as reflecting an emotionally detached or boring individual. In contrast, an optimally functioning social engagement system will have features of high variability in both heart rate (i.e., high-amplitude RSA) and vocal intonations (i.e., high prosody). Lack of prosody is a risk factor similar to low amplitude RSA and both may be used as indications of health risk.

Attention to features of acoustic vocalizations could provide insights into vagal regulation of the heart. For example, the positive features of vocal prosody in social interactions may be synchronized with RSA. The origins of these coordinated functions are most readily appreciated in the context of the evolution of neuroanatomical mechanisms for social engagement and social communication.

Collectively, the muscles of the face and head function as filters that limit social stimuli (e.g., observing facial features and listening to vocalizations) and determinants of engagement with the social environment. The neural control of these muscles determines social experiences by changing facial features (especially in humans and other primates), modulating laryngeal and pharyngeal muscles to regulate intonation of vocalizations (prosody), and coordinating both facial and vocal motor tone with respiratory actions. In addition, the frequency of breathing is encoded into the phrasing of vocalizations, which—independent of the content of speech—may express meaning. For example, urgency may be conveyed by short phrases associated with short exhalations (i.e., rapid breathing), while calmness would be conveyed by long phrases associated with long exhalations (i.e., slow breathing).

NEUROCHEMISTRY AND THE SOCIAL NERVOUS SYSTEM

Neuropeptides regulate sociality, emotion, and the autonomic nervous system. Social behaviors are supported and coordinated by both endocrine and autonomic processes (Grippo, Trahanas, Zimmerman, Porges, & Carter, 2009). The complex networks of biochemical systems necessary for reproduction and homeostasis also are implicated in social behavior. Given the energetic demands of social interactions, it is not surprising that the same neurotransmitters that are involved in social behavior also regulate the autonomic nervous system. Two mammalian hormones/neuromodulators, oxytocin and vasopressin, have been shown to be of particular importance to mammalian sociality. There is increasing evidence that the functions of these same molecules, especially oxytocin, are central to the causes and consequences of positive social behaviors, including sensitivity to social cues in others and constructs such as trust and caregiving (Heinrichs, von Dawans, & Domes, 2009).

Oxytocin and vasopressin are small neuropeptides that differ from each other in only two of nine amino acids (Landgraf & Neumann, 2004). Oxytocin is produced primarily in hypothalamic nuclei, including the supraoptic and paraventricular nuclei. Vasopressin is synthesized in the supraoptic and paraventricular nuclei as well as other brain regions implicated in the regulation of emotional behaviors, as well as circadian rhythms. In addition, and especially in males, vasopressin also is abundant in brain regions (e.g., amygdala, bed nucleus of the stria terminalis, and lateral septum) of particular importance to social and emotional regulation and self-defense (De Vries & Panzica, 2006).

Oxytocin and vasopressin are transported from the hypothalamus (i.e., supraoptic and paraventricular nuclei) to the mammalian posterior pituitary where they are released into the bloodstream and act as hormones on peripheral target tissues, such as the uterus or mammary tissue. Within the brain, these same chemicals also serve as neuromodulators, affecting a broad range of neural processes. Both oxytocin and vasopressin are capable of moving throughout the central nervous system, probably by passive diffusion (Landgraf & Neumann, 2004). Receptors for these molecules are found in various brain areas implicated in social behavior (Gimpl & Fahrenholz, 2001). In contrast to most biologically active compounds, oxytocin has only one receptor. Vasopressin has at least three distinct receptor subtypes with separable functions. However, the oxytocin peptide also may affect the vasopressin receptors and vice versa.

The neuroanatomy of the oxytocin system allows a coordinated effect on behavior, autonomic functions, and peripheral tissues. In some, but not all cases, vasopressin and oxytocin have opposite functions, possibly because they are capable of acting as antagonists to each other's receptors, while in other cases these peptides have similar effects. Dynamic interactions between oxytocin and vasopressin may in turn regulate physiology and behavior, allowing shifts between positive social behaviors and defensive states (Viviani & Stoop, 2008).

EVOLUTION OF OXYTOCIN AND VASOPRESSIN

It is likely that the essential elements on which sociality are based arose from physiological processes fundamental to the need to conserve water and minerals. Among these are adaptations allowing the transition from aquatic to terrestrial life, including internal fertilization and eventually pregnancy and placental reproduction. Although vasopressin is also known as the "antidiuretic hormone," both oxytocin and vasopressin influence kidney function in adults to conserve water and minerals. The capacity to maintain or reabsorb water was a critical element in the evolution of terrestrial mammals. The capacity for internal fertilization and the development of the placenta and lactation required a well-developed water regulation system. This shift also provided a protective environment for offspring before and after birth, and the emergence of contemporary versions of the neocortex and cognition.

Genes for the synthesis of oxytocin and vasopressin are very ancient, estimated to be over 700 million years old (Donaldson & Young, 2008). These genes existed before the split between vertebrates and invertebrates. The original molecular structure from which the peptides evolved is believed to be vasotocin. Vasotocin differs from oxytocin and vasopressin by only one amino acid. Vasotocin is found in mammalian fetuses, although its expression is reduced at the time of birth.

The specific coding sequences that define oxytocin and vasopressin may have evolved more than once, but the current form probably evolved around the time that mammals first emerged. Oxytocin, through its functions in birth and lactation, assists in maternal nurturing of a comparatively immature infant (Brunton & Russell, 2008; Numan, 2007). The capacity of oxytocin to induce uterine contractions may have allowed the expansion of the human skull and cortex, and eventually cognition. These changes contribute to the elaboration of human vocalizations into speech and other forms of social communication that rely on cognitive function and cortical structures (Hrdy, 2008).

NEUROPEPTIDES INFLUENCE AUTONOMIC FUNCTIONS THROUGH EFFECTS ON THE BRAINSTEM

The paraventricular nucleus of the hypothalamus (including cells that synthesize oxytocin and vasopressin) is an important site of convergence for neural communication coordinating endocrine and cardiovascular responses to various forms of challenge (Michelini, Marcelo, Amico, & Morris, 2003). At the level of the paraventricular nucleus, oxytocin may influence both the hypothalamic-pituitary-adrenal axis and autonomic functions. The presence of oxytocin receptors in the dorsal vagal complex has been verified by autoradiography in rodents (Gimpl & Fahrenholz, 2001). The amygdala, with connections to cortex, hypothalamus, and lower brainstem, integrates sensory, cognitive, and emotional information. The central nucleus of the amygdala also contains oxytocin and vasopressin as well as their receptors, and projections to and from the central nucleus of the amygdala may be critical determinants of emotional reactivity. Thus, the central nucleus of the amygdala is one site (among several) where shifts from positive to negative emotions may be managed. Receptors for oxytocin and vasopressin are found in the amygdala, providing an opportunity for these peptides to integrate social and emotional functions.

Oxytocin and vasopressin also can influence emotions and behavior through their effects on the autonomic nervous system. A growing literature implicates oxytocin and vasopressin and their interactions with vagal circuits. For example, there is evidence for interactions between oxytocin and vasopressin at the level of the central nucleus of the amygdala, which has inputs to lower brainstem nuclei controlling vagal circuits. These processes explain in part the capacity of oxytocin to down-regulate activity in the amygdala (measured by functional magnetic resonance imaging), especially under conditions of fear or emotional dysregulation (Meyer-Lindenberg, 2008). Vasopressin plays a complex role in behavior through effects on blood pressure and heart rate, as well as on the sympathetic-adrenal axis and parasympathetic functions. Both the vasopressin peptide and the vasopressin receptor (V1aR) have been identified in the central nucleus of the amygdala, and implicated in the regulation of brainstem areas including the myelinated vagus, with source nuclei in the ventral vagal complex, where oxytocin-containing processes have been observed.

Receptors for both oxytocin and vasopressin are found in pathways regulating the myelinated vagus. However, oxytocin receptors are particularly abundant in the dorsal vagal complex, which regulates the unmyelinated vagus. As described, the unmyelinated vagus can slow the heart and, as part of a primitive defense system, could even trigger massive drops in blood pressure and fainting. However, under normal conditions the myelinated vagal system restrains the unmyelinated vagus, protecting this system from stopping the heart (Porges, 2007b). Under extremely stressful conditions, such as birth, oxytocin may act (on neural targets including the dorsal vagal complex) to protect the autonomic nervous system from reverting to this more primitive vagal system, which could lead to shutting down and reduced emotional, social, and cognitive function. Evolutionary changes in functions of neuropeptides, including the emergence of oxytocin and vasopressin as separate neuropeptides, facilitated the mammalian birth process (Brunton & Russell, 2008), and, in turn, these peptides fostered the reciprocal regulatory features of mammalian social behavior (Carter, 1998; Numan, 2007). A summary of the above model is illustrated in Figure 19.1.

FIGURE 19.1. The polyvagal theory: Hierarchal organization of neuroendocrine and autonomic processes implicated in social behavior and the adaptive management of stressful experiences. Neuropeptides, including oxytocin (OT), vasopressin (AVP), corticotropin-releasing factor (CRF), and endogenous opioids, as well as neurotransmitters such as serotonin (5-HT) and norepinephrine (NE) influence behavior and emotions through direct actions on the brain, as well as indirect effects on different components of the autonomic nervous system, including the ventral vagal complex (VVC), the dorsal vagal complex (DVC), and the hypothalamic-pituitary-adrenal (HPA) axis. Oxytocin, serotonin, and endogenous opioids acting in the brainstem may be protective during or against shutting down and immobilization.

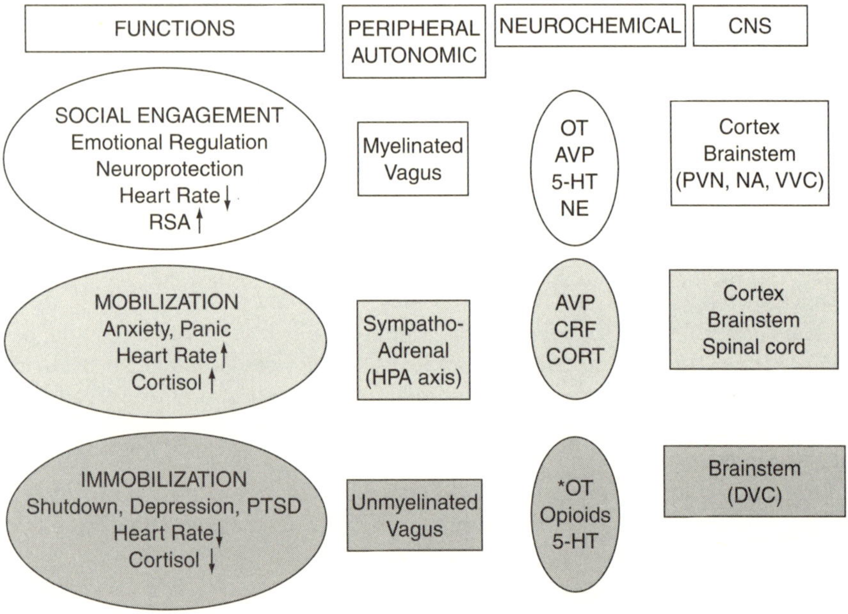

NEUROPEPTIDES AND THE MANAGEMENT OF STRESSFUL EXPERIENCES

The hypothalamus, especially the paraventricular nucleus, is an important site of convergence for neural communication relating stress, affect, and cardiovascular regulation to social behavior. Thus, it is not surprising that oxytocin influences the hypothalamic-pituitary-adrenal axis and autonomic function (Carter, 1998; Viviani & Stoop, 2008). Oxytocin-deficient mice show disruptions in sympathetic-vagal balance and are impaired in their ability to manage stress (Michelini et al., 2003). In addition, oxytocin generally suppresses the activity of the hypothalamic-pituitary-adrenal axis (Neumann, 2008).

Oxytocinergic projections from the paraventricular nucleus to key brainstem regions are important in cardiovascular control. Oxytocin binding sites are found in the dorsal vagal complex, and oxytocin increases the excitability of vagal neurons (Viviani & Stoop, 2008). In addition, oxytocin receptors in the brainstem have been shown to modulate baroreflex control of heart rate by facilitating the bradycardic response to pressor challenges. Thus, under optimal conditions, systems that rely on oxytocin may modulate and constrain overarousal, which would allow optimal management of challenges and also be permissive for social engagement and caregiving (Porges, 2007b).

Peripheral oxytocin administration is able to reduce heart rate and blood pressure (Michelini et al., 2003). The protective effects of oxytocin or its absence may be most readily observed in the face of adversity or a stressful environment. For example, in highly social prairie voles (Carter, DeVries, & Getz, 1995) exogenous oxytocin ameliorated isolation-induced changes in behavior and heart rate (Grippo et al., 2009). This suggests that while *endogenous* increases in oxytocin are not sufficient to ameliorate isolation-induced changes in autonomic function, additional supplementation with *exogenous* oxytocin may have measurable effects. It is important to note that additional supplementation of oxytocin did not lower heart rate in prairie voles that were not isolated. Thus, at least some of the beneficial actions of oxytocin may only become apparent under conditions of stress and adversity.

Centrally released oxytocin can counter the defensive behavioral strategies associated with stressful experiences. Oxytocin also may inhibit the central effects of vasopressin and other adaptive peptides, such as corticotropin-releasing factor, which plays a major role in the hypothalamic-pituitary-adrenal axis (Neumann, 2008). Generally, but not always, the effects of endogenous oxytocin are neuroprotective. We have found, in studies done with the prairie vole, that intense stressors (such as restraint and exposure to a social intruder) can release both oxytocin and vasopressin. Milder stressors, such as handling, increase blood levels of vasopressin, but not usually oxytocin. Experiences, such as exposure to an infant vole, also may transiently release oxytocin, especially in reproductively naive males. Infant exposure concurrently blocks stress-induced increases in adrenal steroids and has the capacity to facilitate subsequent pair-bond formation (Carter, Grippo, Pournajafi-Nazarloo, Ruscio, & Porges, 2008). These and other examples support the general hypothesis that oxytocin plays a critical role in the management of stressful experiences, while also facilitating social behavior.

Animal research suggests that oxytocin affects the immune system, acting during development to "educate" the thymus. Oxytocin can also be a powerful anti-inflammatory agent, with the capacity to reduce inflammatory processes both in vivo and in vitro. For example, oxytocin can restore tissue following exposure to burns, protect against sepsis, and reduce the response to pathogens. At comparatively high levels endogenous oxytocin may promote wound healing, even in humans (Gouin et al., 2010). These functions of oxytocin could provide another set of mechanisms through which caregiving, under conditions that allow the release of oxytocin, might protect and heal both those who give and receive nurture.

SEX DIFFERENCES IN CAREGIVING AND STRESS MANAGEMENT

Sex differences in either the capacity to nurture or be nurtured are frequently observed and often debated. Women are more likely to give direct nurture, sometimes through their role as a spouse or parent, or in a professional capacity, such as nursing. In males, nurturance may be expressed through less direct caregiving behaviors, such as defense or protection of the family or resources.

Culture and experience play an important role in the development, expression, and maintenance of sex differences. However, it is also likely that male and female differences in the capacity to nurture are based in part on biology, which may in turn influence sexually dimorphic behavioral traits and states (Carter, Boone, Pournajafi-Nazarloo, & Bales, 2009).

Gonadal steroid hormones and their receptors can affect sex differences, especially in early development. In addition, sex differences in endogenous neuropeptides, such as oxytocin and vasopressin, or their receptors could influence sexually dimorphic social behaviors. For example, differential exposure to estrogen across the life span might be expected to enhance the availability of oxytocin. However, remarkably little research has actually addressed these questions and, at least in blood, oxytocin often does not differ between males and females. In addition, both the effects of estrogen and oxytocin are context-dependent (Grippo et al., 2009). Thus, other systems, including the hormones of the hypothalamic-pituitary-adrenal and gonadal axes, and autonomic states associated with activation or mobilization may influence the consequences of oxytocin of both endogenous and exogenous origins.

Vasopressin levels in blood also do not reliably differ between the sexes. However, sex differences do exist in *central* vasopressin, especially in a neural axis that includes the amygdala, bed nucleus of the stria terminalis, and lateral septum (De Vries & Panzica, 2006). This system is important to determining reactions to negative and positive stimuli, and may help explain select behavioral features of various disorders including autism, which are highly sexually dimorphic and also characterized by differences in social behavior and emotional reactions to stressful experiences (Carter, 2007). The effects of vasopressin may be dynamically influenced by oxytocin and vice versa (Viviani & Stroop, 2008).

Social experiences are likely to be major factors regulating both the synthesis of oxytocin and vasopressin and their receptors. Thus, the social history of an individual may be translated into an ontogenetic recalibration of neuropeptidergic functions with potential consequences for both physiology and behavior. Developmental exposure to exogenous oxytocin or vasopressin also can have lifelong consequences (Carter et al., 2009). These developmental influences interact with sex, because males and females often have differential responses to exogenous peptides, and have the potential to modify behavioral patterns across the life span. It seems likely that epigenetic changes in peptides and their receptors are one of the mechanisms through which social experiences are converted into long-lasting individual differences. Social behaviors, including alloparenting, are especially sensitive to social and hormonal experiences in early life. Thus, the fundamental components of caregiving may have evolved with the capacity to be modified by an interaction between early experience and hormones, such as oxytocin and vasopressin, that are capable of regulating sociality and emotional reactivity in later life.

CLINICAL IMPLICATIONS OF POSITIVE SOCIAL EXPERIENCES

Contemporary medicine, especially over the past century, has focused on mechanisms of disease. Medical advances have been largely technical. The natural mechanisms underlying health and healing remain remarkably poorly understood. Sophisticated neural mechanisms, based on ancient bodily systems that are unique to mammals, allow the human body to constantly monitor, manage, and restore its own health. However, humans are highly social creatures. Our capacity to heal ourselves is physically linked to our relationships with other people. When social bonds are absent or disrupted by the loss of a loved one, our health also is at risk.

In the context of caregiving, the quality of the person-to-person interactions between a caretaker and those being cared for is critical for survival. Often this involves contingent and "appropriate" gesture, facial expression, prosody, proximity, and touch. In addition to specific clinical treatments, social support and social engagement behaviors by friends and relatives may also be capable of reversing illness and maintaining health (Harris, 2009). It is likely that oxytocin is important to the positive consequences of social support, possibly through effects on the autonomic nervous system and immune system. For example, it has been shown in humans that immune responses to an endobacterial challenge (lipopolysaccaride) can be significantly blocked by concurrent treatment with oxytocin (Clodi et al., 2008).

Person-to-person interactions that trigger neural circuits promoting calm physiological states can contribute to health, healing, and growth processes. Alternatively, threatening interactions trigger defensive strategies associated with physiological states supporting mobilization (e.g., flight-or-fight behaviors) or immobilization (e.g., behavioral shutdown, syncope, death feigning). As described, the nervous system is constantly assessing the environment as being safe, dangerous, or life-threatening (see chapter 1). Through this process of neuroception, neural circuits are triggered that will either support health and healing or support defensive strategies of fight-or-flight or shutdown. Neuroception involves brain structures, including the amygdala, that can be modulated by neuropeptides including oxytocin and vasopressin. Under optimal conditions, person-to-person interactions can be innate triggers within the human nervous system for adaptive biobehavioral systems that support health and healing. Both the giving and receiving of caregiving or love has the capacity to protect, heal, and restore. The mechanisms underlying these processes are only now becoming apparent.

SUMMARY

As we look at social behavior across the life span, we notice long periods in which self-regulated behaviors, including spontaneous social engagement behaviors, are readily expressed. In contrast, we note that this timeline is anchored on both sides by a dependence on caregiver. This dependence on caregiver is paralleled by limitations in the neural regulation of autonomic state via the myelinated vagus. Whether the periods of caregiver dependence are modulated by neuropeptides is a question for future research. Perhaps the regulation of oxytocin during these periods may enable the infant or the elderly to be less selective of caregiver and to be able to be soothed and comforted by a variety of caregivers. As the neural control circuits develop and there are more opportunities to engage socially, then perhaps oxytocin and vasopressin play a more important role in modulating state to promote the establishment of strong social bonds.

As a species, humans are highly social mammals, dependent on others for survival and reproduction. Under optimal conditions, this dependency is both symbiotic and reciprocal. The evolved neural, autonomic, and endocrine underpinnings of sociality are shared with other species, permitting a cross-species analysis of the processes responsible for sociality. Awareness of the neurobiology of social engagement and social bonding also offers insights into human concepts, such as social support and caregiving, which in turn can be associated with good health and recovery from illness. These systems are integrated throughout the body, including at the level of the brainstem, where hormones, such as oxytocin and vasopressin, influence behavior, the autonomic nervous system, and immune system. Projections to and from these ancient systems are experienced by more modern brain structures, including the cortex, as diffuse and sometimes powerful feelings or emotions. The same neuroendocrine and autonomic systems that permit high levels of social behavior and social bonds regulate the management of stressful experiences and the capacity of the mammalian body to heal itself. However, the activities of brainstem and autonomic systems are context-dependent. In a context of safety or comparatively mild or acute stressors, the release of oxytocin can promote health and restoration. In the context of chronic stress or fear, the actions of these same adaptive systems might have consequences that appear detrimental or destructive. Knowledge of the evolutionary origins and neurobiology of sociality provides a contextual perspective for understanding both the causes and consequences of mammalian caregiving behaviors.

Co-author for this chapter was C. S. Carter.

Epilogue

With increasing knowledge from the neurosciences and continuous feedback from clinicians, the polyvagal theory continues to evolve. In the future, the polyvagal theory (Porges, 2007a, 2007b) will expand into an integrated theory of neurovisceral regulation that will incorporate the role specific brain structures play in the neural regulation of the immune, endocrine, and autonomic systems. This integration will enable a more succinct understanding of the influence of both mental processes on bodily functions and health and bodily functions on mental processes. On a neuroanatomical level the integration of these systems is obvious and long overdue. Although these systems share common neuroanatomical structures, research communities have independently emerged with paradigms designed to maximize select response systems (i.e., immune, endocrine, or autonomic) as if they were independent. By proposing an expanded polyvagal theory, immune and endocrine responses will be interpreted within a phylogenetic hierarchy, similar to the three circuits outlined in the initial statement of the polyvagal theory (see chapter 2). Moreover, rather than interpreting immune and endocrine responses as being stressful or injurious, the responses will be interpreted within a phylogenetic framework and the adaptive function of these responses emphasized. The expanded theory will provide a better understanding of the bidirectional mind–body and brain–body responses that would explain important processes, such as the body's own ability to heal and the relation between physical disease and mental health.

Clinicians, especially traumatologists, have found the polyvagal theory useful in understanding mental health symptoms and in developing interventions and treatment models respecting the client's quest for safety. The theory also leads to a better understanding of the strategies an individual uses to regulate physiological state and feel safe. Within the realm of mental health, the polyvagal theory has already directed clinicians to look at the core features related to the social engagement system that are depressed in virtually all psychiatric illnesses. In the future, clinicians will be trained to be more sensitive to these features and will be skilled to attend to prosody of voice, facial expressivity, gaze, and auditory hypersensitivities as both diagnostic and prognostic indicators.

With an expanded polyvagal theory, easily monitored measures (e.g., heart rate, facial muscle activity, acoustic features of vocalization) may provide variables that reflect the same integrated systems involving endocrine and immune regulation as well as the function of brain structures and compromises due to white matter disease and other aspects of brain dysfunction. Moreover, in the future it may be possible to monitor these variables with noncontact technologies such as high-resolution infrared cameras. In our laboratory we are moving to the next generation of technologies and are able to measure with infrared cameras beat-to-beat heart rate and breathing. Our goal is to incorporate these noncontact measures into a polyvagal monitor that could be used to indicate when a client shifts from a physiological state that either supports defensive strategies (i.e., fear-induced mobilization or immobilization behaviors) or supports calm states associated with safety and social engagement. The technology would be helpful in increasing the awareness of therapists to the rapidly changing and often vulnerable physiological states of their clients.

The polyvagal theory, by centering its organizing constructs on current knowledge of neuroanatomy and evolution of the vertebrate autonomic nervous system, has led to a reinterpretation of autonomic reactions as a neural platform on which specific behaviors and psychological processes may occur. Within this model, many behaviors and psychological processes are neither learned nor correlates of neurophysiological processes. Rather, the model emphasizes that many behaviors and psychological processes are contingent emergent properties of well-defined neurophysiological states. Thus, neurophysiological state is a necessary but not sufficient condition for specific spontaneous behaviors and psychological processes to occur, including the symbiotic neurobehavioral regulation between two people that is often labeled as caring and loving (see chapters 18 and 19). Given this model, new therapies for mental and physical health would focus on manipulating neurophysiological state to provide an appropriate platform for mental and physical health and social behavior.

The polyvagal theory challenges the scientist to think in terms of both bidirectional and hierarchical neural feedback circuits involving the communication between peripheral organs and various structures in the brain. The theory challenges the clinician to interpret atypical behaviors and physiological reactions as adaptive. With these organizing principles, the polyvagal theory will be helpful in understanding the features that facilitate and optimize human social behavior and health.

Credits

PART I: THEORETICAL PRINCIPLES

Chapter 1. Porges, S. W. (2004). Neuroception: A subconscious system for detecting threat and safety. *Zero to Three Journal, 24*(5), 9–24. Copyright © 2004 ZERO TO THREE. Reprinted by permission of Zero to Three.

Chapter 2. Porges, S. W. (1995). Orienting in a defensive world: Mammalian modifications of our evolutionary heritage. A polyvagal theory. *Psychophysiology,* 32, 301–318. Reprinted by permission of John Wiley and Sons.

Chapter 3. Porges, S. W. (2009). The polyvagal theory: New insights into adaptive reactions of the autonomic nervous system. *Cleveland Clinic Journal of Medicine, 76*(Suppl 2), S86–S90. Reprinted with permission. Copyright © 2009 Cleveland Clinic Foundation. All rights reserved.

PART II: BIOBEHAVIORAL REGULATION DURING EARLY DEVELOPMENT

Chapter 4. Porges, S. W. (1992). Vagal tone: A physiological marker of stress vulnerability. *Pediatrics, 90,* 498–504. Reprinted by permission of the American Academy of Pediatrics.

The preparation of this chapter and much of the research described have been supported, in part, by grant HD 22628 from the National Institute of Child Health and Human Development. The construct of cardiac vagal tone described in this chapter has been measured with patented methods. These methods have been developed with support from National Institutes of Health grants HD-15968 and HD-05951 and National Institute of Mental Health grants MH-00054 and MH-18909 awarded to Dr. Porges. The methods have been incorporated in a vagal tone monitor that can evaluate vagal tone in real time. (Details regarding the vagal tone monitor can be obtained from Delta-Biometrics, Inc., 9411 Locust Hill Road, Bethesda, MD 20814-3960.)

Chapter 5. Porges, S. W. (1993). The infant's sixth sense: Awareness and regulation of bodily processes. *Zero to Three Journal, 14,* 12–16. Copyright © 1993 ZERO TO THREE. Reprinted by permission of Zero to Three.

Chapter 6. Porges, S. W. (1996). Physiological regulation in high-risk infants: A model for assessment and potential intervention. *Development and Psychopathology*, *8*, 43–58. Reprinted by permission of Cambridge University Press.

Chapter 7. Porges, S. W., Doussard-Roosevelt, J. A., Portales, A. L., & Greenspan, S. I.. (1996). Infant regulation of the vagal "brake" predicts child behavior problems: A psychobiological model of social behavior. *Developmental Psychobiology*, 29, 697–712. Reprinted by permission of John Wiley and Sons.

Chapter 8. Porges, S. W., & Furman, S. A. (2010). The early development of the autonomic nervous system provides a neural platform for social behavior: A polyvagal perspective. *Infant and Child Development*. [Article first published online April 22, 2010.] Reprinted by permission of John Wiley and Sons.

The research described in this chapter was supported, in part, by NIH Grant R01 HD053570 from the National Institute of Child Health and Human Development and NIH Grant T32 MH18882 from the American Psychological Association Diversity Program in Neuroscience.

PART III: SOCIAL COMMUNICATION AND RELATIONSHIPS

Chapter 9. Porges, S. W., Doussard-Roosevelt, J. A., & Maiti, A. K. (1994). Vagal tone and the physiological regulation of emotion. In N. A. Fox (Ed.), *The development of emotion regulation: Behavioral and biological considerations*, Monographs of the Society for Research in Child Development, 59(2–3, Serial No. 240), 167–186. Reprinted by permission of John Wiley and Sons.

Chapter 10. Porges, S. W. (1997). Emotion: An evolutionary by-product of the neural regulation of the autonomic nervous system. *Annals of the New York Academy of Sciences*, 807, 62–77. Reprinted by permission of John Wiley and Sons.

Special thanks are extended to Sue Carter for encouraging me to formalize the ideas presented in this chapter. In addition, I would like to thank Jane Doussard-Roosevelt for commenting on earlier drafts and the students in my graduate seminar who provided a forum for the discussion of the concepts described in the polyvagal theory of emotion.

Chapter 11. Porges, S. W. (1998). Love: An emergent property of the mammalian autonomic nervous system. *Psychoneuroendocrinology*, 23, 837–861. Reprinted by permission of Elsevier.

The preparation of this chapter was supported in part by grant HD 22628 from the National Institute of Child Health and Human Development and by grant MCJ 240622 from the Maternal and Child Health Bureau. Special thanks are extended to Sue Carter for encouraging me to formalize the ideas presented here. In addition, I would like to thank Jack Clark, Jane Doussard-Roosevelt, Jaak Panksepp, and Kerstin Uvnas-Moberg for commenting on earlier drafts.

Chapter 12. Porges, S. W. (2003). Social engagement and attachment: A phylogenetic perspective. *Annals of the New York Academy of Sciences*, *1008*, 31–47. Reprinted by permission of John Wiley and Sons.

This study was supported in part by a grant from the National Institutes of Health (MH60625). Several of the ideas presented in this article are the product of discussions with C. Sue Carter.

Chapter 13. Porges, S. W., & Lewis, G. F. (2010). The polyvagal hypothesis: Common mechanisms mediating autonomic regulation, vocalizations, and listening. In S. M. Brudzynsk (Ed.), *Handbook of mammalian vocalizations: An integrative neuroscience ap-*

proach (pp. 255–264). Amsterdam: Academic Press. Reprinted by permission of Academic Press.

PART IV: THERAPEUTIC AND CLINICAL PERSPECTIVES

Chapter 14. Porges, S. W. The vagus: A mediator of behavioral and physiologic features associated with autism. In M. L. Bauman & T. L. Kemper (Eds.), *The neurobiology of autism* (2nd ed.), (pp. 65–78). © 1994, 2005 The Johns Hopkins University Press. Reprinted with permission of The Johns Hopkins University Press.

The preparation of this chapter was supported in part by grant MH60625 from the National Institutes of Health. The author gratefully acknowledges the assistance of George Nijmeh in the preparation of this manuscript.

Chapter 15. Austin, M. A., Riniolo, T. C., & Porges, S. W. (2007). Borderline personality disorder and emotion regulation: Insights from the polyvagal theory. *Brain and Cognition, 65*, 69–76. Reprinted by permission of Elsevier.

A special thanks to Katherine C. Johnson for her input with this chapter, and to Janice Laben. The preparation of this manuscript was supported in part by a grant from the National Institutes of Health (MH60625).

Chapter 16. Dale, L. P., Carroll, L. E., Galen, G., Hayes, J. A., Webb, K. W., & Porges, S. W. (2009). Abuse history is related to autonomic regulation to mild exercise and psychological wellbeing. *Applied Psychophysiology and Biofeedback, 34*, 299–308. Reprinted by permission of Springer.

The authors wish to acknowledge the support of the administrators and participants at the local yoga studio. We are also grateful to Amanda Bliss, Allison M. Mattison, Lorinn M. Inserra, and Rebekah Jackson who helped with data collection; Jordana Klein and James DiLoretto who helped with data scoring; Rachel Schein who helped oversee the data scoring and entry; and Drs. Keri Heilman and John Denver for help with the physiological data.

Chapter 17. Porges, S. W (2010). Music therapy and trauma: Insights from the polyvagal theory. In K. Stewart (Ed.), *Music therapy & trauma: Bridging theory and clinical practice* (pp. 3–15). New York: Satchnote Press. Reprinted by permission of Satchnote Press.

PART V: SOCIAL BEHAVIOR AND HEALTH

Chapter 18. Porges, S. (2009). Reciprocal influences between body and brain in the perception and expression of affect: A polyvagal perspective. In D. Fosha, D. Siegel, & M. Solomon (Eds.), *The healing power of emotion: Affective neuroscience, development, and clinical practice* (pp. 27–54). New York: Norton. Reprinted by permission of W. W. Norton & Company.

Chapter 19. Porges, S. W., & Carter, C. S. (in press). Neurobiology and evolution: Mechanisms, mediators, and adaptive consequences of caregiving. In S. Brown, R. Brown, & L. Penner (Eds.), *Self interest and beyond: Toward a new understanding of human caregiving*. New York: Oxford University Press. Reprinted by permission of Oxford University Press.

References

Achenbach, T. M. (1988). *Child behavior checklist for ages 2–3*. Burlington, VT: University Associates in Psychiatry.

Administration on Children Youth and Families Children's Bureau. (2006). *Child maltreatment.* Retrieved from http://www.acf.hhs.gov/programs/cb/pubs/cm06/index.htm April 15, 2008.

Adolphs, R. (2002). Trust in the brain. *Nature Neuroscience*, 5, 192–193.

Agostoni, E., Chinnock, I. E., DeBurgh Daly, M., & Murray, I. G. (1957). Functional and histological studies of the vagus nerve and its branches to the heart, lungs and abdominal viscera in the cat. *Journal of Physiology*, *135*, 182–205.

Ainsworth, M., Blehar, M., Waters, E., et al. (1978). Patterns of attachment: A psychological study of the strange situation. Hillsdale, NJ: Erlbaum.

Allen, M. T., & Crowell, M. D. (1989). Patterns of autonomic response during laboratory stressors. *Psychophysiology, 26*, 603–614.

Althaus, M., Mulder, L. J. M., Mulder, G., et al. (1999). Cardiac adaptivity to attention-demanding tasks in children with a pervasive developmental disorder not otherwise specified (PDD-NOS). *Biological Psychiatry*, *46*,799–809.

American National Standards Institute. (1997). *Methods for calculation of the speech intelligibility index* (ANSI Publication no. S3.5). New York: Acoustical Society of America.

American Psychiatric Association. (1994). *Diagnostic and statistical manual of mental disorders* (4th ed.). Washington, DC: Author.

American Psychiatric Association. (2000). *Diagnostic and statistical manual of mental disorders* (4th ed., text revision). Washington, DC: Author.

Anderson, A. K., & Phelps, E. A. (2000). Expression without recognition: Contributions of the human amygdala to emotional communication. *Psychological Science, 11*, 106–111.

Andrews, P. L. R., & Lawes, I. N. C. (1992). A protective role for vagal afferents: An hypothesis. In S. Ritter, R. C. Ritter, & C. D. Barnes, C. D. (Eds.), *Neuroanatomy and physiology of abdominal vagal afferents* (pp. 280–302). Boca Raton, FL: CRC Press.

Apgar, V. (1953). A proposal for a new method of evaluation of the newborn infant. *Current Researches in Anesthesia and Analgesia*, 32, 260–268.

Arata, C. M., Langhinrichsen-Rohling, J., Bowers, D., & O'Farrill Swails, L. (2005). Single versus multitype maltreatment: An examination of the long term effects of child abuse. *Journal of Aggression, Maltreatment & Trauma, 11*, 29–52.

Ardic, F. N., Topaloglu, I., Oncel, S., Ardic, F., & Uguz, M. Z. (1997). Does the stapes reflex remain the same after Bell's palsy? *American Journal of Otology, 18*, 761–765.

Arletti, R., Benelli, A., & Bertolini, A. (1992). Oxytocin involvement in male and female sexual behavior. In C. A. Pedersen, J. D. Caldwell, G. F. Jirikowski, & T. R. Insel (Eds.), *Oxytocin in maternal, sexual, and social behaviors.* New York: Annals of the New York Academy of Sciences.

Ax, A. F. (1953). The physiological differentiation between fear and anger in humans. *Psychosomatic Medicine, 15*, 433–442.

Ayres, A. J. (1972). *Sensory integration and learning disorders.* Los Angeles: Western Psychological Services.

Bagge, C., Nickell, A., Stepp, S., Durrett, C., Jackson, K., & Trull, T. J. (2004). Borderline personality disorder features predict negative outcomes 2 years later. *Journal of Abnormal Psychology, 113*, 279–288.

Bárány, E., 1938. A contribution to the physiology of bone conduction. *Acta Otolaryngology Supplement*, 26, 1–233.

Barbas-Henry, H. A., & Lohman, A. H. M. (1984). The motor nuclei and primary projections of the IXth, Xth, XIth, and XIIth cranial nerves in the monitor lizard, *Varanus exanthematicus. Journal of Comparative Neurology, 226*, 565–579.

Bates, J. E. (1980). The concept of difficult temperament. *Merrill-Palmer Quarterly*, 26, 299–319.

Bates, J. E. (1984). *The infant characteristics questionnaire.* Unpublished manuscript, Indiana University.

Bayley, N. (1969). *Bayley scales of infant development: Birth to two years.* New York: Psychological Corporation.

Bazhenova, O. V., Plonskaia, O., & Porges, S. W. (2001). Vagal reactivity and affective adjustments in infants during interaction challenges. *Child Development*, 72, 1314–1326.

Bear, D. M. (1983). Hemispheric specialization and the neurology of emotion. *Archives of Neurology, 40*, 195–202.

Becker, L. E., Zhang, W., & Pereyra, P. M. (1993). Delayed maturation of the vagus nerve in sudden infant death syndrome. *Acta Neuropathologica*, 86, 611–622.

Behrman, R. E., & Vaughan, V. C. (1987). *Nelson textbook of pediatrics* (13th ed.). Philadelphia: Saunders.

Bennett, J. A., Ford, T. W, Kidd, C., & McWilliam, P. N. (1984). Characteristics of cat dorsal motor vagal motoneurones with axons in the cardiac and pulmonary branches. *Journal of Physiology, 351*, 27.

Benjamin, L. S. (1996). *Interpersonal diagnosis and treatment of personality disorders* (2nd ed.). New York: Guilford Press.

Berlyne, D. E. (1960). *Conflict, arousal, and curiosity.* New York: McGraw-Hill.

Bernard, C. (1973). Lessons on the phenomena of life common to animals and vegetables. Second lecture, The three forms of life. In L. Langley, Ed., *Homeostasis; Origins of the concept* (pp. 129–151). Stroudsburg, PA: Dowden Hutchinson & Ross.

Berntson, G. G., Cacioppo, I. T., & Quigley, K. S. (1991). Autonomic determinism: The modes of autonomic control, the doctrine of autonomic space, and the laws of autonomic constraint. *Psychological Review*, 98, 459–487.

Berntson, G. G., Cacioppo, J. T., & Quigley, K. S. (1993a). Cardiac psychophysiology and autonomic space in humans: Empirical perspectives and conceptual implications. *Psychological Bulletin, 114*, 296–322.

Berntson, G. G., Cacioppo, J. T., & Quigley, K. S. (1993b). Respiratory sinus arrhythmia: Autonomic origins, physiological mechanisms, and psychophysiological implications. *Psychophysiology, 30*, 183–196.

Berntson, G. G., Cacioppo, J. T., & Quigley, K. S. (1994). Autonomic cardiac control. I. Estimation and validation from pharmacological blockades. *Psychophysiology, 31*, 572–585.

Bieger, D., & Hopkins, D. A. (1987). Viscerotropic representation of the upper alimentary tract in the medulla oblongata in the rat: The nucleus ambiguus. *Journal of Comparative Neurology, 262*, 546–562.

Bigger, J. T., Jr., Fleiss, J. L., & Rolnitsky, L. M. (1993). The ability of several short-term measures of RR variability to predict mortality after myocardial infarction. *Circulation, 88*, 927–932.

Billman, G. E., & DuJardin, J.-P. (1990). Dynamic changes in cardiac vagal tone as measured by time-series analysis. *American Journal of Physiology, 258*, H896–H902.

Bjork, E., Nevalainen, T., Hakumaki, M., & Voipio, H.-M. (1999). R-weighting provides better estimation for rat hearing sensitivity. *Laboratory Animals, 34*, 136–144.

Blair, R. J. R., & Cipolott, L. (2000). Impaired social response reversal. A case of "acquired sociopathy." *Brain, 123*, 1122–1141.

Blanchard, E. B. (1990). Elevated basal levels of cardiovascular responses in Vietnam veterans with PTSD: A health problem in the making? *Journal of Anxiety Disorders, 4*, 233–237.

Boon, P., Vonck, K., De Reuck, J., et al. (2001). Vagus nerve stimulation for refractory epilepsy. *Seizure, 10*, 448–455.

Borg, E., & Counter, S. A. (1989). The middle-ear muscles. *Scientific American, 261*, 74–80.

Bowlby, J. (1973). *Attachment and loss: Vol 2. Separation: Anxiety and anger*. New York: Basic Books.

Bowlby, J. (1982). *Attachment and loss: Vol. 1. Attachment*. New York: Basic Books.

Bowlby, J . (1988.). *A secure base: Parent-child attachment and healthy human development*. New York: Basic Books.

Bray, G. A. (1985). Autonomic and endocrine factors in the regulation of food intake. *Brain Research Bulletin, 9*, 279–286.

Brazelton, T. B. (1984). *Neonatal behavioral assessment scale* (2nd ed.). Philadelphia: Lippincott.

Bremner, J. D., & Vermetten, E. (2001). Stress and development: Behavioral and biological consequences. *Development and Psychopathology, 13*, 473–489.

Brems, C., Johnson, M. E., Neal, D., & Freemon, M. (2004). Childhood abuse history and substance use among men and women receiving detoxification services. *American Journal of Drug and Alcohol Abuse, 30*, 799–821.

Brown, J. W. (1974). Prenatal development of the human chief sensory trigeminal nucleus. *Journal of Comparative Neurology, 156*, 307–335.

Brown, J. W. (1990). Prenatal development of the human nucleus ambiguus during the embryonic and early fetal periods. *American Journal ofAnatomy, 189*, 267–283.

Brudzynski, S. M. (2007). Ultrasonic calls of rats as indicator variables of negative and positive states: acetylcholinedopamine interaction and acoustic coding. *Behavior and Brain Research, 182*, 261–273.

Brunton, P. J., & Russell, J. A. (2008). The expectant brain: Adapting for motherhood. *Nature Review of Neuroscience*, 9, 11–25.

Buckley, T. C., & Kaloupek, D. G. (2001). A meta analytic examination of basal cardiovascular activity in posttraumatic stress disorder. *Psychosomatic Medicine*, 63, 585–594.

Bueno, L., Gue, M., Fargeas, M. J., Alvinerie, M., Junien, J. L., & Fioramonti, J. (1989). Vagally mediated inhibition of acoustic stress-induced cortisol release by orally administered kappa-opioid substances in dogs. *Endocrinology, 124*, 1788–1793.

Bulloch, K., & Pomerantz, W. (1984). Autonomic nervous system innervation of thymic-related lymphoid tissue in wildtype and nude mice. *Journal of Comparative Neurology*, 228, 58-68.

Buss, D. M., Larsen, R. J., Westen, D., & Semmelroth, J. (1992). Sex differences in jealousy: Evolution, physiology, and psychology. *Psychological Science*, 3, 251–255.

Buwalda, B., Koolhaas, J. M., & Bohus, B. (1992). Behavioral and cardiac responses to mild stress in young and aged rats: Effects of amphetamine and vasopressin. *Physiology and Behavior*, 51, 211–216.

Byrne, E. A., & Porges, S. W. (1993). Data-dependent filter characteristics of peak-valley respiratory sinus arrhythmia estimation: A cautionary note. *Psychophysiology*, 30, 397–404.

Cacioppo, J. T., Berntson, G. G., Binkley, P. E, Quigley, K. S., Uchino, B. N., & Fieldstone, A. (1994). Autonomic cardiac control II. Noninvasive indices and basal response as revealed by autonomic blockades. *Psychophysiology*, 31, 586–598.

Cacioppo, J. T., Malaarkey, W. B., Kiecolt-Glaser, J. K., et al. (1995). Heterogeneity in neuroendocrine and immune responses to brief psychological stressors as a function of autonomic cardiac activation. *Psychosomatic Medicine*, 57, 154–164.

Calkins, S. D., Graziano, P. A., & Keane, S. P. (2007). Cardiac vagal regulation differentiates among children at risk for behavior problems. *Biological Psychology*, 74, 144–153.

Cannon, W. B. (1927). The James-Lange theory of emotions: A critical examination and an alternative theory. *American Journal of Psychology*, 39, 106–124.

Cannon, W. B. (1928). The mechanism of emotional disturbance of bodily functions. *New England Journal of Medicine*, 198, 877–884.

Cannon, W. B. (1929a). *Bodily changes in pain, hunger, fear and rage. An account of recent researches into the function of emotional excitement.* New York: Appleton.

Cannon, W. B. (1929b). Organization for physiological homeostasis. *Physiology Reviews*, 9, 399–431.

Cannon, W. B. (1957). "Voodoo" death. *Psychosomatic Medicine*, 19, 182–190. (Reprinted from *American Anthropology*, 44 [1942], 169–181.)

Carpenter, D. O. (1990). Neural mechanisms of emesis. *Canadian Journal of Physiology and Pharmacology*, 68, 230–236.

Carter, C. S. (1998). Neuroendocrine perspectives on social attachment and love. *Psychoneuroendocrinology*, 23, 779–818.

Carter, C. S. (2007). Sex differences in oxytocin and vasopressin: Implications for autism spectrum disorders? *Behavioural Brain Research*, 176, 170–186.

Carter, C. S., & Altemus, M. (1997). Integrative functions of lactational hormones in social behavior and stress management. *Annals of the New York Academy of Sciences*, 807, 164–174.

Carter, C. S., Boone, E. M., Pournajafi-Nazarloo, H., & Bales, K. L. (2009). The consequences of early experiences and exposure to oxytocin and vasopressin are sexually-dimorphic. *Developmental Neuroscience, 31*, 332–341.

Carter, C. S., Devries, A. C., & Getz, L. L. (1995). Physiological substrates of mammalian monogamy: The prairie vole model. *Neuroscience Biobehavioral Reviews, 19*, 303–314.

Carter, C. S., DeVries, A. C., Taymans, S. E., Roberts, R. L., Williams, J. R., & Getz, L. L. (1997). Peptides, steroids, and pair bonding. *Annals of the New York Academy of Sciences, 807*, 260–272.

Carter, C. S., Grippo, A. J., Pournajafi-Nazarloo, H., Ruscio, M. G., & Porges, S. W. (2008). Oxytocin, vasopressin and social behavior. *Progress in Brain Research, 170*, 331–336.

Carter, C. S., & Keverne, E. B. (2002). The neurobiology of social affiliation and pair bonding. In D. W. Pfaff et al. (Eds.), *Hormones, brain, and behavior* (pp. 299–337). San Diego: Academic Press.

Carver, C. S., Scheier, M. F., & Weintraub, J. K. (1989). Assessing coping strategies: A theoretically based approach. *Journal of Personality and Social Psychology, 56*, 267–283.

Cassidy, J., & Shaver, P. R. (1999). *Handbook of attachment: Theory, research, and clinical application*. New York: Guilford Press.

Chen, T., & Rao, R. R. (1998). Audio-visual integration in multi-modal communication. *Proceedings of the IEEE, 86* (5), 837–852.

Cheng, G., Zhou, X., Qu, J., Ashwell, K. W. S., & Paxinos, G. (2004). Central vagal sensory and motor connection: Human embryonic and fetal development. *Autonomic Neuroscience: Basic and Clinical, 114*, 83–96.

Chisholm, K. (1998). A three year follow-up of attachment and indiscriminate friendliness in children adopted from Romanian orphanages. *Child Development, 69*, 1092–1106.

Chugani, H. T., Behen, M. E., Muzik, O., Juhász, C., Nagy, F., & Chugani, D. C. (2001). Brain functional activity following early deprivation: A study of postinstitutionalized Romanian orphans. *NeuroImage, 14*, 1290–1301.

Cicchetti, D. (1993). Developmental psychopathology: Reactions, reflections, projections. *Developmental Review, 13*, 471–502.

Cicchetti, D., & White, J. (1990). Emotion and developmental psychopathology. In N. Stein, B. Leventhal, & T. Trabasso (Eds.), *Psychological and biological approaches to emotion* (pp. 359–382). Hillsdale, NJ: Erlbaum.

Clodi, M., Vila, G., Geyeregger, R., Riedl, M., Stulnig, T. M., Struck, J., et al. (2008). Oxytocin alleviates the neuroendocrine and cytokine response to bacterial endotoxin in healthy men. *American Journal of Physiology: Endocrinology and Metabolism, 295*, E686–391.

Cloitre, M., Stovall-McClough, C., Miranda, R., & Chemtob, C. (2004). Therapeutic alliance, negative mood regulation, and treatment outcome in child abuse-related post-traumatic stress disorder. *Journal of Consulting and Clinical Psychology, 72*, 411–416.

Cloitre, M., Stovall-McClough, C., Zorbas, P., & Charuvastra, A. (2008). Attachment organization, emotional regulation, and expectations of support in a clinical sample of women with childhood abuse histories. *Journal of Traumatic Stress, 21*, 282–289.

Coccaro, E. F. (1989). Central serotonin in impulsive aggression. *British Journal of Psychiatry, 155*, 52–62.

Coccaro, E. F., & Kavoussi, R. J. (1991). Biological and pharmacological aspects of borderline personality disorder. *Hospital and Community Psychiatry*, 42, 1029.

Cooper, C., Katona, C., & Livingston, G. (2008). Validity and reliability of the brief COPE in carers of people with dementia: The LASER AD study. *Journal of Nervous and Mental Health*, *1*, 838–843.

Corballis, M. (2003). From mouth to hand: Gesture, speech, and the evolution of right-handedness. *Behavior and Brain Science*, *26*, 199–260.

Corona, R., Dissanayake, C., Arbelle, S., et al. (1998). Is affect aversive to young children with autism? Behavioral and cardiac responses to experimenter distress. *Child Development*, *69*, 1494–1502.

Cottingham, J. T., Porges S. W., & Lyon, T. (1988). Soft tissue mobilization (Rolfing pelvic lift) and associated changes in parasympathetic tone in two age groups. *Physical Therapy*, *68*, 352–356.

Cournand, A. (1979). Claude Bernard's contributions to cardiac physiology. In E. D. Robin (Ed.), *Claude Bernard and the internal environment* (pp. 97–121). New York: Marcel Dekker.

Craig, A. D. (2005). Forebrain emotional asymmetry: A neuroanatomical basis? *Trends in Cognitive Sciences*, *9*, 566–571.

Crews, D. (1997) Species diversity and the evolution of behavioral controlling mechanisms. *Annals of the New York Academy of Sciences*, *807*, 1–21.

Critchley, H. D. (2005). Neural mechanisms of autonomic, affective, and cognitive integration. *Journal of Comparative Neurology*, *493*, 154–166.

Critchley, H. D., Wiens, S., Rothstein, P., Ohman, A., & Dolan, R. J. (2004). Neural systems supporting interoceptive awareness. *Nature Neuroscience*, *7*, 189–195.

Dale, L. P., O'Hara, E. A., Schein, R,, Inserra, L., Keen, J., Porges, S. W. (in press). Infant measures of behavioral and physiological state regulation predict 54-month behavior problems. *Journal of Infant Mental Health.*

Daley, S. E., Burge, D., & Hammen, C. (2000). Borderline personality disorder symptoms as predictors of four-year romantic relationship dysfunction in young women: Addressing issues of specificity. *Journal of Abnormal Psychology*, *109*, 451–460.

Daly, M. deBurgh. (1991). Some reflex cardioinhibitory responses in the cat and their modulation by central inspiratory neuronal activity. *Journal of Physiology*, *422*, 463–480.

Damasio, A. (1999). *The feeling of what happens.* New York: Harcourt, Brace.

Dammeijer, P., Dijk, P., Chenault, M., Manni, J., & Mameren, H. (2007). Stapedius muscle fibre characterization in the noise exposed and auditory deprived rat. *Hearing Research*, *233*, 54–66.

Daniels, D., Miselis, R. R., & Flanagan-Cato, L. M. (1999). Central neuronal circuit innervating the lordosis-producing muscles defined by transneuronal transport of pseudorabies virus. *Journal of Neuroscience*, *19*, 2823–2833.

Darrow, C. W. (1929). Differences in the physiological reactions to sensory and ideational stimuli. *Psychological Bulletin*, *26*, 185–201.

Darrow, C. W. (1943) Physiological and clinical tests of autonomic function and autonomic balance. *Physiological Reviews*, *23*, 1–36.

Darrow, C. W., Jost, H., Solomon, A. P., & Mergener, J. C. (1942). Autonomic indicators of excitatory and homeostatic effects on the electroencephalogram. *Journal of Psychology*, *14*, 115–130.

Darwin, C. (1872). *The expression of the emotions in man and animals.* New York: D. Appleton. (Reprint: Chicago: University of Chicago Press, 1965.)

Davis, M. (1992) The role of the amygdala in conditioned fear. In J. P. Aggleton (Ed.), *The amygdala: Neurobiological aspects of emotion, memory, and mental dysfunction* (pp. 255–306). New York: Wiley.

Dawson, G. (1994). Frontal electroencephalographic correlates of individual differences in emotion expression in infants: A brain systems perspective on emotion. In N. A. Fox (Ed.), *Emotion regulation: Behavioral and biological considerations.* Monograph of the Society for Research in Child Development, 59(2–3): 135–151.

DeGangi, G. A., DiPietro, J. A., Greenspan, S. I., & Porges, S. W. (1991). Psychophysiological characteristics of the regulatory disordered infant. *Infant Behavior and Development, 14,* 37–50.

deJong, F., Kingma, H., Wirtz, P., Berge, H., & Marres, E. (1988). Indications of a differentiated regulation of sound transmission by the middle ear muscles of the rat. *American Journal of Otology,* 9, 70–75.

Dellinger, J. A., Taylor, H. L., & Porges, S. W. (1987). Atropine sulfate effects on aviator performance and on respiratory-heart period interactions. *Aviation Space Environment Medicine,* 58, 333–338.

De Meersman, R. E. (1993). Aging as a modulator of respiratory sinus arrhythmia. *Journal of Gerontology: Biological Sciences,* 48, B74–B78.

Denver, J. W., Reed, S. F., & Porges. S. W. (2007). Methodological issues in the quantification of respiratory sinus arrhythmia. *Biological Psychology,* 74(2) 286–294.

Desai, S., Arias, I., Thompson, M. P., & Basile, K. C. (2002). Childhood victimization and subsequent adult revictimization assessed in a nationally representative sample of women and men. *Violence and Victims, 1,* 639–653.

De Vries, G. J., & Panzica, G. C. (2006). Sexual differentiation of central vasopressin and vasotocin systems in vertebrates: Different mechanisms, similar endpoints. *Neuroscience, 138,* 947–955.

De Wied, D. (1971) Long-term effect of vasopressin on the maintenance of a conditioned avoidance response in rats. *Nature,* 232, 58–60.

Dewsbury, D. A. (1987) The comparative psychology of monogamy. In D. W. Leger & N. E. Lincoln (Eds.), *Nebraska symposium on motivation* (pp. 1–50). Lincoln: University of Nebraska Press.

Dexter, E., Levy, M. N., & Rudy, Y. (1989). Mathematical model of the changes in heart rate elicited by vagal stimulation. *Circulation Research,* 65, 1330–1339.

DiPietro, J. A., Larson, S. K., & Porges, S. W. (1987). Behavioral and heart-rate pattern differences between breast-fed and bottle-fed neonates. *Developmental Psychology,* 23, 467–474.

DiPietro, J. A., & Porges, S. W. (1991). Vagal responsiveness to gavage feeding as an index of preterm status. Pediatric Research, 29, 231–236.

Djupesland, G. (1976). Nonacoustic reflex measurement: Procedures, interpretations and variables. In A. Feldman & L. Wilber (Eds.), *Acoustic impedance and admittance: The measurement of middle ear function* (pp. 217–235). Baltimore, MD: Williams and Wilkins.

Donald, D. E., Samueloff, S. L., & Ferguson, D. (1967). Mechanisms of tachycardia caused by atropine in conscious dogs. *American Journal of Physiology,* 212, 901–910.

Donaldson, Z. R., & Young, L. J. (2008). Oxytocin, vasopressin and neurogenetics of sociality. *Science, 322*, 900–904.

Donchin, Y., Constantini, S., Szold, A., Byrne, E. A., & Porges, S. W. (1992). Cardiac vagal tone predicts outcome in neurosurgical patients. *Critical Care Medicine, 20*, 941–949.

Donchin, Y., Feld, J. M., & Porges, S. W. (1985). Respiratory sinus arrhythmia during recovery from isoflurane-nitrous oxide anesthesia. *Anesthesia and Analgesia, 64*, 811–815.

Doussard-Roosevelt, J. A., McClenny, B. D., & Porges, S. W. (2001). Neonatal cardiac vagal tone and school-age developmental outcome in very low birth weight infants. *Developmental Psychobiology, 38*, 56–66.

Doussard-Roosevelt, J. A., Porges, S. W., Scanlon, J. W., Alemi, B., & Scanlon, K. B. (1997). Vagal regulation of heart rate in the prediction of developmental outcome for very low birth weight preterm infants. *Child Development, 68*, 173–186.

Doussard-Roosevelt, J. A., Walker, P. S., Portales, A. L., Greenspan, S. I., & Porges, S. W. (1990). Vagal tone and the fussy infant: Atypical vagal reactivity in the difficult infant [Abstract]. *Infant Behavior and Development, 13*, 352.

Doyle, C. (2001). Surviving and coping with emotional abuse in childhood. *Clinical Child Psychology and Psychiatry, 6*, 387–402.

Dozier, M., Stovall, K. C., & Albus, K. E. (1999). Attachment and psychopathology in adulthood. In J. Cassidy & P. R. Shaver (Eds.), *Handbook of attachment: Theory, research, and clinical applications* (pp. 497–519). New York: Guilford Press.

Drossman, D. A., Leserman, J., Nachman, G., Li, Z., Gluck, H., Toomey, T. C., & Mitchell, C. M. (1990). Sexual and physical abuse in women with functional or organic gastrointestinal disorders. *Annals of Internal Medicine, 113*, 828–833.

Dufey, M., Hrtado, E., Fernandez, A. M., Manes, F., & Ibanez, A. (in press). *Social Neuroscience, 23*, 1–15. [Epub ahead of print]

Duffy, E. (1957). The psychological significance of the concept of "arousal" or "activation." *Psychological Review, 64*, 265–275.

Eberl, E. M. (2010). Control of gestures and vocalizations in primates. In S. M. Brudzynski (Ed.), *Handbook of mammalian vocalization: An integrative neuroscience approach* (vol. 19). Amsterdam: Elsevier.

Ekman, P. (1978). *Facial action coding system: A technique for the measurement of facial movement.* Palo Alto, CA: Consulting Psychologists Press.

Ekman, P., Levenson, R. W., & Friesen, W. V. (1983). Autonomic nervous system activity distinguishes among emotions. *Science, 221*, 1208–1210.

Else, P. L., & Hulbert, A. J. (1981). Comparison of the "mammal machine" and the "reptile machine": Energy production. *American Journal of Physiology, 240*, R3–R9.

Elsesser, K., Sartoy, G., & Tackenberg, A. (2004). Attention, heart rate, and startle response during exposure to trauma relevant pictures: A comparison of recent trauma victims and patients with posttraumatic stress disorder. *Journal of Abnormal Psychology, 1*, 289–301.

Eluvathingal, T. J., Chugani, H. T., Behen, M. E., Juhász, C., Muzik, O., Magbool, M., et al. (2006). Abnormal brain connectivity in children after early severe socioemotional deprivation: A diffusion tensor imaging study. *Pediatrics, 117*, 2093–2100.

Engelmann, M., Wotjak, C. T., Neumann, I., Ludwig, M., & Landgraf, R. (1996). Behavioral consequences of intracerebral vasopressin and oxytocin: Focus on learning and memory. *Neuroscience Biobehavioral Review, 20*, 341–358.

Eppinger, H., & Hess, L. (1917). *Vagotonia: A clinical study in vegetative neurology.* Nervous and Mental Disease Monograph Series No. 20. New York: The Nervous and Mental Disease Publishing Company.

Faris, P. L., Kim, S. W., Meller, W. H., et al. (2000). Effect of decreasing afferent vagal activity with ondansetron on symptoms of bulimia nervosa: A randomised, double-blind trial. *Lancet, 355*, 792–797.

Fay, R. R. (1988). Comparative psychoacoustics. *Hearing Research, 34*, 295–306.

Feldman, R., & Eidelman, A. I. (2003). Skin-to-skin contact (kangaroo care) accelerates autonomic and neurobehavioural maturation in preterm infants. *Developmental Medicine & Child Neurology, 45*, 274–281.

Ferguson, A. V., & Lowes, V. L. (1994). Functional neural connections of the area postrema. In I. R. A. Barraco (Ed.), *Nucleus of the solitary tract* (pp. 147–157). Boca Raton, FL: CRC Press.

Field, T., Woodson, R., Greenberg, R., & Cohen, D. (1982). Discrimination and imitation of facial expressions by neonates. *Science, 218*, 179–181.

Finger, T. E., & Dunwiddie, T. V. (1992). Evoked responses from an in vitro slice preparation of a primary gustatory nucleus: The vagal lobe of goldfish. *Brain Research, 580*, 27–34.

Fitts, W. H., & Warren, W. L. (1996). *Tennessee self concept scale* (2nd ed.). Los Angeles: Western Psychological Services.

Fletcher, H., & Munson, W. A. (1933). Loudness: Its definition, measurement, and calculation. *Journal of the Acoustical Society of America, 5*, 82–108.

Ford, T. W., Bennett, J. A., Kidd, C., & McWilliam, P. N. (1990). Neurons in the dorsal motor vagal nucleus of the cat with non-myelinated axons projecting to the heart and lungs. *Experimental Physiology, 75*, 459–473.

Forsman, K. A., & Malmquist, M. G. (1988). Evidence for echolocation in the common shrew, *Sorex araneus*. *Journal of Zoology, 216*, 655–662.

Fouad, E. M., Tarazi, R. C., Ferrario, C. M., Fighaly, S., & Alicandro, C. (1984). Assessment of parasympathetic control of heart rate by a noninvasive method. *American Journal of Physiology, 246*, H838–H842.

Fox, N. A. (1989). Psychophysiological correlates of emotional reactivity during the first year of life. *Developmental Psychology, 25*, 364–372.

Fox, N. A. (1994) Dynamic cerebral processes underlying emotion regulation. In N. A. Fox (Ed.), *Emotion regulation: Behavioral and biological considerations.* Monograph of the Society for Research in Child Development, 59, 152–166.

Fox, N. A., & Davidson, R. J. (1984). Hemispheric substrates of affect: A developmental model. In N. A. Fox & R. J. Davidson (Eds.), *The psychobiology of affective development*. Hillsdale, NJ: Erlbaum.

Fox, N. A., & Gelles, M. (1984). Face-to-face interaction in term and preterm infants. *Infant Mental Health Journal, 5*, 192–205.

Fox, N. A., & Porges, S. W. (1985). The relationship between developmental outcome and neonatal heart period patterns. *Child Development, 56*, 28–37.

Fracasso, M. P., Porges, S. W., Lamb, M. E., & Rosenberg, A. A. (1994). Cardiac activity in infancy: Reliability and stability of individual differences. *Infant Behavior and Development, 17*, 277–284.

Frysinger, R. C., & Harper, R. M. (1986). Cardiac and respiratory relationships with neural discharge in the anterior cingulate cortex during sleep-waking states. *Experimental Neurology, 94*, 247–263.

Frysinger, R. C., & Harper, R. M. (1989). Cardiac and respiratory correlations with unit discharge in human amygdala and hippocampus. *Electroencephalography and Clinical Neurophysiology*, 72, 463–470.

Frysinger, R. C., Zhang, J. X., & Harper, R. M. (1988). Cardiovascular and respiratory relationships with neuronal discharge in the central nucleus of the amygdala during sleep-waking states. *Sleep*, *11*, 317–332.

Futa, K. T., Nash, C. L., Hansen, D. J., & Garbin, C. P. (2003). Adult survivors of childhood abuse: An analysis of coping mechanisms used for stressful childhood memories and current stressors. *Journal of Family Violence*, *18*, 227–239.

Fuxe, K., Agnati, L. F., Covenas, R., Narvaez, J. A., Bunnemann, B., & Bjelke, B. (1994). Volume transmission in transmitter peptide costoring neurons in the medulla oblongata. In I. R. A. Barraco (Ed.), *Nucleus of the solitary tract* (pp. 75–89). Boca Raton, FL: CRC Press.

Galen, G., Dale, L. P., Ruzansky, B., Inserra, L., Jackson, R., Wawrzyniak, K., et al. (2007). *The yoga experience scale: A measure of experience with and benefits of yoga*. Paper presented at the 21st Annual Connecticut Psychological Association Convention, Windsor, CT.

Garcia, J., Lasiter, P. S., Bermudez-Rattoni, F., & Deems, D. A. (1985) A general theory of aversion learning. *Annals of the New York Academy of Sciences*, *443*, 8–21.

Gellhorn, E. (1964). Motion and emotion: The role of proprioception in the physiology and pathology of the emotions. *Psychological Review*, *71*, 457–472.

Gellhorn, E. (1967). *Principles of autonomic-somatic integrations; Physiological basis and psychological and clinical implications*. Minneapolis: University of Minnesota Press.

Gentile, C. G., Jarrell, T. W., Teich, A., McCabe, P. M., & Schneiderman, N. (1986). The role of amygdaloid central nucleus in the retention of differential Pavlovian conditioning of bradycardia in rabbits. *Behavior and Brain Research*, 20, 263–273.

George, D. T., Nutt, D. J., Walker, W. V., Porges, S. W., Adinoff, B., & Linnoila, M. (1989). Lactate and hyperventilation substantially attenuate vagal tone in normal volunteers: A possible mechanism of panic provocation? *Archives of General Psychiatry*, *46*, 153–156.

George, M. S., Sackeim, H. A., Rush, A. J., et al. (2000). Vagus nerve stimulation: A new tool for brain research therapy. *Biological Psychiatry*, *47*, 287–295.

Gibbins, I. (1994). Comparative anatomy and evolution of the autonomic nervous system. In S. Nilsson & S. Holmgren (Eds.), *Comparative physiology and evolution of the autonomic nervous system* (pp. 1–68). Singapore: Harwood Academic Publishers.

Gimpl, G., & Fahrenholz, F. (2001). The oxytocin receptor system: Structure, function and regulation. *Physiological Reviews*, *81*, 629–683.

Goldberger, J. J., Ahmed, M. W., Parker, M. A., & Kadish, A. H. (1994). Dissociation of heart rate variability from parasympathetic tone. *American Journal of Physiology*, *266*, H2152–H2157.

Gonzalez Gonzalez, J., & de Vera Porcell, L. (1988). Spectral analysis of heart rate variability of lizard, *Gallotia galloti*. *American Journal of Physiology*, *254*, R242–R248.

Gouin, J. P., Carter, C. S., Pournajafi-Nazarloo, H., Glaser, R., Malarkey, W. B. Loving, et al. (2010). Marital behavior, oxytocin, vasopressin and wound healing. *Psychoneuroendocrinology*, 35, 1082–1090.

Graham, E. K., & Clifton, R. K. (1966). Heart-rate change as a component of the orienting response. *Psychological Bulletin*, *65*, 305–320.

Gray, J. A. (1971). *The psychology of fear and stress*. New York: McGraw-Hill.
Greenspan, S. I. (1992). *Infancy and early childhood: The practice of clinical assessment and intervention with emotional and developmental challenges*. Madison, CT: International Universities Press.
Greenspan, S. I., Portales, A. L., & Walker, P. S. (1987). *Fussy baby questionnaire*. Unpublished assessment tool.
Gribben, B., Pickering, T. G., Sleight, P., & Peto, R. (1971). Effect of age and high blood pressure on baroreflex sensitivity in man. *Circulation Research, 29*, 424–431.
Grippo, A. J., Lamb, D. G., Carter, C. S., & Porges, S. W. (2007). Cardiac regulation in the socially monogamous prairie vole. *Physiological Behavior, 90*, 386–393.
Grippo, A. J., Trahanas, D. M., Zimmerman II, R. R., Porges, S. W., & Carter, C. S. (2009). Oxytocin protects against isolation-induced autonomic dysfunction and behavioral indices of depression. *Psychoneuroendocrinology, 34*, 1542–1553.
Grossman, P., Karemaker, J., & Weiling, W. (1991). Prediction of tonic parasympathetic cardiac control using respiratory sinus arrhythmia: The need for respiratory control. *Psychophysiology, 28*, 201–216.
Grossman, P., & Kollai, M. (1993). Respiratory sinus arrhythmia, cardiac vagal tone, and respiration: Within- and between-individual relations. *Psychophysiology, 30*, 486–495.
Gunderson, J. G. (1996). The borderline patient's intolerance of aloneness. Insecure attachments and therapist availability. *American Journal of Psychiatry, 153*, 752–758.
Gunderson, J. G., Kolb, J. E., & Austin, V. (1981). The diagnostic interview for borderlines. *American Journal of Psychiatry, 138*, 896–903.
Gunnar, M. R., Porter, F. L., Wolf, C. M., et al. (1995). Neonatal stress reactivity: Predictions to later emotional temperament. *Child Development, 66*, 1–13.
Hachinski, V. C., Oppenheimer, S. M., Wilson, J. X., Guiraudon, C., & Cechetto, D. F. (1992). Asymmetry of sympathetic consequences of experimental stroke. *Archives of Neurology, 49*, 697–702.
Hager, J. C., & Ekman, P. (1985). The asymmetry of facial actions is inconsistent with models of hemispheric specialization. *Psychophysiology, 22*, 307–318.
Harper, R. M., Frysinger, R. C., Trelease, R. B., & Marks, J. D. (1984). State-dependent alteration of respiratory cycle timing by stimulation of the central nucleus of the amygdala. *Brain Research, 306*, 1–8.
Harris, J. C. (2009). Toward a restorative medicine—the science of care. *Journal of the American Medical Association, 301*, 1710–1712.
Haselton, J. R., Solomon, I. C., Motekaitis, A. M., & Kaufman, M. P. (1992). Bronchomotor vagal preganglionic cell bodies in the dog: An anatomic and functional study. *Journal of Applied Physiology, 73*, 1122–1129.
Heilman, K. M., Bowers, D., & Valenstein, E. (1985). Emotional disorders associated with neurological diseases. In K. M. Heilman & E. Valenstein (Eds.), *Clinical neuropsychology* (pp. 377–402). New York: Oxford University Press.
Heilman, K. M., Schwartz, H. D., & Watson, R. T. (1978). Hypoarousal in patients with neglect syndrome and emotional indifference. *Neurology, 28*, 229–233.
Heilman, K. M., & Van Den Abell, R. (1980). Right hemisphere dominance for attention: The mechanism underlying hemispheric asymmetries of inattention (neglect). *Neurology, 30*, 327–330.
Heinrichs, M., von Dawans, B., & Domes, G. (2009). Oxytocin, vasopressin and human social behavior. *Frontiers in Neuroendocrinology, 30*, 548–557.

Hemilä, S., Nummela, S., Reuter, T., 1995. What middle ear parameters tell about impedance matching and high frequency hearing. *Hearing Research*, *85*, 31–44.

Hering, H. E. (1910). A functional test of heart vagi in man. *Menschen Munchen Medizinische Wochenschrift*, 57, 1931–1933.

Herpertz, S. C., Kunert, H. J., Schwenger, U. B., & Sass, H. (1999). Affective responsiveness in borderline personality disorder: A psychophysiological approach. *American Journal of Psychiatry*, *156*, 1550–1556.

Hess, W. R. (1954). *Diencephalon, autonomic and extrapyramidal functions*. New York: Grune & Stratton.

Hickey, J. E., Suess, P. W., Newlin, D. B., Spurgeon, L., & Porges, S. W. (1995). Vagal tone regulation during sustained attention in boys exposed to opiates in utero. *Addictive Behaviors*, 2, 43–59.

Hodges, S. (2003). Borderline personality disorder and posttraumatic stress disorder: Time for integration? *Journal of Counseling & Development*, *81*, 409–417.

Hofer, M. A. (1970) Cardiac respiratory function during sudden prolonged immobility in wild rodents. *Psychosomatic Medicine*, 32, 633–647.

Hofer, M. (2006). Psychobiological roots of early attachment. *Current Directions in Psychological Science*, *15*, 84–88.

Hoffman, P. D., Buteau, E., Hooley, J. M., Fruzzetti, A. E., & Bruce, M. (2003). Family members' knowledge about borderline personality disorder: Correspondence with their levels of depression, burden, distress, and expressed emotion. *Family Process*, *42*, 469–478.

Hofheimer, J. A., Wood, B. R., Porges, S. W., Pearson, E., & Lawson, E. E. (1995). Respiratory sinus arrhythmia and social interaction patterns in preterm newborns. *Infant Behavior and Development*, *18*, 233–245.

Hopkins, D. A. (1987). The dorsal motor nucleus of the vagus nerve and the nucleus ambiguus: Structure and connections. In R. Hainsworth, P. N. Williams, & D. A. G. G. Many (Eds.), *Cardiogenic reflexes: Report of an international symposium* (pp. 185–203). Oxford: Oxford University Press.

Horvath, K., & Perman, J. A. (2002). Autism and gastrointestinal symptoms. *Current Gastroenterology Reports*, *4*, 251–258.

Hoshino, Y., Yokolyama, F., Hashimoto, S., et al. (1987). The diurnal variation and response to dexamethasone suppression test of saliva cortisol level in autistic children. *Japan Journal of Psychiatry and Neurology*, *41* 227–235.

Hrdy, S. B. (2008). *Mothers and others: The evolutionary origins of mutual understanding*. Cambridge, MA: Belknap Press.

Huffman, L. C., Bryan, Y. E., del Carmen, R., Pedersen, F. A., Doussard-Roosevelt, J. A., & Porges, S. W. (1998). Infant temperament and cardiac vagal tone: Assessments at twelve weeks of age. *Child Development*, *69*, 624–635.

Hugdahl, K., Franzon, M., Andersson, B., & Walldebo, G. (1983). Heart-rate responses (HRR) to lateralized visual stimuli. *Pavlovian Journal of Biological Science*, *18*, 186–198.

Humphrey, T. (1970). Function of the nervous system during prenatal life. In U. Stave (Ed.), *Physiology ofthe perinatal period* (pp. 751–796). New York: Appleton-Century-Crofts.

Hutt, C., Forrest, S. J., & Richer, J. (1975). Cardiac arrhythmia and behavior in autistic children. *Acta Psychiatric Scandinavia*, *51*, 361–372.

Insel, T. R., & Young, L. J. (2001). The neurobiology of attachment. *Nature Reviews Neuroscience*, 2, 129–136.

Izard, C. E. (1979). *The maximally discriminative facial movement coding system (MAX)*. Newark: University of Delaware Instructional Resource Center.

Izard, C. E., Porges, S. W., Simons, R. F., Parisi, M., Haynes, O. M., & Cohen. B. (1991). Infant cardiac activity: Developmental changes and relations with attachment. *Developmental Psychology*, 27, 432–439.

Jackson, J. H. (1958). Evolution and dissolution of the nervous system. In J. Taylor (Ed.), *Selected writings of John Hughlings Jackson* (pp. 45–118). London: Stapes Press.

Jacob, J. S., & McDonald, H. S. (1976). Diving bradycardia in four species of North American aquatic snakes. *Comparative Biochemistry and Physiology*, 53, 69–72.

Jansen, L. M. C., Gispen-de Wied, C. C., Van der Gaag, R. J., et al. (2000). Unresponsiveness to psychosocial stress in a subgroup of autistic-like children, multiple complex developmental disorder. *Psychoneuroendocrinology*, 25, 753–764.

Jaycox, L. H., Foa, E. B., & Morral, A. R. (1998). Influence of emotional engagement and habituation on exposure therapy for PTSD. *Journal of Consulting and Clinical Psychology*, 66, 185–192.

Jennings, J. R., & McKnight, J. D. (1994). Inferring vagal tone from heart rate variability. *Psychosomatic Medicine*, 56, 194–194.

Jensen, J. B., Realmuto, G. M., & Garfinkel, B. D. (1985). The dexamethasone suppression test in infantile autism. *Journal of the American Academy of Child and Adolesccent Psychiatry*, 24, 263–265.

Jerrell, T. W., Gentile, C. G., McCabe, P. M., & Schneiderman, N. (1986). Sinoaortic denervation does not prevent differential Pavlovian conditioning of bradycardia in rabbits. *Brain Research*, *100*, 3–10.

Jones, J. F. K., Wang, X. Y., & Jordan, D. (1995) Heart rate responses to selective stimulation of cardiac vagal C fibers in anesthetized cats, rats and rabbits. *Journal of Physiology*, 489, 203–214.

Jordan, D., Khalid, M. E. M., Schneiderman, N., & Spyer, K. M. (1982). The location and properties of preganglionic vagal cardiomotor neurones in the rabbit. *Pflügers Archive*, 395, 244–250.

Jyonouchi, H., Sun, S., & Le, H. (2001). Proinflammatory and regulatory cytokine production associated with innate and adaptive immune responses in children with autism spectrum disorders and developmental regression. *Journal of Neuroimmunology*, *120*, 170–179.

Kagan, J. (1994) On the nature of emotion. In N. A. Fox (Ed.), *Emotion regulation: Behavioral and biological considerations*. Monograph of the Society for Research in Child Development, 59, 7–24.

Kalia, M. (1981). Brain stem localization of vagal preganglionic neurons. *Journal of the Autonomic Nervous System*, 3, 451–481.

Kalia, M., & Mesulam, M.-M. (1980). Brain stem projections of sensory and motor components of the vagus complex in the cat. II. Laryngeal, tracheobronchial, pulmonary, cardiac, and gastrointestinal branches. *Journal of Comparative Neurology*, 193, 467–508.

Kapp, B. S., Frysinger, R. C., Gallagher, M., & Haselton, J. R. (1979) Amygdala central nucleus lesions: Effect on heart rate conditioning in the rabbit. *Physiology and Behavior*, 23, 1109–1117.

Katona, P. G., & Jih, R. (1975). Respiratory sinus arrhythmia: A noninvasive measure of parasympathetic cardiac control. *Journal of Applied Physiology*, 39, 801–805.

Keay, K. A., & Bandler, R. (2001). Parallel circuits mediating distinct emotional coping reactions to different types of stress. *Neuroscience and Biobehavioral Reviews*, 25, 669–678.

Kintraia, P. I., Zarnadze, M. G., Kintraia, N. P., & Kashakashvili, I. G. (2005). Development of daily rhythmicity in heart rate and locomotor activity in the human fetus. *Journal of Circadian Rhythms*, 3, 1–12.

Koch, K. L., Summy-Long, J., Bingaman, S., Sperry, N., & Stern, R. M. (1990) Vasopressin and oxytocin responses to illusory self-motion and nausea in man. *Journal of Clinical Endocrinology and Metabolism*, 71, 1269–1275.

Komisaruk, B. R., & Whipple, B. (1995) The suppression of pain by genital stimulation in females. *Annual Review of Sex Research*, 6, 151–186.

Kovacs, G. L., & Telegdy, G. (1982) Role of oxytocin in memory and amnesia. *Pharmacology and Therapeutics*, 18, 375–395.

Kryter, K. D. (1962). Methods for the calculation and use of the articulation index. *Journal of the Acoustical Society of America*, 34, 1689–1697.

Kryter, K. D. (1985). *The effects of noise on man*. New York: Academic Press.

Kuypers, H. G. J. M. (1958). Corticobulbar connexions to the pons and lower brain-stem in man. An anatomical study. *Brain*, 81, 364–388.

Lacey, B. C., & Lacey, J. I. (1978). Two way communication between the heart and the brain. *American Psychologist*, 33, 99–113.

Lacey, J. I. (1967). Somatic response patterning and stress: Some revisions of activation theory. In M. H. Appley & R. Trumbull (Eds.), *Psychological stress: Issues in research* (pp. 14–37). New York: Appleton-Century-Crofts.

Landgraf, R., Mallkinson, T., Horn, T., Veale, W. L., Lederis, K., & Pittman, Q. J. (1990). Release of vasopressin and oxytocin by paraventricular stimulation in rats. *American Journal of Physiology*, 258, 155–159.

Landgraf, R., & Neumann, I. D. (2004). Vasopressin and oxytocin release within the brain: A dynamic concept of multiple and variable modes of neuropeptide communication. *Frontiers in Neuroendocrinology*, 25, 150–176.

Lane, R., & Schwartz, G. (1987). Induction of lateralized sympathetic input to the heart by the CNS during emotional arousal: A possible neuro-physiologic trigger of sudden cardiac death. *Psychosomatic Medicine*, 49, 274–284.

Langley, J. N. (1921). *The autonomic nervous system*. Cambridge: Heffer & Sons.

Larson, S. K., & Porges, S. W. (1982). The ontogeny of heart period patterning in the rat. *Developmental Psychobiology*, 15, 519–528.

Lawes, I. N. C. (1990). The origin of the vomiting response: A neuroanatomical hypothesis. *Canadian Journal of Physiology and Pharmacology*, 68, 254–259.

LaBar, K. S., & LeDoux, J. E. (1996). Partial disruption of fear conditioning in rats with unilateral amygdala damage: Correspondence with unilateral temporal lobectomy in humans. *Behavioral Neuroscience*, 110, 991–997.

Leckman, J. F., Grice, D. E., Boardman, J., Zhang, H., Vitale, A., Bondi, C., et al. (1997). Symptoms of obsessive-compulsive disorder. *American Journal of Psychiatry*, 154, 911–917.

LeDoux, J. E., Iwata, J., Cicchetti, P., & Reis, D. J. (1988). Different projections of the central amygdaloid nucleus mediate autonomic and behavioral correlates of conditioned fear. *Journal of Neuroscience*, 8, 2517–2519.

Lee, S. W., Mancuso, C. A., & Charlson, M. E. (2004). Prospective study of new participants in a community-based mind-body training program. *Journal of General Internal Medicine, 19,* 760–765.

Leite-Panissi, C. R., Coimbra, N. C., & Menescal-de-Oliveira, L. (2003). The cholinergic stimulation of the central amygdala modifying the tonic immobility response and antinociception in guinea pigs depends on the ventrolateral periaqueductal gray. *Brain Research Bulletin, 60,* 167–178.

Leslie, R. A. (1985). Neuroactive substances in the dorsal vagal complex of the medulla oblongata: Nucleus of the tractus solitarius, area postrema, and dorsal motor nucleus of the vagus. *Neurochemistry International, 7,* 191–211.

Leslie, R. A., Reynolds, D. J. M., & Lawes, I. N. C. (1992). Central connections of the nuclei of the vagus nerve. In S. Ritter, R. C. Ritter, & C. D. Barnes (Eds.), *Neuroanatomy and physiology of abdominal vagal afferents* (pp. 81–98). Boca Raton, FL: CRC Press.

Lester, B. M., & Zeskind, P. S. (1982). A biobehavioral perspective on crying in early infancy. In H. E. Fitzgerald, B. M. Lester, & M. W. Youngman (Eds.), *Theory and research in behavioral pediatrics* (pp. 133–180). New York: Plenum.

Levenson, R. W., Ekman, P., & Friesen, W. V. (1990). Voluntary facial action generates emotion-specific autonomic nervous system activity. *Psychophysiology, 27,* 363–384.

Levy, M. N. (1977). Parasympathetic control of the heart. In W. C. Randall (Ed.), *Neural regulation of the heart* (pp. 95–129). New York: Oxford University Press.

Levy, M. N. (1984). Cardiac sympathetic-parasympathetic interactions. *Federation Proceedings, 43,* 2598–2602.

Li, P., Chang, T. M., & Chey, W. Y. (1998). Secretin inhibits gastric acid secretion via a vagal afferent pathway in rats. *American Journal of Physiology, 275,* G22–G28.

Lindsley, D. (1951). Emotion. In S. S. Stevens (Ed.), *Handbook of experimental psychology* (pp. 473–516). New York: Wiley.

Linnemeyer, S. A., & Porges, S. W. (1986). Recognition memory and cardiac vagal tone in 6-month-old infants. *Infant Behavior, 9,* 43–56.

Lonstein, J. S., & Stern, J. M. (1998). Site and behavioral specificity of periaqueductal gray lesions on postpartum sexual, maternal, and aggressive behaviors in rats. *Brain Research, 804,* 21–35.

Lu, Y., & Owyang, C. (1995). Secretin at physiological doses inhibits gastric motility via a vagal afferent pathway. *American Journal of Physiology, 268,* G1012–G1016.

Luo, Z. X. (2007). Transformation and diversification in early mammal evolution. *Nature, 450*(7172), 1011–1019.

Luo, Z. X., Crompton, A. W., & Sun, A. L. (2001). A new mammaliaform from the early Jurassic and evolution of mammalian characteristics. *Science, 292,* 1535–1540.

Lyoo, K., Han, M. H., & Cho, D. Y. (1998). A brain MRI study in subjects with borderline personality disorder. *Journal of Affective Disorders, 50,* 235–243.

Machado, B. H., & Brody, M. J. (1988). Effect of nucleus ambiguus lesion on the development of neurogenic hypertension. *Hypertension, 11,* 135–138.

MacLean, P. D. (1990). *The triune brain in evolution.* New York: Plenum Press.

Malik, M., & Camm, J. A. (1993). Components of heart rate variability—What they really mean and what we really measure. *American Journal of Cardiology, 72,* 821–822.

Malmo, R. B. (1959). Activation: A neurophysiological dimension. *Psychological Review, 66,* 367–386.

Marangell, L. B., Rush, A. J., George, M. S., et al. (2002). Vagal nerve stimulation (VNS) for major depressive episodes: One year outcomes. *Biological Psychiatry, 51,* 280–287.

McAllen, R. M., & Spyer, K. M. (1976). The location of cardiac vagal preganglionic motoneurones in the medulla of the cat. *Journal of Physiology,* 258, 187–204.

McAllen, R. M., & Spyer, K. M. (1978). Two types of vagal preganglionic motoneurones projecting to the heart and lungs. *Journal of Physiology,* 282, 353–364.

McCabe, P. M., Yongue, B. G., Porges, S. W., & Ackles, P. K. (1984). Changes in heart period, heart period variability and a spectral analysis estimate of respiratory sinus arrhythmia during aortic nerve stimulation in rabbits. *Psychophysiology, 21,* 149–158.

McConaughy, S. H., & Achenbach, T. M. (1988). *Practical guide for the child behavior checklist and related materials.* Burlington, VT: University of Vermont Department of Psychiatry.

McDonald, H. S. (1974). Bradycardia during death-feigning of *Heterodon plalyrhinos* Latreille (Serpentes). *Journal of Herpetology,* 8, 157–164.

McEwen, B. S., & Wingfield, J. C. (2003). The concept of allostasis in biology and biomedicine. *Hormones and Behavior,* 43, 2–15.

McGurk, H., & MacDonald, J. (1976). Hearing lips and seeing voices. *Nature,* 264, 746–748.

McLeod, D. R., Hoehn-Saric, R., Porges, S. W., Kowalski, P. A., & Clark, C. M. (2000). Therapeutic effects of imipramine are counteracted by its metabolite, desipramine, in patients with generalized anxiety disorder. *Journal of Clinical Psychopharmacology,* 20, 615–621.

McLeod, D. R., Hoehn-Saric, R., Porges, S. W., & Zimmerli, W. D. (1992). Effects of alprazolam and imipramine on parasympathetic cardiac control in patients with generalized anxiety disorder. *Psychopharmacology, 107,* 535–540.

McNair, D. M., Lorr, M., & Droppleman, L. F. (1992). *POMS manual: Profile of mood states.* San Diego: Edits/Education and Instructional Testing Service.

Mera, E., Wityk, R., & Porges, S. W. (1995, May). *Abnormal heart variability in brainstem injury.* Paper presented at the American Academy of Neurology, Seattle, WA.

Mesulam, M. M. (1981). A cortical network for directed attention and unilateral neglect. *Annals of Neurology, 10,* 309–325.

Meyer-Lindenberg, A. (2008). Impact of prosocial neuropeptides on human brain function. *Progress in Brain Research, 170,* 463–470.

Miao, F. J.-P., Janig, W., Green, P. G., et al. (1997). Inhibition of bradykinin-induced plasma extravasation produced by noxious cutaneous and visceral stimuli and it modulation by vagal activity. *Journal of Neurophysiology,* 78, 1285–1292.

Michelini, L. C. (1994) Vasopressin in the nucleus tractus solitarius: A modulator of baroreceptor reflex control of heart rate. *Brazilian Journal of Medical and Biological Research,* 27, 1017–1032.

Michelini, L. C., Marcelo, M. C., Amico, J., & Morris, M. (2003). Oxytocin regulation of cardiovascular function: studies in oxytocin-deficient mice. *American Journal of Physiology: Heart and Circulatory Physiology, 284,* H2269–2276.

Mitchell, G. A. G., & Warwick, R. (1955). The dorsal vagal nucleus. *Acta Anatomica,* 25, 371–395.

Molfese, D. L., & Segalowitz, S. J. (Eds.). (1988). *Brain lateralization in children: Developmental implications.* New York: Guilford Press.

Moore, G. A., & Calkins, S. D. (2004). Infants' vagal regulation in the still-face paradigm is related to dyadic coordination of mother–infant interaction. *Developmental Psychology, 40*, 1068–1080.

Morris, J. L., & Nilsson, S. (1994). The circulatory system. In S. Nilsson & S. Holmgren (Eds.), *Comparative physiology and evolution of the autonomic nervous system* (pp. 193–240). Chur, Switzerland: Harwood Academic Publishers.

Morris, J. S., Ohman, A., & Dolan, R. J. (1999). A subcortical pathway to the right amygdala mediating "unseen" fear. *Proceedings of the National Academy of Sciences USA, 96*, 1680–1685.

Movius, H. L., & Allen, J. J. B. (2005). Cardiac vagal tone, defensiveness, and motivational style. *Biological Psychology, 68*, 147–162.

Mulder, L. J. M., & Mulder, G. (1987). Cardiovascular reactivity and mental workload. In O. Rompelman & R. J. Kitney (Eds.), *The beat-by-beat investigation of cardiovascular function* (pp. 216–253). Oxford: Oxford University Press.

Munhall, K. G., Jones, J. A., Callan, D. E., Kuratate, T., & Vatikiotis-Bateson, E. (2004). Visual prosody and speech intelligibility: Head movment improves auditory speech perception. *Psychological Science, 15*, 133–137.

Murphy, J. V., Wheless, J. W., & Schmoll, C. M. (2000). Left vagal nerve stimulation in six patients with hypothalamic hamartomas. *Pediatric Neurology, 23*, 167–168.

Nara, T., Goto, N., & Hamano, S. (1991). Development of the human dorsal nucleus of vagus nerve: A morphometric study. *Journal of the Autonomic Nervous System, 33*, 267–276.

Nelson, N. M. (1976). Respiration and circulation before birth. In C. A. Smith & N. M. Nelson (Eds.), *The physiology of the newborn infant* (4th ed, pp. 15–116). Philadelphia: Thomas.

Neuheuber, W. L., & Sandoz, P. A. (1986). Vagal primary afferent terminals in the dorsal motor nucleus of the rat: Are they making monosynaptic contacts on preganglionic efferent neurons? *Neuroscience Letters, 69*, 126–130.

Neumann, I. D. (2008). Brain oxytocin: A key regulator of emotional and social behaviours in both females and males. *Journal of Neuroendocrinology, 20*, 858–865.

New, A. S., & Siever, L. J. (2002). Neurobiology and genetics and borderline personality disorder. *Psychiatric Annals, 32*, 329–336.

Newman, J. D. (1988). *The physiological control of mammalian vocalizations*. New York: Plenum Press.

Ni, H., Zhang, J. X., & Harper, R. M. (1990). Respiratory-related discharge of periaqueductal gray neurons during sleep-waking states. *Brain Research, 511*, 319–325.

Nissen, R., Cunningham, J. T., & Renaud, L. P. (1993). Lateral hypothalamic lesions alter baroreceptor-evoked inhibition of rat supraoptic vasopressin neurones. *Journal of Physiology (London), 470*, 751–766.

Nolte, J. (1993). *The human brain: An introduction to its functional anatomy* (3rd ed.). St. Louis, MO: Mosby-Year Book.

Numan, M. (2007). Motivational systems and the neural circuitry of maternal behavior in the rat. *Developmental Psychobiology, 49*, 12–21.

Obrist, P. A. (1976). The cardiovascular behavioral interaction—As it appears today. *Psychophysiology, 13*, 95–107.

Obrist, P. A. (1981). *Cardiovascular psychophysiology*. New York: Plenum Press.

Ogden, P., Minton, K., & Pain, C. (2006). *Trauma and the body: A sensorimotor approach to psychotherapy*. New York: Norton.

Owley, T., McMahon, W., Cook, E. H., et al. (2001). Multisite, double-blind, placebo-controlled trial of porcine secretin in autism. *Journal of the American Academy of Child Psychiatry, 40,* 1293–1299.

Pagani, F. D., Norman, W. P., & Gillis, R. A. (1988). Medullary parasympathetic projections innervate specific sites in the feline stomach. *Gastroenterology,* 9, 277–288.

Palkovitz, R. J., Wiesenfeld, A. R. (1980). Differential autonomic responses of autistic and normal children. *Journal of Autism and Developmental Disorders, 10,* 347–360.

Pang, X.D., Guinan, J.J., 1997. Effects of stapedius-muscle contractions on the masking of auditory-nerve responses. *Journal of the Acoustic Society of America, 102,* 3576–3586.

Panksepp J. (1998). *Affective neuroscience.* New York: Oxford University Press.

Panksepp, J. (2009). Brain emotional systems and qualities of mental life: From animal models of affect to implications for psychotherapeutics. In D. Fosha, D. J. Siegel, & M. F. Solomon (Eds.), *The healing power of emotion: Affective neuroscience, development, clinical pratice* (pp. 1–26). New York: Norton.

Paris, J., Zweig-Frank, H., Ng, Y. K., Schwartz, G., Steiger, H., & Nair, N. P. V. (2004). Neurobiological correlates of diagnosis and underlying traits in patients with borderline personality disorder compared with normal controls. *Psychiatry Research, 121,* 239–252.

Parmeggiani, P. L. (1985) Homeostatic regulation during sleep: Facts and hypotheses. In D. H. McGinty et al. (Eds.), *Brain mechanisms of sleep* (pp. 385–397). New York: Raven Press.

Pereyra, P. M., Zhang, W., Schmidt, M., & Becker, L. E. (1992). Development of myelinated and unmyelinated fibers of human vagus nerve during the first year of life. *Journal of Neurological Sciences, 110,* 107–113.

Pessoa, L., McKenna, M., Gutierrez, E., & Ungerleider, L. G. (2002). Neuroprocessing of emotional faces requires attention. *Proceedings of the National Academy of Sciences USA, 99,* 11458–11463.

Pianta, R., Egeland, B., & Adam, E. (1996). Adult attachment classification and self-reported psychiatric symptomatology as assessed by the Minnesota Multiphasic Personality Inventory-2. *Journal of Consulting and Clinical Psychology, 64,* 273–281.

Pigott, L. R., Ax, A. F., Bamford, J. L., et al. (1973). Respiration sinus arrhythmia in psychotic children. *Psychophysiology, 10,* 401–414.

Pimental, P. A., & Kingsbury, N. A. (1989). *Neuropsychological aspects of right brain injury.* Austin: Pro-Ed.

Pilz, P. K., Ostwald, J., Kreiter, A., & Schnitzler, H. U. (1997). Effect of the middle ear reflex on sound transmission to the inner ear of rat. *Hearing Research, 105,* 171–182.

Porges, S. W. (1972). Heart rate variability and deceleration as indexes of reaction time. *Journal of Experimental Psychology,* 92, 103–110.

Porges, S. W. (1973). Heart rate variability: An autonomic correlate of reaction time performance. *Bulletin of the Psychonomic Society, 1,* 270–272.

Porges, S. W. (1983). Heart rate patterns in neonates: A potential diagnostic window to the brain. In T. M. Field & A. M. Sostek (Eds.), *Infants born at risk: Physiological and perceptual responses* (pp. 3–22). New York: Grune & Stratton.

Porges, S. W. (1985). U.S. Patent No. 4,520,944: Method and apparatus for evaluating rhythmic oscillations in aperiodic physiological response systems.

Porges, S. W. (1986). Respiratory sinus arrhythmia: Physiological basis, quantitative methods, and clinical implications. In P. Grossman, K. Janssen, & D. Vaitl (Eds.), *Cardiorespiratory and cardiosomatic psychophysiology* (pp. 101–115). New York: Plenum Press.

Porges, S. W. (1988). Neonatal vagal tone: Diagnostic and prognostic implications. In P. N. Vietze & H. G. Vaughn (Eds.), *Early identification of infants with developmental disabilities* (pp. 147–159). Philadelphia: Grune & Stratton.

Porges, S. W. (1991). Vagal tone: An autonomic mediator of affect. In J. A. Garber & K. A. Dodge (Eds.), *The development of affect regulation and dysregulation* (pp. 111–128). New York: Cambridge University Press.

Porges, S. W. (1992). Autonomic regulation and attention. In B. A. Campbell, H. Hayne, & R. Richardson (Eds.), *Attention and information processing in infants and adults* (pp. 201–223). Hillsdale, NJ: Erlbaum.

Porges, S. W. (1995). Cardiac vagal tone: A physiological index of stress. *Neuroscience and Biobehavioral Reviews, 19,* 225–233.

Porges, S. W. (2001a). The polyvagal theory: Phylogenetic substrates of a social nervous system. *International Journal of Psychophysiology, 42,* 123–146.

Porges, S. W. (2001b). Is there a major stress system at the periphery other than the adrenals? In D. M. Broom (Ed.), *Dahlem workshop on coping with challenge: Welfare in animals including humans* (pp. 135–149). Berlin: Dahlem University Press.

Porges, S. W. (2007a). A phylogenetic journey through the vague and ambiguous Xth cranial nerve: A commentary on contemporary heart rate variability research. *Biological Psychology, 74,* 301–307.

Porges, S. W. (2007b). The polyvagal perspective. *Biological Psychology, 74,* 116–143.

Porges, S. W., Arnold, W. R., & Forbes, E. J. (1973). Heart rate variability: An index of attentional responsivity in human newborns. *Developmental Psychology, 8,* 85–92.

Porges, S. W., & Bohrer, R. E. (1990). Analyses of periodic processes in psychophysiological research. In J. T. Cacioppo & L. G. Tassinary (Eds.), *Principles of psychophysiology: Physical, social, and inferential elements* (pp. 708–753). New York: Cambridge University Press.

Porges, S. W., & Doussard-Roosevelt, J. A. (1997). The psychophysiology of temperament. In J. D. Noshpitz (Ed.), *Handbook of child and adolescent psychiatry* (pp. 250–268). New York: Wiley.

Porges, S. W., Doussard-Roosevelt, J. A., Portales, A. L., & Suess, P. E. (1994). Cardiac vagal tone: Stability and relation to difficultness in infants and three-year-old children. *Developmental Psychobiology, 17,* 289–300.

Porges, S. W., Doussard-Roosevelt, J. A., Stifter, C. A., McClenny, B. D., & Riniolo, T. C. (1999). Sleep state and vagal regulation of heart period patterns in the human newborn: An extension of the polyvagal theory. *Psychophysiology, 36,* 14–21.

Porges, S. W., & Greenspan, S. I. (1991). Regulatory disordered infants: A common theme. In National Institutes of Drug Abuse workshop report on Methodological Issues in Controlled Studies on Effects of Prenatal Exposure to Drugs of Abuse, *National Institution Drug Abuse Research Monograph, 114,* 173–181.

Porges, S. W., & Lipsitt, L. P. (1993). Neonatal responsivity to gustatory stimulation: The gustatory-vagal hypothesis. *Infant Behavior and Development, 16,* 487–494.

Porges, S. W., & Maiti, A. K. (1992). The smart and vegetative vagi: Implications for specialization and laterality of function [Abstract]. *Psychophysiology, 2,* S7.

Porges, S. W., McCabe, P. M., & Yongue, B. G. (1982). Respiratory-heart rate interactions: Psychophysiological implications for pathophysiology and behavior. In J. Cacioppo & R. Petty (Eds.), *Perspectives in cardiovascular psychophysiology* (pp. 223–264). New York: Guilford Press.

Porges, S. W., & Raskin, D. C. (1969). Respiratory and heart rate components of attention. *Journal of Experimental Psychology, 81*, 497–503.

Porges, S. W., Riniolo, T. C., McBride, T., et al. (2003). Heart rate and respiration in reptiles: Contrasts between a sit-and-wait predator and an intensive forager. *Brain Cognition*, 52, 88–96.

Porges, S. W., Stamps, L. E., & Walter, G. F. (1974). Heart rate variability and newborn heart rate responses to illumination changes. *Developmental Psychology, 10*, 507–513.

Portales, A. L., Porges, S. W., Doussard-Roosevelt, J. A., Abedin, M., Lopez, R., et al. (1997). Vagal regulation during bottle feeding in low-birthweight neonates: Support for the gustatory-vagal hypothesis. *Developmental Psychobiology*, 30, 225–233.

Porter, F. L., & Porges, S. W. (1988). Neonatal cardiac responses to lumbar punctures [Abstract]. *Infant Behavior, 11*, 261.

Porter, F. L., Porges, S. W., & Marshall, R. E. (1988). Newborn pain cries and vagal tone: Parallel changes in response to circumcision. *Child Development*, 59, 495–505.

Potter, E. K., & McCloskey, D. I. (1986). Effects of hypoxia on cardiac vagal efferent activity and on the action of the vagus nerve at the heart in the dog. *Journal of the Autonomic Nervous System, 17*, 325–329.

Prims, A., Kaloupek, D. G., & Keane, T. M. (1995). Psychophysiological evidence for autonomic arousal and startle in traumatized adult populations. In M. J. Friedman, D. S. Charney, & A.Y. Deutsh (Eds.), *Neurobiological and clinical consequences of stress: From normal adaptation to PTSD* (pp. 291–313). Philadelphia: Lippincott-Raven.

Pynoos, R. S., Frederick, C. J., Nader, K., Arroyo, W., Steinberg, A., Eth, S., et al. (1987). Life threat and posttraumatic stress in schoool age children. *Archives of General Psychiatry, 44*, 1057–1063.

Randall, W. C., & Rohse, W. G. (1956). The augmenter action of the sympathetic cardiac nerves. *Circulation Research, 4*, 470–477.

Raymond, N. C., Eckert, E. D., Hamalainen, M., et al. (1999). A preliminary report on pain thresholds in bulimia nervosa during a bulimic episode. *Comprehensive Psychiatry, 40*, 229–233.

Raymond, N. C., Faris, P. L., Thuras, P. D., et al. (1999). Elevated pain threshold in anorexia nervosa subjects. *Biological Psychiatry, 45*, 1389–1392.

Reed, S. F., Ohel, G., David, R., & Porges, S. W. (1999). A neural explanation of fetal heart rate patterns: A test of the polyvagal theory. *Developmental Psychobiology, 35*, 108–118.

Regal, P. J. (1978). Behavioral differences between reptiles and mammal: An analysis of activity and mental capabilities. In N. Greenberg & P. D. MacLean (Eds.), *Behavior and neurology of lizards* (pp. 183–202). Rockville, MD: National Institute of Mental Health.

Ren, K., Randich, A., & Gebhart, G. F. (1990). Electrical stimulation of cervical vagal afferents. I. Central relays for modulation of spinal nociceptive transmission. *Journal of Neurophysiology, 64*, 1098–1114.

Richards, J. E. (1985). Respiratory sinus arrhythmia predicts heart rate and visual responses during visual attention in 14- and 20-week-old infants. *Psychophysiology*, 22, 101–109.

Richards, J. E. (1987). Infant visual sustained attention and respiratory sinus arrhythmia. *Child Development*, 58, 488–496.

Richards, J. E., & Casey, B. L. (1991). Heart rate variability during attention phases in young infants. *Psychophysiology, 28,* 43–53.
Richter, C. P. (1957). On the phenomenon of sudden death in animals and man. *Psychosomatic Medicine, 19,* 191–198.
Richter, D. W., & Spyer, K. M. (1990). Cardiorespiratory control. In A. D. Loewy & K. M. Spyer (Eds.), *Central regulation of autonomic function* (pp. 189–207). New York: Oxford University Press.
Riniolo, T., Doussard-Roosevelt, J., & Porges, S. W. (1994). The relation between respiratory sinus arrhythmia and heart period during waking and sleep [Abstract]. *Psychophysiology, 31*(Suppl.), S81.
Riniolo, T., & Porges, S. W. (1997). Inferential and descriptive influences on measures of respiratory sinus arrhythmia: Sampling rate, R-wave trigger accuracy, and variance estimates. *Psychophysiology, 34,* 613–621.
Rinn, W. E. (1984). The neurophysiology of facial expression: A review of the neurological and psychological mechanisms for producing facial expressions. *Psychological Bulletin, 95,* 52–77.
Rinne, T., de Kloet, E. R., Wouters, L., Goekoop, J. G., ReRijk, R. H., & van den Brink, W. (2002). Hyperresponsiveness of hypothalamic pituitary adrenal axis to combined dexamethasone/corticotrophin-releasing hormone challenge in female borderline personality disorder subjects with a history of sustained childhood abuse. *Biological Psychiatry, 52,* 1102–1112.
Rizvi, T. A., Ennis, M., Behbehani, M. M., & Shipley, M. T. (1991). Connections between the central nucleus of the amygdala and the midbrain periaqueductal gray: Topography and reciprocity. *Journal of Comparative Neurology, 303,* 121–131.
Rodier, P. M., Ingram, J. L., Tisdale, B., et al. (1996). Embryological origin for autism: Developmental anomalies of the cranial nerve motor nuclei. *Journal of Comparative Neurology, 370,* 247–261.
Rogers, R. C., & Hermann, G. E. (1992). Central regulation of brainstem gastric vagovagal control circuits. In S. Ritter, R. C. Ritter, & C. D. Barnes (Eds.), *Neuroanatomy and physiology of abdominal vagal afferents* (pp. 99–134). Boca Raton, FL: CRC Press.
Rosen, J. B., Hamerman, E., Sitcoske, E., Glowa, J. R., & Schulkin, J. (1996). Hyperexcitability: Exaggerated fear-potentiated startle produced by partial amygdala kindling. *Behavioral Neuroscience, 110,* 43–50.
Rosenzweig, M. R., & Amon, A. H. (1955). Binaural interaction in the medulla of the cat. *Cellular and Molecular Life Science, 11,* 498–500.
Ross, E. D. (1981). The aprosodias: Functional-anatomic organization of the affect components of language in the right hemisphere. *Archives of Neurology, 38,* 561–569.
Ross, E. D., Homan, R. W., & Buck, R. (1994). Differential hemispheric lateralization of primary and social emotions. *Neuropsychiatry, Neuropsychology, and Behavioral Neurology, 7,* 1–19.
Ross, E. D., & Mesulam, M. (1979). Dominant language functions of the right hemisphere? Prosody and emotional gesturing. *Archives of Neurology, 36,* 144–148.
Rothschild, B. (2000). *The body remembers: The psychophysiology of trauma and trauma treatment.* New York: Norton.
Rothschild, L., Haslam, N., Cleland, C., & Zimmerman, M. (2003). A taxometric study of borderline personality disorder. *Journal of Abnormal Psychology, 112,* 657–666.
Rottenberg, J., Solomon, K., Gross, J. J., & Gotlib, I. H. (2005). Vagal withdrawal to a sad film predicts subsequent recovery from depression. *Psychophysiology, 42,* 277–281.

Rowe, T. (1996). Coevolution of the mammalian middle ear and neocortex. *Science, 273*, 651–654.

Rowell, L. B. (1993). Central circulatory adjustments to dynamic exercise. In L. B. Rowell (Ed.), *Human cardiovascular control* (pp. 162–203). New York: Oxford University Press.

Sachis, P. N., Armstrong, D. L., Becker, L. E., & Bryan. A. C. (1982). Myelination of the human vagus nerve from 24 weeks postconceptional age to adolescence. *Journal of Neuropathology and Experimental Neurology, 41*, 466–472.

Sack, M., Hopper, J. W., & Lamprecht, F. (2004). Low respiratory sinus arrhythmia and prolonged psychophysiological arousal in posttraumatic stress disorder: Heart rate dynamics and individual differences in arousal regulation. *Biological Psychiatry, 55*, 284–290.

Sacks, O. (2007). *Musicophilia: Tales of music and the brain*. New York: Random House.

Sahar, T., Shalev, A. Y., & Porges, S. W. (2001). Vagal modulation of responses to mental challenge in posttraumatic stress disorder. *Biological Psychiatry, 49*, 637 643.

Santer, R. M. (1994). Chromaffin systems. In S. Nilsson & S. Holmgren (Eds.), *Comparative physiology and evolution of the autonomic nervous System* (pp. 97–117). Switzerland: Harwood Academic Publishers.

Sargunaraj, D., Lehrer, P. M., Carr, R. E., Hochron, S. M., & Porges, S. W. (1994). The effects of paced resistance breathing [Abstract]. *Psychophysiology, 31*(Suppl.), S85.

Sargunaraj, D., Lehrer, P. M., Hochron, S. M., Rausch, L., Edelberg, R., & Porges, S. W. (1996). Cardiac rhythm effects of .125 Hz paced breathing through a resistive load: Implications for paced breathing therapy and the polyvagal theory. *Biofeedback and Self-Regulation, 21*, 131–147.

Saul, J. P., Berger, R. D., Chen, H., & Cohen, R. J. (1989). Transfer function analysis of autonomic regulation. II. Respiratory sinus arrhythmia. *American Journal of Physiology, 256*, HI53–HI61.

Sawchenko, P. E., & Swanson, L. W. (1982). The organization of noradrenergic pathways from the brainstem to the paraventricular and supraoptic nuclei in the rat. *Brain Research Reviews, 4*, 275–325.

Schachter, J. (1957). Pain, fear, and anger in hypertensives and normotensives: A psychophysiological study. *Psychosomatic Medicine, 19*, 17–29.

Schachter, S., & Singer, J. E. (1962). Cognitive, social, and physiological determinants of emotional state. *Psychological Review, 69*, 379–399.

Scherlel, E. R., Brourman, J. D., Kling, S. M., Schmall, L. M., Tobias, T. A., & Myerowitz, P. D. (1994). Vagal innervation influences the whole body oxygen consumption-delivery relationship in the dog. *Shock, 2*, 127–132.

Schmahl, C. G., Elzinga, B. M., Ebner, U. W., Simms, T., Sanislow, C., Vermetten, E., et al. (2004). Psychophysiological reactivity to traumatic and abandonment scripts in borderline personality and posttraumatic stress disorders: A preliminary report. *Psychiatry Research, 126*, 33–42.

Schmahl, C. G., Vermetten, E., Elzinga, B. M., & Bremner, J. D. (2003). Magnetic resonance imaging of hippocampal and amygdala volume in women with childhood abuse and borderline personality disorder. *Psychiatry Research: Neuroimaging, 122*, 193–198.

Schneiderman, N. (1974). The relationship between learned and unlearned cardiovascular responses. In P. A. Obrist, A. H. Black, J. Brener, & L. V. DiCara (Eds.), *Cardiovas-*

cular psychophysiology: Current issues in response mechanisms, biofeedback, and methodology (pp. 190–210). Chicago: Aldine.

Schneirla, T. C. (1959). An evolutionary and developmental theory of biphasic processes underlying approach and withdrawal. In M. R. Jones (Ed.), *Nebraska symposium on motivation* (vol. 7, pp. 1–42). Lincoln: University of Nebraska Press.

Schore A. (1994). *Affect regulation and the origin of the self: The neurobiology of emotional development.* Hillsdale, NJ: Erlbaum.

Schore A. (2003). *Affect dysregulation and disorders of the self.* New York: Norton.

Schuck, A. M., & Widom, C. S. (2001). Childhood victimization and alcohol symptoms in females: Causal inferences and hypothesized mediators? *Child Abuse and Neglect, 25,* 1069–1092.

Schumm, J. A., Hobfoll, S. E., & Keough, N. J. (2004). Revictimization and interpersonal resource loss predicts PTSD among women in substance-use treatment. *Journal of Traumatic Stress, 17,* 173–181.

Schwaber, J. S. (1986). Neuroanatomical substrates of cardiovascular and emotional-autonomic regulation. In A. Magro, W. Osswald, D. Reis, & P. Vanhoutte (Eds.), *Central and peripheral mechanisms of cardiovascular regulation* (pp. 353–384). New York: Plenum Press.

Schwaber, J. S., Kapp, B. S., & Higgins, G. (1980). The origin and the extent of direct amygdala projections to the region of the dorsal motor nucleus of the vagus and the nucleus of the solitary tract. *Neurosci Letters, 20,* 15–20.

Selye, H. (1936). A syndrome produced by diverse nocuous agents. *Nature, 138,* 32.

Selye, H. (1956). *The stress of life.* New York: McGraw-Hill.

Shaver, P. R., & Mikulincer, M. (2002). Attachment-related psychodynamics. *Attachment & Human Development, 4,* 133–161.

Siegel, D. (2007). *The mindful brain.* New York: Norton.

Silberman, E. K., & Weingartner, H. (1986). Hemispheric lateralization of functions related to emotion. *Brain and Cognition, 5,* 322–353.

Skodol, A. E., Gunderson, J. G., Pfohl, B., Widiger, T. A., Livesley, W. J., & Siever, L. J. (2002). The borderline diagnosis I: Psychopathology, cornorbidity, and personality structure. *Biological Psychiatry, 51,* 936–950.

Skodol, A. E., Siever, L. J., Livesley, W. J., Gunderson, J. G., Pfohl, B., & Widiger, T. A. (2002). The borderline diagnosis II: Biology, genetics, and clinical course. *Biological Psychiatry, 51,* 951–963.

Smith, D. E. P., Miller, S. D., Stewart, M., et al. (1988). Conductive hearing loss in autistic, learning-disabled, and normal children. *Journal of Autism and Developmental Disorders, 18,* 53–65.

Smotherman, M., Schwartz, C., & Metzner, W. (2010). Vocal–respiratory interactions in the parabrachial nucleus. In S. M. Brudzynski (Ed.), *Handbook of mammalian vocalization: An integrative neuroscience approach* (vol. 19, pp. 383–392). Amsterdam: Elsevier.

Smyke, A. T., Dumitrescu, A., & Zeanah, C. H. (2002). Attachment disturbances in young children. I: The continuum of caretaking casualty. *Journal of the American Academy of Child and Adolescent Psychiatry, 41,* 972–982.

Sokolov, E. N. (1963). *Perception and the conditioned reflex.* Oxford: Pergamon Press.

Sostek, A. M., Glass, P., Molina, B. C., & Porges, S. W. (1984). Neonatal vagal tone and subsequent sleep apnea in preterm infants [Abstract]. *Psychophysiology, 21,* 599.

Sovik, R. (2000). The science of breathing—The yogic view. *Behavior Modification, 27*, 710–730.

Spitzer, R. L., Williams, J. B. W., Gibbon, M., & First, M. B. (1990). *Structured clinical interview for DSM-III-R*. Washington, DC: American Psychiatric Press.

Spitzer, R. L., Williams, J. B. W., Gibbon, M., & First, M. B. (1992). The structured clinical interview for DSM-III-R (SCID) I: History, rationale, and description. *Archives of General Psychiatry, 49*, 624–629.

Spyer, K. M., & Jordan, D. (1987). Electrophysiology of the nucleus ambiguus. In R. Hainsworth, P. N. Williams, & D. A. G. G. Many (Eds.), *Cardiogenic reflexes: Report of an international symposium* (pp. 237–249). Oxford: Oxford University Press.

Stamps, L. E., & Porges, S. W. (1975). Heart rate conditioning in newborn infants: Relationships among conditionality, heart rate variability, and sex. *Developmental Psychology, 11*, 424–431.

Stansbury, K., & Gunnar, M. R. (1994). Adrenocortical activity and emotion regulation. In N. A. Fox (Ed.), *Emotion regulation: Behavioral and biological considerations*, Monograph of the Society for Research in Child Development, 59, 108–134.

Stern, J. M. (1997). Offspring-induced nurturance: Animal-human parallels. *Developmental Psychobiology, 31*, 19–37.

Stifter, C., & Corey, J. (2001). Vagal regulation and observed social behavior in infancy. *Social Development, 10*, 189–201.

Stifter, C. A., & Fox, N. A. (1990). Infant reactivity: Physiological correlates of newborn and 5-month temperament. *Developmental Psychology, 16*, 582–588.

Stifter, C. A., Fox, N. A., & Porges, S. W. (1989). Facial expressivity and vagal tone in five- and ten-month-old infants. *Infant Behavior and Development, 12*, 127–137.

Streeck-Fischer, A. & van der Kolk, B. (2000). Down will come baby, cradle and all: Diagnostic and therapeutic implications of chronic trauma on child development. *Australian and New Zealand Journal of Psychiatry, 34*, 903–918.

Suess, P. E., Alpan, G., Dulkerian, S. J., Doussard-Roosevelt, J., Porges, S. W., & Gewolb, I. H. (2000). Respiratory sinus arrhythmia during feeding: A measure of vagal regulation of metabolism, ingestion, and digestion in preterm infants. *Developmental Medicine and Child Neurology, 42*, 353.

Sumby, W. H., & Pollack, I. (1954). Visual contribution to speech intelligibility in noise. *Journal of the Acoustical Society of America, 26*, 212–215.

Surguladze, S. A., Calvert, G. A., Brammer, M. J., Campbell, R., Bullmore, E. T., Giampietro, V., et al. (2001). Audio-visual speech perception in schizophrenia: An fMRI study. *Psychiatry Research, 106*, 1–14.

Swanson, L. W., & Sawchenko, P. E. (1977). Hypothalamic integration: Organization of the paraventricular and supraoptic nuclei. *Annual Review of Neuroscience, 6*, 269–324.

Swartz, M., Blazer, D., George, L., & Winfield, I. (1990). Estimating the prevalence of borderline personality disorder in the community. *Journal of Personality Disorders, 4*, 257–272.

Takahashi, L. (1992). Ontogeny of behavioral inhibition induced by unfamiliar adult male conspecifics in preweanling rats. *Physiology & Behavior, 52*, 493–498.

Tanaka, T., & Asahara, T. (1981). Synaptic actions of vagal afferents on facial motoneurons in the cat. *Brain Research, 212*, 188–193.

Taylor, E. W. (1992). Nervous control of the heart and cardiorespiratory interactions. In

W. S. Hoar, D. J. Randall, & A. P. Farrell (Eds.), *Fish physiology: The cardiovascular system* (vol. 12, pp. 343–387). New York: Academic Press.

Taylor, E. W., Jordan, D., & Coote, J. H. (1999). Central control of the cardiovascular and respiratory systems and their interactions in vertebrates. *Physiological Reviews, 79,* 855–916.

Tebartz van Elst, L., Hesslinger, B., Thiel, T., Geiger, E., Haegele, K., Lemieux, L., et al. (2003). Frontolimbic brain abnormalities in patients with borderline personality disorder: A volumetric magnetic resonance imaging study. *Biological Psychiatry, 54,* 163–171.

Teicher, M. H., Andersen, S. L., Polcari, A., Anderson, C. M., Navalta, C. P. & Kim, D. M. (2003). The neurobiological consequences of childhood maltreatment. *Neuroscience and Biobehavioral Reviews, 27,* 33–44.

Teplin, L. A., Abram, K. M., McClelland, G. M., Dulcan, M. K., & Mericle, A. A.(2002). Psychiatric disorders in youth in juvenile detention. *Archives of General Psychiatry, 59,* 1133–1143.

Thayer, J. F., & Lane, R. D. (2000). A model of neurovisceral integration in emotion regulation and dysregulation. *Journal of Affective Disorders, 61,* 201–216.

Thomas, W. G., McMurry, G., Pillsbury, H. C. (1985). Acoustic reflex abnormalities in behaviorally disturbed and language delayed children. *Laryngoscope,* 95, 811–817.

Thompson, M. E., Felsten, G., Yavorsky, J., & Natelson, B. H. (1987). Differential effect of stimulation of nucleus ambiguus on atrial and ventricular rates. *American Journal of Physiology,* 253, R150–R157.

Thorndike, E. L. (1911). *Animal intelligence.* New York: Macmillan.

Tomkins, S. S. (1962). *Affect, imagery, consciousness. Vol. I: The positive affects.* New York: Springer.

Tomkins, S. S. (1963). *Affect, imagery, consciousness. Vol. II: The negative affects.* New York: Springer.

Torgersen, S., Kringlen, E., & Cramer, V. (2001). The prevalence of personality disorders in a community sample. *Archives of General Psychiatry,* 58, 590–596.

Trevarthen, C. (1999–2000). Musicality and the intrinsic motive pulse. In *Rhythms, musical narrative, and the origins of human communication* (pp. 155–215). *Musicae Scientiae* [special issue]. Liège: European Society for the Cognitive Sciences of Music.

Truex, R. C., & Carpenter, M. B. (1969). *Human neuroanatomy,* 6th ed. Baltimore, MD: Williams & Wilkins.

Tucker, D. M. (1981). Lateral brain function, emotion, and conceptualization. *Psychological Bulletin,* 89, 19–46.

Umhau, J. C., George, D. T., Reed, S., Petrulis, S. G., Rawlings, R., & Porges, S. W. (2002). Atypical autonomic regulation in perpetrators of violent domestic abuse. *Psychophysiology,* 39, 117–123.

Uvnas-Moberg, K. (1987). Gastrointestinal hormones and pathophysiology of functional gastrointestinal disorders. *Scandinavian Journal of Gastroenterology,* 22(Suppl. 128), 138–146.

Uvnas-Moberg K. (1989). Gastrointestinal hormones in mother and infant. *Acta Paediatrica Scandinavica* Suppl., 351, 88–93.

Uvnas-Moberg, K. (1994). Role of efferent and afferent vagal nerve activity during reproduction: Integrating function of oxytocin on metabolism and behaviour. *Psychoneuroendocrinology,* 19, 687–695.

Uvnas-Moberg, K. (1997). Physiological and endocrine effects of social contact. In C. S. Carter, I. I. Lederhendler, & B. Kirkpatrick (Eds.), *The integrative neurobiology of affiliation* (pp. 46–163). New York: Annals of the New York Academy of Sciences.

Uvnas-Moberg, K. (1998). Oxytocin may mediate the benefits of positive social interaction and emotions. *Psychoneuroendocrinology*, 23, 819–835.

van der Kolk, B. A. (1994). The body keeps the score. *Harvard Review of Psychiatry*, *1*(5), 253–265.

Vanhoutte, P. M., & Levy, M. N. (1979). Cholinergic inhibition of adrenergic neurotransmission in the cardiovascular system. In C. M. Brooks, K. Koizumi, & A. Sato (Eds.), *Integrative junctions of the autonomic nervous system* (pp. 159–176). Tokyo: University of Tokyo Press.

Viviani, D., & Stoop, R. (2008). Opposite effects of oxytocin and vasopressin on the emotional expression of the fear response. *Progress in Brain Research, 170*, 207–218.

Voeller, K. (1986). Right-hemisphere deficit syndrome in children. *American Journal of Psychiatry, 143*, 1004–1009.

Völlm, B., Richardson, P., Stirling, J., Elliott, R., Dolan, M., Chaudhry, I., et al. (2004). Neurobiological substrates of antisocial and borderline personality disorder: Preliminary results of a functional fMRI study. *Criminal Behavior and Mental Health, 14*, 39–54.

Wakefield, A. J., Puleston, J. M., Montgomery, S. M., et al. (2001). Review article: the concept of entero-colonic encephalopathy, autism and opioid ligands. *Alimentary Pharmacological Therapy, 16*, 663–674.

Wakerley, J. B., Clarke, G., & Summerlee, A. J. S. (1994). Milk ejection and its control. In E. Knobil & J. D. Neill (Eds.), *The physiology of reproduction* (pp. 1131–1177). New York: Raven Press.

Wang, Y., Hu, Y., Meng, J., & Li, C. (2001). An ossified Meckels cartilage in two Cretaceous mammals and origin of the mammalian middle ear. *Science, 294*, 357–361.

Warwick, R., & Williams, P. L. (Eds.) (1975). *Gray's anatomy*. Philadelphia: Saunders.

Weaver, T. L., & Clum, G. A. (1993). Early family environments and traumatic experiences associated with borderline personality disorder. *Journal of Consulting and Clinical Psychology, 61*, 1068–1075.

Weiling, W., van Brederode, J. F. M., de Rijk, L. G., Borst, C., & Dunning, A. J. (1982). Reflex control of heart rate in normal subjects in relation to age: A data base for cardiac vagal neuropathy. *Diabetologia*, 22, 163–166.

Weinberg, M. K., & Tronick, E. Z. (1996). Infant affective reactions to the resumption of maternal interaction after the still-face. *Child Development*, 67, 905–914.

Weiner, N. (1948). *Cybernetics*. New York: Wiley.

Weise, F., & Heydenreich, F. (1991). Age-related changes of heart rate power spectra in a diabetic man during orthostasis. *Diabetes Research and Clinical Practice, 11*, 23–32.

Weisz, J., Szilagyi, N., Lang, E., & Adam, G. (1992). The influence of monocular viewing on heart period variability. *International Journal of Psychophysiology, 1*, 2, 11–18.

Widom, C. S., & Maxfield, M. G. (1996). A prospective examination of risk for violence among abused and neglected children. *Annals of the New York Academy of Sciencees, 794*, 224–237.

Williams, P. (1989). *Gray's anatomy* (37th ed.). New York: Livingstone.

Winslow, J. T., & Insel, T.R. (2002). The social deficits of the oxytocin knockout mouse. *Neuropeptides*, 36, 221–229.

Winston, J. S., Strange, B. A., O'Doherty, J., & Dolan, R. J. (2002). Automatic and intentional brain responses during evaluation of trustworthiness of faces. *Nature Neuroscience*, 5, 277–283.

Woodworth, R. S. (1928). Dynamic psychology. In C. Murchison (Ed.), *Psychologies of 1925*. Worcester, MA: Clark University Press.

Woolley, D. C., McWilliam, P. N., Ford, T. W., & Clarke, R. W. (1987). The effect of selective electrical stimulation on non-myelinated vagal fibres on heart rate in the rabbit. *Journal of the Autonomic Nervous System*, *21*, 215–221.

World Health Organization. (1992). *International statistical classification of diseases and related health problems*. Geneva: Author.

Wormald, P. J., Rogers, C., & Gatehouse, S. (1995). Speech discrimination in patients with Bell's palsy and a paralysed stapedius muscle. *Clinical Otolaryngology*, *20*, 59–62.

Wozniak, W., & O'Rahilly, R. (1981). Fine structure and myelination of the human vagus nerve. *Acta Anatomica*, *109*, 118–130.

Yagi, N., & Nakatani, H. (1987). Stapedial muscle electromyography in various diseases. *Archives of Otolarynogology Head and Neck Surgery*, *113*, 392–396.

Yanowitz, F., Preston, J., & Abildskov, J. (1966). Functional distribution of right and left stellate innervation to the ventricles: Production of neurogenic electrocardiographic changes by unilateral alterations of sympathetic tone. *Circulation Research*, *18*, 416–428.

Yokoyama, K., Jennings, R., Ackles, P., Hood, P., & Boller, F. (1987). Lack of heart rate changes during an attention-demanding task after right hemisphere lesions. *Neurology*, 37, 624–630.

Zanarini, M. C., & Grankenbrug, F. R. (2001). Treatment histories of borderline inpatients. *Comprehensive Psychiatry*, 42, 144–150.

Zeanah, C. H. (2000). Disturbances of attachment in young children adopted from institutions. *Journal of Developmental and Behavioral Pediatrics*, *21*, 230–236.

Zero to Three: National Center for Clinical Infant Programs. (1994). *Diagnostic classification: 0–3. Diagnostic classification of mental health and developmental disorders of infancy and early childhood*. Arlington, VA: Zero to Three Publications.

Zahn, T. P., Rumsey, J. M., & Van Kammen, D. P. (1987). Autonomic nervous system activity in autistic, schizophrenic, and normal men: Effects of stimulus significance. *Journal of Abnormal Psychology*, 96, 135–144.

Zavaschi, V., Pires, D., Winkler, S., Carvalho, R. H., Rohde, L. A., & Eizirik, C. L. (2006). Adult mood disorders and childhood psychological trauma. *Revista Brasileira de Psiquiatria*, 28, 184–190.

Zurif, E. G. (1974). Auditory lateralization: Prosodic and syntactic factors. *Brain and Language*, *1*, 391–404.

Zweig-Frank, H., & Paris, J. (2002). Predictors of outcome in a 27-year follow-up of patients with borderline personality disorder. *Comprehensive Psychiatry*, 43, 103–107.

Zwislocki, J. J. (2002). Auditory system: Peripheral nonlinearity and central additivity, as revealed in the human stapedius-muscle reflex. *Proceedings of the National Academy of Science USA*, 99, 14601–14606.

Index

[Page numbers in italic refer to illustrations.]

Also available from

The Norton Series on Interpersonal Neurobiology

The Birth of Intersubjectivity: Psychodynamics, Neurobiology, and the Self
Massimo Ammaniti, Vittorio Gallese

Neurobiology for Clinical Social Work: Theory and Practice (Second Edition)
Jeffrey S. Applegate, Janet R. Shapiro

Mind–Brain–Gene
John B. Arden

The Heart of Trauma: Healing the Embodied Brain in the Context of Relationships
Bonnie Badenoch

Being a Brain-Wise Therapist: A Practical Guide to Interpersonal Neurobiology
Bonnie Badenoch

The Brain-Savvy Therapist's Workbook
Bonnie Badenoch

The Neurobiology of Attachment-Focused Therapy

Jonathan Baylin, Daniel A. Hughes

Coping with Trauma-Related Dissociation: Skills Training for Patients and Therapists

Suzette Boon, Kathy Steele, and Onno van der Hart

Neurobiologically Informed Trauma Therapy with Children and Adolescents: Understanding Mechanisms of Change

Linda Chapman

Intensive Psychotherapy for Persistent Dissociative Processes: The Fear of Feeling Real

Richard A. Chefetz

Timeless: Nature's Formula for Health and Longevity

Louis Cozolino

The Neuroscience of Human Relationships: Attachment and the Developing Social Brain (Second Edition)

Louis Cozolino

The Neuroscience of Psychotherapy: Healing the Social Brain (Second Edition)

Louis Cozolino

Why Therapy Works: Using Our Minds to Change Our Brains

Louis Cozolino

From Axons to Identity:
Neurological Explorations of the Nature of the Self
Todd E. Feinberg

Loving with the Brain in Mind:
Neurobiology and Couple Therapy
Mona DeKoven Fishbane

Body Sense:
The Science and Practice of Embodied Self-Awareness
Alan Fogel

The Healing Power of Emotion:
Affective Neuroscience, Development & Clinical Practice
Diana Fosha, Daniel J. Siegel, Marion Solomon

Healing the Traumatized Self:
Consciousness, Neuroscience, Treatment
Paul Frewen, Ruth Lanius

The Neuropsychology of the Unconscious:
Integrating Brain and Mind in Psychotherapy
Efrat Ginot

10 Principles for Doing Effective Couples Therapy
Julie Schwartz Gottman and John M. Gottman

The Impact of Attachment
Susan Hart

Art Therapy and the Neuroscience of Relationships, Creativity, and Resiliency: Skills and Practices

Noah Hass-Cohen and Joanna Clyde Findlay

Affect Regulation Theory: A Clinical Model

Daniel Hill

Brain-Based Parenting: The Neuroscience of Caregiving for Healthy Attachment

Daniel A. Hughes, Jonathan Baylin

Sex Addiction as Affect Dysregulation: A Neurobiologically Informed Holistic Treatment

Alexandra Katehakis

The Interpersonal Neurobiology of Play: Brain-Building Interventions for Emotional Well-Being

Theresa A. Kestly

Self-Agency in Psychotherapy: Attachment, Autonomy, and Intimacy

Jean Knox

Infant/Child Mental Health, Early Intervention, and Relationship-Based Therapies: A Neurorelational Framework for Interdisciplinary Practice

Connie Lillas, Janiece Turnbull

Play and Creativity in Psychotherapy

Terry Marks-Tarlow, Marion Solomon, Daniel J. Siegel

Clinical Intuition in Psychotherapy: The Neurobiology of Embodied Response

Terry Marks-Tarlow

Awakening Clinical Intuition: An Experiential Workbook for Psychotherapists

Terry Marks-Tarlow

A Dissociation Model of Borderline Personality Disorder

Russell Meares

Borderline Personality Disorder and the Conversational Model: A Clinician's Manual

Russell Meares

Neurobiology Essentials for Clinicians: What Every Therapist Needs to Know

Arlene Montgomery

Borderline Bodies: Affect Regulation Therapy for Personality Disorders

Clara Mucci

Neurobiology and the Development of Human Morality: Evolution, Culture, and Wisdom

Darcia Narvaez

Brain Model & Puzzle:
Anatomy & Functional Areas of the Brain
Norton Professional Books

Sensorimotor Psychotherapy:
Interventions for Trauma and Attachment
Pat Ogden, Janina Fisher

Trauma and the Body:
A Sensorimotor Approach to Psychotherapy
Pat Ogden, Kekuni Minton, Clare Pain

The Archaeology of Mind:
Neuroevolutionary Origins of Human Emotions
Jaak Panksepp, Lucy Biven

The Polyvagal Theory:
Neurophysiological Foundations of Emotions,
Attachment, Communication, and Self-regulation
Stephen W. Porges

The Pocket Guide to Polyvagal Theory:
The Transformative Power of Feeling Safe
Stephen W. Porges

Foundational Concepts in Neuroscience:
A Brain-Mind Odyssey
David E. Presti

Right Brain Psychotherapy

Allan N. Schore

The Development of the Unconscious Mind

Allan N. Schore

Affect Dysregulation and Disorders of the Self

Allan N. Schore

Affect Regulation and the Repair of the Self
Allan N. Schore

The Science of the Art of Psychotherapy
Allan N. Schore

Mind:
A Journey to the Heart of Being Human

Daniel J. Siegel

The Mindful Brain:
Reflection and Attunement in the Cultivation of Well-Being

Daniel J. Siegel

The Mindful Therapist:
A Clinician's Guide to Mindsight and Neural Integration

Daniel J. Siegel

Pocket Guide to Interpersonal Neurobiology:
An Integrative Handbook of the Mind

Daniel J. Siegel

Healing Moments in Psychotherapy

Daniel J. Siegel, Marion Solomon

Healing Trauma:
Attachment, Mind, Body and Brain

Daniel J. Siegel, Marion Solomon

Love and War in Intimate Relationships:
Connection, Disconnection, and Mutual Regulation in Couple Therapy

Marion Solomon, Stan Tatkin

How People Change:
Relationships and Neuroplasticity in Psychotherapy

Marion Solomon and Daniel J. Siegel

The Present Moment in Psychotherapy and Everyday Life

Daniel N. Stern

The Neurobehavioral and Social-Emotional
Development of Infants and Children

Ed Tronick

The Haunted Self:
Structural Dissociation and the Treatment of Chronic Traumatization

Onno Van Der Hart, Ellert R. S. Nijenhuis, Kathy Steele

Prenatal Development and Parents' Lived Experiences:
How Early Events Shape Our Psychophysiology and Relationships

Ann Diamond Weinstein

Changing Minds in Therapy: Emotion, Attachment, Trauma, and Neurobiology
Margaret Wilkinson

For all the latest books in the series, book details (including sample chapters), and to order online, please visit the Series webpage at wwnorton.com/Psych/IPNB Series